WITHDRAWN

B
945
.J24
B37
1983

Barzun, Jacques
A stroll with
William James

BRADNER LIBRARY
SCHOOLCRAFT COLLEGE
LIVONIA, MICHIGAN 48152

# A STROLL WITH WILLIAM JAMES

# A STROLL WITH WILLIAM JAMES

## Jacques Barzun

1817

**HARPER & ROW, PUBLISHERS, New York**

Cambridge, Philadelphia, San Francisco, London
Mexico City, São Paulo, Sydney

B
945
.J24
B 37
1983

To
the
gentle
rereader

Portions of this work appeared first in *American Heritage, The American Scholar, Encounter, National Review,* and *The St. John's Review.*

A STROLL WITH WILLIAM JAMES. Copyright © 1983 by Jacques Barzun. All rights reserved. Printed in the United States of America. No part of this book may be used or reproduced in any manner whatsoever without written permission except in the case of brief quotations embodied in critical articles and reviews. For information address Harper & Row, Publishers, Inc., 10 East 53rd Street, New York, N.Y. 10022. Published simultaneously in Canada by Fitzhenry & Whiteside Limited, Toronto.

FIRST EDITION

Designer: C. Linda Dingler

Library of Congress Cataloging in Publication Data

Barzun, Jacques, 1907–
  A stroll with William James.

  Includes bibliographical references and index.
  1. James, William, 1842–1910.   I. Title.
B945.J24B37  1983      191      82-48108
ISBN 0-06-015090-4


83 84 85 86 87 10 9 8 7 6 5 4 3 2 1

# Contents

# A Personal Note

This book is the record of an intellectual debt. If it does other things too—gives pleasure or knowledge, or brings light into some of the dark places of our present world—I shall be glad. But while telling here at what a high rate I have benefited from keeping an open account with William James, I know I cannot hope to do justice to the man or to the fullness of his thought. The libraries contain many valuable works which, if properly trimmed and laid end to end, would go a good way toward that important goal. Even if I were tempted to take on the task of biographer and critic of philosophy, I think I should resist and, in this year which is seeing the first scholarly edition of James's works, simply show what those works have meant to me and can mean to others.

This is not the first time I have written about James. I find in my files a thick bundle of book reviews, lecture notes, encyclopedia and periodical articles dating back forty years; and in nearly all my books, beginning with *Of Human Freedom* in 1939, there are hints or discussions of James's relevance. The present book is but one more tribute to his relevance, as a whole.

By way of lifelong preparation, I have also spoken—I mean conversed—about James with many persons, greatly to my profit: with Whitehead, Learned Hand, F. J. E. Woodbridge, Bertrand Russell, Herbert Read, C. Wright Mills, Horace Kallen, Jerome Frank, Mortimer Adler, Herbert Schneider, W. P. Montague, Mason Gross, Richard Kroner, C. H. Waddington, B. A. G. Fuller, Harry Murray, Polykarp Kusch, Martin Newhouse, Louis Arnaud Reid, Charles Scribner, Jr., Mrs. Winthrop Ames (a former student of James's), and with James's son William, who until his death lived in his father's Cambridge house at 95 Irving

Street. I remember, too, a long discussion with a transplanted German philosopher who had become in this country an admirer of James's work and who punctuated our remarks on various aspects of it with the mysterious refrain "... and also Death!," an amplification I was bound to respect each time it came.

Several of my students and colleagues by their words on James over the years have added to my understanding and my pleasure, chief in this group being Lionel Trilling, Gail Kennedy, and Justus Buchler. One brilliant student I also recall, whose powerful mind all too soon destroyed itself and who would shake his head in wonder at anybody's willingness to be satisfied by the Jamesian open universe—so many loose ends, so little comfort in the idea that the great unities had to be *made*, and then were never guaranteed. With another congenial disputant, much the same temperament expressed itself in pure impatience: James simply did not "take care" of all the pressing uncertainties, and when it came right down to it, did not, like a proper academic, put forth a system one could "study oneself into." This plaintiff was at any rate performing like a proper critic in giving the correct hostile view, which is the very ground of the favorable view when the observer's expectation shifts: Walt Whitman and the Metaphysical poets may satisfy equally, but not the same wants.

One last word of reminiscence and acknowledgment: in 1943 the then new publishing firm of Duell, Sloan, and Pearce undertook to publish a series of small books on American Men of Letters. Charles Pearce, who had just read my article in the issue of *The New Republic* celebrating the centenaries of the two Jameses, asked me to do the volume on William for his projected series. I accepted with delight at the thought of dealing with James as prose stylist and critic of literature. But the publishing scheme did not weather wartime difficulties; so that, luckily perhaps, I postponed the book. But I kept reading and pondering, until the editor of another series, Dr. Ruth Nanda Anshen, kindly invited me to contribute to "World Perspectives" on a subject of my choice. I had but one to propose. As things turned out, my "stroll" exceeded the limits of a series volume. Now I can only hope that the repeated delay in carrying out a cherished plan has made the product clearer, lighter, truer.

# Prologue

To Whitehead, he was "that adorable genius, William James"; to John Jay Chapman, himself a genius of no mean order, James was "simply the only man [in America] who wasn't terrified at ideas, moonstruck at a living thought, but alive himself." To Gertrude Stein, he was "the important person in her life" at college and medical school, while to another contemporary, who published a supposed diary anonymously month by month in an English magazine, he was "Mr. James, I mean Mr. William James, the humorist who writes on Psychology, not his brother, the psychologist who writes novels." Oliver Wendell Holmes, Jr., a friend of James's youth, called him "a Celt and therefore illogical," though Holmes himself lived to glory in his own inconsistencies. In the eyes of brother Henry, the novelist, younger by fifteen months, William remained "my protector, my backer, my authority, and my pride."

To the American public at the turn of the century William James was the well-known professor at Harvard—was it of philosophy or psychology?—who was also in demand as a lecturer to general audiences, something like the late Mr. Emerson, but not so preacher-like, much more argumentative and lively. The works of this Cambridge notable were said to bring the United States a great deal of prestige—"the first American thinker with a European reputation." He was indeed the head and founder of a school of thought most easily—too easily—described as "characteristically American: something to do with energy, you know"—practicality, the individual, the pioneer optimism of those who by geographical good fortune see the road indefinitely open before them.

But there was more to be said about James—and it was said—that did not fit these clichés: he could be a stern critic of American traits and for all his apparent optimism and energy he certainly espoused the tragic view of life. Great thinkers are so confusing! Anyhow, thanks to this particular thinker, the word *pragmatic* suddenly came back into use after 150 years, this time with an honorific meaning—though not for long, as we shall see.

Meanwhile, as usual, professional opinion was divided about what he really meant, though rarely about the man himself. His courtesy, broad and quick sympathies, depth of reflection and study, vivacity of mind and speech, evident generosity of spirit—all these fostered many lifelong friendships, even with opponents. James seemed to *like* being opposed, just as he liked to flutter the academic dovecotes with extraordinary questions—"Does Consciousness Exist?"—to which he produced reasoned and revolutionary answers. Was he not the very embodiment of this new century—the so-called twentieth—with its passion for building anew after clearing the ground of nineteenth-century errors and preconceptions?

The old guard was anything but silent. They said with confidence that the Jamesian propositions could hardly be taken seriously, a conclusion that was somewhat flawed by the long and serious arguments written to prove it. What could not be denied was that William James's *Principles of Psychology*, which appeared in 1890, established the subject once for all as a distinct scientific discipline. But impressive as it was by its experimental findings and introspective depth, it was also a very provoking work. Some of the examples in it came from literature (a whole page from Jane Austen!), from the fine arts, from the philosophers and mystics, from history, from the trivialities of common life. Every page being in fact alive with actuality, it might be called a work of genius, but was it science?

Sixty years later, on its reissue in paper covers, leading psychologists writing in their learned journals paid tribute to the work's lasting power and undimmed relevance: "a classic"; "it brings a sense of perspective and even a little humility to our regard for more modern achievements"; "the republication is an important event."

Other professional thinkers—philosophers, moralists, theologians— also continue to find James a source of ideas adapted to contemporary debate. They hold symposiums and devote issues of periodicals to the main heads of his thought. The popular press, too, is kept mindful of him through biographies, new selections from his works, or articles reviewing his achievements. The tone throughout is one of respect, but it is mingled with surprise: James's stature when measured afresh seems so much greater than his reputation as it is commonly remembered. To this emotional discrepancy is added intellectual uncertainty as to a final estimate. Perhaps it is due to words: Pragmatism and Pluralism have become common nouns without exact significance. And psychology, one assumes, must have greatly changed since 1890. In short, James is in that twilight which for the great may follow death for fifty or a hundred years.

That position in the shadows is well shown in the use made by President Carter, in an early message about the national need to conserve energy, of James's essay title "A Moral Equivalent of War." The phrase could not be said to be familiar to the public and its meaning in James was obviously not clear to the speech writer. Yet the borrowing gave no one the feeling that an obscure thinker had been drawn upon. Rather, it was a "well-known" American figure whose words were conveniently misapplied to the current emergency.

In the same vein and not long after, one of the best-read among Washington political writers began his column by reminding his readers of what "James named Pragmatism at the turn of the century: What works is good." This "essence" of the "philosophy" was then ascribed to all those Americans who attack the principle of upholding "human rights" in our foreign policy by saying: "It won't work." If that thought-cliché came anywhere near being a tenable interpretation of Jamesian thought, it would indeed be hard to see why his name should be remembered, or why so many and such diverse observers should have paid him uncommon tributes.

I remember in an academic discussion of the welfare state, not many years ago, one of the speakers asserting with great warmth that "William James had what we need now—genius, plus being the most quantitative social scientist of his time." That odd description left me speechless at first but on reflection struck me as indicative. Certain types of genius are clearly seen or felt to be such, but their species, their essence—to use the columnist's term—eludes classification. Range of interest and fertility of imagination disturb the observer's judgment and give rise to extravagance in both praise and detraction. I first met this phenomenon in surveying the literature about Berlioz; it occurs again about Diderot. It is not merely that the magnitude of the mind upsets the balance of those who judge; it is that the magnitude conceals the unifying principle. And thus it is with our subject. Who, or what, was this Protean creature William James? How did he come to project so many different images, to inspire such a variety of passions? An obvious way to begin answering these questions is for me to show how he still serves me after half a century of meditation on him and on contemporary life.

I am not the fortunate sort of person who can feed his mind and guide his moral conduct with the aid of a single book or author. I am naturally polytheistic and fastidiously (I hope) promiscuous. When I read philosophy, or to put it more modestly, read in philosophy, whether gymnastically for muscle tone or hedonistically for the wild circus of thought, I am as likely to pick up Montaigne as Aquinas, Rousseau as Pascal, Berkeley as Whitehead. What then is the difference when I go back to James? The answer is that his ideas, his words, his temperament speak to me with intimacy as well as force. Communication is direct; I do not "derive benefit" from him, he "does me good." I find him visibly and testably right—right in intuition, range of considerations, sequence of reasons, and fully rounded power of expression. He is for me the most inclusive mind I can listen to, the most concrete and the least hampered by trifles. He is moreover entirely candid and full of gaiety, lovable through his words as he was in life to his friends. As if this were not enough, he helps me to understand what his contemporaries and mine were and are doing. I stroll with him again and again because he knows better than anyone else the material and spiritual country I am traveling through.

The tone and temper of his thought, aside from its purport and contents, is a prop to independence of mind, an antidote to the opium of modern ideologies, a tonic in the resistance to the sludge of "modern communications," popular and advanced. His resolving lucidity in analysis, his hard-won freedom that frees others (a rare consequence of liberation movements) enables me better to endure or enjoy whatever befalls me—and all this in the simplest way of making actual and unmistakable what I would otherwise grope toward or dimly sense.

Take a modest example bearing on the old question of science versus the humanities. For too many years the conflict has exercised both scientists and humanists. Can they, will they, ever come together on common ground, understand each other? Coexistence has been a fact from the beginning, but not détente. When I became interested in the issue, half a century ago, mutual comprehension was inconceivable—scientists claimed possession of the only truth; humanists pretended to despise what they took no trouble to understand. A few of us historians thought we saw a means of rapprochement in the history of science. We were told that science has no use for history; only the latest findings are science; what went before has no value and has thus lost interest. Meanwhile, our brother humanists sulked and muttered under their breath about the arrogant, narrow-gauge scientific mind.

In this crossfire, argument was scarcely listened to; no philosophic voice was heard to put the case for either side or even to state the division clearly. I then came across James's discussion of what the humanities signify—not Greek and Latin as such, but the literature of those languages "and in a still broader sense the study of masterpieces in almost any field of human endeavor. Literature keeps the primacy; for it not only consists of masterpieces, but is largely *about* masterpieces, being little more than an appreciative chronicle of human master-strokes, so far as it takes the form of criticism and history. You can give humanistic value to almost anything by teaching it historically. Geology, economics, mechanics are humanities when taught with reference to the successive achievements of the geniuses to which these sciences owe their being. Not taught thus, literature remains grammar, art a catalogue, history a list of dates, and natural science a sheet of formulas and weights and measures. The sifting of human creations!—nothing less than this is what we ought to mean by the humanities."

Once stated, the principle seems obvious, but the encompassing mind was needed to make it so, by putting the humanities themselves among the non-humanities when they are taken or taught in the wrong way—"art a catalogue"—from which it followed that the sciences as human achievements, as masterpieces of the mind, belong no less than poetry to the humanistic tradition.

Since the crusade which some of us launched five decades ago, the history of science has become part of the curriculum in many colleges, and the monumental *Dictionary of Scientific Biography*, recently completed under the editorship of an historian of science, has proved that James's grasp and statement of the point still holds a lesson for culture. It will continue to do so as long as intellectual provincialism rules any discipline or profession.

This example, small as it is, shows the master in the easy handling of a superfluous difficulty. But it also suggests the originality and force of mind by which James met and subdued some of the old Sphinxes who challenge the earthly traveler, as always on pain of death.

# The Man

The year is 1890 and the place Cambridge, Massachusetts. On one of
the streets leading northeast along Harvard Yard a man in early middle
age—he is, in fact, forty-eight years old, of slight build and medium
height but vigorous motion—is walking with a pair of students, boy and
girl, who have followed him out of his class in experimental psychology. His face is bearded and his eyes bright blue, and his features reflect
the rapidity of his thought. He is William James, the scientist and philosopher. The two, who plan to do advanced work in his laboratory, are
pursuing him with questions and he is replying as equal to equals with
his customary fullness of illustration. The girl is short and pretty and
very noticing, and it occurs to her, apropos of the point being discussed,
to remark on the large, imposing figure coming toward them. His long
white beard blowing, cane swinging, he seems in a world of his own,
talking to himself, or else to some invisible listener. He will mow them
down if they do not get off the narrow sidewalk. "Whoever he is," says
the girl, sure of his not overhearing, "he's the epitome of the absent-
minded professor."

"What you really mean," says James, "is that he is present-minded
somewhere else." As usual, the Jamesian observation inspires silent
thought, and at the next corner he leaves them to turn left. He has
remembered that young What's-his-name, that uncommonly original
undergraduate, lives in one of the dormitories nearby and is reported
sick. The young fellow probably hasn't bothered about a doctor and his
ailment may be something that should not be neglected.*

---

* "One of James's colleagues believed that only Dean Briggs had climbed more stair-
ways to the third floor of houses to visit sick students." (Rollo Walter Brown, *Harvard
Yard in the Golden Age*, New York, 1948, p. 78.)

The resolve to pay this visit is not prompted solely by professional feeling—that of a teacher who is also an M.D. True, the atmosphere of Harvard College is still family-like; the place is as yet a largely local institution, not the Olympus among universities, to which academic demigods aspire so as to be gods-in-full before they die. But the fact is that at any time or place William James behaves by nature and habit like no one else. He differs even from people who are out of the ordinary by not remembering that he is one of them. Spontaneous, unaffected, his character is to act on any full-fledged emotion provided others' feelings are not hurt. His conscience will approve, and conventions will not stop him. So independent a personality did not please everybody. George Santayana recalled in his memoirs of Harvard that although James's "position was established" it had seemed at first "questionable and irregular." James "had had to be swallowed." Once this was done, he began to be seen as "a marvellous human being"—tolerant, generous, tender to others' difficulties, and yet strongly affirmative, combative even. His spirit seemed all-embracing, though too secular to be called saintly. There is a word for such a character: it is the Magnanimous Man.

This year 1890 marks the midpoint in James's creative life. Since the late 1870s, when his long search for a vocation and a social role came to end, his work has been abundant and intense. Now he has summed it up in a treatise that is about to come out. On either side of this median date, his work as teacher, experimenter, writer, and public lecturer takes effect on three generations of students, colleagues, audiences, readers, and correspondents. From their recollections, and from his unmistakable voice showing through the written word, we draw our impression of the man we are to accompany.

It is thanks to physical mischance suffered at the right time by a pair of brothers that this country can now boast of the achievements of two of her greatest sons. William and Henry James had turned twenty by the height of the Civil War, and in the normal course would no doubt have enlisted on the Union side like their two brothers, their cousins, and their friends. But Henry was disabled after an injury to his back and William was a prey to a recurrent nervous ailment. The younger brothers, Wilky and Bob, who came back shattered from Fort Wagner and other places, and whose later lives were sad and ineffectual, serve as a "control" in this small test of the consequences of war upon the culture of nations.

Such accidents of chronology are seldom made enough of. Likewise, the successive details of William's upbringing are given in all the books, but the point they suggest has not been sufficiently insisted on. To say that as a child William was moved from school to school too often for good results conveys no special image, nor does it define the sort of mind that emerged from his globe-trotting and broken schooling. There have been, after all, many hotel-bred children of no more than ordinary capacity. But genius, especially genius in which intellect is fused with imagination, cannot be well understood without recapturing the quality of its earliest experience. For experience is an instinct of life, as Oscar Wilde said, and what matters is the way life is "taken" by the experiencer. We know St. Augustine, Rousseau, and Berlioz as we do not "know" Aristotle, St. Thomas, and Bacon, because the first three wrote autobiographies whose opening chapters give us a direct view of the "taking" in childhood. To know William James we go to his early letters and find there not only the quality of his power to experience, but also the germs of almost all his original ideas.

Young James's nervous instability or neurasthenia, as it was then called, was no temporary trouble of late adolescence.* It was a deep-rooted depression which held up his choice of career till his mid-twenties, which he overcame in part by an heroic effort of will, and which periodically returned, though less crippling, throughout his life.

Whatever the cause, it cannot have been lack of parental love. The Jameses were an uncommonly united and affectionate family. As the letters show, every member of it took enormous pleasure in the person and the company of the others. The father, Henry James, Sr., was a genial, unworldly man with a humorous eye and an extraordinary way with words. He also had a cork leg, the consequence of an accident in boyhood. Having independent means, he divided his time between domesticity and writing works of theology and social reform. He had a wide circle of friends among intellectuals, in particular Ralph Waldo Emerson. But his family was his paradise. Once, having left home for a visit of some length, the first steps toward separation brought him such a foretaste of homesickness that part way to his destination he turned and hurried back.

In a sane man of forty this feeling and behavior are unusual. But then nothing about the Jameses was usual. This father was what we should call a permissive parent in an age when fathers knew their "rights." Like a man of the twentieth century, he wanted not to repeat the mistakes his father had made in rearing him; so he indulged his children with a sublime confidence that their characters were indestructible. Regular schooling was fitful, the slackness of tutors was tolerated, free-

---

*Neurasthenia, or "nervous exhaustion," was so named by the American physician George Beard to describe the frequent disorder he found among Americans after the Civil War. The affliction apparently led to the surge of "mind cures" that James later took note of in his psychopathology.

dom of speech and movement at home and outside was pushed to the limit, and extravagant, paradoxical opinions were bandied about to stimulate thought. The system—or absence of system—would either ruin or make strong original minds. Judging by William, Henry, and Alice, it succeeded, though at a cost, as we shall see.

Willy, the eldest, was an active, talkative, willful little boy, whose lust for exploring, trying out, and uttering his discoveries soon shattered the household calm that his studious father had once enjoyed, even though *his* restlessness was also an obsessive trait. The Jameses are often thought of as New Englanders, because one has read about William teaching at Harvard or about Henry living with his cousins at Newport. The fact is that they were originally from New York and soon from everywhere. The grandfather (the first William), who had come from Ireland "to see a revolutionary battlefield," settled in Albany in 1789. He became one of the builders of that city, a promoter of the Erie Canal, and the possessor not only of wealth but of cultivation. His son, our Henry Sr., born in Albany in 1811 and a graduate of the new Union College in Schenectady, happened to be in New York with his wife when his first son was born, at the old Astor House, on January 11, 1842. Later, that same building had the further honor of bringing together Lincoln on his way to the White House and Walt Whitman in the crowd of citizen gapers.*

The James family shortly moved into a three-story brick house near Washington Square, where Emerson gazed at the three-month-old Willy in his cradle, and where Henry was born fifteen months later. The brothers' closeness in age was an element in their intense, lifelong devotion, which had important intellectual and artistic consequences for them both.

When Willy was about a year and a half, the paternal wanderlust asserted itself and the family was whisked off to Europe—Paris, England, Paris again—for a visit that lasted two and a half years. Abroad, Henry Sr. met Carlyle, Tennyson, Lewes, Mill, Thackeray, and others, and he also experienced a severe mental crisis—almost a total break-

---

* Whitman gave an account of the unusual scene: "The broad spaces, sidewalks, and streets in the neighborhood ... were crowded with solid masses of people, many thousands. The omnibuses and other vehicles had all been turn'd off, leaving an unusual hush in that busy part of the city. Presently, two or three shabby hack barouches ... drew up at the Astor House entrance. A tall figure step'd out of the centre of these barouches, paused leisurely on the sidewalk, look'd up at the granite walls and looming architecture of the grand old hotel—then, after a relieving stretch of arms and legs, turn'd round for over a minute to slowly and good-humoredly scan the vast and silent crowds. There were no speeches—no compliments—no welcome—as far as I could hear, not a word said.... The President-elect ... possessed no personal popularity in New York City, and very little political.... The result was a sulky, unbroken silence, such as certainly never before characterized so great a New York crowd." (Lecture on April 14, 1879, reprinted in *Walt Whitman's Memoranda During the War and Death of Abraham Lincoln*, ed. Roy P. Basler, Bloomington, Ind., 1962, pp. 3-4 [after facsimile].)

down—that resisted medical treatment. The chance discovery of Swedenborg's works began to effect a cure and also redirected his thought and writings. After some two years he regained his composure permanently, but for those months the tension and anxiety of both parents doubtless affected the two uncommonly perceptive boys. Back in this country, the family lived first in Albany; then, for an unexampled stretch of seven years, in New York, on West Fourteenth Street, where Alice was born in 1848.

But the cosmopolitan ideal still ruled the father's mind, and Willy was sent, for his first schooling (other than to kindergarten for a few weeks), to a French institution in New York, where he learned nothing but the art of dodging the books hurled by perpetually angry masters. Shifted after a while to another school, he enjoyed being taught to draw. His brother Henry remembered Willy in Fourteenth Street "drawing and drawing, always drawing, not as with a plodding patience ... but easily, freely, and, as who should say, infallibly." Both had begun to "write," that is to say original "works," spurred no doubt by the abundant conversation of interesting visitors in the parlor and of the family at table, where a free-for-all was encouraged between their own and "Father's ideas." A dinner guest has recorded a somewhat later scene of the children's vehement disputes at mealtimes drowning out the voice of the father-moderator and accompanied by alarming gesticulations, knife or fork in hand. Mrs. James would reassure the visitor: "Don't be disturbed; they won't stab each other. This is usual when the boys come home."

If one asks, What did they argue about so fiercely, the most likely answer would be "Everything," for they were all-observant, perceptive, articulate, and "philosophical" in the sense of wanting to ascertain the "hang of things." William Dean Howells, in a letter about dining at the Jameses—"a very pleasant evening"—told how the old sage would listen to his bright brood and now and then "say something that each of the others had to modify and explain away," after which the father would be "clapped back into durance again." One can imagine the youthful mob, having united to dispose of the older generation in the person of Henry Sr., redividing to settle its own differences, and one may be sure that William talked his full share, or more, in the debate, despite "being sick for such a long time." But it is equally evident that for such a chorus to perform so fluently and so discordantly each was able to take his own part with practiced strength.

If early school was no intellectual goad, frequent attendance at near-by theatres (which Henry Sr. shocked his friends by allowing) may well have been: a strong dramatic sense pervades the work of both Henry and William; and the former, despite ill-success as a playwright, kept

on conceiving his fiction in dramatic—indeed, melodramatic—scenes.*
Clearly, for the third generation of Jameses, "culture" in and out of the
home was so much a matter of course as to cease being culture at all; it
was simply everyday life like eating and sleeping. This state of affairs,
so far in advance of the American cultural awakening of the 1920s and
'30s, could not help marking them off from the vast majority of their
American contemporaries.

In June 1855 Europe beckoned again and the family trooped over. By
then it included the last two children, Garth Wilkinson (Wilky) and
Robertson (Bob), equally cherished and appreciated by the rest, and not
less mentally alert, but soon to be overtaken by ill-chance. From this
trip forward—Willy now in his teens—the story of the Jameses, and
especially the oldest boys, is an account of perpetual motion. It has to
be summarized quickly, if only to avoid protracted dizziness: Geneva,
Paris, London; tutors and governesses. A year at Boulogne-sur-mer
(1857–58), where Willy at the excellent lycée earned praise for work in
science and bought a microscope. Back in the States (for no more than a
year), a new setting and new friends, at Newport, Rhode Island. It was
there that the beautiful child cousin, Minny Temple, became for William and Henry a beloved emblem of the beauty of life, and by her
early death, the very figure of tragedy.

At Newport, the leading American painter William Morris Hunt had
his studio, in which a young man of French origin, John La Farge, was a
pupil with a future. From him William took fire and decided he too
must be a painter. There ensued a disagreement between Willy and his
father which must be unique in the annals of fathers and sons quarrel-
ing over careers. For Henry Sr.'s strenuous opposition to Willy's desire
was not because being an artist was "unpractical," unlikely to bring in
the livelihood that was now needed, owing to family losses and the
prospective division of the estate among five children; nor was it because the father doubted his son's talent and chances of success. What
he feared was that the profession of artist would not bring Willy the
intellectual and spiritual satisfactions he craved and deserved.

This incident beautifully shows how the position of art has shifted in
modern times. Henry Sr. as an advanced thinker did believe that "the
artist or producer is the only regenerate image of God in nature," but
the artist's career was still questionable. When art came to be accepted
in our century as the fit replacement of religion—a source of wisdom as
well as the highest expression of the human spirit—the old philosopher's reasonable apprehension could no longer be understood. William belonged to the first generation that accorded art the high serious-

* See "Henry James the Melodramatist," in The Question of Henry James, ed. Frederick W. Dupee, New York, 1945.

ness we now take for granted, an attitude that we shall see playing a part in his philosophy.

But by 1859, the year of Darwin's *Origin of Species*, of *Tristan*, and of Marx's *Critique*, the cult of art was still confined to those directly engaged in its production and Willy was so far only an aspirant to that role. He was seventeen and in need of further general education. Hence Europe again—Geneva, this time—where he entered the university (then still called "the Academy") and distinguished himself in anatomy (including dissection), a discipline in which his good draftsmanship served him well. Then, Germany for the summer, to learn the language. Willy "soaked it up" while living with a family in Bonn. Geneva had afforded him a reading knowledge of Italian, in addition to perfecting his French. But the urge to paint still throbbed inside him and his arguments virtually forced a return to Newport, where, in 1860, he joined Hunt and La Farge as an apprentice.

William's odyssey was by no means over, but despite some formidable breakers ahead, this first part of it matters most for seeing the later achievement in perspective. James had been acclimated to Europe virtually from birth, was at home in four of its greatest capitals, was fluent in French at fourteen and German at eighteen, and not as a tourist merely, but as a resident who could also read and write the educated language. He had somehow acquired a thorough grounding in Latin, too, and in enough other parts of the European curriculum to attend a lycée and a university of the first rank. Voracious reading, besides, had filled his mind with the literature of the West, old and new. It is clear that when critics later on spoke of James's philosophy as "typically American"—a sort of homespun product of the backwoods—they were ignorantly jumping at conclusions, perhaps from reading his birth certificate rather than his works.

At the same time it will not do to forget that, except for not undergoing the full strain of national anxiety that preceded the outbreak of Civil War, William—unlike Henry—never lost touch with his native land. Its ways and speech were deep in him, fused with those that came from the whole civilization to which he had been bred. I mean by this not only that his home nurture had made ideas as concrete as tables and chairs; I mean also that even lacking the valuable lesson of American public-school life as it was then, James picked up the true spirit of democracy in the unsupervised rambles in downtown New York that his father—an absolute democrat if ever there was one—encouraged as impartially as theatre-going.

The zest for being in the rough and tumble of life, and not just a moralizing spectator, was a temperamental trait, an element of the

young boy's energy and love of action. It may be read into the episode
of his brother Henry's wanting to share in some boyish expedition. As
the older and less shy, Willy had naturally assumed the role of model
and guardian, and he turned down the request with the final rebuff: 'I
play with boys who curse and swear.' Later on, William's impatience
with conventional goodness and propriety affords the rare spectacle of
a philosopher gifted, Lincoln-like, with the common touch. Santayana is
again a good witness, for he never really liked or understood James
and, like a good critic, objected to what others also find present but not
objectionable: "He was so extremely natural that there was no knowing
what his nature was, or what to expect next; . . . I found no foothold, I
was soon fatigued."

James's childhood hide-and-seek with schoolmasters here and abroad
had certainly developed a critical judgment that gave short shrift to
received opinion and professional routines. When William in his twenty-fifth year encountered German academic ways in philosophy and
science, he wrote home: 'You never saw such a mania for going deep
into the bowels of truth, with such an absolute lack of intuition and
perception of the skin thereof.'* The 'skin' is the plain concrete feel of
things, and James gives to the Germans' uniformly abstract and verbal
ways of explaining them a revealing series of epithets: 'disgusting and
disheartening . . . corrupt and immodest.'

Father Henry's transatlantic shuttle had provoked or facilitated or reinforced all these attitudes. If they led in some fashion to the coming
breakdown of the young mind called upon to organize and assess them,
they were at the same time the best preparation for a genius who was
not, after all, going to be another Delacroix, William's favorite painter
in Paris. When the elder James's sons were little, they were sometimes
embarrassed at being asked what their father did. He, when consulted
for the right answer, gave one that did not help at all: "Say I'm a philosopher, say I'm a seeker for truth, say I'm a lover of my kind, say I'm an
author of books, if you like; or best of all, just say I'm a Student." When
William gavé up painting, he was already halfway to a career that could
be described in identical terms.

The second part of James's odyssey occupied less than a decade, from
1861 to '69, and though full of drama and adventure, it set off almost at
once on the right course. For painting with Hunt took up just one year:

---

* Here and later, quotations from James are distinguished from all others by single
quotation marks, and the usual sign of ellipsis is omitted. The reference notes, pp. 315–
335, direct the interested reader to the passage in full.

giving it up expressed the pupil's sound judgment that talent is not enough:* 'Nothing is more contemptible than a mediocre artist.' William turned to his other interests and abilities; he enrolled in the Lawrence Scientific School of Harvard and, after three years there, entered the Medical School in 1864. Then came a providential interruption: the famous naturalist Louis Agassiz, subsidized by a Boston patron and the Emperor of Brazil, outfitted an expedition to study the fauna of the Amazon. By invitation—the older Agassiz children being his friends—William joined as one of the seven volunteer aides making up the exploring party of seventeen. We get a glimpse of him from a letter Mrs. Agassiz wrote to her younger children in Cambridge: "He is a delightful travelling companion. You know how bright, intelligent, cultivated he is—a fellow of vivid, keen intellect. He works hard and is ready to turn his hand to anything for your father."

The fifteen months spanning 1865 and 1866—three in Rio and the rest up country—were a test of endurance, punctuated for William by smallpox (or varioloid), eye trouble, and the accidents of life in the wilds. There was drudgery too and some doubt as to any benefit he might be reaping. Before the end, though, he concluded that he was indeed profiting from the disciplining of his natural quickness and speculative power: 'No one,' he wrote home, 'sees farther into a generalization than his own knowledge of details extends.' The statement prefigures one of the seminal principles of his later philosophy—the passion for concreteness and the riddling not merely of false but of misused generality. In the same message, William also shows that appreciation of others, regardless of their faults, which struck so many observers of his behavior throughout his life: Agassiz talks a great deal of nonsense, thinks James, and at once corrects that impression: 'I saw only his defects at first, but his wonderful qualities throw them quite in the background. He had great personal tact too, and I see that in all his talks with me he is pitching into my loose and superficial way of thinking.'

One finds also in these letters from Brazil the early-matured style, strong in the picturesque exaggeration that was a family trait. In William the tone varies easily from reflectiveness (as above) to irony ('I speak Portuguese like a book and am ready to converse for hours on any subject. To be sure, the natives seem to have a slight difficulty in understanding me, but that is their lookout') and to extravagance ('I am writing to you in a room 120 ft. long—just about large enough for one

* Though a surviving portrait in oils of Katharine Temple is nothing short of superb, neither prentice work nor mere "talented effort." Half a century later, La Farge told Royal Cortissoz, the art critic, that James could draw beautifully, repeating the word three times. (R. Cortissoz, *John La Farge*, Boston, 1911, p. 117.) The training, as we shall see, was not wasted.

man'). Then it may go on to self-searching tenderness about one or other member of the family or even a public figure: 'I can't tell why, but albeit unused to the melting mood, I can hardly think of Abraham Lincoln without feeling on the point of blubber. Is it that he seems the representation of pure simple human nature against all conventional additions?' And looking at the devastation, moral and physical, of the war at home and hoping nobody still wants to hang Jefferson Davis, he concludes: 'Can anyone think of revenge now?'

James came back to finish his medical studies, sandwiching in an internship at the Massachusetts General Hospital that confirmed his preference for practical study. He read medical theory eagerly, but the school's teaching of therapy and bedsidery left him cold. Even before finishing the course, he was sure he did not want to be a physician. Intervening experiences had redirected his scientific interests. Besides, his neurasthenia had worsened soon after his return from Brazil in 1866—trembling weakness, pain in the lower back, and, as one or two intimates knew, persistent thoughts, for a whole winter, of 'the pistol, the dagger, and the bowl.' Believing that the physical part of the trouble could be cured abroad at a spa, William, encouraged as usual by his father, went off to Paris and then to Germany in April 1867. He wound up far from cured, but still studying hard in Berlin and making his German as much second nature as his French. That he was 'a mere wreck, bodily' did not stop mental activity, and though feeling a 'deadness' that made him wish for 'hibernation,' he decided to take up 'the nervous system and psychology' from the physiological point of view which the Germans were making their own.

The person before us, then, is a greatly gifted youth of twenty-five, favored by fortune in every respect but that of health, who yet at every turn encountered the experience that he needed for his still uncharted development.

If I were attempting a biographical sketch instead of merely making introductions for a first acquaintance, I would show by extracts from letters how James's recurrent impulse to quit life was grounded equally in his sense of failure and in the reigning philosophy that life is meaningless, both these proofs of futility being reinforced by knowing that he was a moral and financial burden on his generous father. But even without the details of this complex agony one can imagine William's states of mind—the periods of concentration on new and captivating facts and ideas, the bouts of wearily self-centered thought caused by physical pain, the fits of hope at surcease followed by despair, the waves of shame when thinking of the family and seeing himself a social nullity: in short, an intellectual-emotional chaos in which the young man James floundered for months on end, sustained chiefly by the unstinted love that came from those at home and that he felt for them; sustained also by some inner determination to learn, to think, and to leave his mark.

James received his M.D. in 1869. The training, he thought, had shown him chiefly how society molds and directs an apparently independent profession and requires a pretense of science from its practitioners. He nevertheless hoped to use his medical knowledge to get rid of his crippling back pains and general anxiety. He did not suspect that his worst trial, or rather, the best because the deepest, was just around the corner, and that he would meet it victoriously.

For James did not take to being an invalid. He hated the 'tedious egotism' of sickness and solitude; his natural bent was toward activity—and not simply the normal kind, but exuberant activity. Since some time, too, he had struggled with strong sexual impulses, which in his social and ethical view must lead to marriage, a step he could not take if he were to continue ailing and morbid. He experimented with drugs, exercise, and rest, including less study. From his New-Year's-day reflection for 1870, the measure of this reduced effort appears dubious: if during the year he finished reading his father's works in thirteen volumes, plus Schopenhauer, Fechner, Fichte, Spencer (the biology), and half a dozen lesser lights, he thought he would have done enough.

There was a point to all this reading and philosophizing. The young man had come to think that regaining health might have some connection with the problem of free will, which he had been pondering and arguing with friends. The scientific dogma of the day was mechanistic materialism—the great push-pull system of the physical universe by which every event was deemed to be completely determined in an endless chain of previous events, with 'not a wiggle of our will' taking part. Soon the dread Huxley, "Darwin's Watchdog," was to assert that man was an automaton. His consciousness of choosing, of having a purpose, of thinking before acting, was an illusion, an "epiphenomenon"—so to say: the flame of burning brandy on the plum pudding; it plays lightly over the lump beneath, but has no control over it.

To this day, this is the scheme of things that is taken for granted by the majority of unreflective minds—by thousands of scientists, journalists, and their docile listeners. It seems to fit what we see, feel, and (especially) hear. For William James, this issue of material causation was urgent and inescapable: if reason meant anything, the automaton theory was wrong; and if it meant nothing, then an effort to get well was also a meaningless phrase. Yet despising self-pity and sensing within him energies that were being mysteriously dammed up, James considered it a duty to save himself and thus release them. Since he no longer had the help of traditional religion—'seeing into the purposes of

God'—he could only cling to 'the thought of my having a will and of my belonging to the brotherhood of men.' With these two convictions he might overcome the melancholia and the 'evil of restlessness' which he hid from all but one chosen correspondent.

The reality of the will he found confirmed by an argument in the French philosopher Renouvier, whom James had discovered a couple of years before: to will was to sustain a particular thought when one had other thoughts equally sustainable, in short, to choose a goal and hold on to it by attending. As for the significance of mankind—as against the contention of current science that all but matter is illusion—James found it demonstrated by the evidence of history: every thought and act 'owes its complexion to the acts of your dead and living brothers.' The importance of history for James grew with his expanding thought; it never left him; and I have no doubt that the congeniality of his views to my own mind is due to the strong sense of time, place, and concrete particulars which underlies all his work.

James goes on to his friend: 'Man is *the best we know*; and your loathing for what you call the vulgarity of human life is furnished by your manhood; your ideal is made up of traits suggested by past men's words and actions.' In other words, the quality of life was determined not by matter but by man. It followed that the justification of life was 'by hook or by crook, to make my *nick*, however small a one, in the raw stuff the race has got to shape, and so assert my reality.'

Such are James's starting point and philosophical base, which mark him out as what came in the twentieth century to be known as an existential thinker; that is, one who philosophizes from the need to survive intellectually and emotionally in a universe that the collapse of traditional religion and the tyranny of science have laid waste. James had defined the task as early as his twenty-third year, in a letter to his father: 'Men's activities are occupied in two ways—in grappling with external circumstances, and in striving to set things at one in their own topsy-turvy mind.' And five years later, by the time of the impending crisis, he knew the full extent of mankind's dependence on itself: '*Everything* we know and are is through men. We have no revelation but through men.'

The great test of these convictions came in the form of two unrelated events in the spring of 1870. At some time in March he touched the rock bottom of depression and was seized by the same sort of mindless terror that his father had experienced in England twenty-five years before. William described his own case later under the guise of a 'communication from a French correspondent':

'Whilst in this state of philosophic pessimism and general depression of spirits about my prospects, I went one evening in a dressing-room in the twilight to procure some article that was there; when suddenly there fell upon me without warning, just as if it came out of the darkness, a horrible fear of my own existence. Simultaneously there arose in my mind the image of an epileptic patient whom I had seen in the asylum, a black-haired youth with greenish skin, entirely idiotic, who used to sit all day on one of the benches, or rather shelves against the wall, with his knees drawn up against his chin, and the coarse grey undershirt, which was his only garment, drawn over them inclosing his entire figure. . . . This image and my fear entered into a species of combination with each other. *That shape am I,* I felt, potentially. Nothing that I possess can defend me against that fate, if the hour for it should strike for me as it struck for him. There was such a horror of him, and such a perception of my own merely momentary discrepancy from him, that it was as if something hitherto solid within my breast gave way entirely, and I became a mass of quivering fear. After this the universe was changed for me altogether. I awoke morning after morning with a horrible dread at the pit of my stomach, and with a sense of the insecurity of life that I never knew before, and that I have never felt since. It was like a revelation; and although the immediate feelings passed away, the experience has made me sympathetic with the morbid feelings of others ever since. It gradually faded, but for months I was unable to go into the dark alone.'

The close of the report may well be a literary rounding-off of the central event, for it took more than "fading" for James to recover. In the figure of the idiot on his bench, he had, like a painter, objectified Huxley's view of man as automaton, giving visual equivalents for the horror, vacancy, and desolation that the conception implied. No such vision could be counted on to recede by degrees, like the storybook cat, without long intellectual analysis and a heroic "sustaining of the idea" of himself as an active and rational being.

It was during this effort—or as some have surmised, before the crisis—that the news came of Minny Temple's death. For him as for Henry, the fact was a devastation. It struck at their tenderest feelings of love, of course, but also at their imagination of love, at the poetry of human excellence, at any trust they might have in life itself. William's renewed struggle to will his recovery seems to be linked with that loss, turning it into a source of energy through the recognition of the tragic and the resolve to accept himself. A diary entry dated two weeks after Minny's death gives the contents of this emotional upturn: 'By that big part of me that's in the tomb with you, may I realize and believe in the immediacy of death! May I feel that every torment suffered here passes and is a breath of wind—every pleasure too. *Acts and examples* *stay....* * Is our patience so short-winded, *our curiosity so dead or our grit so loose* that that one instant snatched out of the endless age should not be cheerfully sat out? Minny, your death makes me feel the nothingness of all our egotistic fury. The inevitable release is sure; wherefore take our turn kindly whatever it contain. Ascend to *some sort of partnership with fate* and since *tragedy is at the heart of us,* go to meet it, work it in to our ends, instead of dodging it all our days.... Use your death (or your life, it's all one meaning).'

This Nietzschean declaration of *amor fati,* the love of fate, owes nothing, of course, to Nietzsche, then unknown. In carrying out the demands of his new vision, James discovered the potency of habit. It enables us to 'advance to really interesting fields of action' by supporting unfamiliar feelings and attitudes. 'My belief, to be sure, can't be optimistic—but I will posit life,' by which he means 'the self-governing resistance of the ego to the world.' Though far from wholly rescued, and subject to relapses ('I am again as melancholy as a whippoorwill'), James in his twenty-eighth year had forged in the throes of adversity a set of working principles by which to build a character. They were at the same time to determine the shape of a philosophy.


To outward view the young wastrel nearing thirty was not the wretched, impulse-torn creature that he knew himself to be. Shortly before her death Minny had written to a friend about William: "What a *real* person he is! ... in all respects a head and shoulders above other people." And somewhat earlier: "He has the largest heart as well as the largest head." That head he kept filling with knowledge covering many subjects, for which he finally found a use in his first consecutive, recognized, official occupation. James had attended a course of lectures on Optical Phenomena and the Eye, which led him to some experiments of his own in a lab he borrowed at the medical school. His initiative attracted notice. Those were the days when American colleges began to blossom into universities in a mood of come-one, come-all. Holding out "free electives" with one hand, President Eliot corralled students for Harvard, and with the other he gathered the best young talents he could find to build a faculty. When in 1872 James was offered and accepted an instructorship in anatomy and physiology, the colleagues of his generation in other departments included Henry Adams, John Fiske, and Oliver Wendell Holmes, Jr.

The odyssey was over: James had found a niche for his unique, single vocation of experimental-scientist-psychologist-philosopher. To say so

* Italics in this fragment are added.

may surprise those who have read about James that "he came to philosophy late," after digesting several tougher disciplines. That conclusion
rests on the familiar biographical fallacy—the recounting of a subject's
life by means of dates marking conventional steps: *studying* chemistry
and medicine, *assisting* Agassiz as naturalist in Brazil, *teaching* physiology, then psychology; *establishing* the first American laboratory in that
science, and finally *publishing* its *Principles* in 1890. It thus seems as if,
released by the act, James ascended to the clouds, like Socrates in his
basket in the play by Aristophanes. The sequence, formally correct, is
significantly false. Five years before his M.D., in 1864, James had read
and assimilated as much philosophy as many professors of the subject
possess at their retirement. His preoccupation with ideas had begun in
childhood, at father's table, if not at his knee, and it was never interrupted. As he announced to his brother before leaving Brazil: 'When I
get home, I'm going to study philosophy all my days.'

Nor was it for long an amateur concern—witness the score of articles
he published on philosophical subjects between 1870 and 1889, which
was also his productive period of "hard science." In retrospect it is
clear that all James's diverse studies were never put aside but kept
feeding convergent interests. President Eliot had noted, when James
studied chemistry with him, how frequent were this student's "excur-
sions into other sciences and realms of thought . . . ; his mind was excur-
sive, and he liked experimenting, particularly novel experimenting." In
parallel fashion, depression, the backaches, eyestrain, career flounder-
ings, foreign scenes and languages, painterly longings, cousin-and-
brother idolatry, Brazilian adventure, and passionate bull sessions*
merged into an encyclopedic experience of the kind that forms great
artists and epoch-making thinkers. James found himself philosophizing,
not: decided to become a philosopher.

But apart from his existential need to come to terms with life, how
did James conceive the task of philosophy at large? He tells us in a book
review of 1875: 'All philosophic reflection is essentially skeptical at the
start. To common sense, and in fact to all living thought, matters actually thought of are held to be absolutely and objectively as we think them.
Every representation becomes relative, flickering, insecure, only when
reduced, only in the light of *further* consideration which we may con-
front it with. This may be called its *reductive*.** Now the reductive of
most of our confident beliefs is that they are *our* beliefs; that we are

* Chiefly with Wendell Holmes and Chauncey Wright, variously inclined to skeptical
materialism.

** The term is borrowed from Taine (*De l'Intelligence*), who himself borrows it from
chemistry to denote an agent that reduces a compound to a simpler substance by removing oxygen. In its figurative use (as here), it suggests a device for clarifying or verifying
thought.

turbid media; and that a form of being may exist uncontaminated by the touch of the fallacious knowing subject. The motive of most philosophies has been to find a position from which one could *exorcise the reductive,* and remain securely in possession of a secure belief.'

It is perhaps worth noting about these words that James when he wrote them had just begun teaching his first course in psychology; it must have brought home to him more strongly than ever that the relation of the mind to objects is not a simple one and that any contribution of psychology to philosophy must be made as definite as possible by experiment. Now, of the current "reductives" scientific materialism was favored by James's closest friends; to James it was not good enough. As he had told Wendell Holmes more than once: 'I'm blest if I'm a Materialist: the materialist posits an X for his ultimate principle. Were he satisfied to inhabit this vacuous X, I should not at present try to disturb him. But that atmosphere is too rare; so he spends all his time on the road between it and sensible realities, engaged in the laudable pursuit of degrading every (sensibly) higher thing into a (sensibly) lower. . . . It availeth little that he should at the end put in his little caveat that, after all, the low denomination is as unreal as the unreduced higher ones were. . . . What balm is it, when instead of my High you have given me a Low, to tell me that the Low is good for nothing?'

This allusive critique of reductionism deserves a word of explanation, for it is central to James's thought: reality is not found by replacing some full experience with a list of its smaller components. Analysis and reduction distort. In other words, James affirms the main insight of Gestalt psychology and philosophy long before its birth.

But what is X and what are the 'sensible realities' that Holmes or Wright kept pushing one grade lower "laudably," says James with irony? X is matter, which no one has ever seen, heard, or touched; its existence is an assumption made by the materialist to provide a backstop for his actual sensations—what is seen, heard, touched, and so on—the "sensible" (sensed) elements of all experience, behind which no one can go. The supposition that "matter" is the ultimate reality Berkeley had shown untenable in a manner that cannot be got around. Dr. Johnson missed the point when he kicked a large stone, as Boswell relates, and thought he had refuted Berkeley. No one has ever denied that a stone is hard and real. But the question remains, Is there behind or below the hardness an "invisible pincushion" that holds together all the sensible "pins" (hard, rough, round, grayish brown etc.) of ordinary experience? * If so, what is it? Matter, answers the materialist. Mind (or God's mind), says the idealist, each a man of faith unable to bring his hypothesis to the proof. In the *Psychology* and later, we shall see James

---

* "Invisible Pincushion" was Coleridge's analogy for matter.

at war with both those hitherto prevalent views of the century he was born in.

Meanwhile he is unwilling to see any part of experience "lowered" by any kind of analysis, as if the experience thereby became "more real" or "ultimate." This Jamesian resistance to reductionism, like the role of psychology in his thought, is the mark of his contribution to the intellec- tual revolution of the 1880s and '90s. By then, the great nineteenth-century achievements in physics and biology had generated a scientific orthodoxy that professed to explain all of reality by the laws of evolution and thermodynamics. Given a little time, every question in the natural, social, and moral worlds would be answered with finality. The promised explanations, moreover, were simple—within any thoughtful person's grasp, being no more than organized common sense. Against this established faith, as against the other pieties now called Victorianism, the young men of James's generation everywhere directed their critical and constructive genius. James fired his first shot in the campaign when at the age of thirty-six he reviewed Spencer's *Psychology*.

In that massive work the evolution of the human mind is explained as the progressive "adjustment of inner to outer relations." The vagueness of this large "law" was enough to arouse James to combat, though to most of his advanced contemporaries the formula sounded plausible. The blessed words "adaptation" and "evolution" seemed to put every living thing in its place, from the humble polyp to H. Spencer himself. 'The picture drawn,' says James, 'is so vast and simple, it includes such a multitude of details in its monotonous framework, that it is no wonder that readers of a passive turn of mind are, usually, more impressed by it than by any portion of the book. But on the slightest scrutiny its solidity begins to disappear. In the first place, one asks, what right has one, in a formula embracing "the entire process of mental evolution," to mention only phenomena of cognition, and to omit all sentiments, all aesthetic impulses, all religious emotions and personal affections? The ascertainment of outward fact constitutes only one species of mental activity. [Yet think] how much of our mental life is occupied with this matter of a better or a worse? How much of it involves preferences or repugnances on our part? We cannot laugh at a joke, we cannot go to one theatre rather than another, take more trouble for the sake of our own child than our neighbor's; we cannot long for vacation, show our best manners to a foreigner, or pay our pew rent, without involving in the premises of our action some element which has nothing whatever to do with simply cognizing the actual.' We note here that the late twentieth-century objections to overvaluing the cognitive did not begin yesterday. James was early in challenging the crude evolutionism that interpreted mind as nothing more than a gatherer of useful facts. 'Mind, as we actually find it, contains all sorts of laws—those of logic, of fancy, of wit, of taste, decorum, beauty, morals, and so forth, as well as perception of fact.'

The words 'as we actually find it' are characteristic of the Jamesian questioning. It insists on all the evidence, and the result is an enlargement of the issue Spencer thought he was swiftly settling: 'Every living man would instantly define right thinking as thinking in correspondence with reality. But Spencer, in saying that right thought is that which conforms to outward relations, and this exclusively, undertakes to decide what reality is. In other words, under cover of an apparently formal definition he really smuggles in a material definition of the most far-reaching import. For the stoic, to whom *vivere convenienter naturae** was also the law of mind, the reality was an archetypal Nature; for the Christian, whose mental law is to discover the will of God, and make one's actions correspond thereto, *that* is the reality. In fact, the philosophic problem which all the ages have been trying to solve in order to make thought in some way correspond with it, and which disbelievers in philosophy call insoluble, is just that: What is the reality?'

Spencer's attempt to 'forestall discussion by a definition' is thus 'a proceeding savoring more of piracy than philosophy.' What is more, Spencer vacillates about what we ought to think. 'At one time "scientific" thought, mere passive mirroring of outward nature; at another time, thought in the exclusive service of survival. Let us consider the latter ideal first, since it has the polyp's authority in its favor: "We must survive—that end must regulate all our thought." The poor man who said to Talleyrand, "Il faut bien que je vive!" expressed it very well. But criticize that ideal, or transcend it as Talleyrand did by his cool reply, "Je n'en vois pas la nécessité,"** and it can say nothing more for itself. A priori it is a mere brute teleological affirmation on a par with all others. Vainly you should hope to prove it to a person bent on suicide, who has but one longing—to escape, to cease. Vainly you would argue with a Buddhist or a German pessimist, for they feel the full imperious strength of the desire, but have an equally profound persuasion of its essential wrongness and mendacity. Vainly, too, would you talk to a Christian, or even to any believer in the simple creed that the deepest meaning of the world is moral. For they hold that mere conformity with the outward—worldly success and survival—is not the absolute and ex-

---

* Living conformably to Nature.

** It was in fact D'Argenson who said he saw no necessity for the survival of the scribbler who was excusing himself for having written a libel against one of his benefactors. Voltaire reports the incident in the preface to *Alzire* (1736).

clusive end. In the *failures* to adjust—in the rubbish heap, according to Spencer—lies, for them, the real key to the truth, the sole mission of life being to teach that the outward actual is not the whole of being.'

The vehemence of James's prose must not be misunderstood. It is directed against Spencer's ideas, not toward the support of any of the beliefs cited. The range from the suicide to the Buddhist or moralist simply illustrates James's perception of the plural "realities" within which individuals do in fact live and choose their goals—realities that overlap, to be sure, but do not merge to constitute one Reality, whether abstract or concrete. James in effect makes the unusual demand that diversity as we find it be acknowledged until a better criterion than Spencer's pseudo-scientific one shall bring the suicide and the Christian into unforced agreement as to what *the* reality is.

With this wide-angled perception, James was early led to conclude that 'our opinions about the nature of things belong to our moral life.' This formulation implies that a philosophy is inadequate when it professes to be a flat, toneless, photographic report on a supposed reality. When such a report is made, other elements in experience have first been suppressed. It is plain, moreover, that by the time a man starts to philosophize he has long been "embarked" (as Pascal said) or *engagé* (as the existentialists put it), and his being there is part of the situation to be observed—as in quantum mechanics. Only, in James the proper analogy is not with the scientist but with the artist. He himself did not boast of the fact, but nothing is clearer in his writings than the recurrent esthetic attitude. In that regard, too, James is a "man of the nineties," as we shall see more amply later.*

The esthetic is of course but one part of the moral life. The passions, ethics, and religion claim their share of our being, and merely because cognition is overvalued one must not exclude from the passions the desire to know—curiosity and its companion: doubt or skepticism. In a letter of his twenty-fifth year addressed to his father on the subject of an article by the elder James, William explains why he cannot agree. His skepticism springs from his cognitive interest in the 'natural constitution of things,' which he refuses to regard as separated from the moral universe. 'I can understand no more than ever the world-wide gulf you put between "Head" and "Heart"; to me they are inextricably entangled together, and seem to grow from a common stem.' This declaration not only goes against all the common cliches about head and heart and about people who "are emotional" whereas others are "coldly intellectual"; but it also opposes the traditional ethics, as old as Plato, which teach that one ought to control the emotions by reason in the way that

* See also "William James and the Clue to Art" in my book *The Energies of Art*, 2nd ed., New York, 1962.

an expert rider controls a bucking bronco. Already at that early date, James perceived the admixture of emotion in all the workings of mind and saw in the false separation of feeling from thought a cause of the distrust people feel for one another's realities.* What is more, his power of introspection showed him what much later came to be known as ambivalence: 'The closest human love incloses a potential germ of estrangement or hatred.'

His difference from his father on this point reflects the different ways each took his mental crisis. As a result of his own, Henry Sr. read Swedenborg and was led to attribute true actuality solely to the realm of spirit. Nature for him as for Blake was a kind of superstition—a product of the sensuous imagination, an expression of the lowest form of intelligence, meant by Divine Wisdom to spur us onward to spiritual understanding. William, on the contrary, had painfully taught himself the principle of total acceptance—not to subordinate or explain away anything but to welcome the contents of every kind of experience. Starting with the given, he would find the meaning or meanings of any of its aspects. For his own sake, to overcome neurasthenia, he had had to pay attention to the idea of sanity, not dismiss it and give up his soul to the chaotic circumstances of life. His first obligation was to accept himself. His future pluralist empirical philosophy follows this same rule of keeping the gates of experience wide open without fear or favor.

Self-acceptance is not egotism; it is in fact modest when compared with self-contempt, for the latter may well result from an overblown estimate of one's powers, which "circumstances," "fate," or "the system" have kept from blossoming. At the same time, the self-accepting must beware of complacency while honoring the impulses of ambition and self-improvement. It is a tightrope performance in which the awareness of oneself is kept from becoming the crippling self-consciousness that is so characteristic of the intelligent in modern culture. James saw—and will make any good reader see—that the endless dialogue with the "second man" inside oneself, the debunking voice within, far from showing a modest and judicious spirit, prevents true modesty, leads from self-contempt to contempt of others, fails to subdue envy, and chills sympathy and tolerance into mere indifference.

Of course, William acquired some of his lovable traits and intellectual powers from his father, but their divergence about the makeup of man and the world is important and instructive. Henry Sr. had chafed under his father's rigid Calvinist upbringing and had accordingly reared his own offspring in the utmost freedom. Having found both

* It is a pity that western languages lack a word such as the Chinese hsin, which "conveys both cognitive and affective functions." (W. Theodore DeBary, Neo-Confucian Orthodoxy and the Learning of the Mind-and-Heart." (New York, 1981, p. 67.)

Union College and the Princeton Theological Seminary intellectually stifling, he was ever after "extremely tepid" about schools and colleges for his children. As a result, native genius and originality in William, Henry, and Alice flourished, not without harm. William in his maturity diagnosed his father's crisis as the outbreak of long-repressed hostile feelings against the paternal tyranny, but he suggested no cause for his own bout of total dread. One may plausibly surmise that it was the intolerable pressure of not being able to rebel against a father who exerted no tyranny but that of love.

Admiring as well his father's range and power of mind, William may have felt that for all his freedom to act, he had really no room, no role ahead of him. In his time of great fear, the idiot may have been the image of his own double powerlessness. Alice, too, was a victim of the same godlike affection and latitude, complicated by the presence of brothers and the mutually enveloping devotion of all the members of the family, a perfectly self-sufficient erotic-intellectual commune. Except by chance, it seems, there is no way to bring up children right—though some ways may be a little better than others.

At any rate, William's revolt against love yielded a more inclusive world view than his father's revolt against coldness; though here again it must be said that William's victory owed something to "Father's ideas." The elder James, as a disciple of Fourier the socialist, believed in the latter's "harmony of the emotions" and showed his children that this goal required a democratic equality of spirit and manners as well as of conditions—no distinctions based on class or wealth or religion; no sense of privileged access to God. "Society" in that sense, the good society, was "the redeemed form of man," and none could enjoy its blessings if he maltreated himself in his own mind.

William likewise acquired the parental notion that 'doing determines being,' character depends on action; we make ourselves as we go, by our choices. We are not wound-up mechanical toys performing within set limits, much less are we "chosen" ahead of time by a Calvinist deity. It follows that novelty can occur in the universe, mankind being the carrier of unknown possibilities, the germs of which deserve notice and nurture. Such convictions encourage a bias against systems, churches, social machineries—or at least those proclaimed as fixed and final.

A thinker moved by this rich cluster of feelings, experiences, and ideas logically comes to see reality as a series of postulates—as a group of realities, each of which risks its fortune in competition with the rest. Each 'depend[s] on experience as a whole to bear out its validity. The formula which proves to have the most massive destiny will be the true one.' History is again the court of appeals, but in no crude sense of temporary victory. For 'most massive' does not mean simply largest majority vote; it means wide acceptance and also most comprehensive coverage, widest satisfaction of the claims of head-and-heart.

Meanwhile, each thinker and doer must take a chance on the one conception that strikes him as most likely true, or right, or just. That is the tragic in history—everybody (or nearly) is sincere, pursues a legitimate end, a worthy cause; not everybody is right, but in the right, as in a good stage play, and few live to see the dénouement. Such is the permanent spectacle of the world and condition of our thought, for 'what umpire can there be between us but the future? In other words, we are all fated to be a priori teleologists, whether we will or not.* Interests which we bring with us, and simply posit or take our stand upon, are the very flour out of which our mental dough is kneaded. The organism of thought, from the vague dawn of discomfort or ease in the polyp to the intellectual joy of Laplace among his formulas, is teleological through and through. Not a cognition occurs but feeling is there to comment on it, to stamp it as of greater or less worth.'

The rest of this remarkable essay-review of 1878 goes further into reasons why James sees the mind as not merely serving but setting ends. His reasons at that point were far from fully documented or statable. The study of the many intricate ways in which the mind perceives and uses reality, the complexity of its performances from ordinary adapting to creating art and philosophy, were to occupy James for the next dozen years. Experiment, reading, debate, and reflection furnished the materials which he shaped first in chapter-articles for advance publication and which after this long gestation appeared as the inclusive Principles of Psychology, the work a sober modern critic has called "the important event of 1890."

By that pivotal date 1890, we find James full professor of philosophy at Harvard, happily married and father of four, as well as newly installed in a house he built in a new part of Cambridge, at 95 Irving Street, where during the next twenty years so many people of note sought him out, first as students perhaps, or as strangers, distant colleagues, or steady correspondents.**

James married Alice Howe Gibbens in 1878, and as usual with the Jameses, the circumstances were in several ways unusual, beginning with the background of the young woman herself. She was the daughter

---

* That is, awaiters of such proofs as apply to the goal we aim at.
** Across the street from No. 95 a minister and his wife shortly came to live. Their son, born in 1894, was later the poet e. e. cummings.

of a country doctor of the hearty type, who had died and left his family poorly off. To make do on their small income, the widow and two daughters went to live in Germany, at the very time of William's wanderings there. He and Alice might have met in Heidelberg or Dresden. After five years, during which Alice learned to speak German fluently and studied the piano with Clara Schumann, the ladies returned to Boston, where Alice began to teach school. These were all predisposing conditions for a romance with William, but its astonishing feature is that it was foretold by Henry Sr. before William and Alice ever met. Mr. James regularly attended the Radical Club, which was a Unitarian group intent on making religion pure of meaningless ritual and superstition. Alice was a member, and one evening talked at some length with Henry Sr. He came home and announced that he had met William's future wife.

At that time William, aged thirty-four, still considered himself to be in poor health and anything but a conspicuous success. Reluctantly he let himself be persuaded to meet Miss Gibbens. His old philosophical friend Thomas Davidson introduced the pair, for whom it was love at first sight as well as first love. They exchanged books; they read Browning together (at that date the equivalent of joining forces to work through *Finnegans Wake*); they found they enjoyed both poetry and thought. Henry Sr. had been right, no doubt because he understood the two natures; for their mutual attraction owed little to outward appearance. William did not look like a matinee idol. Alice was twenty-seven years old, stocky, and only her eyes, in a face without delicate features, revealed her intelligence, character, and vitality. These, of course, and her wit, appeared in her talk, uttered in a resonant, well-modulated voice that hearers noticed and did not forget.

William had at last met his unlikely but 'not impossible she,' as he himself said, remembering Crashaw's lyric. When Henry Sr. saw his son's inclination checked by inner doubts, he guessed that the inadequacy of an assistant professor's salary was one of the causes. Unlike the traditional father, he urged marriage and offered to supply the means. But in action as in thought William was ever fastidious and demanding of himself. What held him back now was a second scruple: his health. He thought it unfair to bind Alice to a quasi-invalid, periodically crippled by backaches, eye failure, and nervous irritability. Seeing him tortured by the conflict between apprehension and love, she decided that the only way to restore his peace of mind was to give him up. She even went to Canada for a time, to leave him untempted. For two years they fought out this struggle of conscience. Fortunately, love prevailed over self-distrust and from the outset the marriage justified itself, despite the occasional clash of two strong temperaments equally adept at verbalizing their feelings.

William's latest and best biographer, G. W. Allen, was the first to bring out what Alice Gibbens contributed to William's work and inward serenity. It was not merely that she made a home for him, became his amanuensis, and protected him from unwelcome intrusions; nor was it the additional good fortune of his adoring his mother-in-law, who returned his affection.* It was that Alice instinctively understood his genius, his mercurial moods, and emotional needs. A genius is never housebroken, and if a writer, he is always too much in the house, with his overflowing books and papers that must not be touched, and his odd visitors, and his superhuman need of quiet—or of immediate comforting companionship. James knew with all his powers of feeling exactly what Alice meant in his life and he let her know his gratitude and devotion.

We can gauge how remarkable Alice and William were, and their union also, from one of his letters to her during his trip to Europe in 1882, when he first made the acquaintance of leading thinkers and was received as one of them. Among impressions other than intellectual that he brought back from Germany, the deepest, he wrote, was of 'the indefatigable beavers of old wrinkled peasant women, striding like men through the streets, dragging their carts or lugging their baskets, minding their business, seeming to notice nothing in the stream of luxury and vice, but belonging far away, to something better and purer. They are the venerable ones whom we should reverence. All the mystery of womanhood seems incarnated in their ugly being—the Mothers! the Mothers! Ye are all one! Yes, Alice dear, what I love in you is only what these blessed old creatures have.'

Was James thinking of the scene of the Mothers in Goethe's *Faust* and counting on Alice's knowledge of it to interpret his words? At any rate, that a woman of thirty-two and not long married could accept a comparison with wrinkled old peasants is as noteworthy as William's feeling confident that she would understand it.

And as to her place in his uncommon taking of experience, William must again have relied on Alice's perfect understanding, for he writes to her after a visit to the Brighton aquarium that 'the impression which will perhaps outlast everything on this trip, was four cuttle-fish (octopus). I wish we had one of them for a child—such flexible intensity of life in a form so inaccessible to our sympathy.' This fancy was not a sign of indifference to children. The loss of his 'little Humster' [Her-

---

* James dedicated to her The Varieties of Religious Experience "In filial gratitude and love."

man, eighteen months old] affected him deeply. 'He was a broad, generous, patient little nature, with a noble head, who would doubtless
have done credit to his name.' But 'the great part of the experience to
me has been the sight of Alice's devotion. I thought I knew her, but I
didn't, nor did I fully know the meaning of that old human word *moth-
erhood*. Six weeks with no regular sleep, nine days with never more
than three hours in the twenty-four, and yet bright and fresh and ready
for anything as much on the last day as on the first. She is so essentially
*mellow* a nature that when the excitement is gone and the collapse sets
in, it will be short and have nothing morbid about it.'

William's letters were also sprinkled with spontaneous love-touches,
such as this one apropos of gardens: 'Like all human things (except
wives) they grow banal if one stays long in their company.' But the
greater part of what he wrote to her consisted of social, moral, and
philosophical observations that plainly show the companion she was on
the plane of intellect.

This affinity and community of tastes remained solid and effectual.
William now had a collaborator in the literal sense of the term. As early
as their honeymoon he felt free to work, as he wrote to his older friend
Francis Child, the folklorist whose name is now attached to the monumental collection of English and Scottish popular ballads. The latter
replied teasingly about this industriousness at such a time, to which
William rejoined: 'What is this mythological and poetical talk about psychology and Psyche and keeping back manuscripts composed during a
honeymoon? The only Psyche now recognized by science is a decapitat-
ed frog whose writhings express deeper truths than your weak-minded
poets ever dreamed. *She* (not Psyche but the bride) loves all these doctrines which are quite novel to her mind. She swears entirely by reflex
action now and believes in universal *Nothwendigkeit* [Necessity]. Hope
not with your ballad-mongering ever to gain an influence. We have
spent, however, a ballad-like summer in this delicious cot among the
hills [Keene Valley]. We only needed crooks and a flock of sheep.'

The work and manuscript referred to were the beginnings of the textbook in psychology for which James had signed a contract a month
earlier. It was to be a volume in Henry Holt's American Science Series
and the publisher wanted it in one year. James pleaded for two. It took
twelve. The egregious delay was due to the scope of the author's plan
and the originality and abundance of his materials. Indeed, the year
1878 marks James's coming into full possession of his riches of knowledge and talent. In February, word having gone out that the work of
this young man's psychological laboratory at Harvard (the first in the
country) was of prime quality, Daniel Coit Gilman invited James to lec-

ture at Johns Hopkins on "The Brain and the Mind." Immediately afterwards Gilman tried to acquire him for his faculty, but Eliot persuaded James to stay at Harvard. In the ensuing months James published three essays—"Remarks on Spencer's Definition of Mind" (which we have already sampled); "Quelques Considérations sur la Méthode Subjective" (in James's own French); and "The Sentiment of Rationality." Taken together, these hundred pages contain in embryo the leading ideas of James's psychology, philosophy, and moral science.

These three papers thus mark the birth of an original philosophy, nurtured (as we have seen) by reading, debate, and scientific work. James continued his research and his critique of current psychologies. In November 1878 James repeated his Johns Hopkins lectures at the Lowell Institute in Boston. From 1879 to the publication of the *Principles* in 1890, he contributed to professional and other journals no fewer than thirty-eight articles and reviews on topics ranging from mind in the lower animals to reaction time in the hypnotic trance, and from the origin of right-handedness to "The Hidden Self" (i.e., the unconscious), while also keeping the readers of *The Nation* informed of developments in evolution theory. It was in that period that he discovered the relation of dizziness to the malfunction of the semicircular canals of the ear and deduced remedies for seasickness and certain ailments in deafmutes. In that decade, too, he edited a volume of his father's writings on social theory and religion, which he introduced in a long, detailed study of their significance.

This pace of teaching and research was kept up despite continued trouble with his eyes, and Alice's secretarial help became indispensable in dealing with his ever-enlarging correspondence. In 1879, their first child was born and named Henry. The expectable addition to expenses compelled James to take on more outside lecturing, then called "popular," though it would seem high-academic today. At Harvard he continued his regular offering in psychology, with laboratory work, plus (that same year) a new course that soon became famous, Philosophy 3. The thought of the textbook for Holt no doubt kept hammering at his conscience. And then, too, a university exacts committee work, and there are students, with infinite demands on time and energy that are not infinitely elastic. Still, it was by any standard a happy life. The only possible flaw in the wonderful Jamesian harmony was the antagonism between the two Alices, wife and sister—a mysterious fact, for William's wife was much loved by all others in the family, Henry especially.

In 1881, the book still unwritten, James began to yearn for a break in routine, a year's leave abroad. He was eager for new or closer intellectual acquaintance with the men whose work he followed or with whom he corresponded. He sensed that he and they and yet others were bringing about a great cultural change. When the leave came, Alice was expecting a second child and he knew that leaving her, in excellent health and with her mother close by, to deal alone with the birth and the necessary recasting of domestic arrangements, would be a relief to her. She thought him clumsy and useless around the house, and the very depth and force of his sympathy could be trying.

The result was a trip of six months in 1882-83, during which he made the rounds of the intellectual centers—after Venice (for the paintings), Vienna, Salzburg, Prague, Berlin and other German universities, Liège, London, Oxford. He attended laboratory sessions and lectures and gave some when invited. He met Ewald Hering, Ernst Mach, Carl Stumpf, Carl Ludwig, the famous Wundt, Delboeuf, Pillon, Shadworth Hodgson, Leslie Stephen, Frederic Maitland, Edmund Gurney, Croom Robertson, Carveth Read, Frederick Pollock, and the young R. B. Haldane—a cross-section of the German and English intellectual establishments—as well as a number of Belgian scientists and philosophers who could have modified Baudelaire's contemptuous idea of "l'esprit belge."

All through the trip, James kept writing of his experiences to his "master," Charles Renouvier, whom he had hoped to see at last. But the old philosopher was not strong enough to come from the South to Paris, where James was attending the lectures by Charcot that were later to redirect Freud's career. News then came of Henry Sr.'s grave illness, which brought William to London, ready to sail home. He was urged not to break his leave as "the peril was not immediate." But a few days later he heard from his wife of his father's death and of the startling fact she had so far kept from him: old Henry, tired of physical existence and yearning to be pure spirit, had deliberately, in the course of several weeks, starved himself to death.

Throughout his voyage of mental refreshment, James had been plagued by insomnia and eyestrain, by concern for those at home, by an irritating argument in letters to and from his brother Henry—a very rare occurrence, at the end of which Henry admitted to having been "meddlesome." The subject was William's opinion that English society was "stuffy" and life in Cambridge better for his work. To Henry, settled in London, this was blasphemy; he tried to talk William into staying on with him, or at least in Europe for the remainder of the academic year. On top of these worries came their father's death and difficulties involving the other brothers, the unhappy ones, about the inheritance. The conflict, Jamesian fashion, was one between generous proposals, not selfish intentions, and it did not last long.

In retrospect, James's foray abroad proved extremely beneficial. Despite his unsteady nerves, it gave him renewed confidence in himself. Thanks to his fluency in French and German, he was able not merely to make his ideas known and valued, but also to gauge with precision the "state of the art" in European psychology and philosophy. 'I learned a good many things, both in the way of theory and fact. They are not so different from us as we think. But I found that I had a more *cosmopolitan* knowledge of modern philosophical literature than any of them, and shall on the whole feel much less intimidated by the thought of their like than hitherto.' This was about his German colleagues. In England, he was spurred to present some of his new ideas, and the lectures he sketched there developed into important sections of the *Psychology*, the writing of which was obsessively on his mind. The metaphor "stream of thought," "stream of consciousness" came to him then. 'Yesterday,' he wrote to his wife, 'I was parturient of psychological truth, being in one of my fevered states you wot of, when ideas are shooting together and I can think of no finite things. I wrote a lot at headlong speed, and in the evening, having been appointed, gave an account of it at the Scratch Eight' (an informal group of philosophers and psychologists).

After his return to the United States, James expanded these talks into complete lectures, which he delivered at the Concord (Mass.) School of Philosophy. He also published an important essay on "The Association of Ideas." But in spite of the growing material for his "big book," he was surprised to find that the writing of it did not go forward at speed as he had hoped. One reason was certainly the resumption of academic work, always an obstacle to consecutive thought. Another was the need to digest what he had learned abroad. James was the psychologist who said that we learn to skate in summer and to play tennis in winter, meaning that the inner integration of experience takes place slowly and during inactivity. In the same way, Wordsworth attributed the making of poetry to "emotion recollected in tranquillity." Then (what is often forgotten in quoting this familiar tag) a long contemplation of the experience gradually dispels the tranquillity and a kindred experience comes to occupy the mind. "In this mood," says Wordsworth, "successful composition generally begins."

In other words, in the minds we call creative (as against mere data processors), a great work takes its own time for incubation. So it was with James's *Principles of Psychology*, which, as we were told before by the historian of the Unconscious, was "the important event of the year 1890."

# The Masterpiece

The work that James gave to the world in 1890 is an American masterpiece which, quite like *Moby Dick*, ought to be read from beginning to end at least once by every person professing to be educated. It is a masterpiece in the classic and total sense—no need of a descriptive or limiting word before or after: not "of observation," or "of prose writing," not more "scientific" than "humanistic." One can point to these and other merits if one is so minded, but the fused substance defies reduction to a list of epithets. No matter how many unexpected qualities are found in it—wit, pathos, imaginative understanding, polemical skill, moral passion, cosmic vision, and sheer learning—the work remains always greater than their sum.

The book is again like *Moby Dick* in being the narrative of a search. When well launched on either, one reads on and on for the sake of the plot. At once simple and grandiose, it makes the vast erudition not merely easy to absorb but a bulwark of verisimilitude. And in James, the object of the pursuit is as elusive, as intimate, as momentous for Everyman as anything symbolized by the white whale: it is the human mind; or how, from multiple sensation—the 'one great blooming, buzzing confusion' of the infant's encounter with the world—comes such an extraordinary entity as the warm particular self each of us knows, with its perceptions, will, judgment, habits, emotions, preferences; and its undetermined powers: its capacity to abstract and remember, to suffer and utter in myriad languages, to create art and philosophize, to invent systems of writing and of algebra; and with the aid of puny limbs and muscles to bore through mountains, bridge abysses, and reach the moon.

It is no wonder the book is long, yet not so long as *War and Peace*, with which it shares one possibly obstructive feature. Readers of Tolstoy will remember how in their first acquaintance with *his* masterpiece the setting of the stage seemed long and dull—fifty pages of three-layered Russian names and no clear direction for our interest. Near the beginning of James's *Principles* there are also some pages that may at first seem rather dry. The opening proper is most enticing, but roughly between pages 30 and 65* with their diagrams and technical words the impression may arise that one is becalmed in a textbook. James had every reason—and Tolstoy no excuse—for putting us through this discipline. If we are interested, I will not say simply in the mind, but in conscious life, art, thought, the passions and the illusions of mankind, we must know something about the presumable seat of these activities. Hence the discourse about brain function and its physical conditions.

Nor is that subject as James treats it so much dull as temporarily forbidding by its terminology. But whoever happens to be ignorant of the neurology of the reflex arc will quickly become interested in learning why he drops the hot handle of the skillet and jumps up when he sits on a tack; while the sophisticated may be surprised to discover why it is inaccurate to speak of one's "reaction" to people or ideas, and why the familiar "conditioned reflex" is not a true reflex: it can be made to disappear by repeating the stimulus without reward—or, as Pavlov found out, by a sudden emergency, as when his trained dogs were caught in a fire.

The larger significance of the reflex arc is as the pattern or, better, as the scaffolding of our mental activity. Brain function is the physical response to the myriad stimuli that arouse it—the things we call "the world outside." The mind, which is *not* brain function, depends upon that response for its very different activity. The assumption is that 'every sensorial excitement propagated to a lower center tends to spread upwards and arouse an idea. Every idea tends ultimately either to produce a movement or to check one which otherwise would be produced.' What marks off the simple nerve-and-muscle mechanism of the reflex from the scaffolding above is that 'the lower centers act from present sensational stimuli alone; the hemispheres of the brain act from perceptions and considerations, the sensations which they receive serving only as suggesters of these.'

The originality of James's psychology is that it is written throughout from the empirical or naturalist's point of view without its being "reductive." He finds in experience alone the constituents of the mind and

* Of the 1890 edition, New York, Henry Holt, 2 vols., 1890. At the writing of this chapter, the new Harvard edition had not yet appeared.

the explanations of its performance. But beware of taking "experience" too narrowly or equating it with one or another philosophy of knowledge or behavior. Not the least revelation of the *Principles* is its demonstration of what astonishing things do or do not occur in experience.

This being so, one looks back on those introductory pages and diagrams with something like the affection one feels for the unfamiliar rules that taught one a new game or the complex instructions for assembling a useful and diverting piece of equipment—except that here the game and the equipment have been ours from birth, and the wonder is that after so long a use we are learning to thread their intricacy for the first time.

But if we come to *The Principles of Psychology* in the mood suited to a *Moby Dick* or *War and Peace*, may we also expect the solid disclosures of science? We may: "the big event of 1890" was awaited by contemporary psychologists because they knew from the author's published papers dating as far back as 1868 how much research and experimentation had gone into its making. As we saw, sixty years later a professional reviewer could still speak of its power to strike humility in the modern researcher. Recent studies have extended our understanding of the neurons and confirmed James's evidence that the brain fosters the range and rapidity of thought thanks to the wide flooding of whole regions of it by neural impulses. But science today is no nearer than in James's time to explaining how the physiological processes are related to the contents and workings of consciousness. 'Thought is not the brain, closely as it seems to be connected with it.'*

Where then is the science in psychology? This question will occur to some, because we have grown used to looking for explanations "from below," on some darker level than the one surveyed, where it is hoped things may be simpler. But the first duty of science is to its own domain. Make *that* clear and perhaps other connections will be disclosed. James established psychology as an independent science by adhering to this principle, which meant refusing to treat psychology as a branch of physiology, keeping a steady eye on a distinct subject matter, and making only those assumptions appropriate to it.

The subject matter can be defined simply enough: thoughts and feelings as experienced. And the main assumption is that these experiences occur 'in a physical world existing in time and space, with which the thoughts and feelings co-exist and which they "know."' Such is the *nat-*

---

* It is a pity that the terms that James adopted—*neurosis* for the nerve action and *psychosis* for the mental event—were diverted by heedless psychiatrists into the meanings now attached to them. For they made clear the brain-mind distinction now so persistently blurred. See James's usage in the *Principles*, I, p. 243.

uralist's point of view. I revive the old word and avoid "naturalistic," because the term has come to stand for accounts of experience based on the analogy of man and machine—the materialist interpretation. James throughout is dead against such imports from philosophy—and not the materialist alone, but the idealist, associationist, and (as in Spencer) the crudely evolutionist. 'To explain our phenomenally given thoughts as products of deeper-lying entities is metaphysics,' and thus belongs outside his book. James was well fitted by his long study of philosophy to detect its secret influence where it had no business. He shows again and again how it has beclouded psychology and distorted our ideas. And because of that age-old entanglement which he must undo, the *Psychology* gives us along the way a virtual history of the warring conceptions of the mind since Plato.

Happy as one may be at the thought of such a grand panorama having been composed by a man of genius, the question may nevertheless occur, "Why come closer and scan it in detail?" The reissue of James's *Psychology* in 1950 was considered "an important event" for a psychologist, as one who reviewed it said, but what benefit is the layman to expect? A sufficient answer is that becoming acquainted, through James, with the workings of the conscious mind will open up new vistas on every subject of interest, general and special. Unsuspected facets of one's intelligence, feelings, and memory; of language and opinion, art, education, and society will be successively disclosed. At the same time, persons who have taken too trustingly the various (and inconsistent) teachings that our thoughts and acts are fated by physical or sub-psychic forces (glands, genes, the unconscious) will become reacquainted with a most interesting part of themselves, whose workings "explain" fully as much as blind forces, chemical or animal, and often in more succulent detail.*

The first task of a naturalist psychology is obviously to describe with accuracy. 'There is no closed system in this book.' But psychology calls for special methods and faces characteristic snares. The methods are: introspection, difficult and fallible as it is; the study of abnormal minds and of normal ones under hypnosis, drugs, or stress; and experiments, both on animals and on human beings—to determine reaction time, perceptual discrimination, optical illusions, and generally all modes of sensory response. The several methods often give divergent results; what settles doubts is 'the final consensus of our farther knowledge.' In

---

* One student of James's work sums up the effect of psychoanalytic interpretations of mind: "Our horizon has been progressively restricted by a set of theoretical pre-conceptions." This judgment could apply as well to the physiological preconceptions that have restricted the interpretation of acts and feelings. (Norman Cameron in *William James, the Man and the Thinker*, Addresses on His Centenary, Madison, Wis., 1942, p. 81.)

this part of his work James had the advantage of drawing on more than a hundred years of abundant observation. Yet in reading him one has no feeling of being choked with raw data; all has been sifted, corrected, digested into a wonderfully smooth and orderly exposition—a formidable task, as one can see by noting the array of authors who survived scrutiny for citation in his pages.*

As for the snares, the greatest is what James calls "the psychologist's fallacy." It consists in 'thinking that the mind he is studying must necessarily be conscious of the object after the fashion in which the psychologist himself is conscious of it.' The psychologist here includes anyone looking at a thought or feeling from the outside. When we do so 'we have the inveterate habit of dropping the thought as it is in itself and talking of something else. We describe the things that appear to the thought, and we describe other thoughts *about* those things—as if these and the original thoughts were the same. If, for example, the thought be "the pack of cards is on the table," we say, "Well, isn't it a thought of the pack of cards? Isn't it of the cards as included in the pack? Isn't it of the table? And of the legs of the table as well? . . . Hasn't our thought, then, all these parts—one part for the pack and another for the table? And within the pack-part a part for each card, as within the table-part a part for each leg? And isn't each of these parts an idea? And can our thought, then, be anything but an assemblage or pack of ideas, each answering to some element of what it knows?"

'Now not one of these assumptions is true. The thought is, in the first place, not of "a pack of cards." It is of "the pack-of-cards-is-on-the-table," an entirely different subjective phenomenon, whose Object implies the pack and every one of the cards in it, but whose conscious constitution bears very little resemblance to that of the thought of the pack *per se*. What a thought *is*, and what it may be developed into, or explained to stand for, and be equivalent to, are two things, not one.'

This difference is the first great lesson of James's work; for the psychologist's fallacy carries over into all modes of thought and feeling and

---

* The classics are present to begin with, including: Plato, Aristotle, the Scholastics, Hobbes, Descartes, Locke, Malebranche, Berkeley, Hume, Condillac, Rousseau, Diderot, Destutt, Priestley, Reid, Thomas Brown, Hartley, Kant, Hegel, Mill, Herbart, and Schopenhauer. One finds also many contemporaries of James's who are still remembered, among them: Darwin, Huxley, Bain, Galton, Hartmann, Hodgson, Lotze, Bradley, Tarde, Taine, Mach, Royce, Ward, Grant Allen, Romanes, Ribot, O. W. Holmes, Wundt, E. H. Weber, Fechner, Lewes, Bagehot, Charcot, Janet, Mantegazza, Helmholtz, Gurney, Cattell, Münsterberg, and Weismann. Finally, one encounters a host of obscure indispensables, who make one feel (with all respect) like Oscar Wilde's hero in *The Importance of Being Earnest*, "What names these people have!": A. Moll, Hack Tuke, Plateau, Piderit, Mosso, Volkman von Volkmar, Kussmaul, Blix, Bubnoff, Stumpf, Lipp, Lipps, Boxt, Azam, Bleek, Gley, Grashey, Munk, Naunyn, Neiglick, Pitres, Strümpell, Fick, Nothnagel, Vierordt, Vennum, Orschansky, Wunderli, Tschisch, and Urbantschitsch.

is the unending source of mankind's deepest and bloodiest errors. The familiar failure to see ourselves as others see us is bad enough, but the reverse blindness is even more dangerous: we scarcely begin to know what reality the multitude of selves around us perceive. Yet we either bestow on them our reality or, when they act contrary to it, we impute to them all manner of folly and wickedness for not seeing and doing what is so plain to us. The psychologist aware of the fallacy simply states that to know something and to know about it belong to separate spheres of experience, and these must be carefully reconciled before understanding can be attained. In some languages the discrepancy is recorded in two unlike verbs, both meaning "to know": *kennen* and *wissen, connaître* and *savoir, conocer* and *saber,* etc. Our being and our experience we know by direct awareness; the rest is second-hand, by observation and inference: compare notes with your dentist after he has hurt you more than he expected.

To sum up the naturalist view of psychology: its proper subject and sole material is what happens in the mind, not some assumed identity between this and any behavior of the organism, muscular or neural. For what happens is certainly not that a thought or feeling is *of* a nerve current or *of* a muscular movement. True, the mind inside the skull, in the dark, is 'incited by nerve changes and nothing else,' but 'of these it knows nothing.' How thoughts accompany the brain's workings, or the relations of a mind to its own brain are 'of a unique and utterly mysterious sort.' They can 'only be written down empirically, confessing that no glimmer of explanation is yet in sight.' The chances are that the connection eludes us because of the very power by which the mind knows reality and itself as well. Think of the eye, too busy to see how it performs its own seeing; all it can ever see of sight is the dissected optic nerve on the laboratory table, the retina, lens, and other parts, no longer seeing.

What is more, in this act of observation, the mystery of mind persists, for how it knows objects "outside itself" is not explained either. Common speech assumes that "sensations" (which most of us would find it hard to define clearly) are the signals that enable us to navigate in a universe of solid objects, and it is clear that the mind learns to handle as objects the confused and continuous mass of stimuli that bombard our outer covering. But apart from the speculations of philosophers there is nothing to be said but that they occur. 'Sensations, aware of mere qualities, involve the mystery as much as thoughts, aware of complex systems, involve it.' No "machinery" imaginable will solve the riddle, as one may realize by stopping to think of 'the effect of the word "Wake!" on a patient in a hypnotic trance.' Minds are objects in a world of objects, and somehow related as inhabitants of a real space and real time. How these relations are possible is not the business of psychology. But the interest of the question is such that James as philosopher will tell us later his formulation of an answer.

Compared with the empirical psychologist's rigorous program, the subject as it is understood today gives the impression of a relapse into primitive ideas. Few among the educated show much knowledge of the mind's performance; the language used to deal with ideas and feelings, especially in criticism and social theory, follows ancient misconceptions. In popular use, psychology means guessing or playing upon other people's motives and characters. "It's such a psychological thing between pitchers and hitters," says a famous baseball player. "When they're using something other than psychology alone, when they apply a substance to the ball or make a naughty mark on it, pitchers have aerodynamics and other elements of science working for them."

These casual remarks fairly represent the common view that "psychology" means wiliness and "science" means "substance"—physical objects. Popular magazines, relying on the same assumptions, thrive by proffering alarm, hope, and advice based on "studies" that reveal endlessly, month after month, the inexhaustible secrets of "the" human mind. There are methods for augmenting one's attractiveness or ability to love and for strengthening the memory, will power, or concentration—old family recipes rewritten in the mixed jargon of couch psychiatry and laboratory psychology. The old mechanistic superstition occurs again in ordinary fiction—Hercule Poirot's "little gray cells" *telling him* what to think; or, by a simple shift to newer clichés, "my unconscious" dictating this or that attitude and behavior.*

As professional disciplines, academic psychology and its nervous sister, psychiatry, have divided into many sects, some approaching a religious strictness and fervor of belief, and most of them falling into the psychologist's fallacy by confusing thoughts or feelings with their surmised origins and causes. Current jargon shows how the psychiatries have indoctrinated the public mind through literature and the press. "Neurosis," "complex," "fixation," have become popular means of "psychologizing," which is to say discovering secret agents at work in thought and behavior, others' and one's own.**

---

* Similar assumptions influence even highly educated minds. A distinguished sculptor and critic once wrote of a fellow-artist that in him could be found "some chromosomes of Breughel or Hieronymous Bosch." The remark was figurative, but its imagery reveals the under-belief that one's style or view of the world comes from one's genes.

** Should we attribute this prevailing mode of thought to a "substitution compulsion"?

It is a life of unmasking, which, in its suspicion of all appearances, destroys the true ones along with the false. For unmasking takes as the chief signs of truth that it is hidden, complicated, surprising, and unpleasant. "Depth analysis" is here at one with behaviorist psychology in pushing back the mind (which, as James says, is but 'a class name for distinct individual minds') into the pre-Jamesian condition of an appliance moved by hidden wires. This desire to bodify the mind is unchecked, because it chimes in with the common conception of "what science says" and because it serves the convenience of laboratory experiments—those that seek to pull habits out of rats by mechanical traps; or that demonstrate changes in behavior by physical tampering, such as implanting electrodes in the brains of monkeys. The treatment makes them understandably ill-tempered, poor mothers, or oversexed, but their minds as such are still far from intimately known.

Again, physicians have marked off a portion of their domain as psychosomatic medicine, thus giving the public the idea that whereas some diseases are altogether events of the soma or body, a few others regrettably stem from the psyche or mind. But no doctor has yet been found who ever saw a patient walk in as a free soma without a psyche, or vice versa. These simplifying doctrines suit our age, which seeks formulas for classification and control, faced as it is with a mass of men in unmanageable numbers and irreconcilable states of mind. Brainwashing, reconditioning by drugs or surgery, or in any other way forcibly manipulating behavior go with the theory of mechanical causation; each supports the other.

James had to deal in his book with the related but more extreme idea; it should study only that the mind and its states were no concern of science, mentioned earlier, the changes that take place in the tangible parts of organism. "We are conscious automata," said Huxley in 1872; and he found the "explanation" wonderfully simplifying. It had the further advantage of making human and animal psychology into one field, for as Huxley said: "the consciousness of brutes would appear to be related to the mechanism of their body simply as a collateral product of its workings . . . and the argumentation which applies to brutes holds good of men."

James's verdict was: the Automaton Theory springs from 'a sort of philosophic faith, bred like most faiths from an esthetic demand. Mental and physical events are on all hands admitted to present the strongest contrast in the entire field of being. Why not then call it an absolute chasm, and say that the two worlds are independent? This gives us the comfort of all simple and absolute formulas.' The desire of laboratory men 'not to have their physical reasonings mixed up with such incommensurable factors as feelings is certainly very strong. Feeling constitutes the "unscientific" half of existence.' But, James goes on, to ignore that half is to ignore half the difficulties of the subject. 'For this "concomitance" in the midst of absolute separateness is an utterly irrational notion. It is to my mind quite inconceivable that consciousness should have *nothing to do* with a business which it so faithfully attends.'

In the biological branch of laboratory psychology, present-day students of the brain and nervous system work with similar postulates about the mind. Some labor to refine our knowledge of brain functions by localizing them very exactly, finding in one region the so-called "nose-brain," whose specialty is smelling. Others push their search into the supposed "oldest part of the brain," the R-complex, to discover with the aid of lizards what "natural behaviors" are embedded there. Referring to one investigator, *Science* says he "believes that to understand ourselves, we have to figure out what our animal brains are up to." Another has learned that "in goldfish, the M-cell is a command neuron that mediates the fastest forms of startle responses, in which a strong flip causes the fish to yaw abruptly." And pursuing the secret of structure and activity in a single cell is the present business of cellular neurobiology.

All these experiments are wonderful to follow; they testify to immense ingenuity and patience and are buttressed by a broad system of supports in related sciences. They have the one inconvenience of leaving the manifold activities of the human mind rather in the distance. Even if we were willing to postpone our curiosity about the mind, we would remain uneasily aware that the brain is often able to reassign or recover functions after injury or amputation; that it can "perceive different color sensations from identical stimuli," and that one can display an IQ of 126 "and have virtually no brain." None of this squares with the premise that the gears and levers are in sole control.

Nor do these uncertainties encourage belief in other writers, who are not neurologists (including the ever-speculative Marshall McLuhan), but who take inspiration from the division of the brain into two hemispheres to build great theories of culture and individual types, telling us what the left or the right lobe has "dictated" to human history and where it is taking us now.*

The most thoughtful of recent investigators say among other things: "The cerebral cortex is virtually terra incognita." And they go on to confirm what James perceived as all-important—in his words 'the insta-

---

* See Julian Jaynes, *The Origin of Consciousness in the Breakdown of the Bicameral Mind* (Boston, 1977), and my review of it in the *Times Literary Supplement*, May 19, 1978.

bility of the molecular system in that blood-soaked sponge,' the brain. Because it is unstable and ever-ready to form and re-form itself, it permits the infinity of interconnections that accompany, *no one knows how,* our endless shifting thoughts.*

Given this ignorance, which few admit, and the equal resistance of mind and of brain to being made interchangeable on easy terms, the tempting way out is to discard the more troublesome of the pair. In the study of sensation known as psycho-acoustics, this goal appears to have been reached. This science has shown that "a mathematically ideal observer and a simple energy detector, although worlds apart conceptually, behave rather alike. The net outcome is that the listener can be painted out of the picture in the ideal way that sensory psychologists strive to discover." In other words, "Back to the automaton!"

The principle that in order to know the mind scientifically we must get rid of it is as noteworthy as the remark that a living listener is *conceptually* different from a piece of equipment. How he differs concretely in the world of experience is nobody's business. As for the triumph of replacing the mind by a detector, it is on a par with replacing it by an unconscious that does all the work and leaves us the role of a talkative puppet. Reductive schemes of this kind have one trait in common: they work indirectly. The mind is not there under study, something else is: lobe or nerve or cell; or not the human mind but a monkey's or a lizard's or "a reliable detector." James's naturalist outlook and method, by contrast, aim at satisfying human curiosity about the organ and agent of curiosity itself, of *knowing,* and of its amazing experiences—what it learns of objects, space, and time; how it comes to feel, choose, and move; how it remembers, changes mood, makes errors, loses direction and control, splits into disparate halves, as well as performs seeming miracles of judgment, reasoning, and imagination.

Once the distinction is clear between brain function and mind, the question of paramount interest is: what sort of thing is mind? It is in fact not a thing in the ordinary sense, not a switchboard or a computer circuit, these being analogies applicable only to brain and brain function.

---

* James's observation brought up to date is put in the following technical terms by the recent investigators quoted above: "Of course, complexity as such need not necessarily result in 'plasticity' or modifiability, which is yet another attribute of higher brain function. . . . The new view of the neuron, based primarily on recent electron microscope evidence . . . holds that the dendrite, far from being only a passive receptor surface, may also be presynaptic, transmitting information to other neurons. . . . Such neurons may simultaneously be the site of many electrotonic current pathways. . . . A crucial feature of local circuits is their high degree of interaction both through specialized junctional structures and through the extracellular fields generated by local and more distant brain regions." (F. O. Schmidt, P. Dev, B. H. Smith, "Electrotonic Processing of Information by Brain Cells," *Science,* vol. 193 [July 9, 1976], pp. 114, 120.)

Nor is mind a ghostly kind of presiding officer recognizing speakers from the floor, or a sovereign receiving messages from couriers, as earlier psychologies used to teach. The mind is first of all a stream: 'Chain or train does not express it; it flows.' From James's now famous phrase ... "the stream of consciousness" have also flowed many novels, good and bad, which profess to recapture the mind in its natural state.*

Such an attempt is impossible, for the mental stream is of a peculiar sort. At every moment a central wave or swirl in it is most prominent and vivid, is surrounded by a fringe of fainter presences, and is endlessly fading away, to be replaced by some portion of what was faint a moment before. The whole motion is orgasmic: it works up to a peak of emphasis, forging ahead to the goal of its desire, neglecting or rejecting the rest. As each wave recedes, its remembered actuality may form part of the next. There is no limit to the number of items—ideas, objects, memories—that may coexist in a single pulse of consciousness. To set all these down on paper is beyond anyone's attention and memory and the result would be unreadable even if reproducible. In reaching its peak of vividness each pulse seems endowed with a direction of its own—it tends toward we know not what, but we translate this feeling as our *interest* or *focus of attention*: the stream feels as if moving with a purpose.

All these terms, of course, are figures of speech—necessarily, for consciousness is unique and so infinitely variable that all the words one could apply to what happens there fall short of the experience. James himself never ceased to marvel at its character; he calls it the 'wonderful stream of our consciousness' of which the components may move each at its own pace; there are 'flights and perchings,' which human language expresses in part by its rhythms, by its sentences stopped and begun. To match the 'magical, imponderable streaming of our ideas,' the agglutinative languages, which string together a series of vocables into one interminable word, would clearly be closest, though otherwise inconvenient. In another way, highly inflected languages such as Greek and Latin fit thought more faithfully than French or English, because in their declensions and conjugations the words do not stay the same but change their endings so that "the same but different" is rendered in tangible form.**

* The phrase, foreshadowed as 'stream of mental action' in an essay of 1879, occurs here and there in the *Principles* (e.g. I, 239), though the main treatment is in a chapter headed "The Stream of Thought." In the shorter version of the work, a year later, that same chapter is entitled "The Stream of Consciousness." The term appears to have been first used in literary criticism—to describe a novelistic device—by May Sinclair in 1918. (Kenneth Hopkins, *The Powys Brothers*, Fairleigh Dickinson Press, 1967, p. 156.)

** It is a striking fact that the more primitive the language the more faithfully does it reflect this feature of thinking. As languages progress and drop inflections, they resemble rather a shorthand than a contour map of thought.

No words, of course, can ever reproduce the 'shimmering of consciousness,' mysteriously linked with the 'infinite inward iridescences' of the brain cells under stimulation. These two sets of terms together define the 'concrete and total manner of regarding the mind,' and James's choice of words also suggests the likeness between the stream of thought and an Impressionist canvas—no hard contours, but fringes around every object or cluster, all of them aglow with the feeling of interest, with meaning. But despite its flowing quality, the mind also experiences sharp contrast or difference, the glow often being the result of the contrast, as when thunder is felt, not as such, but as 'thunder-breaking-upon-silence-and-contrasting-with-it,' or when after a steady noise 'silence sounds delicious.'

In the light of this description the analogy so passively received nowadays, of the mind as computer, is manifestly fallacious. A computer does not think, it feels nothing, and what it is said to "know"—bits of information all cast in the digital mode—has no fringe. Nor has it a memory, only storage room. On any point called for, the answer is all or none. Vagueness, intelligent confusion, original punning on words or ideas never occur, the internal hookups being unchangeable; they were determined once for all by the true minds that made the machine and the program.* When plugged in, the least elaborate computer can be relied on to work to the fullest extent of its capacity; the greatest mind cannot be relied on for the simplest thing; its variability is its superiority. Homer nods, Shakespeare writes twaddle, Newton makes mistakes, you and I have been known to talk nonsense. But they and we can (as the phrase goes) surpass ourselves, invent, discover, create. The late John von Neumann, mathematician, logician, and inventor of game theory, would not allow one to liken the mind to a computer. He knew how his mind worked and he understood his computer. So goodbye to all the bright remarks, in fiction and conversation, about programming oneself to pass an interview.

Mechanical and electronic analogies, then, are alike false to the fluidity of the stream. But even worse, they mistakenly assume that the contents of the mind are "ideas" or pictures corresponding to their "object" in a one-to-one relation, each idea summoned up by the object outside or by the memory of it inside. This model James explicitly rejects. That is the first of his revolutions. His account of the mind is 'meant to impeach the entire English psychology derived from Hume and Locke, and the entire German psychology derived from Herbart, so

---

* "Intelligent confusion" is not a paradox. As James points out, 'confusion and reasoning are generically the same process. The difference between a muddle-head and a genius is that between extracting [from experience] wrong characters and right ones. All *eminently* muddle-headed persons have the temperament of genius.' (*Principles*, II, pp. 352n.–353n.).

far as they treat "ideas" as separate subjective entities that come and go.'*

To begin with, 'what are things? Nothing but special groups of sensible qualities which happen practically or esthetically to interest us, to which we therefore give substantive names, and which we exalt to this exclusive status of independence and dignity. But in itself, apart from my interest, a particular dust-wreath on a windy day is just as much of an individual thing, and just as much or as little deserves an individual name, as my own body does.' One could add that "things" felt as more solid than the swirl of dust are no less changeable in their "sensible qualities." Anyone brought up in the Alps and taking trips among them knows that "a mountain" is never twice the same—in shape, color, and "character." It is "one thing" by a fiat helped by a name.

James's denial of one idea for one object also corrects the old confusion between the thought of an object's recurring as the same object—something we experience, obviously—and the sameness of the recurring thought, which in a living being is impossible. For as one cannot step into a river twice—the water has flowed on—so one can never think the same thought twice: the stream of thought has flowed on. But the new thought can acknowledge the return of its object: "This is my hat, my good old hat." The present pulse of consciousness takes cognizance of the present object simultaneously with previous (and different) thoughts of the hat, charged with the feeling of sameness.

The importance of this account of mind is, first, that it accords better with what we experience—the variableness of each of our "takings" of reality. And it is also important because it destroys the notion that our mental states are put together from bits of material poking in from outside—a color, a sound, a smell—each distinct and unchanging, then somehow fitted together by the mind into permanent shapes and stored in cubby holes for later reference. Such "ideas" by definition could have no "fringe," no varying intensity or warmth—in short, no feeling-tone—and such lumps would not flow.

The idea-psychology was a prime example of the psychologist's fallacy. We know what this is: the observer conceives and tags the mental state by reference to the object which he knows to be fixed in name and nature. He knows all this not naïvely, but for his adult purposes as philosopher and man of science. This being my hat in front of us, you as psychologist look at it abstractly and with contempt—it is your first

* Did psychology cling to "ideas" because the word suggests a fixed and neatly rounded "thing"? In English, "thinking" has been freely used as a synonym for thought or idea as far back as 1382. Since James's time, the verbal form in -ing, which renders the streaming, has taken the lead over thought, and one may hear: "Give me your thinking and I'll give you mine"—a pledge that might well inspire a popular song.

sight of the battered thing—whereas I as owner see it with a careless eye full of affection, fringed by fond memories of travel together. These are two distinct mental states, each a complete and single whole, and in neither is there a pure, detachable image to be labeled "gray hat."

Several issues are disposed of by this fundamental view of a mental stream: no need to argue whether perceptions "represent" things or only present them; or what form a thing assumes in the mind when only a general notion (concept) of it is held there; or whether ultimate reality resides in things or names or concepts. All of experience—concept, name, or thing—is real exactly as someone experiences it. The "all" includes dreams, visions, trances, and hallucinations. As naturalist the psychologist deals with them as with everything else that occupies or affects mind, any failing or abnormality, good or bad—color-blindness, echolalia, insanity, genius, perfect pitch, synesthesia, total recall: he has no right to dismiss from experience any observed event as it is delivered in and through the mind. He may of course account for it, classify it as more or less stable, more or less usual, more or less true in relation to a given purpose. That is why he will need a really subtle test of truth, which we shall find on a later page.

Remembering now that the streaming contents of the mind arise in some way from the exposure of nerve and brain to stimuli, we are led to ask how the random bombardment turns finally into something like an ordered view of—let us not say *the* world, but *a* world, each person's world. It is clear that from the first moments of infant consciousness, choice takes place. The body receives too many sensations for all to be attended to; without selection, experience would remain chaos. As James says: 'My experience is what I agree to attend to.' What governs choice is *interest* in its double sense: we follow what is interesting and what looks like serving our interest. In either appeal lies a purpose, however dim. To say this is also to say that the stream of thought surges forward along the path of meaning. The mind *means*, intends—is intent upon. 'The sense of our meaning is an entirely peculiar element of thought. No one can turn on himself and catch it' by looking inward. It pertains to the fringe, and is a feeling of tendency, whose neural counterpart is 'a lot of dawning and dying processes too faint and complex to figure.'

What the stream finds meaning in is a miscellany—every kind of object—'singular, particular, indefinites, and universals mixed in every way.' But the 'rush of thought is headlong and brings us to conclusions regardless.' Now comes a curious fact. Because conclusions are about substantive matters, it is usual to ascribe "more reality" to subject-matter than to its connections, to the physical object rather than to the fringe. But the actual objects of the mind are not the mere core, physical or abstract, that language makes pre-eminent. The stream of thought, let it be said again, consists of "wholes," a fullness of feeling, sight, idea, desire, shape, memory, what not. With the growth of mind these wholes become naturally more complex until there hardly seems a limit to the number of elements that an experienced mind can take in during one pulse of thought—witness a general in battle or a musician conducting.

Among the so-called elements—"so-called" because they are not present as "parts" until artificially separated in hindsight—are the relations that appear to hold them together and to organize local meanings within the total meaning. These relations are given, not added; that is, they belong from the start to the "whole" and make it what it is. 'Not a preposition, conjunction, syntactic form, vocal inflection but expresses a shading or other of relation' corresponding to our experience of things. 'We ought to say a feeling of *and*, a feeling of *if*, *but*, *by*, and so on, as much as a feeling of *blue* or a feeling of *cold*.'*

In demonstrating that consciousness is of wholes self-formed, not assembled from various sources of supply, not held together by "relations" brought in or tacked on, James was reversing a postulate of psychology and philosophy which had prevailed since Descartes, two and a half centuries before—the separation of the "thinking subject" from the "external objects" supposedly "copied" by the mind. Whitehead called this old dualism "the bifurcation of Nature," a split condition that thinkers had attempted to repair without success. To overcome the supposed difficulty and put an end to the bifurcation, James grasped the nettle: that is, he made consciousness-as-we-feel-it the starting point instead of the end product; he derived the elements from the activity instead of the activity from the elements.**

The image "grasp the nettle" (a favorite with James) aptly describes what Newton and Einstein did when the one postulated gravitation and the other, relativity, instead of deriving these from assumed causes.

* This is strikingly confirmed by the differences between one European language and another in the use of the "same" preposition, differences which make learning a foreign tongue so arduous. When Americans took up the French *mais* in the slang affirmative "But definitely," it was as a new feeling added to the old *but*, previously a pure adversative. The smartness of the phrase, quite absent in French, came from this addition to our "feeling of *but*."

** Fifty years later Bertrand Russell could write: "The dualistic view of perception, as a relation of a subject to an object, is one which, following the leadership of William James, empiricists have now for the most part abandoned." (*Human Knowledge: Its Scope and Limits*, New York, 1948, p. 205.)

James's way with consciousness is in exact parallel, and that is why Whitehead attributed to James a revolution in philosophy, the end of Descartes's undisputed rule. James had solved the bedeviling question, How does the world "out there" get into so narrow and unlikely a container as my mind "in here"?

So strongly does James wish to stress the irreducibility of the stream that he tells us there ought to be in language an impersonal form "it thinks," similar to "it rains." Thought goes on, rather than "*I* think" in the manner of "I fish, I pay taxes, I watch television," or any other action that may be withheld—as thought cannot.* This psychological observation is the root of one of his subsequent philosophical positions—Does Consciousness exist?—that is, as an *entity* distinct from a *function.*

The self-sufficiency of the stream, of thinking as a natural working that needs no additional "operator" to produce its effects, is what enables James to repel the intrusion of all metaphysics. It disposes of the old empiricists' assumption of a "combining power" that puts together separate sensations into an idea; of the materialist doctrine of a "monad" or supervising brain cell or structure, also for uniting the obviously scattered responses of the nerves;** of the idealists' notion of a Transcendental Ego, whose sole responsibility is to make experience possible; and finally of the traditionalists' postulate of a soul which does the thinking and uses our organs temporarily for its purposes. The soul is simply the earlier version of the materialist device: 'all the arguments for a "pontifical cell" or an "arch-monad" are also arguments for that well-known spiritual agent in which scholastic psychology and common-sense have always believed.'

It is important for a naturalist psychology that all these assumptions be seen as equivalent. For modern scientism has become the common sense of the day, and any rejection of its materialist formula is suspected of being a means to "slip in the soul," or some other "vital principle." There is no need of it. The 'bare phenomenon, the immediately known is the state of consciousness' itself. So, for the science of psychology proper, unmixed with explanatory metaphysics, 'the thought is the thinker' and nothing can or need be added.

---

* The archaic forms *methinks* and *meseems* carry a suggestion of what James is saying. We still say "it occurs to me," which reproduces faithfully the arrival of an unbidden thought, as do its synonyms: "it popped into my head that, etc." The French say "*il me vient à l'idée*" and "*il m'en souvient*," and the Germans "*es dünkt mich, mir dünkt.*"

** An alternative for modern materialists is "the whole-brain activity." But as James points out 'the entire brain process is not a physical fact at all. "Entire brain" is nothing but our name for the way in which a million molecules arranged in certain positions may affect our sense. On the principles of the mechanical philosophy, the only realities are the separate molecules, or at most the cells.' (*Principles*, I, p. 178.)

But do not on that account imagine that your precious self has been lost in some impersonal flood. When the stream is closely examined its features are found to be these: '1. Every thought is part of a personal consciousness. 2. Within each consciousness, thought is always changing. 3. It is sensibly [i.e., felt as] continuous. 4. It appears to deal with independent objects. 5. It is interested in some and rejects others continually.'

The thinking stream belongs to the thinker, because it is felt as separate from other streams, a quality which is present from the start. The self is thus 'a system of memories, purposes, strivings, fulfilments or disappointments.' Except in pathological cases, the feeling of ownership of the stream is its one constant feature; no other mental state recurs so steadily. Otherwise, the system is in perpetual agitation—"irritable," in the sense that it is forever ready to respond to stimuli here, there, or elsewhere.

To see the stream for the incessantly varying thing it is makes us revise our ideas in many different realms, as I hope to show when a few other features of the mind are clear. Here it is enough to note in passing that the stream explains without moralizing what that wonderful self-observer Montaigne found as the chief mark of man: he is *ondoyant et divers*—wavering and diverse—a creature of moods and changing views, not a passive recorder of the surrounding world but a congenital "perspectivist," and thus easily thrown off in judgment, memory, and purpose—a specialist (as it were) in misunderstanding. The cause is not "the passions" overcoming "Reason"; it is the native flooding of thought, which in its irregularity also contains the uncharted powers we call imagination and intellect.


The mind, of course, finds as it goes correctives to its waywardness. Perceptions are products developed and checked by experience. In ordinary speech the words *perception* and *sensation* tend to be used interchangeably, but the psychologist distinguishes. Sensations are the items of consciousness—a color, a weight, a texture—that we tend to think of as simple and single. Perceptions are complex affairs that embrace sensation together with other, associated or revived contents of the mind, including emotions. James says categorically: 'No one ever had a simple sensation by itself. The activity by which we perceive always gives a *figured* consciousness.' The adult mind's simplest awareness is of things "organized"—the first and most enduring results of the infant's exploration.

With the child, to think is but to act, to put in the mouth, fiddle, throw down, get entangled with. Out of this trial and error, things (which, owing to the construction of the eye, it sees upside down) are put right side up forever, distances are related to apparent size, tangible shapes are inferred from a lopsided perspective, and so on down the list of perceptions enabling the creature to move about safely yet casually amid the dangers of objects. After a time, experienced senses and well-worn brain patterns enable consciousness to recognize and recall the multitude of "things" we are confident exist independently of ourselves. In other words, no one can merely open his eyes and see; for all ordinary purposes 'every perception is an acquired perception.' Later, nearly everything we see is the fruit of pre-perception: when we hunt for a mislaid object, we visualize it in order to find it.*

Again, the perception of any thing is never its full reproduction. The "thing," for the mind, does not resemble either what we would discover if we examined it thoroughly with all our senses and from a number of points of view, nor yet what we see from a single one. The perceived is a pattern of hints and signs, memories and notions. 'When I get, as now, a brown eye-picture with lines not parallel, and with angles unlike, and call it my big solid rectangular walnut library table, that picture is not the table. It is not even like the table as the table is for vision, when rightly seen. It is a distorted perspective view of three of the sides of what I mentally *perceive* (more or less) in its totality and undistorted shape. The back of the table, its square corners, its size, its heaviness, are features of which I am conscious when I look, almost as I am conscious of its name. The suggestion of the name is of course due to mere custom. But no less is that of the back, the size, weight, squareness, etc.'

The difference between a perception and a set of unorganized, unpreperceived sensations is easily tested by holding a familiar painting upside down: it is at once unrecognizable and more vivid. We attend now to color and shape without the benefit of habit and with no distraction from "meaning" or "beauty," which owe their force to custom and past associations. Painters have often used this device to "verify" their composition or values. The same break with perceiving and partial return to original sensation occurs also with words and inarticulate sounds. Detach yourself from a certain headlong faith, and any passage in a quartet or symphony can suddenly seem silly ding-dong. Repeat a word a dozen times and the emphasized sound kills meaning. Or again, a word stares at you from the paper, says James, 'like a glass eye, with no speculation in it.'

---

* When the near-blind Aldous Huxley came upon the Bates method for improving eyesight, he was redisovering (as Bates had done) the role of preperception in adult vision. (See "The Mental Side of Seeing," ch. 13 of Huxley's *Art of Seeing*, New York, 1942.)

Indeed, so fitful (not to say flighty) is the relation of our mind to things that an imaginative person can easily fall prey to the feeling that reality is a dream—*la vida es sueño*, as Calderón showed symbolically in his famous play and as some philosophers have maintained. Physical needs bring most of us back to the insistent streaming of perceptions that we must call real, but even the workaday mind has its uneasiness, as Eddington remarked when he read in an account of a speech: "... reality! (Loud cheers)." We cheer on getting reassurance, even from the rhetoric of a speech. Hence there is hardly a more foolish word in our mouths than *realistic* when we use it to flatter ourselves or summon somebody else to see things as we do. "Be realistic!" means "go by my experience"—as if experience were uniform and universal—egotism masquerading as argument. The very question is what—or where—the reality is.

The "practical man" takes the uniformity of experience for granted, but his strong awareness of what is real would seem full of gaps and defects to the philosopher—faulty connections, doubts not raised, well-known errors swallowed whole. And, in reverse, the worldly man could point out ranges of ignorance and illusion in the philosopher's well-cultivated field. At the same time, for each thinker, the world is continuous, not full of holes, which shows again that our experience is not a faithful impersonal mirror of things but a personal selective one.

How does selection take place? It used to be thought that by chance and the force of repetition certain things and thoughts grouped themselves to form the contents of our minds. The "great law of association" did the work, and this automatic device meant that "the environment"—whatever it might include—was all-powerful in shaping mind and character. Well, association does account for some of our memories and feelings—a scent brings up the thought of a place, the word "table" brings up "chair," and a certain set of features brings up the name of a friend. But perception is a curious function, dependent less on specific energies than on modes of attention.

Attention, long ignored by psychologists, for whom the mind was a passive receiver, is another name for 'the glaring fact of subjective interest.' By 'laying its weighty index-finger on particular items of experience' it may give 'the least frequent associations far more power to shape our thought than the most frequent ones possess. The interest itself, though its genesis is doubtless perfectly natural, *makes* experience more than it is made by it.' The mind, in other words, "takes" from possible experiences the portions that become its own experience. If repetition, mere numerical reinforcement of impressions, were the whole story, says James with a characteristic twist, then a 'strain of dogs bred in the Vatican would become connoisseurs of sculpture—the odors at the base of the pedestals would organize their consciousness into a system of knowledge.'

Anyone who reflects on what James has so far told us about the mind will see at once the important bearing his facts have on all that we may say and think about art. Tastes and theories of criticism alike assume a fixed object and the beholder's "seeing it as it really is." The encounter is vastly more complicated and we must return here to James for more details.

What this "interest" is that commands our attention we all know from the inside but would be hard put to it to define; we are interested in varying degrees—or not at all, and that ends our account. But, as James shows in his chapter on the subject, attention can also be voluntary. We turn it on at the call of courtesy, duty, habit, pride, or other motives when interest is slight or absent. Two kinds of interest are commonly distinguished, which include those secondary motives of voluntary attention. We find interesting what relates to our well-being, physical or other, and indeed we speak of such matters as "our interests." And clearly, this perpetual "taking," which means considering less than the whole, and these "purposes," which seem so self-centered, are by no means always to be deplored. 'The human mind is essentially partial,' but its success comes from the very 'necessity of limiting our view.' For there are 'different cycles of operation in nature that are relatively independent of one another. The mould on the biscuit in the store-room of a man-of-war vegetates in absolute indifference to the nationality of the flag.' And 'the captain who in manoeuvering the vessel through a naval fight should think it necessary to bring the mouldy biscuit into his calculations would very likely lose the battle by reason of the excessive thoroughness of his mind.'

But in addition to the practical, we respond to what James calls the esthetic interest, using the term broadly to mean order, shapeliness, unity, smooth transition, the fulfillment of curiosity, and generally anything that we (aptly) call "attractive"—pulling on us by reason of qualities not related, as far as we can see, to our common needs.

Gradually, the particular items seized on by our ever-wakeful interest come together to form our intellectual tendencies, our biases, our temperament. These particulars include our growing knowledge, and the whole is colored by the feelings inseparable from every thought. For example, the perception of pain varies with one's ideas about it, one's make-up and past experiences. (The brain, incidentally, is not sensitive to pain.)

In these ways, the possibilities of any human being, which at first seemed infinite, narrow down to each man's modest limits. Every new experience is given the coloring of that one mind. The new item is assimilated—i.e., made like the previous ones—and perhaps distorted in the very act of being added to the stock.* That stock is known as the "apperceptive mass," because it screens and adjusts all fresh perceptions. The man who looked at a giraffe for the first time and said there was no such animal vividly expressed the response of a weak apperceptive mass. It assigned to quadrupeds only a few shapes and proportions; beyond them the mind preferred to deny the phenomenon rather than doubt its own modes of seeing.

In ordinary life, repeated experience and social pressure slowly correct individual narrowness, though there is such a thing as invincible ignorance. But what is rightly called a stamp of the mind, a deep-rooted way of "taking," in short a literal "pre judice," is the usual mark of a sect or a class, a time or a region. We know it as "national character" or "the limitations of the age." Consider the April poets of English literature. Chaucer at its beginning is happy

When April with his showers sweet

reawakens the frozen energies. But T. S. Eliot at the end avers that

April is the cruellest month

because it inspires hope and action, which are doomed to defeat—the same object in two takings.**

The inertia of the intaking mass is tremendous. One can feel it in what I think of as the rubber-band effect. Explain to someone why something is not as he thinks, giving reasons, facts, and authorities, and if he is intelligent and interested, he will follow and even take pleasure in his new acquirement. But ten minutes later he will say something that shows he has snapped back to his old misconception as if nothing had been said.

This common occurrence helps to explain why new ideas, new art, new attitudes to life take so long to be understood, let alone accepted.***

* An example of the power of "mere idea" to alter perception may be found in the journal kept by John Stuart Mill as a boy of fourteen during his first trip to France. He was, as everybody knows, highly trained in languages and logic by his father, and he was learning French. He read Racine and other classics, as he notes, but in his writing of French he always put an acute accent on the commonest verb form *est*. This accent he cannot have seen anywhere, in print or in handwriting—except in his own. It was a product of a wholly original and false preperception. (See *John Mill's Boyhood Visit to France*, ed. A. J. Mill, Toronto, 1960.)

** Compare Rainer Maria Rilke, a few years before Eliot: "as anguishing as the growth of children and as sad as the beginning of Spring" (*Letters to a Young Poet*, December 23, 1903). Shakespeare, farmer-like, sees "spongy April" without moralizing, and lists the cereals and riverbank vegetation that come with it (*The Tempest*, IV, 1, 65).

*** Max Planck says in his autobiography that *really* new ideas in science do not get *accepted*. Rather, old scientists die, and with them their impregnable apperceptions.

To change an intellectual tradition one must change the apperceptive mass. That is why in my work on Berlioz and Romanticism I had to surround these subjects with a massive array of recognized facts and views in order to link the well-known minutely with the unknown and the ignored, and thus form a new apperceptive mass.

In guarding its own thoughts so simply and stubbornly, the mind is duly saving its energy and preserving its individuality. In the day-to-day routine it has no occasion to doubt that the world is as perceived. Hence the actual chaos of men and opinions, so evident to the historian, is only to be expected, a natural result of perception as it develops individually.

When one is reminded of this native discord, perhaps when walking a busy city street and scanning the host of faces advancing—open countenances, most of them—one grows dizzy trying to imagine, behind the endlessly different features, the contents of the "streams" animating them. If one had access, a residue of similarities would be found, but how small!—or rather, how artificial and misleading: old platitudes, fashionable thought-clichés, pieties acquired early in life and fixed by thoughtless repetition. The true character of these strangers, their strong intimate thoughts and feelings, would show the tangled luxuriance of a jungle.

The best minds themselves work and apperceive as much with error, superstition, and perverse fancy as with sound knowledge and decent feeling. As any biography shows, no grade of intelligence or education makes us free of these deformities. We are all bundles of wild and warrantless convictions, especially about one another, and when one gets an accidental glimpse of someone else's candid mind, the sight is dread-inspiring. For his cozy chamber of horrors—and particularly his facts—are owned and enjoyed in complete good faith. They are to him *the* reality of whatever subject—the stars, the good life, art, money, God, child rearing, or the etiology of migraine headaches.

Such "honest beliefs" are our undoing, singly and collectively. Even within a group calling itself a league, a union, a party—hence somehow agreeing—the perpetual dissensions are signs of different worlds honestly perceived.* Among nations it is for these worlds, manifestly true and right, that wars are fought. "Interests," for good and evil, govern us from the start of the simplest perceptions.

It is clear that for society to survive, the individual "takings" must

---

* A vivid example comes to hand while reading proof: the Palestine Liberation Organization is as closely knit a body of men as the passion of nationalism and the pressure of the terrorist life can make it. Yet three members of the force, recently interviewed, "joined under different circumstances, the invasion [of Lebanon] meant something different to each of them, and each had a different hope for the future." (*New York Times*, August 11, 1982.)

somehow be made to overlap. That is why states and churches snatch the young—to create a uniform apperception early in its making. Ideologies coin slogans and enforce the party line to repair in adults the divergent, wayward streams. A free society itself can subsist only with the aid of conventions, of beliefs tacitly held in common, whether or not they jibe with individual perceptions and preferences. When they do not, they must be respected under social pressure—lip service is as good as belief; from which it follows that because the mind works as it does, society cannot endure without customary and beneficial hypocrisy.

Though ever-varying perception is the rule, the mind is not wholly adrift in experience. It is guided by the sense of sameness in things and it has a way of noting this down in permanent fashion. The means to this end is called Conception, the making of concepts. These are abstractions, not objects but ideas "drawn away" from objects, on the strength of one or more points of similarity. Sameness is 'the very keel and backbone of our thinking.' The sense of personal continuity—each thought being felt as belonging to the same self—rests on it, just as the understanding of the world, physical and mental, depends on connecting as similar whole groups of facts in a way that only concepts permit. The original meaning of "identify" records this procedure. Thus does the mind, having first made a world of objects out of stimuli, make a universe out of the welter of objects. Whether any of these are the same or remain the same, the mind through concepts *intends* their sameness by 'singling out some one part of the mass of matter for thought and holding fast to it without confusion.'

Conceiving is made firm with the aid of words—tree, fear, dog, mankind, love, liberty: our stock of nouns largely consists of terms that point not to single items of experience but to classes of particulars taken as being the same. No guarantee exists that things or persons so taken by the mind are in fact the same. A woman will call a middle-aged gentleman her son and maintain he is the same being that she dandled on her knee. We accept her meaning, but reserve the right to say he was once our friend but is no longer, "because he is utterly changed." To us he is *not* the same. Each party intends a different meaning and can explain it with the aid of concepts commonly accepted: son, friend. In a world where nothing stays put, where form and substance alter with time and perspective, sameness is clearly no passive registration of what is. Rather, we may call it the mind's act of self-defense against universal drift and decay.

Concepts can be constructed at will to serve our convenience. By their nature they are unmistakably distinct from each other. The concept *whiteness* differs forever from the concept *blackness*. In other words, every concept is 'the vehicle of a decision that can be expressed as: I mean this and I don't mean that.' Concepts stay put; that is their great value. Though a white thing may turn black, the concept of white does not pass into the concept of black. But as things change, fresh perceptions add features to our thought of that thing. 'New conceptions come from new sensations, new movements, new emotions, new associations, new acts of attention, and new comparisons of old conceptions.'

It is a pity that careless modern speech has blurred the meaning of *concept* by using the word for every sort of idea or opinion. The advertiser trying to sell some article boasts of "a new concept"—in sleeping pills or desk chairs. These new products represent at best *conceptions*, that is to say schemes for carrying out the abstract idea of "seat" or "sedative."* True concepts are primary ideas such as these. The concepts of taxation, crime, or health each signify a general topic of thought. The physical acts or facts that they cover—this tax, that crime, his poor health—are so many concrete particulars linked by the concept which, whenever thus actualized, ceases to be a concept.

One way to grasp the difference is to remember the tradition going back to Plato which maintains that concepts are the only true reality, because their unlimited scope makes them "universals"—significant always and everywhere. Actual things begin, grow, and perish, but their respective concepts are eternal; things are always flawed, concepts perfect. The Platonic aim is therefore to free oneself from attachment to things and persons and attain the love of archetypal ideas, particularly the mathematical. As unchanging forms of being, they promise never to disappoint.

To persons who yearn for security and perfection here below, the realm of the abstract is a refuge. Thinking only in clean-cut concepts they are able to despise the world and the worldly as being not only gross but badly illuded. These yearnings account for the conceptual language of most cults. Love of the All-Good, Union with the Infinite, Inner Light, Total Regeneration are terms that seem to give comfort by their very capital letters and require little or no attention to concrete details.

A psychology of experience gives no warrant for believing in the

---

* James himself was bothered about the word *concept*, but for a different reason. In his time, *concept* was beginning to be used by some writers as if it represented the object somewhat as a blueprint represents a house. He accordingly preferred for psychological clarity to use the word *conception*—to show what is plainly an *act of mind*. By now, *conception* is used by careful writers to mean precisely the comprehensive plan, the blueprint, and *concept* has lost exact meaning: Here I shall use *concept* in its oldest sense, e.g.: "The concept Identity means complete sameness, which is never found in experience."

greater reality (whatever that might mean) of concepts over objects. It is an error to regard a concept as if it stood for the object in a better version, more complete and clearer in form; it is rather the reverse. A concept only expresses a relation seen between certain *parts* of objects and used for a given purpose. This relation is as real and important as any other, but not superior. 'From every point of view,' says James, 'the overwhelming and portentous character ascribed to universal conceptions is surprising. Why, from Plato and Aristotle downwards, philosophers should have vied with each other in scorn of the knowledge of the particular and in adoration of that of the general, is hard to understand, seeing that the more adorable knowledge ought to be that of the more adorable things and that the things of worth are all concretes and singulars. The only value of universal characters is that they help us, by reasoning, to know new truths about individual things. The restriction of one's meaning, moreover, to an individual thing probably requires even more complicated brain-processes than its extension to all the instances of a kind; and the mere mystery, as such, of the knowledge is equally great, whether generals or singulars be the things known. In sum, the traditional universal-worship can only be called a bit of perverse sentimentalism.'

Concepts, then, are *of* things, *of* events, *of* qualities, not the things or qualities themselves. Looking thus at only one or two features gives but a thin idea of the original. 'Concepts are shorthand notes taken on reality,' and like notes they may be misleading even when perfectly definite in themselves.

Besides, not all concepts are true universals, not all are even generalities. Some are merely familiar impressions. 'If I abstract *white* from the rest of the wintry landscape this morning, it is a perfectly definite conception,* a self-identical quality which I may mean again; but, as I have not yet individualized it by expressly meaning to restrict it to this particular snow, nor thought at all of the possibility of other things to which it may be applicable, it is so far nothing but a "that," a floating adjective. Properly it is, in this state, a singular—I have "singled it out"; and when, later, I universalize or individualize its application and my thought turns to mean either *this* white or *all possible* whites, I am in reality meaning two things and forming two new conceptions.'*

Who, when letting his ideas stream in the ordinary way, would stop to make this distinction? Yet, it might matter. As we all know, desperate arguments take place about a wallpaper being blue or green, though by definition blue cannot be green. It is a cliché of debate that if people

* Read "concept" to avoid confusion.

want to argue responsibly, they must define their terms. Definitions sometimes help to clear away gross differences in conceiving, but they are powerless in the face of "blue"; and when definitions are attempted of such concepts as Freedom or Duty, they usually consist of other abstract terms that need defining. The more careful and elaborate the definition, the harder it is for the arguing parties to remember and observe it. In the end, human agreement depends on good speechways, that is, on controlling one's language by visualizing—and not switching—the same concrete embodiments of the concepts being tossed about in discussion.

For it is easy to think and talk without the image of anything at all present to the mind; words—the bare familiar sounds ending in -tion or -ity or -ness—will keep thought moving and make the thinker feel rational though he literally does not know what he is talking about. If the user of concepts—which is to say everybody—habitually fails to think of persons, things, events as they happen in the world of particulars, steady abstraction will land him in sheer nonsense or dangerous folly.* For abstractions form a ladder which takes the climber into the clouds, where diagnostic differences disappear.

Take, for example, this small, hard, round red object that fills your present sight, touch, and sense of smell, and that you immediately "identify" as a McIntosh apple. By naming it you merge it with millions of similar items, each in some way different from the one in your hand. If you use only the word "apple," the concept now includes yellow and green color and possible elongated forms of unlike size and taste. Your apple has twice been lost sight of. If anyone goes on to speak of "a piece of fruit," the term lacks all power to compel a correct image of what is in your hand. By the time "foodstuff" is invoked, only the most general idea of function remains. Then comes "organic matter," and the next step is bare "object," at which point all things whatever are "the same."

Concepts are not the work of adult minds exclusively. As James surmises, even low forms of life may be able to frame concepts if they recognize events as "the same"; and one has only to observe children to see how great their appetite for abstraction is, for they are brought up on words well ahead of their knowledge of life. Story books and television teach them to ask whether so-and-so is "a bad man." It is reassuring to classify. Concepts also take care of fears. I have seen a small boy,

---

* One more point about usage: it is regrettable that particular(s) is so rarely used in the place of specific(s), for the first is unmistakable, whereas the second, derived form species, suggests the features or traits of a class. "Give me the specifics" should mean something else than "Give me the particulars." And why not just say details?

much upset by the knocking noises in a radiator, quite reassured when the girl sitter told him it was "the expansion." Her own understanding went no farther, but both were comforted, because they sensed that concepts are mankind's fundamental means of charting experience.

The ladder of increasing generality is traveled up and down by the mind a dozen times an hour without one's noticing it. If from love of abstraction new conceptual terms are substituted for common ones, it often happens that the power of words to direct thought approaches zero. "Serious love affair" used to be a good enough phrase to indicate a whole range of feelings and actions. We have substituted "meaningful relationship," which is so indefinite that it could cover the association of a hunter and his dog—or even that of oxygen and hydrogen in water. What image can one form of "the largest consumer-oriented financial service entity"? It is on record that the advertising agencies now recommend, and compose, phraseology that abstracts from familiar objects to the very edge of the ludicrous: "America's personal driving machine" stands for a Dodge car, and a Pentax camera has become "an exhilarating photographic instrument."*

Our age is enamored of concept-making, concept-work. Most of our day-to-day dealings with the world and with one another are cushioned and often blanketed by concepts. The jargon that blocks communication is conceptual verbiage. The "plain man" of an earlier day, who spoke in concrete terms and suspected that highfalutin language concealed trickery, is now a steady consumer and creator of concepts. They add dignity to his person and his job, while confusing his mind and misguiding his steps.** Indeed, it would astonish most speakers, educated or not, to discover how many of the conceptual terms that they combine in clearly grammatical sentences actually represent only some vague attitude, often unrelated to the concept invoked. "Creativity," for instance, which should surely imply some product, is generally no more than a gesture of praise—or it stands for a wish not to take orders from anyone. Does "a job with creativity" ever call up the image of successive acts of *creation*?

For lack of exercise, the ability to summon up some solid contents for

* Mr. William Safire, in his usual incisive way, denounced these absurdities in the *New York Times* for December 6, 1981. But one fears that ridicule will not kill a practice that appeals to minds already drugged with concepts.

** When President Truman came to Columbia University on a lectureship in political science, the most striking fact of his performance on the platform and in discussion with students was the unfailing concreteness of his thought and speech. His experience seemed to be stored up in examples, incidents, or factual suppositions which he had apparently felt no need to translate into concepts or generalities. This trait may have limited his philosophic range, it also wonderfully limited his capacity for talking nonsense.

every concept that one hears or uses disappears. People think from word to word instead of imagining from word to fact. True intelligence fuses the two functions, which is why many intelligent people make poor academic records. For learning is mostly words. The public school has increased everybody's stock of them without increasing the capacity to imagine. As for higher education, what it teaches is largely the terminology of theories. Add the verbal fallout of science and technology, and the habit of living only by general terms becomes the norm.

One would have hoped that knowledge about humankind, created as it has been by successive intuitions and not by geometrical reasoning, might have kept free of needless abstraction. But in order to imitate science, the modern studies of man and society, of the arts and humanities, have all pitched in to frame new concepts and in such forms that they prove even more slippery than the terms of the accepted language.

They resemble scientific concepts only in the free use of Greek and Latin roots. Psychology and sociology were the first to succumb;* then pedagogy, by losing its mind to educational theory, denatured education; finally, business on one side and linguistics, literature, and criticism on the other have joined the rest to wallow in the bog: personnel theory, management theory, information theory, and literary theory envelop in phraseology the last vestiges of the practical, the concrete, the immediate, and the appreciable.

The parallel tendency in politics has long been at work. Think of the force, magnified by vagueness, of the terms *exploitation, imperialism, colonialism, racism, sexism;* and in some parts of the world, of the still vaguer *deviationism, adventurism, revisionism,* plus a host of isms attached to proper names—Marx, Lenin, Trotsky, Tito, Mao. All these mean whatever one wants or nothing in particular.** There has not been such bloody verbalizing since the two centuries of religious wars after Luther, when concepts such as consubstantiation and prevenient grace aroused men to civil and foreign war. Those times had the excuse that their abstractions dealt with the hereafter, about which it is diffi-

---

* For example, here is a description of the reason for punishing crime: "If enforcible deprivations are provided for deviational conduct, the mature members of the community are expected to take these possible deprivations into account as potential costs in assessing the balance of indulgence and deprivation attendant upon behavioral alternatives." (H. D. Lasswell and R. C. Donnelly, quoted in *Criminal Law* by Donnelly, Goldstein, and Schwartz, New York, 1962, p. 869.)

The language illustrates the conceptual jargon; the concept itself carries out the attempt to be "neutral"—i.e., scientific—by following Durkheim and conceptualizing crime as "deviant behavior" that society visits with unpleasant consequences. Under this definition it is clear that the life and work of an original genius in art come under the head of crime.

** The cellist and conductor Mstislav Rostropovich and his wife were stripped of Soviet citizenship on grounds of "ideological degeneracy."

cult to be concrete, whereas we profess to be handling or bettering the here and now.

Concepts classify facts by *imposing* "sameness." This act necessarily conceals individuality. The danger of what I long ago described as "race thinking," which includes sexism and all other forms of group denigration, is that the classifying sign—color, sex, or whatever—acts as a barrier to seeing what is in front of one's nose, the person with his or her qualities and defects. And blindness works in reverse. There is no less prejudice in making sex, race, or nationality an automatic sign of merit. Nor is it any better to turn the single instance into a horrendous truth denoted by a concept: the nationalist partisan who cries out that the lawful conviction of a fellow terrorist is "genocide" will probably not convince many people. But the dishonesty is not less when cases of police brutality or abuse of power, disclosed by a free press, are used to show that this or that western nation is a police state with a population exploited and oppressed.

Concealment by concept is likewise the source of our disgusting euphemisms: the disadvantaged, the developing nations, the undocumented alien. Our collective cowardice sees less reproach in the mealy-mouthed phrase (as if reproach were relevant at all) and it hopes to suggest a problem well in hand, when what we are struggling with is a permanent difficulty. This falsification is now habitual: if a new experience startles us, quick! throw over it the hushcloth of a shoddy concept. With its help we manage to unperceive, not carelessly once in a while, but infallibly all the time.

When I had learned from James what he had learned from Agassiz about generalities and particulars, I used to warn my students in history against all forms of "misplaced abstraction." History is the realm in which the particular is the center of interest. Generalities help to organize and relate, but reification—making agents or forces out of generalities—is the unforgivable fault. Hence so-called philosophies of history—the attempt to distill from the facts any fundamental cause or "law," whether based on economics, or climate, or the unconscious—deceive by misplaced abstraction.* The discipline of history—and its value—is to keep the mind turned in the other direction.

The proverb should read: "A person's character is known by the concepts he keeps." To James, 'the difference between all possible abstrac-

---

* Later I discovered in Whitehead that he called the same error "the fallacy of misplaced concreteness." His is the more vivid and memorable phrase, mine the more pedagogical and closer to the subject I was engaged in teaching. That both terms, seemingly opposite, refer to the same error may help to keep the warning present to the mind.

tionists and all livers in the light of the world's concrete fullness' was one that 'he was never able to forget.' And indeed, his intellectual struggle against his time is one long illustration of this contrast. Yet keeping hold of the concrete and the particular is not to take sides against concepts and conceptions, ideas and general truths. On the contrary, it is to value these so much that one remembers to be fastidious in their use and demanding as to their quality.

Having seen how like fire and knife blades concepts are, we can look at them again as instruments enhancing the power of the mind. The most striking example of their worth in this guise is natural science, whose progress has been made by the steady creation *and criticism* of concepts. The first step is to classify phenomena by their effects. Molière made fun of the doctors who gave as the reason for the effect of opium its "dormitive power," but the ridicule applies only when the phrase is offered as a cause. To bring into one view all the things that are "dormitive" is of immense value. Science progresses by gathering an ever-wider range of phenomena under concepts more and more inclusive so that they become fewer and fewer. To see as instances of "the same" the bubbling of water on the boil, the light of the sun, the fire in the grate, the shifting of continents, and the bodily glow after a hard run—in short, heat, motion, energy, and finally mass, as interchangeable—is the result of successive conceptual feats.

That desirable end comes from conceiving rightly, and so does the simple beginning—measurement. To measure anything it must be taken as homogeneous—the same—and it is because the common things of experience differ endlessly in appearance and behavior that science goes down and down, ever farther from the surface, to find what is—or what may be taken as—uniform. As such, in the atomic or subatomic level, differences in kind no longer exist and handling the identical units becomes mathematicians' play.

If as Descartes said three hundred years ago, "the mathematical is alone free from the taint of falsity," the path to truth seems plain: reduce everything in life as close as possible to bare figure and number by concepts. This reasoning is one cause of the extravagant proliferation of concepts today, but as we saw, their use only creates confusion. It was another genius in Descartes's day who showed why: the reliability of the mathematical is not due to the finer poise and colder blood of the specializers we call scientists; it comes from the material that they choose to carve out of experience. In an early section of his *Pensées*, Pascal describes two divergent orientations of the human mind, which he calls the geometrical and the intuitive (*esprit de finesse*). The former works exclusively with elements resulting from clear-cut definitions—a line, a number, a molecule. Being abstract, these "things" stay put in any context. Their interrelations may be complicated but (if one may use the word for contrast) never *complex*. As more than one great physicist has said: "If it isn't simple it isn't physics." That sort of simplicity enables scientific debate to be clear, open to inspection and correction by any other mind familiar with the relevant and immobile concepts.

Contrariwise, the subjects of intuitive thought cannot be conceived "geometrically"; they are inherently complex. They can be talked about—and must be—but they slip out from under the most painstaking description and they resist the making of measurable units. Who could define and measure a degree of hate, a sphere of influence, a volt of sexual attraction? The things are patently real, but they shift, mingle, vanish, and return in a way we can understand but not compute. It takes, as we say, subtlety, judgment, finesse, to find one's way among such subjects—poetry, politics, love, and even science at the stage just preceding the framing of a new concept. For mathematics, physics, biology—all the sciences—begin with intuition and are creations, too. But to grasp those other matters calls for nothing less than the unlimited stream of mind. They are in fact the expression in various social and individual forms of the stream's fullness and instability.*

This radical distinction has a bearing on one of the complaints heard more and more frequently about the quality of life in modern civilization. It maintains that owing to the cultural prestige and widespread imitation of science, the "geometrical" way of thought has denatured our intellectual and emotional life. It has spoiled pleasure, wasted talent, and bewildered the public mind. For example, the scientific habit of "seeing" one kind of phenomenon as the equivalent of another— heat as motion—has turned into a trick that destroys the wholeness of experience. We "see" voluntary acts as the work of the unconscious. The literary critic "sees" everything as something else—language as gesture, a Shakespeare play as a long metaphor, a painting as the image of a neurosis, a novel as the elaboration of a thematic catalogue. And the journalist soon echoes him by seeing fashion in dress as "movable sculpture," "nature as fiction," and "the economy as theatre."

Nothing scientific such as experiment or calculation keeps this analogy-mongering in check; nothing, that is, but a healthy *esprit de finesse*. Consider the first "as" above: if there is anything that is clear in human experience it is that language is not a gesture but an extraordi-

---

* In some parts of human knowledge the two modes are jointly used, for example in medicine, psychology, sociology, and even archeology. In all these the "art" is as indispensable as the "science." On the inherent unfitness of sociology to be a wholly empirical science, see Theodore Caplow, "The Middle Range," Institute for the Study of Social and Legal Change, Charlottesville, Va., 1982 (mimeographed).

nary improvement upon it. To a true mind the details that differentiate the two are vastly more important than the conceptual husk of "communication" that they share.*

With such pseudo-scientific "analysis" incessantly distorting thought and wrenching emotion from their place in the intuitive domain, it is no wonder that a sort of underground movement is developing against "science and intellect." It appeals to the rights of feeling, immediacy, spontaneity, and it proclaims that modern civilization will collapse—or should be brought down—because it tramples on these human traits and desires.

The grievance is just, though its cause is not "science and intellect," as should be evident from what has just been shown. The evil comes from a one-sided view and use of the mind, from ignoring Pascal's distinction and James's description of experience, from believing that because geometry (science) is indeed wonderful, its form of thought should hold sway over all of life. For that is the creed of our times, all the stronger for being implicit. It is the faith we reveal when we regard all the difficulties of existence as "problems" and teach the young that the goal of all they learn is "problem-solving."

We go astray, then, and suffer from not knowing our James. For if we assemble his findings to draw up a characterization of mind at large, before it is narrowed into types by vocation or training, the summary that fits best is: mind is the aboriginal artist. It works by selection; it fashions percepts and concepts charged with meanings and associations; it handles and recalls them by signs and symbols. Around each object of consciousness a fringe of feelings perpetually flows, which assigns to each pulse its quality and importance, the whole unrolling scene unified by the sense of self-identity and directed by attention and interest. This sweep of activity is obviously broader than any special use that can be made of it, and notably broader than the numerical and conceptual uses of science. If 'the larger part of all we see comes out of our heads' and the mind works by 'reactive spontaneity,' then it may be said to create, and the shorthand term "artist" is not fanciful.

So the complaint that society today puts too much value on intellect and knowledge and not enough on feeling and impulse overlooks the fact that these are not separable except abstractly speaking. If there is one truth that James makes forever clear, it is that mind and emotion, head and heart, are not contending parties, one of which may lose by

* As we saw, at a high enough rung on the ladder of abstraction, disparate things become the same: a song and a spinning top are, after all, but two ways of setting air waves in motion; and if we like we may "see" as identical in that same respect a shouted greeting and a shouted insult.

the decision of some inner umpire. 'The current opposition of Feeling to Knowledge is quite a false issue. If every feeling is at the same time a bit of knowledge, we ought no longer to talk of mental states differing by having more or less of the cognitive quality; they only differ in knowing more or less, in having much fact or little fact for their object. The feeling of a broad scheme of relations is a feeling that knows much; the feeling of a simple quality is a feeling that knows little. But the knowing itself, whether of much or little, has the same essence and is as good knowing in the one case as in the other. Concept and image, thus discriminated through their objects, are consubstantial in their inward nature as modes of feeling.'

Indeed, among the subtlest emotions is one that, if common speech were to be believed, is the enemy of all feeling. I mean reason, rationality. Depending on the speaker and the situation, it is praised as "cool reason" or condemned as "cold reason," these modulated temperatures being meant to distinguish it from such sources of heat as sympathy and lust. But one has only to look around the world or consult history to discover that the most passionate fanatics are the devotees of reason. As for the basis of all reasoning, it is no more than a feeling—the conviction of obviousness that we experience in self-evident truths: "equals added to equals give equals." Whoever doubts or denies makes us angry or contemptuous (more passion!) by questioning not so much our thought as the irresistible force of our feeling, which is not an act of reason at all.

That astute mathematician, our helpful Pascal, also remarked that "the propositions of geometry become sentiments": he had observed the inseparable fringe of feeling around the idea, just as the young James had remarked in arguing psychology with his father. To say, then, that somebody is "emotional" and somebody else "intellectual" is to misdescribe. The "emotional" is full of ideas, too, though the observer may overlook these as being too simple or crude—they would not move *him*. As for persons called "too intellectual," it may be the range, variety, and strength of their ideas that disconcert, while the force of feeling attached to each goes unperceived; we measure by our own standards, and pint pots rarely credit the reality of quarts.

The whole art of life might be said to reside in linking rightly, for self and circumstance, one's ideas and one's feelings.* For their attachments are detachable: our adult passions no longer cling to the games and toys

---

* This is the meaning of Wordsworth's lines in *The Prelude* (Conclusion):

> ... and he whose soul has risen
> Up to the height of feeling intellect
> Shall want no humble tenderness.

of our infancy. We subdue a feeling by other feelings that we learn to prefer while we develop (as we say) new intellectual interests. These transformations are not mechanically imposed from outside. They are us, *seeking and trying*, responding to curiosity, ambition, social approval, or the pleasure of mastery—over ourselves or over the difficulties of a trade or an art. At no point is any interest without its feeling: it feels at least interesting, and perhaps more; and at no point is the feeling of—say—boredom, exhilaration, bewilderment without some idea that it colors through and through.

And this flow of feeling-thought, rich or thin, is as variable as our perceptions. Man is inconstant despite all sincerity and *la donna e mobile* as well. On this topic James gives us one of his evocative digressions: 'We wonder how we ever could have opined as we did last month about a certain matter. We have outgrown the possibility of that state of mind, we know not how. From one year to another we see things in new lights. What was unreal has grown real, and what was exciting is insipid. The friends we used to care the world for are shrunken to shadows; the women, once so divine, the stars, the woods, and the waters, how now so dull and common; the young girls that brought an aura of infinity, at present hardly distinguishable existences; the pictures so empty; and so for the books, what *was* there to find so mysteriously significant in Goethe or in John Mill so full of weight?'

On this subject of reason and emotion the twentieth century is fond of using a pair of clichés that can only mislead. One is "wishful thinking," which is meant to scout an idea by attacking the way it was reached.* James shows that *all* thinking is wishful. The Wright brothers had to wish while thinking how to fly. Even in mental wandering, the stream wants to get there, wherever "there" may be; and the more consciously the mind directs itself—be it in research or in playing bridge—the stronger must be the wish. What, then, are we to call the thought that a lover is faithful, or that the backyard has oil beneath it, just because one wishes it were so? Different words will apply, from "hope and trust" to "self-delusion," depending on the thought's scope and outcome; its origin is irrelevant. Judge by the airplane's flight, not the inventor's wish.

The other charge often made to discredit an idea is to call it a rationalization. The term implies a makeshift to cover up a "real" feeling or belief. When the fox in the fable could not reach the grapes, he

---

* The phrase seems to owe its origin to a remark of T. H. Huxley's in his "Credo," which begins: "To think wishfully, to rest in comfortable illusion . . ." (*Life and Letters of Thomas Huxley*, I, pp. 233–39). Oddly enough, Huxley insisted elsewhere that he very much "wanted to believe," i.e., in God.

said they were sour. Here again the proper point of attack is not the
fox's second thoughts (rationalization), but his accuracy and truthful-
ness. As in all that the mind does, the quality of the rationalizing depends on how far the thinker has been fastidious and demanding. For
any frustration of desire makes us think again and suggests alternatives
from which to choose. Rationalization is thus a large source of new
truth: balked in one direction, we discover a better way. Many an illness has brought the sufferer philosophic insight, accidents have led to
new careers, grievous loss has turned out to be gain—all by rationalizing.

Both wishful thinking and rationalization illustrate the generality that
the mind works to serve wants, ideas are the product of desire. James
did not discover this truth; Plato admitted it with regret; Hume asserted
it with vehemence: "The mind is and ought to be the slave of the passions." But it was James who showed that desire, taking the form of
interest, pursues not simply practical ends but also theoretical and esthetic. At the same time, by the operation of the response pattern of the
nervous system, all thought terminates in action, even if it is no more
than frowning, jingling keys in the pocket, or jumping up with impatience.

This last conclusion leads to several others that will appear in due
course. Here it supplies an answer to still another question about the
human emotions. What is sentimentality? Offhand you will be told that
it is "too much emotion" or "wallowing in emotion." These are unsatisfactory tests, for who is to say how much is the right amount and when
wallowing begins. James's criterion is: appropriate action. The senti-
mentalist is the person who fails to act on his or her fine sentiments—
'the weeping of a Russian lady over the fictitious personages in the play
while her coachman is freezing to death on his seat outside.' This particular failure to act is also, of course, a failure to connect feeling-
thoughts rightly, to join the concepts "suffering" and "sympathy" in
some concrete image and deed. The critic would sum up: sentimentality
is no excess of anything; it is a deficiency of the imagination that should
lead to action. This is what we find also in the work of art judged sentimental.

Unlike most books on psychology before and after his, James's devoted but little space to the several emotions distinguished in common
speech—rage, love, fear, hatred, and the rest. His reason was that the
descriptive literature of the emotions is 'not only tedious, but you feel
that its sub-divisions are to a great extent either fictitious or unimpor-
tant and that its pretence to accuracy is a sham. As emotions are described in novels, they interest us, for we are made to share them; literary works of aphoristic philosophy also flash lights into our emotional

life and give us a fitful delight. But as far as a "scientific philosophy" of the emotions goes, I should as lief read verbal descriptions of the shapes of the rocks on a New Hampshire farm.'

This familiarity with the novelists and moralists enabled James to see how misleading the names given to our feelings are. They make us regard them 'as absolutely individual things, as so many eternal and sacred entities,' whereas 'the internal shadings merge endlessly into each other'—and into the reactions of instinct as well. In fact, there are either too many names or not enough for our emotional experiences, whether strong or weak; and apart from the detailed account of a scene (as in fiction) the words 'hatred, antipathy, animosity, dislike, aversion, malice, spite, vengefulness' convey no clear and distinct information.

James's original contribution to the subject of emotion is his physiological account of their 'constitution and conditioning.' It is known as the James-Lange theory, because the Danish psychologist Carl Lange published similar conclusions a year after James had broached his. When baldly stated, the theory sounds like a paradox: we do not feel grief and then weep nor are seized by fear and then run, but the reverse. Yet if the stimulus-and-response system is the unchanging model in any triggering of feeling-thought, the James-Lange view must be right. 'Without the bodily states following on the perception [of the bad news or the frightening sight] the latter would be purely cognitive in form, pale, colorless, destitute of emotional warmth. We might then see the bear and judge it best to run, receive the insult and deem it right to strike, but we would not actually *feel* afraid or angry.'

That is the point to keep in mind: the theory refers not to the mere assessing of the situation but to the feeling experienced in it. Normally we use "feel" in loose fashion for the faint fringe of a passing thought: "I feel you ought to call up and find out." But with strong emotions we *feel* we feel—the hot flush or cold trembling. Those bodily conditions *are* the emotion, the *motion*, in fact, of our nerves, muscles, blood, adrenalin, or whatever. What the James-Lange theory implies is that objects and ideas directly excite bodily changes, thanks to instinct or habit. 'These changes are so indefinitely numerous and subtle that the entire organism may be called a sounding board, which every change of consciousness, however slight, may make reverberate.'

Later students have disputed the theory and some have retained it with modifications.* For my part I find no difficulty in accepting it. If,

* Notably Professor Gerald E. Myers of Queens College, New York, in "William James's Theory of Emotion: a Critical Study." (Sidore Lecture Series, University of New Hampshire, December 12, 1966.) See also Nina Bull's "Attitude Theory of Emotion," reported in the *New York Times*, October 8, 1951.

as James suggests, I recall a moment of strong emotion and try to sub-tract mentally the surge of bodily feelings, nothing is left to think of except the typical "situation" or the name it goes by. If the occasion was recent, the image of it may be so vividly recalled that the emotion—the bodily sensation—is re-aroused, sometimes stronger than before, as when one relives the terror of a near-accident and finds oneself shud-dering.

What adds to my confidence in James's description is the light it throws on various aspects of art. Why is it a commonplace that the nov-elist must not tell but show? Obviously because the emotions are better stirred by objects than by ideas, and a good narrator wants instant re-sponse. Stronger confirmation still is the ability of James's theory to explain the mystery of dramatic art. There "showing" is the root idea, and when it is effectively done several hundred people can be made to feel by turns anxious, indignant, appalled, exhilarated, and often liter-ally breathless.

These emotions are genuine, physical; one can leave a play in a sweat, or exhausted and at peace, as after a good workout. From Aris-totle down it has been taken for granted that the theatrical emotions are of the same kind as those of life and that a good play, by detaching them from certain ideas and attaching them to others, makes for emo-tional order within the spectator. But how can this change be brought about by make-believe? Simply enough on James's view: the objects presented act directly on the perceiving organism. At the knocking on the gate in *Macbeth*, the spectator is as petrified as the newly hatched murderer—and he believes apprehensively in the witches too; the visi-ble and audible objects work on the senses, whose stirring *is* the dra-matic emotion.

Why then don't we jump on the stage to stop the murder? The answer is that we have been taught to resist the impulse. But small children are often thoroughly alarmed and bewildered at their first play, and the tales about cowboys in the audience threatening the villain in the melo-drama are not all jokes. I therefore venture to dispute Coleridge's ex-planation of the theatrical effect as due to "the willing suspension of disbelief." Nobody is born disbelieving what he sees happening in front of his eyes. The reason for the sophisticated spectator's staying in his seat is *an acquired suspension of belief.* This is so true that staged inci-dents to test accuracy of perception in the psychology classroom invari-ably fool the unprepared students; they leap to defend the "victim." And instances have occurred of movie making in the street which has been interrupted from the same spontaneous response.

In drama, then, passions and actions affect us directly, though with less force when we keep a check on them by the thought of artifice; and with least force when, as in amateurish acting, the objects fail to be like life. In life itself, the leader, the advocate, the salesman moves us by *acting*, in both senses of the word. A related sidelight on this last point may be read in Poe's story of "The Purloined Letter," where he tells how the boy won all the marbles at school in the guessing game of Odd or Even: he imitated every opponent's facial expression so as to feel within himself the other's intention, the principle being that the bodily configuration would reproduce the feeling.* Mimicry is certainly one of the modes by which infants learn to feel others' attitudes and the performing mime often induces matching grimaces in us as we catch his moods.

It is indeed the age-old advice of moralists and friendly comforters that we should "go through the motions" of the feeling-state that is appropriate or desirable—dry the tears, erase the hangdog look and try to put on a cheerful face, hold up the head, keep a stiff upper lip, clench the jaw against fear, whistle in the dark as we would in sunshine—and with luck we shall feel the right emotion taking hold of us.

It was hinted earlier that James's panorama of the mind at work had implications for art, that the mind, in fact, dealt with experience like an artist. And we saw just now what probably happens to our sensorium when we witness a play. But James's great book has something more fundamental and comprehensive to say about art, even though it contains no chapter on esthetics. Certainly my reading in youth the pages on sensation, perception, and attention; on the stream of thought and the nature of concepts; and on habit and association, weaned me from the doctrines I had grown up with and that still prevail. Having learned that perception is fused sensation and thought, surrounded by a fringe of memories and fluid emotions, I realized that in looking at works of art, or hearing and reading them, the object cannot be seen "as it really is," no matter how familiar one may be with the technique of the art or the principles of criticism. The person, the moment, the mood, the past—the apperceptive mass, in short—are inseparable from "the object," as in every experience.

* Poe then refers to the seventeenth-century writer Campanella as psychologist. How Poe came across this author's little-known writings was a puzzle until I found in Edmund Burke's essay "On the Sublime and the Beautiful" the very passage Poe relies on. It quotes a French writer who quotes Campanella, whom Burke also uses as authority in describing what happens "when we have before us such objects as incite love . . . ; the head inclines . . . the eyelids are more closed . . . the eyes roll gently, etc. . . . All this is accompanied with an inward sense of melting and languor." (Part IV, Sec. 4.) Evidently, the germ of the James-Lange theory dates back a couple of centuries.

The facts, then, disallow the theories that proclaim art "autonomous," each work of art obeying laws of its own and disclosing a "realm apart," "the opposite of life." These ideas are empty concepts; they do not fit what art is—a purposeful arrangement of concrete objects. Art is made to assail our senses and is thus an extension of experience. So it is sheer paradox, affectation, to want to limit the proper encounter with art to something called the "esthetic experience" based on or leading to the appreciation of "pure form." Perhaps these fashionable attitudes do not positively prevent the enjoyment of art; indeed, they probably add a touch of snob relish to it; but they corrupt critical thought, distort or obscure artistic meaning, and often serve to deny the merits of certain genres and certain artists.

This finding is important to the critic and connoisseur; James also has something to say to the esthetician. We know that it was from James's teachings that Bernard Berenson derived his own critical system based on the notion of "tactile values" in painting.* Yet when James reviewed (in *Science*) his former student's book on *The Florentine Painters*, which was the first use of psychology in modern art criticism, James questioned 'whether we shall ever define just what the superior significances are in the better of two pictures.' As he had written to a colleague, his belief was that 'no good will ever come to Art as such from the analytic study of Aesthetics—harm rather, if the abstractions could in any way be made the basis of practice. We should get stark things done on system with all the intangible personal *je ne sais quaw* left out. The difference between the first- and second-best things in art absolutely seems to escape verbal definition—it is a matter of a hair, a shade, an inward quiver of some kind—yet what miles away in point of preciousness!' More formally, James asked: 'Is not the conception of "Aesthetics" far too wide for any profitable treatment in general terms? Have the classically beautiful, the interestingly ingenious, the emotionally exciting, the neatly accurate, the grotesquely unreal, and the humorous, anything in common except that they are *welcome,* and is it likely that the welcomeness is in all cases due to the same kind of process being aroused?'

Such were his reasons for not devoting a chapter to esthetics in the *Psychology*. The omission alone would imply that James understood the equivalence of life and art, as well as their difference; and it suggests

* "I owe everything to William James," said Berenson. "'Tactile values' was really James's phrase, not mine, although he never knew he had invented it." (Meryle Secrest, *Being Bernard Berenson: a Biography*, New York, 1979, p. 188.) To pursue James's thought on these matters, one should read his reviews of H. R. Marshall and Grant Allen on esthetics, Lucien Arréat (*Psychologie du Peintre*), W. von Bezold on color, and Santayana's *Sense of Beauty*. (See Notes, p. 320.)

also that he considered all known or unknown facts about the mind sufficient to equip a critic. In other words, there is no way to get rid of the perceiver and arrive at an independent conception of what art is. Our best chance of coming to terms with an art object and with one another's opinions about it is to be aware of how we "take" what is presented to us in both art and nature.

"Taking" explains, among other things, the immense variety of styles in every art from the primitive to the surreal. It tells us that all art is "realistic" in the functional sense: every maker, every technique aims at conveying what is there, or more exactly, what the artist, or the age believes important and memorable about what is there. It is only the concentration on one part of experience that has led to equating "realism" with recognizable familiar objects. Recall James's example of the swirl of dust and then think of Turner's later works and you see what "realistic" should embrace.

That is but one ray of light thrown on a large subject by the Jamesian description of mind. Another comes from the process of discrimination: 'difference [between two terms] feels as if incorporated and taken up in the second term, which feels "different-from-the-first" even while it lasts. It is obvious that the second term of the mind in this case is not a bald *n*, but a very complex object; and that the sequence is not simply: first *m*, then *n*; but first *m*, then difference, then *n-different-from-m*.' In music, where immediate repetition is frequent, we obviously find pleasure or tedium in a passage by reason of this curious ability to feel a chord or theme "different" the third time around, though abstractly considered it is "the same" chord or theme.* Indeed, we may discern in the sequence of sameness yet other feelings—suspense, emphasis, obsession, depending on the context. Then again, context may vanish: James cites 'the pleasure of a slow crescendo simply as such.'

Tending toward the same conclusion is the fact James makes prominent, that the fusion of thought and feeling which nothing can undo prevents any ultimate clarity about experience. 'The mixture of things is so pervasive' that 'abstraction is never complete and the analysis of a compound never perfect, because no element is ever given to us absolutely alone. Colors, sounds, smells are just as much entangled with other matter as are more formal elements of experience, such as extension, intensity, effort, pleasure, difference, likeness, harmony, badness, strength, and even consciousness itself. All are embedded in one world.' The best we can do, then, if we want to sharpen our perception

---

* The workings of perception are indeed strange: it appears that one cannot judge differences between two wines while the second is still in the mouth. (*Principles*, I, p. 496.) And 'The word "or" names a genuine reality.' (*A Pluralistic Universe*, p. 324.)

of art, is to observe the direction (so to speak) in which each singled-out element differs from the rest. Something experienceable is always left over and it will hardly be the same for all perceivers. This state of affairs rules out any notion of "purity." Neither the maker nor the beholder nor the critic is a sterilized vessel distilling essences.

At the same time, the greater one's awareness of what does happen in and to the mind, the more acute the resulting judgment of any object, including art. The mind can learn to see itself and to outwit its over-responsive ways. It is as if it helped sensitiveness to reduce its scope. Accordingly, the judge of every kind of art, and not just the visual, should know about the role of after-images: there may be a bright or dark object nearby that starts a train of associations. 'Words, visions, etc. come disconnected with the main stream of thought, but discernible to an attention on the watch for them. A horse's head, a coil of rope, an anchor are, for example, ideas which have come to me unsolicited whilst I have been writing these latter lines. We shall probably never know just what part retinal after-images play in determining the train of our thoughts.'

The whole organism is indeed a "sounding board." Many critics and most devotees of art have noted a curious bodily sensation that may accompany a word or line, a quiet musical phrase, a pictorial detail, when it seems to come at just the moment of perfect fitness. It is a shudder, a physical thrill. We are being literal when we call certain masterpieces, certain performances thrilling. When Victor Hugo first read Baudelaire, he wrote that the younger poet had given the world un frisson nouveau—that is, a new source of James's 'inward quiver.'

But is not this importation of psychology into the enjoyment of art a reduction, a lessening of its reality? Does it not also mean that criticism can never be objective and therefore that it is futile? No, to both questions. Knowing the ways of the mind does not reduce but adds to the number and the nuances of controlled perception. And as to objectivity, though its absolute degree is denied us no matter what we look at, other facts of mind counteract the wayward individuality, save us from the bugbear of "subjectivity." Those facts we may learn, once again, from the Psychology when it takes up Habit, Attention, and Imagination.

For just as the welter of sensation is put in order first by perception, then by concepts, so the variety of possible takings and ideas is limited by habit. This phenomenon is due to the plasticity of the material in which stimulus and response occur. Repeated action along one path of the neural arc digs a channel that later action follows. It is another mystery, for the nerve current uses up the nerve shaft, which is then self-repaired in the usual way of the body. None the less, the habits are engraved on that fresh substance—and from the earliest years, when it is still superbly elastic.

James's chapter on Habit is deservedly famous; it is the masterpiece within the masterpiece and it has often been issued separately, for with its varied illustrations it sheds light on a great many activities of life; it could touch on all of them if a list could ever be drawn up.

The habits that organize our responses to art are the same social ones that create communities and hold them together. 'Habit is the enormous fly-wheel of society, its most precious conservative agent. It alone is what keeps us within the bounds of ordinance, and saves the children of fortune from the envious uprisings of the poor. It alone prevents the hardest and most repulsive walks of life from being deserted by those brought up to tread therein.' (Obviously, crime, once taken up, is one of these occupations, as compelling and change-resistant as the rest.) Habit, again, in the form of tradition and convention creeping up on us from infancy, enables us to see and enjoy the arts as perceptions and emotions shared, rather than anarchically as individual takers. This force is redoubled when the art of an age is closely linked with its religion.

Such has been the norm until recently: in any one period or place only one style of art flourished at a time; the old was discarded and taste altered slowly. It was the historical sense of the nineteenth century that changed all that, and the technology of the twentieth that brought to market the art of the whole past and of the whole globe simultaneously. But although artistic pluralism has become possible, it is remarkable how strong is the urge of art lovers to stay huddled together and "admit," in any given art, only this or that collection of works and masters. The excluded are always far more numerous than the admitted. The criteria, which vary with nationality or politics, with avant-garde habits or those of a main body, suggest that the choice has to do with "elements that are wanted"—in Coleridge's phrase—matters of mood or message that the kind of art in vogue best provides.

But equally remarkable, underneath this shifting consensus there persists a dissensus that shows both the radical diversity of minds and the habit of social conformity, spurred by the fear of being wrong. It is simply not true that "there is general agreement" about the classics or the modern masters.*

But the dissent, when it is conscious, is subdued; and when it is unconscious it is released only like a conspirator's secret to an agent pro-

---

* I have given a sketch of the state of dissensus on Shakespeare, perhaps the most striking example, since it has to do with "the supreme artist." ("From the Shakespeare File" in *The Energies of Art*, New York, 1956.) And one can always meditate about the Nobel Prizes in literature.

vocateur. Yet whoever reads criticism critically is amazed at the general self-assurance that ignores this instructive situation. What it teaches is that for the sake of our congenial habits we use every means to maintain not merely our social and physical environment constant, but also our spiritual and esthetic. Art can contribute to coziness, and it is not surprising that for a good many people music means one composer, literature one author, and so on, while for the critic his matured choice of masters sets the limits of the art.

Clearly, the desirable thing to do is to break through habits when they become shackles; and there lies the difficulty. For habit by its very narrowing is liberating too. We would all go mad if every part of our daily routine—buttoning and unbuttoning—had to be thought about and decided on. Besides, learning, growing, enlarging one's scope mean nothing else than forming new habits; being cast-iron, they had better be good habits. James's warning applies here: 'Could the young but realize how soon they will become mere walking bundles of habits, they would give more heed to their conduct while in the plastic state. We are spinning our fates, good or evil, and never to be undone.'

Yet, as I suggested, there is a role for the habit of breaking habits. I have tried to cultivate it, with varying success and in spite of the feeling of foolishness that comes with it: "how absurd to make a point of this!" To change trivial ways is hardest, of course—to dislocate old arrangements, give up usual foods, or do without breakfast shows in its effects how hag-ridden we are. But such attempts limber up the mind and incidentally explain why cultural changes so often begin with affectation. Before the general rediscovery and enjoyment of medieval architecture some eccentrics had to show the world and *build* gothic ruins in their gardens.

This is but to say that conscious, awkward effort precedes unconscious ease. The piano piece has to be learned bit by bit, with stumblings, then rehearsed until performance calls for none of the attention that went into learning it. Indeed, one part of the mind (or as we inaccurately say, the fingers) can play it while another part carries on a conversation or thinks silently of past or future. Habit is the mind's supreme efficiency, as Samuel Butler implied when he said that a really accomplished thief would steal a horse by reflex action.*

By this test, our intellectual and spiritual doings for the past half century or more must be rated as failing, incomplete. We have learned

---

* Butler did not know that his ideal had been realized in the person of one John Rabon, who in 1835 in South Carolina was indicted on four counts of stealing—horse, bull, hog, and bees—within a few days in one district. (Jack Williams, *Vogues in Villainy*, Columbia, S. C., 1959, p. 43.)

much, thanks to the host of searchers and teachers in all fields, but the conscious effort has left us still self-conscious, like the learner at the piano. The flood of advice, the continual analysis of thought and behavior, have not been assimilated into unconscious habits that might do us good. The arts themselves remain horribly stuck on the conscious—on technique, intention, explanation—so much so that they have to a large extent removed themselves from the list of pleasures and added their burden to the mass of other "problems," proud of being riddles, which an equally self-conscious Criticism then grapples with in language correspondingly dark.

Attention, which presides over the forming of habits, is 'the withdrawal from some things in order to deal effectively with others.' It is that 'reactive spontaneity' that makes of experience our experience. There are kinds of attention—immediate, when the subject is interesting in itself; derived, when, as in some parts of study, the interest comes from a distant goal; reflex or passive, as when some sudden noise breaks in on the stream of thought; voluntary or active, when the stream concentrates itself on a purpose. The voluntary is always derived and varies with the purpose, as well as with age, experience, and training. The proof corrector sees typographical errors that the reader, kept in suspense by the plot, never notices.

In addition, there are differences in attending that go with a sort of bodily specialization in perception, association, and memory. Some people are visual, others auditory, still others muscular or "motor." Habit naturally reinforces what is originally temperament or type—and explanation goes no further. What is curious is that these differences do not wholly determine tastes or careers. Some great painters had poor visual memory. James himself, who was a "motor" and an excellent draftsman, had little or no visual memory.

These divisions and subdivisions of types, it need hardly be said, should make us still more cautious and self-aware in our judgments of art. Others' associations are beyond our ken, but that they are effectively there does matter. Whistler's exclamation "Of course, Friday's yellow!" gives us pause. In Scriabin, absolute pitch was accompanied by matching colors for each note; for him a chromatic scale had a literal meaning. Everybody experiences to some extent such a mixing of the senses and can understand James's remark about a brilliant snow scene: 'The light is shrieking away outside.' Modern poetry in particular relies on this simultaneity. But which senses mix, and how much, within ourselves at any moment taxes the closest attention.

Since attention is by nature selective, the question for any judgment—not simply in art but in the law, business, politics, marriage—is what to attend to? Habit can help or hinder, habit of speech especially. The painter's eye, we say, sees what is really there—details and harmonies to which we are blind. We see the grass as uniformly green (concept-work: "greenness, as in grass"), whereas the painter sees it shading from brown or purple under the tree to greens and yellows under the sun. We wish we had the painter's eye. But the real is not so simple. "Seeing" the grass as all one color has value too: it tells us to expect the same stuff under the tree as under the sun. The painter himself had better see as we do when he crosses the street, for if he sees only patches of color and does not translate them into "large moving object," his painter's eye will land him under the wheels of a truck.

It is by voluntary attention that the double aspect of thinking comes to be noticed, on one side the so-called subjective or transient, which is a feeling or coloring of every passing thought; on the other, the so-called objective or cognitive, which yields the more permanent objects. Both lead to discoveries. When Wilde said that nature ends by imitating art, he meant that after many hints on canvas or in literature (and why not in music?)—hints first occurring as some artist's subjective impressions—we grow attentive to such sensations and spot them easily in experience.

As a good Impressionist, James was fond of noting these 'fringes and halos, inarticulate perceptions, whereof the objects are as yet unnamed, mere nascencies of cognition, premonitions, awarenesses of direction'; and he took some pride in having 'restored the *vague* to its psychological rights.' By so doing he also settled the question, still mooted, whether art has or has not a cognitive function. By the direct action of physical things (words, rhythms, surface appearances) on our "sounding boards," a work of art makes us both feel and think. And since art is an extension of experience, we come to "know," we can "learn about life," from art.

But is this true of the kind of art that is meant only for escape? The question is begged in the asking: what is escape? To attend to anything is to neglect, to escape, something else. Playing records is not studying math and the quality of the music does not nullify the "escape" from duty. Reading the greatest novel will not take care of impending bankruptcy better than reading the cheapest. Either one of them may relieve strain and redirect the practical energies—or weaken them further; only the outcome will tell.

In looking back on the overlapping experience of art and life one is led to generalize, to frame concepts about it; and this in turn often gives rise to the feeling that the themes or parts of a great work have developed by themselves—"inevitably," we like to say. The creator often has the same impression. To hear him, the characters took charge and worked out their own play or novel. To the admiring critic, the plan of the picture or building follows "a rigorous logic." These notions arise because a chunk of experience singled out 'has a way, if the mind is left alone with it, of suggesting other parts of the continuum from which it was torn.' Similarly, the practiced historian speaks of the logic of events and foresees what *his* characters will do.

These "logics" are true, but limited to the single case. Two artists will deal with the same material differently and two historians show events in different configurations. The mind is fertile in handling what it attends to, but no material or concept is fertile in itself. James took it for granted that 'no one would think of saying of any single note [in a chord] that it "developed" of itself into the other notes or into the feeling of harmony.' He was evidently not familiar with the modern cant that regards the time-bound artistic conventions—say, of music—as inherent in its substance and demanding the "logic" we discover by hindsight. He might have cited the fact that until the thirteenth century the major third was not classed as a consonance, or the demonstration by Helmholtz that musical scales and harmonic rules are artistic inventions. They use, but are not dictated by, the physics and mathematics of sound.

If there are any fundamental rules of art, they rest on the simplest psychological facts, such as that 'no one can possibly attend continuously to an object that does not change.' Just as to think of nothing at all is an effort that ends in falling asleep, so does monotony ( = "one note") fatigue and cause slumber. True, minds vary as to what they find capable of holding their interest. In speaking of the Germans' contributions to psychophysics—measuring thousands of reaction times—James says that the results were achievable 'only in a country whose natives could not be bored.' But in art, in oratory, or in factory work, change must be frequent. Certainly in silent, solitary thought attention must perpetually revive itself or die. How is this done? By turning the matter over, as the expressive term goes, circling around its facets, seeing to it that there be "more to it."

What becomes, then, of genius defined as the taking of endless pains? James turns the maxim around: it is genius that makes prolonged taking pains possible. A richly endowed mind attends better and longer than a shallow one, because it has more interests, associations, perceptions, suggestions, purposes, with which to work upon its object. The rare masterpieces in which not a single portion betrays drudgery must yet have been gone over and over relentlessly, the maker each time bending his Will to Attend upon some aspect, meaning, or formal relation and remaking it new.

Other ingredients of genius will receive mention when we consider James himself under that heading. Yet here one of them cannot be postponed—Imagination. Unexpectedly, not much need be said about it, because in the usual honorific sense imagination is a collective name for the full exertion of all the powers of mind at their best: perception, reason, conception, discrimination, emotion, and imagination in its strictly psychological sense. In that sense it is simply the recurrence of images in thought after the stimulus is gone. These imaginings are '"reproductive" when the copies are literal; "productive" when elements from different originals are recombined so as to make new wholes.'

Both kinds are usually imperfect, incomplete, and follow the individual bent described earlier toward visual, auditory, or other bodily inclination. It is from this narrow sense of Imagination that Berenson derived his "tactile values"—images the painter must arouse to give roundedness to the flat surface of color and line. The assumption that imagined sensations are always weaker is true, but not absolute. When the real sensation is weak, it is hard to discriminate from the imagined. 'Certain violin players take advantage of this in diminuendo terminations. After the pianissimo has been reached, they continue to bow as if still playing, but are careful not to touch the strings. The listener hears in imagination a degree of sound fainter still.' And the phenomenon is not confined to hearing.

This fact neatly shows the continuity of experience, subjective and objective. But it is also a fact that nothing can be imagined—sensed anew—without an original external stimulus. Imagination does not "create" in the sense of making out of nothing. Those who are blind from birth have no notion of sight and no visual dreams; whereas the blind who used to see dream and imagine sights. This dependence of the imagination on a triggering from outside one would expect from the inescapable role of the neural arc. At first it seems to set limits to "imagination," the poetic, scientific gift that has rightly been made the queen of human faculties. On second thought, the limitation increases our wonder, for it shows the mind seemingly inexhaustible in its power to play variations, to combine and recombine the givens of sense into a pattern that stretches from the number systems to the untranslatable messages of ordered sound.

The reason for relating to art, science, and society some of the things James tells us of the conscious mind (so unpopular these days) has been to show their high interest and usefulness in almost any consideration of our culture and our lives. The very texture of *The Principles of Psychology* is a lesson in the unity of knowledge, a reproach to our specialisms. Obviously, this sketch, shaped by my own concerns, has not fully represented the contents of the work. The chapters on Association, The Perception of Time, The Perception of Space,* Instinct, Will, and Necessary Truths contain additional treasures of scientific fact and philosophic thought, richly illustrated in the Jamesian way. The discussion of Hypnotism, the pages on abnormal states, the references to sexuality will be taken up later: James at this point has not said his last word on the mind.

Yet to some of his contemporaries at least, he did seem to have said the last word. For the masterpiece when it appeared was both a detailed record of original work and a *summa* of results due to others. The reviews of the work were prompt, numerous, and largely favorable, despite the enormous number of subjects treated. Some critics, as sister Alice wrote in her diary, "reprobate his mental pirouettes and squirm at his daring to go lightly among the solemnities." But there were shortly four requests to translate the work into German, which suggests that the intellectual capers did not bother the most fact-seeking of James's professional colleagues.

James, at any rate, knew what he had done. In announcing to his publisher the arrival of the *Psychology, Briefer Course* a year later, he wrote: 'By adding some twaddle about the senses, by leaving out all polemics and history, all bibliography and experimental details, all metaphysical subtleties and digressions, all quotations, all humor and pathos, all *interest* in short, and by blackening the tops of all the paragraphs, I think I have produced a tome of pedagogic classic, which will enrich both you and me, if not the student's mind.'

Other critics of the full work thought its organization defective. James, who was always ready to admit—even to advertise—his imperfections, stood by his guns on this point. In the preface to the *Briefer Course* he says: 'The order of composition is doubtless unshapely, or it would not be found so by so many. But planless it is not, for I deliberately followed what seemed to me a good pedagogic order in proceeding from the more concrete mental aspects with which we are best acquainted to the so-called elements which we naturally come to know later by way of abstraction. The opposite order, of "building up" the mind out of its "units of composition" has the merit of expository elegance and gives a neatly subdivided table of contents; but it often purchases these advantages at the cost of reality and truth. On the whole, I

---

* For technical originality and brilliance, James's greatest achievement in psychology.

venture to think that the "unsystematic" form charged upon the book is more apparent than profound.'

Later readers have confirmed this judgment. It is the misfortune of those who first criticize works of genius to suppose that there can be no good reason for what they do not immediately understand.

# The Test of Truth

If Experience as natively given in consciousness is fleeting, variable, helter-skelter, and if we have the power to work upon it, by attention, by making concepts, by combining images, then we need a way of making sure that the account we give of any experience, the bearing of any connections we discover, is solid, reliable, permanent because rooted in the nature of things. The common way of saying this is that we need a test of truth.

James's description of the human mind implied such a test. The mind, bent upon action, drives ahead toward a goal and asks: has the goal been reached? have other, unexpected results emerged? James from his earliest studies turned this question into a test, but he gave it no public expression till August 1898, when he delivered a lecture at the University of California in Berkeley. It was this lecture that launched Pragmatism into the world.

It is for Pragmatism that conventional opinion about James gives him the most ample credit—or discredit, as the case may be. Textbook summaries of his thought call Pragmatism the philosophy on which his fame is based. Yet some writers think it an idea unrelated to the rest of his work and which in no way affects his greatness as a psychologist and philosopher. Both views are baseless.

Pragmatism is not a philosophy; it is an attempt to explain how the mind ascertains truth. If correct, this explanation supplies a means of testing truths. Nor did James spend his life expounding Pragmatism; the volume of lectures called by that name was written only four years before his death, and so far from claiming particular merit for the idea, he gave to the published book the subtitle: "A New Name for Some Old Ways of Thinking." He also tried—unsuccessfully as we shall see—to share with two fellow-philosophers any credit that might accrue. To these misconceptions must be added the fact that the daily or newspaper use of the word *pragmatic* connotes a dozen different things, none of them indicative of what James proposed. After sampling this grand confusion a little further on, the reader will decide for himself whether the word *pragmatic* means anything. Perhaps James's definition and test of truth should be baptized anew.

Historically, that is, for James, the term Pragmatism covers the steps we go through before we can say: "This is true; that is not." How do we know? One would suppose that the meaning of *true* and the signs of truth would have been settled long ago. Not so. All thinkers acknowledge that although mankind has always held many truths as permanent and unquestionable, these truths vary none the less, from place to place and mind to mind and especially from time to time. Science, which "makes progress" (i.e., varies), offers a good example of truths changing in time; religions and moral codes show truth's variability from place to place and mind to mind. This predicament calls for an investigation of truth, a bedrock statement of what it is. In the history of western thought two accounts have been repeatedly offered: that is true which copies or matches reality; that is true which is consistent with itself and other truths.

The copy or matching explanation is seen to have a fatal flaw from the moment one understands the stream of consciousness. "Copying reality" must mean that over there is a reality; here in the mind is a copy being made of it; to find the truth, see if the two match. Actually, no "copying" can take place, because no reaching out to "over there" is possible. What the mind sees, feels, gets hold of in whatever way, comes in one continuum—its own experience—not two. So there is nothing to match up, no direct testing of a "copy" with its original.

Consistency or coherence as a test proves just as false in the long run. For, in the first place, how are those earlier truths verified which demand consistency from the new one? And second, it often happens that two or more divergent schemes of thought show equal consistency and leave us wondering which is true. The possibility of different geometries based on opposite axioms is fatal to the test of consistency.

A system coherent within itself can also fail, because fresh experience upsets one part or another, or because the demonstration of coherence depends on words that a hair-splitting mind may find ambiguous—double meanings, distinctions ad infinitum. Many proofs of the existence of God have succumbed in this way, though at first they satisfied not only the inventor but also his critics; the sharpest minds found no flaw.

The problem for James then was: how to account for the variability of truth and how to get around the weakness of the copy and consistency doctrines. It was not his problem alone. It was one of the great preoccupations of the men of his time. Read Nietzsche or Samuel Butler, Poincaré or Mach, or any other speculative thinkers and scientists after 1870, and you find the question recurring in many forms and contexts.

Responding in part to this agitation, the American Charles Sanders Peirce wrote a popular article in 1878 entitled "How to Make Our Ideas Clear." In it he suggested that a good way was to ask whether any practical difference would follow if some change were made in the statement of any idea. If the change left the consequences identical, then there was no difference between the two statements. To this rule of thumb he gave the name Pragmatism, from the Greek *pragma*, meaning "a thing done." Peirce was a neighbor in Cambridge whom James read and admired, corresponded with and befriended.*

The word Pragmatism crystallized in James's mind all his own earlier inklings about a definition of truth and inspired him to set it forth under that name. After expounding his view in the Berkeley lecture of 1898, James presented a fuller account in eight lectures at the newly established Stanford University in 1906. He was there when the great San Francisco earthquake struck, but survived to repeat the lectures at Columbia University the following year; after which they appeared in the book entitled *Pragmatism*. In all these utterances James acknowledged his debt to Peirce, who ultimately would have none of it. James mentioned the influence of another friend, the English philospher Shadworth Hodgson, who also declined shared fatherhood.**

What James did on his own, then, was to enlarge Peirce's and Hodgson's limited uses of the test into a description of all truth-seeking and -finding. When the natural purposiveness of the stream of mind is directed rationally for making sure that an idea is right, the search is "pragmatic" in the sense that it looks chiefly to what follows, not back-

---

* James did all he could to obtain for him a permanent post at Harvard, but Peirce was too unaccommodating for the institution. James helped him tirelessly in other ways, which led Peirce, playfully and gratefully, to change his middle name Sanders to Santiago— "Saint James."

** For Hodgson, see p. 321 below. In *The Thought and Character of William James*, Boston, 1935, R. B. Perry says: "It is clear that the idea that pragmatism originated with Peirce was originated by James." (II, pp. 407 ff.) Peirce rechristened his own brainchild with the still clumsier word Pragmaticism and clung to the copy theory of truth, believing it the view of science. Yet just after reading *Pragmatism* Peirce was apparently satisfied: "I found a statement of my own thoughts, which I can appreciate, having been laboring and crowding my way for months and months—crowding through throngs of technicalities, objections, and stupidities—to try to express. There you have put it on your page with the utmost lucidity and apparent facility. Nothing could be more satisfactory." (Perry, II, p. 436.)

wards to precedent or sideways to an "original." The mind perceives many bewildering things and frames many conceptions of them. To be called true, these ideas must correspond and must agree, as previous thinkers maintained, but with what? Agreement can only be found in the fitness of further experiences—objects seen or actions made possible.

James's description thus supplies the concreteness missing from both the copy and the consistency theories of truth. At the same time, the new definition supplies a standard of judgment: 'The true is only the expedient in the way of our thinking.' Or again: 'Truth is simply a collective name for verification processes, just as health, wealth, strength, etc. are names for other processes connected with life. Truth is *made*, just as health, wealth, and strength are made, in the course of experience.'

The making of truth might also be expressed as: "Go and see if experience *responds*; find out if later perceptions within the same field of interest bear out the interpretation, the formulation given tentatively at the outset. Note also whether the new idea fits in with earlier accepted ones." For 'loyalty to them is the first principle—in most cases it is the only principle.' This use of consistency is no return to an old error; it falls in at a different point in the handling of ideas. 'A new opinion counts as "true" just in proportion as it gratifies the individual's desire to assimilate the novel in his experience to his beliefs in stock. It must both lean on old truth and grasp new fact.' To sum up: 'Ideas (which themselves are but parts of our experience) become true just insofar as they help us to get into satisfactory relation with other parts of our experience.'

For example, when a stick is half dipped in water we see certain lines and colors that makes us think it broken—we know from past experience that that is how a broken stick looks. But if we have any doubt, we slide our hand along the stick in the water and feel no break: the idea "broken stick" is not true; it disagrees with a subsequent, relevant experience. The pragmatic test is repeated when we pull the stick out of the water, see it whole and lean on it—*not* broken.

In this sequence, the role of the idea is to lead us through action toward a fresh and fitting experience. Its power to do that is its truth-value. More generally about theories: 'none is absolutely a transcript of reality, but any one of them may from some point of view be useful. Their great use is to summarize old facts and to lead to new ones. They are only a man-made language, a conceptual shorthand, in which we write our reports of nature.'

In this version of how truths are made we find the explanation of the great variability of truth. The long life of errors, too, is accounted for: mistaken, incomplete views fitted well enough; they fitted all the facts known, all the experiences (or experiments) so far possible; they were useful as far as they went. From this human and historical condition, now or later, it is not likely that we shall emerge.

The shorthand way to describe the supposition of a broken stick is: "that idea won't work"; it does not lead to the expected sequel. By inverting the negative phrase about "working," we get that other shorthand definition: "truth is what works." The amount of ink and toil expended in debating this aphorism during the last seventy-five years would suffice to write out the *Encyclopaedia Britannica* by hand, like Mr. Jabez Wilson in "The Red-Headed League." In that curtailed definition some critics of Pragmatism, early and late, interpret "work" as "get away with": if you manage to sell a stranger a gold brick, your idea has "worked" and the brick has to be acknowledged "pragmatically" as being gold. Since this is obviously a falsehood, Pragmatism is false too. The use of such an argument tells us something about the level of debate to which professional thinkers are willing to descend when given a chance to impute unworthy views to an esteemed colleague.

Others, it is true, greeted James's work as a shaft of light thrown into the darkness by an elegant demonstration. In the capitals of Europe they founded Pragmatic Clubs to discuss all possible implications. But many resisted with a passion suggesting that Pragmatism must violate something like a religious faith. That passion springs from a Platonic judgment, scornful of the imperfect and earthly: how can actions and things be the proving ground of ideas? Instead of the clarity and simplicity long felt to be the sign of truth, human thought was now plunged back into the complex and uncertain. 'Our duty to agree with reality is grounded in a perfect jungle of concrete expediencies.' James's test brought noble truth (often said to be naked, yet just as often clothed in a large capital letter) into the daily moil of practice, which unlike Theory is never perfect. The pragmatic analysis, the pragmatic test offer only variable, incomplete truths. What happens then to sacred, pure, absolute, and eternal Truth?

That question can be left hanging until someone shows where that truth is domiciled. In any case, the stated problem was not about this imaginary creature; it was about the evident variability of the truths we do have and the reason why we need them. First and last, then, the name Pragmatism, for all its Greek aura, was an unfortunate choice. It blurred the fact that the *question* of truth had been redefined, and not just the answer. His answer James had found hints of in many thinkers through the ages.* But none gave it in full and none insisted as he did on the complexities—the rival claims of different kinds of evidence—along the path of discovering truth, let alone the difficulty of stating it unassailably. The pragmatic account of truth thereby disturbed many assumptions and caused much discomfort. It implied, for instance, that we ought to cease deploring the imperfect and approximate and accordingly abate our dogmatism, make room for a plurality of truths.

Naming such consequences only created the impression that here was a new and rather vulgar creed fishing for followers. Actually, what James had established was that all thinking creatures—scientists, philosophers, doctors, ditchdiggers, architects, lawyers, children—alike proceed pragmatically whether they know it or not. But if Pragmatism is not an ism one adopts like Marxism or Zen Buddhism, not a world-view but a description of the common path to truth, there is nothing to join and "believe in." If the description is correct, everybody is a pragmatist, for the same reason that M. Jourdain in Molière's comedy had spoken prose all his life: there was no way he could do anything else.

Other results follow from the recognition that veri-fying—literally, "making true"—is pragmatic work, but they stand out more clearly if we look first at what the world has made of the unblessed word *pragmatic*. Since James's adoption of the term to express gratitude to the first user, the adjective form has been degraded to convey not a description of thought but a moral judgment, largely adverse. During the past months I have culled from books, the press, and casual conversation well over two hundred uses of the word; nearly all contain or imply disparagement. Some do suggest that there is something astute or hard-headed about the pragmatist. But it is always a left-handed compliment; to say pragmatic is to say second-best, below standard for a worthy person. Not one use in my collection has to do with James's historic conception or indeed with mind in search of truth. When "pragmatic test" occurs, it denotes success achieved in a rough-handed way, unhampered by scruples. Here are, from two works of fiction, plain words that show the prevailing bias:

—"That's pragmatism," I said, "and I've been taught that pragmatism's naughty."

---

* In the margin of Locke's *Essay*, which James annotated in 1876, he penciled the word *practicalism* opposite a passage where Locke says it makes no difference what the self is made of provided its functions remain the same. See also below, pp. 107–8.

—"Stick to the concrete. You will be much happier."

"You are a pragmatist," said Mr. Smith.

"Now that really is an unkind thing to say."

During the last presidential campaign, *pragmatic* and *pragmatism* were of course continually bandied about. Applied to candidates for office, the meaning was "getting things done, with or without kid gloves." One hears little of candidates who do not want to get things done—there is no word for them. But all would apparently prefer to achieve by divine grace, without being "pragmatic." Pragmatism, in short, is represented as the antithesis of principle. A columnist justly famed for his keen mind and deft use of words writes: "Frankly the pragmatists have all the fun.... Moralists, on the other hand, are pests." And he goes on to advocate morality in business and foreign policy.

In daily use, the close kin and the opposites of *pragmatic* and *pragmatism* are bewildering, and so are the paired words that seem required to help out the sense:

... largely unencumbered by dogma, modern and pragmatic. Basing foreign policy on pragmatism and idealism ...

The couples take the wait to get married pragmatically as well as philosophically.

As a critic of poetry my position is pragmatical or traditionary.

Stendhal's philosophy is an attitude, a pragmatic and practical combination of theories, reflexions, and observations.

We did not waste time on unrealistic rhetoric or unattainable objectives. We dealt with pragmatic solutions to the problems. (The President of the United States after an international conference.)

Then, too, the reader encounters such phrasings as: the pragmatic conservative/ pragmatism, not conservatism/ a centrist streak of pragmatism/ Socialist pragmatic principles/ professional and pragmatic/ creative and pragmatic ideas/ stubborn instead of passively pragmatic. "Pragmatic pregnancy" is explained as having a child in order to qualify for welfare support. These uses would suggest that ideals, principles, theories are admirable but ineffectual. This is plainly put in another of my cullings: "He said a lot of the right things, but I'm a pragmatist." And to round out the series, a puzzling remark that should interest critics and gourmets: "Those beaded bubbles? Well, Keats was a pragmatic drinker."

Even this overdose of examples does not exhaust the intellectual laxity of the wretched word. But it does prove beyond doubt that the root

idea of pragmatism and the pragmatic test is totally absent from the
current usage.* "Pragmatic," one concludes, is one of those words like
"romantic" that are thrown into a sentence for the small pleasure of
labeling without thinking. In good writers, who avoid empty gestures,
the word is most often used as a needless synonym for practical, with a
connotation of self-interest. Alan Paton, for example, tells us in his
autobiography that one should dedicate one's life to a cause greater
than oneself, but that besides this duty there is "a second reason, purely
pragmatic, namely, that one is going to miss the meaning of life if one
doesn't." It might be supposed that learning the meaning of life was as
lofty a purpose as serving a great cause; or conversely, that both had a
"pragmatic" regard for self in the shape of self-fulfillment.

The lesson to draw from so much verbal floundering is that it betrays
our mixed feelings and shuffling attitude about thought and action. To
strive and make the ideal real and actual is no longer seen to be a high
achievement; it is a low endeavor. Sometimes, the concrete imagination
does reawaken and give praise, grudging, shamefaced, or defiant, to the
person or purpose that aims at accomplishing. Why there should be a
choice between the two, with honor attached to theory and odium to
practice, is not explained. Perhaps it is not even a conscious thought.
Opinion takes it for granted that the practical is faulty, it being so hard
to work with. Few people note that there is usually the error of excess
in the promise of the ideal. As a foreign correspondent truly says: "In
the battle for hearts and minds, pragmatism simply cannot compete
with the ideals, the martyrs, above all the passion, of ideology."


To return to pragmatism in the strict sense of a test in common use and
most often automatic, what we must ask next is how we know the test
has been met. Uncertainties in life are more complex than that of the
broken stick. The effort of thought is usually about probable results not
clearly visible. How does one know that the right conception of the

---

* Readers of Matthew Arnold may be surprised to find him speaking with respect of
"pragmatic poetry," just as students of history will find the famous German Mommsen
calling himself a "pragmatic historian." This usage goes back to the ancients. The scholars
at Alexandria who interpreted myths as having meaning for life, and the historian Poly-
bius, who said his work was pragmatic because it was not solely narrative but dealt with
consequences, gave the word the meaning it had for Arnold—poetry as a criticism of life.
For Mommsen it meant history told for its significant results.

Between the ancients and the nineteenth century, in Shakespeare's time, say, *pragmatical* meant overbusy, meddling, officious; though it was also a term of Roman law denot-
ing a fundamental decree by a ruler, e.g., the "Pragmatic Sanction of Bourges" (1438). All
this uncertainty shows how ill-favored from birth the word has been. It cannot now be
removed from James's work or the ensuing controversy, but it deserves to be dropped
from the common vocabulary.

facts—the useful, necessary truth—has been reached? In an extended essay on "The Sentiment of Rationality," published some twenty years before his first lecture on pragmatism, James replied in psychological terms: 'The only answer can be that he will recognize rationality as he recognizes everything else, by certain subjective marks. What, then, are the marks? A strong feeling of ease, peace, rest, is one of them. The transition from a state of puzzle and perplexity to rational comprehension is full of lively relief and pleasure.'

Some minds, of course, are satisfied sooner than others. They take simple views; others refine and distinguish; but all of them attempt to 'banish uncertainty from the future. The permanent presence of the sense of futurity in the mind has been strangely ignored by most writers, but the fact is that our consciousness at a given moment is never free from the ingredient of expectancy.' That fact accounts for the natural desire to complete supposition or imagined hypothesis by pragmatic testing through action. There is no instantaneous way to "see" the truth or the right. The notion of its sudden discovery as a ready-made thing—something like mislaid spectacles recovered—is an illusion, due either to the long diet of past truths fully formed that we are fed as children, or to the singling out of the moment of illumination after a long search. At any rate, James's account of thought puts an end to the spectator conception of truth and shows Time to be a necessary ingredient of its making. In this feature, incidentally, Pragmatism parallels the other new, time-laden conceptions of the turn of the century, which revolutionized science and the arts as well as philosophy.

This same recognition of futurity has the effect of uniting the various types of search for the rational. Not scientific or empirical truth alone is found and tested by the matching of present experience with earlier and later, but what we call moral truth, artistic truth, historical truth, religious truth, and right policy in any department of life. Including these forms of truth is important, for their omission forces one into the position of certain modern thinkers who say that all statements other than those verifiable by experiment are but "emotional language" having no truth value and expressing nothing more than vagrant preferences.

Yet the faith in "spectator truth" and the urge to equate truth with finality have strong roots in the feeling that thought, in order to be good, must be pure. Many years ago in a socialist journal, John Dewey and Max Eastman (who had attended James's *Pragmatism* lectures in 1907) argued the question "Was Lincoln a Pragmatist?" The main issue was: Has or has not truth anything to do with action? Eastman, who defended Lincoln from the taint of pragmatism, said: "The art of valid thinking must be an art of setting aside not only action but the whole preoccupation with its purposes." The appeal was to serene contemplation; truth reveals itself only if one keeps free from the disturbances of the active world.

Neither contestant quoted Lincoln himself, yet it is evident from all his writings that his thought was consciously pragmatic. It relied on imagined consequences in action. His famous reply to Horace Greeley's public attack is a classic example of the accomplished pragmatist at work:

"My paramount object in this struggle is to save the Union, and is not either to save or to destroy slavery. If I could save the Union without freeing any slave, I would do it; and if I could save it by freeing all the slaves, I would do it; and if I could save it by freeing some and leaving others alone, I would also do that. What I do about slavery and the colored race, I do because I believe it helps to save the Union; and what I forbear, I forbear because I do not believe it would help to save the Union. I shall do less whenever I shall believe what I am doing hurts the cause, and I shall do more whenever I shall believe doing more will help the cause. I shall try to correct errors when shown to be errors and I shall adopt new views so far as they shall appear to be true views. I have here stated my purpose according to my view of official duty, and I intend no modification of my oft-expressed personal wish that all men, everywhere, could be free."

There is something in this progression by short steps that reminds one of a good teacher leading the mind of a poor student. Greeley was far from stupid, but his thought leapt about among familiar "principles" and lost sight of the purpose that touched off the need to think—the purpose (ideal, goal, promise, true policy) that Lincoln sets down in his first sentence. His exact molding of idea to purpose, rare as it is, easily wins our approval when we look at the historical result; and it readily commends itself to those willing to say, "Yes, that is what we want in politics and business, which are practical concerns." But they add: "In higher things the mind must follow a different rule." What rule? Apparently the rule of detached observation, unconcerned with results, or what is called pursuing truth for its own sake and wherever it may lead.

In this vein, Max Eastman, not content with "brushing aside action and purpose" goes even further and says: "it is impractical to mix the purpose of an act with the definition of the facts upon which it is to be based." The remark is a clue to the difficulty of grasping what James said, never mind agreeing or disagreeing with it. His opponents' objection, born of our verbal habits, is: When—as in pure science—a thinker has not the slightest desire to act but only to know, the prospect of action should play no part in his thinking.

In view of the way scientists actually work—"doing one's damndest with one's mind, no holds barred" (as Bridgman put it), this self-denying rule of the guardians of truth seems strange.* Take the discovery of Neptune. Leverrier, finding irregularities in the movements of one planet, surmises the existence, size, and orbit of another. The surmise is of course based on the possession of many antecedent truths. After a general search of the heavens, by numerous observers, there is the new planet. A sense of irrationality had triggered a desire for relief into rationality, a need for action to quiet the trouble. That activity was first the fitting together of thought and consequence; then came the readjustment of earlier truths to the new one, a second fitting of the ever-unfinished garment of truth. For as we all know from recent findings, several hitherto plausible and consistent ideas about the solar system have been upset or modified by sending movable labs into outer space.

Nor is this all. The pragmatic or active view of truth is the only one that will account for the inconsistencies or paradoxes involved in scientific thought—how, for example, light can be said to be waves and particles; or why a table top, which is solid and subject to the "laws" of solids, is, also according to science, a sieve with more empty space than hard matter. Purpose and point of view—perspectivism—inevitably shape our human truths. Familiar phrases record this necessity: "from this angle," "considering this aspect," "relatively to the norms of that time," "all other things being equal," and the like, show how difficult it is to tell the truth without specifying the perspective. The very change in the meaning of "point of view" to its present sense of "opinion" reminds us that true statements vary with the point of sight.

When therefore the pragmatist says that his truth fits his purpose and may not fit others he is not claiming the privilege of being "subjective" or eccentric, he is only pointing to a condition of human thought. In one of his lectures James gave a simple illustration: 'For me, this whole "audience" is one thing, which grows now restless, now attentive. But in your own eyes, ladies and gentlemen, to call you "audience" is an accidental way of taking you. The permanent real things for you are your individual persons. To an anatomist, again, those persons are but organisms, and the real things are the organs. Not the organs so much as the individual cells, say the histologists; not the cells but their molecules, say in turn the chemists.' The "taking," natural and essential to the mind, is what makes truth additive.

* A good example of no holds barred is Bertrand Russell's suggestion after his discovery of a logical paradox involving numbers. His colleague Frege had exclaimed: "Alas, arithmetic totters!" upon which Russell propounded "a rule of safety" by which three would not be the same when applied to different types of entities. Fortunately, another way out was found.

This same versatility—so to speak—is reflected wherever we turn. It occurs, for example, in the well-known conflict between pair after pair of proverbs: "Look before you leap," but "He who hesitates is lost." Both are experientially true, but which should one follow? "It depends" is the only possible answer, which is itself enshrined in the legal dictum "circumstances alter cases." The law is in fact a mass of distinctions based on the diverse perspectives embodied in human conduct. Moralists, poets, and novelists contradict each other in the same helpful way. They truthfully set down their wisdom in maxims that do not jibe. Aristotle's recommendation of the golden mean was an attempt to evade this discouraging inadequacy of absolute maxims. Not too much of anything, even of the virtues, says the apostle of moderation. Courage is splendid, but too much courage is rashness, too much generosity is improvidence, too much accuracy is hairsplitting. Well, but rashness has accomplished great things and so have minute measurement and total self-sacrifice. Who is to tell how much is too much and when? And who, moreover, wants a moderately honest friend, a moderately faithful wife?

That mankind cannot manage without perspectivism is evident from the many conventions long since devised to accommodate divergent observers. We allow small children to act on truths that are "of their age"—and our household pets also. Foreigners among us get the benefit of the doubt. Religious believers nowadays tolerate one another—more or less. Art worshipers less rather than more, which is a sign of the greater fervor we feel about art. Primitive cultures perish when deprived of their truths; and the strange spectacle of our globe as seen from the planet Mars is yet another sign that perspective is the mother of truths.

Do the foregoing illustrations mean that the search for uniform truths and the sharper defining of perspectives might as well stop? Or again, that we must resign ourselves to living without principles? On the contrary.

As novel experience leads to new inquiry, 'the mind engenders truth upon reality,' and that truth often combines with earlier ones to extend the man-made intellectual unities. The increasing store of partial truths, in a civilization that continually propounds and criticizes them, is bound to generate links among them and so to form larger wholes. This progression is helped out by the tendency of human beings to exert a sort of gravitational pull on one another's minds; they compare notes and they like agreement; a truth seems stronger to the first believer when a second adopts it. In short, the conception of one truth, *the* truth, to which we are all so wedded, answers a social even more than an intellectual need.

But the need must not be exaggerated or the depth of the diversity denied. The existential fact is that everybody—scientists and philosophers included—lives comfortably enough with conflicting truths inside him, and this too can serve a useful end. Truth is so difficult to seize and express that the best minds are often those able to hold two opposed and mutually tempering ideas simultaneously. This is the source of all the dicta in praise of inconsistency and against pure logic. The law offers a good example of this virtue. When a judge reconciles the theoretical interest in fixed rule with the practical interest in dealing out justice, he is moved by incompatibles toward a decision he hopes will establish a wider, a truer truth.

That is genuine pragmatics; hence it is a mistake to call by that name the systematic disregard of precedent, of "funded truth," whether for the sake of settling each case on its merits or for the sake of reforming public policy. What judges should do in the conflict of truths has been a violently political issue for a good while. A generation ago a number of American jurists began to advocate "pragmatism and realism in the law," which to them meant deciding in the light of social results. The late judge Jerome Frank was a leader of this "sociological movement," as it was also called, and I remember several arguments in which I failed to persuade him that his pragmatism (as he thought of it) was inadequate.

I was making a case for precedent, stability and impartiality as the strength and virtue of the law. The litigant or accused must feel that his case is about his concerns and not a mere vehicle for social reform. At the same time I argued against those who maintained that the law was a deductive science ruled by logic and into which no thought of social consequences should enter—as if laws were not made for social ends and as if these were all foreseeable by the lawmaker. Each of the two conceptions is true in reason and in right feeling, but neither takes it into account that social consequences loom on *both* sides of the debate. The subtlest pragmatising is needed to accord due influence to past legal truths (pragmatically dependable) and preferred results (pragmatically desirable).*

The tragic element in history comes from the ingrained vice of one idea at a time. Innovation begins by ignoring and ends by ignorance.

---

* The writings of our contemporary Lord Devlin seem to me to supply such teachings with incomparable virtuosity in reasoning and style.

The newmakers are blind to what the institution or idea they attack intended and accomplished. Change comes and we deride past eras, assuming that their arrangements were absurd if not perverse. Dueling seems atrocious, because we never knew it as the device by which family feuds (read *Romeo and Juliet*) were put an end to. The divine right of kings arouses indignation or laughter, because we have forgotten its usefulness in quelling local warlords and in holding the central ruler accountable to the law of God.*

Mankind, in other words, moves by spurts of instinctive pragmatising spoiled by rigid concept-work and weak imagination; usually it is fulfilling in haste a need too long felt and denied. True progress would consist in a change that did not leave behind as many advantages as it offers new ones. But that would call for a pragmatic calculus alien to our notions of principle and our habits of revolution. Why does disillusionment follow the revolutionary victory? Simply because of the prior illusion that the overthrow of the existing regime will not affect present benefits; it will add to them the new ones desired. But once the change has been fought and bled for, it turns out that no addition but only an exchange has taken place, at great cost.

Law and history as the record of human action provide endless examples of the difficulty that pragmatic thought has to grapple with. While others cry "Be realistic!" the pragmatist knows that reality is elusive. In the abstract, reality is a legitimate standard to appeal to; it is the general goal that all truths aim at; but concretely, the real is not there ready to shake hands with the adventurer. He must expect disappointment and bad surprises.

The sour modern views of reality reflect this likelihood but do so from the conventional standpoint that truth is cut-and-dried and available. When T. S. Eliot, in one of his famous prosaic lines, states his discovery that "Human kind/ Cannot bear very much reality," one wonders how he gauged the human muchness or the size of the remainder and what more-than-human hold on the real he judged by. The aphorism is touched with superiority and self-pity combined. As for Freud's contrast, central to his analysis, between the pleasure principle and the reality principle, one must ask, Isn't pleasure real? The assumption that reality always brings pain parallels Eliot's maxim and is simply not true. It can only pass for true among those who have suffered as a

---

* Note an application: the nation state from its inception down to 1914 fought on the dueling principle, using professional armies as its champions. Since the first world war, for technological and democratic reasons, peoples have reverted to the "family feud" system, which involves every man, woman, and child in the great quarrels. And since other groups, ideological or religious, cannot muster whole nations in their cause, they resort to piecemeal raids—terrorism—like feudal chieftains.

result of overconfidence in some established truth and now express their resentment against fickle and heartless "reality."

Clearly, the subject of truth is not the simple thing that our school and laboratory habits have made it seem. In that picture, Truth is a vast collection of statements somewhere to be found. All good minds—our searchers and researchers—dig for truths like Forty-Niners and add their nuggets to the pile. Some dull old ones are replaced with bright new ones, and one day the collection will be complete and systematized, a hoard of propositional truth sitting inside a computer like the Nibelungs' beneath the Rhine.

That popular libretto overestimates the verbal. 'The Truth: what a perfect idol of the rationalistic mind. The whole notion of the truth is an abstraction, a mere useful summarizing phrase like the Latin language or the law. Judges and Latin teachers often speak of these entities as if they were something apart and existing before legal decisions and grammatical ways, but clearly they are nothing of the kind. Both law and Latin are results. Distinctions between the lawful and the unlawful or between correct and incorrect in speech have grown up incidentally among the interactions of men's experiences in detail.'

A proposition, then, is not so much true as truth-ful, a short-hand reminder of how to orient ourselves in experience. A truth is like a map, which does not copy the ground, but uses signs to tell us where to find the hill, the stream, and the village. Truth is the pathway, not the terminus. By our truths we chart "reality," but never exhaust it, however faithful to its contours; and because of this limitation, truth-seeking, individual or collective, is always thrown back upon experience, where we vainly wish that truth might be read like a book.

In life, the way to tie together notion and results or ideal and action is seldom clear either to ourselves or to those who judge our ways. The pragmatic test is at once subtle and laborious. Though we "want to make sure," we do not always look far and wide enough for the consequences that fit the case, or know how to sort them out. Holding on to a purpose amid the distraction of other plausible aims is a capacity given to few. Pragmatism describes the way we think, but to think well is rare, precisely because it is not straight "reasoning" or straight intuition, but a weaving together of all the relevants—abstract and concrete, obvious or recalled, known or imagined.

Everybody understands more or less the need to complete thought by appropriate action, as proverbial wisdom shows. "Deeds, not words"; "The road to Hell is paved with good intentions"; "He means well"; "Handsome is as handsome does"; "The proof of the pudding is in the eating"—all state or imply the pragmatic test. But the failure of our schooling to teach it as a conscious habit lets "ideas" cloud even simple issues. Chesterton gives a stunning example in his *Autobiography*. People in his small town wanted to put up a war memorial. After raising the money, some decided it would be "more practical" to build a meeting hall. The new proposal split the community. Chesterton comments:

"If people thought it wrong to have a memory of the war, let them say so. If they did not approve of wasting money on a War Memorial, let us scrap the War Memorial and save the money. But to do something totally different which we wanted to do, on pretence of doing something else that we did not do, was unworthy of *Homo Sapiens*. . . . I got some converts to my view; but I think that many still thought that I was not practical; though in fact I was very specially practical, for those who understand what is really meant by a Pragma. The most practical test of the problem of unmemorial memorials was offered by the Rector of Beaconsfield, who simply got up and said: 'We already have a ward in the Wycombe Hospital which was supposed to commemorate something. Can anybody here tell me what it commemorates?'"

The case is worth a moment's attention to the pattern it reveals. Discerning the pragma usually requires that we pull apart old links: the townspeople thought of a meeting hall as practical (because you can meet there endlessly) and of a war memorial as unpractical (because you can only look at it). But a monument does memorialize and a hall does not; therefore the bronze group of soldiers ("with an officer about to hurl his binoculars at the post office") *is* practical *for the stated purpose.*

In many modern "studies"—of social fact or of public opinion or of human psychology—the results announced profess to throw light on a subject, but the survey turns out to be of something else. An example in brief is the title Kinsey gave to his work *Sexual Behavior in the Human Male*, though it is based exclusively on facts and attitudes reported by residents of the United States in the first half of the twentieth century. More deceptive are counts of "the thing next door," as when written work is judged for clarity by calculating the proportion of short sentences; or when children are tested for "artistic ability" by measuring their visual memory; or when the degree of literacy of an earlier age is gauged by counting extant signatures on documents (as if literacy had not frequently been limited to signing one's name); or when the life histories of "genius" are tabulated from persons listed in *Who's Who*. Really! pragmatising has to begin with a sense of what's what.


Because natural science, in its searching and its power to predict, illustrates the pragmatic march of thought, and because in ordinary affairs similar procedures are associated with material success, it is easy to conclude that pragmatism is but a version of scientism and utilitarianism, the philosophy of the practical man of business. Accordingly, James and Pragmatism have been branded as typically American, a mind and a doctrine to be expected from a nation of hucksters.

The inference is false. In the first place, it overlooks the value that Pragmatism assigns to acquired truths and to theoretic and esthetic interests. Perhaps still more thoughtless is the mistaken notion of utility. Conventionally speaking, certain things and activities are called useful because they serve an ulterior purpose, and others are said to be ends in themselves because they are simply enjoyed. Food, clothing, and shelter are useful; giving a party, listening to music, sporting with Amaryllis in the shade are done—as the phrase goes—for their own sake. This distinction parallels that which separates the necessary from the optional, and it may pass, provided it does not lead to the false belief that the optional is not pursued for results, exactly like the necessary. For example, to say, "All art is quite useless," and thus to contrast art with a pair of shoes, is to forget that some human beings desire both equally because they feel the need of both. And what fulfills desire has utility.

It should also be evident that many useful objects can be enjoyed as ends—food by the gourmet, shelter by the connoisseur of architecture, clothing by the devotee of conspicuous consumption. Once again, it is language that derails judgment. To say "ends in themselves" about art objects suggests that nothing passes from the object to the beholder, that he does not get good from it as he would in hunger from a piece of bread. But one can and does hunger for art and the "end" of art is inside the beholder, just like the bread. True, one would not perish from lack of music and art, but that fact does not change the other fact of both food and art being useful to man, the one to his body (and spirit) the other to his spirit (and body).*

The phrase "for its own sake" leads astray even more slyly. Suppose the seemingly rational statement: "I go to concerts and listen to music for its own sake," and compare it with: "I go to church on Sunday for my sister's sake." It is at once obvious that music has no "sake" like the sister's. The concert goer is not doing a favor to music by listening to it; he is listening for *his* own sake, for pleasure, excitement, or even "drowsy reverie interrupted by nervous thrills." In short, the music serves his peculiar ends; it is therefore useful. Let it be said again: it does not reach its end *in itself*, it is not devoid of ulterior results. Like-

---

* For surely the effect of a good performance or a good exhibition is physically enhancing, just as their opposites may be debilitating. One can suffer rhythmical indigestion from misconducted music and physical distress from daubs or muddy prose.

wise in other activities called spiritual and not usually thought of as useful. Worship, for example, to those who deem salvation the highest good, is certainly a source of benefit to the self, whatever else it may be; it is of use. God himself is thought to expect it for his glory and it has appreciable results.

The blundering intention in the use of "sake" hopes to suggest a single-mindedness—listening to music for enjoyment, rather than for study, for therapy, for snobbery. That may be a praiseworthy difference, though human motives are usually mixed; but motive is not the point here. The point is utility, which is inescapably a feature of whatever the human mind seeks out. So "useful" requires a qualifier to show what species of utility is being talked about. To the keeper of the museum, the white glove Charles I wore at his execution has historical utility; it differs from that which it had for the king.

To point out these links and nuances is not merely to reprove bad habits of speech. The habits represent rooted opinions and the feelings attached; they come from the Platonizing (and patronizing) attitude toward the body and toward things. It ignores the mind in its wholeness and flies off to perform trapeze work among concepts and conventions. To put it the other way around, the opposite or pragmatic analysis follows from the nature of the stream of consciousness, from thought as it actually occurs. Pragmatism is the expanded description of how we natively think.

So far, the discussion of truth as pragma has led us to illustrations taken from politics, science, and common life, where the test by action and results becomes obvious once the fog of convention is lifted. But "the mind in its wholeness" also includes esthetic interests, and it is no exaggeration to say that, within his art, the artist is the pragmatist par excellence, the very model of unremitting practicality. His whole effort is to realize his aims, formal and intuitive. Art is fashioned for results and is judged by them: noble intentions, fine sentiments, studious technique do not count, only success—success, that is, in making a conception real, making it into an object perceptible to others as the artist wants it to be perceived. To that end, the work is tested at every step, modified part by part until all parts together form one working body full of meanings, intended and emergent.

Most of these meanings are not statable in words; and, again like ordinary experience, the finished object is liable to various takings, indefinitely, on each of its planes—technical, esthetic, moral, spiritual, social, political. That is why great art gives the illusion of being immortal. Because one can go on and on finding new aspects, the work seems to possess the inexhaustibility of experience itself. And for that reason the work changes with the passage of time—new findings, new takings —exactly as happens about life.

In the pursuit of his purposes, which means his effects, the artist acknowledges no restraints; he claims and exercises the right to use any material, to treat any subject, to flout any rule or precedent. The history of art is a tale of violence done to set forms, moral and esthetic imperatives, and public expectations. And the only test of innovation for both creator and beholder is pragmatic. When Turner was criticized by a colleague for pasting a piece of black paper on one spot of a painting, he said: "I'd use something else if it was blacker." Collage is justified by works. Beethoven's critics accused him of smashing the delicate shape of the symphony and imposing on the listener murky confusion and intolerable length. But "it worked"—*ça marche,* as Berlioz said—so that, after the fact, the new rules of the symphony are drawn from his unruly example.

This sequence of trial and triumph in the arts is a commonplace of biography and criticism, but it is rarely shown as the typical pragmatic sequence. Art is thought too fine to be a series of material arrangements that have to "work," though artists have lately come to speak of their work as finding solutions to problems. But when James insisted at every turn that the mind naturally follows esthetic as well as practical interests, he was pointing out that in perceiving, doing, searching, building we prefer pattern to disorder and within pattern certain qualities.* We call them balance, harmony, contrast, variety (and also repetition), unity, simplicity, and other such names, and we assume that they are fixed attributes—and so they are, as concepts. But things—sounds, words, colors—can be arranged in an infinity of different and opposite ways to produce those desired qualities, and nothing in the name "balance" or "order" can predict the new arrangements that are possible. They must be discovered, like truth, pragmatically. And as successive schools of art show, the discoveries express a point of view, a purpose: the Impressionists want to exhibit light and play with it, the Post-Impressionists want to recover solidity and play with that. They are equally right, equally real: all artists of all schools are pragmatists and, as was said before, realists.

Perhaps the best witness to the pragmatic essence of art—and of his

---

* It has not been sufficiently noticed that the revered scientific principle which requires hypotheses or assigned causes to be kept to the smallest possible number is a purely esthetic rule, congenial to man for the pragmatic reason that it gives security through clarity, as well as spurs the mind to invent ever simpler formulas. In art, the same pleasure is given cunningly, by first creating apparent disorder through a diverse collection of themes, ideas, characters, elements, and then reducing the seeming confusion to order and finality.

own art—is Henry James. He has at times been represented as the fine European-esthetic opposite of William, the all-American. The fact is that when *Pragmatism* appeared, Henry expressed in characteristic language his sense of a self-revelation:

"Why the devil I didn't write to you after reading your *Pragmatism*— how I kept from it—I can't now explain save by the very fact of the spell itself (of interest and enthralment) that the book cast upon me; I simply sank down, under it, into such depths of submission and assimilation that *any* reaction, very nearly, even that of acknowledgment, would have had the taint of dissent or escape. Then I was lost in the wonder of the extent to which all my life I have (like M. Jourdain) unconsciously pragmatised. You are immensely and universally *right*, and I have been absorbing a number more of your followings-up of the matter in the *American [Journal of Psychology?]*. . . . I feel the reading of the book, at all events, to have been really the event of my summer."

It will not do to dismiss this adherence as a token of brotherly love, or the sign of a mind subtle in everything but philosophy. Any lifelong reader of both Jameses cannot have helped noticing the degree to which Henry's test of truth and reality resembles William's without anywhere echoing it. And readers of Henry's prefaces will recall the all-importance he attached to "the point of view" in the art of the novel. For the doubting opsimath, there is fortunately an admirable work which demonstrates in close detail "the remarkable congruity between William's philosophical thought and the Jamesian idiom. . . . William James's pragmatistic thought is literally *actualized* as the literary art and idiom of his brother Henry, especially so in the later work. . . . William is the pragmatist; Henry, so to speak, is the pragmatism; that is, he possesses the very mode of thinking that William characteristically expounds."*

Henry James's conception of character and behavior is also evidence of pragmatic demands, as will appear in connection with William's moral philosophy. Here it need only be said that the concurrence of brotherly views suggests a further observation: the relation of art to life is pragmatic exactly as thought is related to truth: both art and thought work with symbols in an effort to master experience. Both know success when by conception and craft a set of concrete particulars endows experience with intelligible shape. Discursive truth can be stated in words or numbers or it can be embodied in habits and prejudices; only art finds permanence in solid matter as well as in words.

The presence of this common element strengthens the answer given

* Richard A. Hocks, *Henry James and Pragmatistic Thought* (Chapel Hill, N.C., 1974), pp. 4–5.

earlier to the question whether art is cognitive or not. Does it record truths or only play about with illusion as Freud and others have maintained? Let us apply the pragmatic test: Art tells or implies truths (to those who know how to scan it) when its shape and contents lead us back to experience more aware and more able to deal with it. Why else should art be "important"? Like thought, art does not copy reality but weaves in and out of it, now as sensation, now as idea. The best truthful thought and the best art are a fused product: we then "feel" the true, the work of art "moves" us—in contrast with those truths we repeat mechanically, or those artistic objects we admire for their skill or surface only, *pragma*, the thing done, being missing.

James remarked in his chapter on the stream that psychologists ought to speak of 'a feeling of *but*' and likewise of other prepositions. Some of his critics would confess to a feeling of "Yes, but," as to the validation of truth by pragma. Their objection is so natural it must be listened to. This is it: Art is man-made; if pragmatic truth is of the same order— comes from the same shop—then it is not the real thing, just as art is not life or nature. The real truth exists independently of man; it imposes itself on him willy-nilly; it existed before him and it lives on with or without his knowledge or assent, an entity not made at all but already there.

A passionate being like James's friend John Jay Chapman (a writer and thinker still greatly undervalued) could not tolerate the idea that he was, as it were, co-author of anything so potent as the truth. "The pragmatist," he cried, "is debarred by his pragmatism from knowing what truth is!" One can sympathize with the quick flash of Chapman's emotion. Instead of the "perfect idol," James shows truths (in the plural) to be halting, imperfect, scarred with the toolmarks of their makers—men, including John Jay Chapman. For *his* love of truth to be requited, the truth must be of nobler origin and more beautiful. How could it claim his whole-souled belief if he knew it came from himself?

There is modesty, perhaps religious humility, in this feeling, and there is some degree of introspection. Every mind remembers times when it fought a truth which it later yielded to with surprise and gratitude. Hence the impression that the truth stands outside, waiting to be recognized and finally compelling submission from all right minds. It is this vision of a stubborn wooing that James dispels. He replaced it by a no less stubborn creation of mind and he cited the derivation of the word *truth* from the archaic verb *I trow, man troweth*. James was wrong in believing that the noun came from the verb instead of the other way around, but the connection is sound. Anglo-Saxon *trow* means "fidelity," "trust"—whence both *troth* and *truth*. The image of experience being "faithful" to our verified expectation, and that expectation therefore being trustworthy, is in keeping with everything else we can observe about thought—not least the variations in truth and in experience which were the starting point of the whole inquiry.

In effect, James asks for a deeper introspection and even more humility than Chapman's, so that the self may recognize its concerns, habits, training, and temperament as conditions of the truths it maintains. In their concreteness, as these truths are held actively and passionately and for use, they are custom-tailored to the individual, even the truths handed down by teaching and tradition. This existential character of truth, which our century learned a good while after James, from Kierkegaard and others, is especially fruitful in morals and politics. Even in science the truth keeps its individuality. The same equations are taken and handled differently by different minds—which is one means by which science makes its great conceptual advances.*

Still, the familiar metaphor "discovering the truth" grips our imagination by picturing the truth as lying hidden and waiting to have the cover taken off. We are lured into saying: "Even before its discovery, it was true that the continent of Australia existed; whether we knew it or not, it was always true that light rays are bent by gravitation in passing around the sun." Such remarks confuse fact with truth. We have good reasons for projecting the *existence* of Australia backward into time, but the *truth* of its being there can only mean something said, or a map being drawn, which did not exist before it was said or drawn. Likewise with the sun's rays: their bending was an occurrence of long standing, but not a truth until Einstein. In other words, what is discovered is fact, which we then combine with earlier ideas and words—"continent," "south seas," "gravitation"—to form a new truth. So to the question "Is the truth less true before it is verified?" James answers with another: 'Surely truth can't inhabit a third realm between realities and statements or beliefs?'

Out of a similar desire to distinguish "realms" and show a flaw in pragmatism, Arthur Lovejoy, the minute historian of thought, famous for his "thirteen pragmatisms" and "eighteen romanticisms," made a point in a letter to James that James in his placatory way accepted. The point was that there is a difference between the consequences of a truth

---

* This and kindred topics are discussed in W. I. B. Beveridge, *The Art of Scientific Investigation* (London, 1955), and A. A. Moles, *La Création Scientifique* (Geneva, 1957), as well as in the essays or reminiscences of Einstein, Max Born, Werner Heisenberg, H. Poincaré, J. Hadamard, E. Chargaff, Max Planck, and others. One of the most vivid statements is James Watson's *The Double Helix* (New York, 1968).

and the consequences of believing and acting on that truth. It is indeed
a logical difference, one between the realm of discourse and the realm
of action. But the difference disappears if the truth and the belief are
held with equal strictness, free of additions and irrelevancies. For example, if Nero Wolfe suspects that a Louis Quinze chair will not bear
his weight and his suspicion is true, then the consequences of the truth
in his mind and of the truth in action are identical. This is but to say
that what is true in theory is true in practice, an old principle which
even Lovejoy could not split into half a dozen kinds of meaning.

In the debate about pragmatism, as in anyone's first natural surprise
and doubt, the main cause of resistance comes from not grasping the
fact—or not retaining it if grasped—that James's purpose is 'to overhaul
the very idea of truth.' James sees truth as a many-faceted *activity* that
includes several varieties of truth-making and truth-naming, from simple reporting ("your umbrella is in the coat closet") or imaging ("the
clock says 3:20") to the special operations and creations that lead to the
symbolism and attitudes we call scientific and moral truth. Most of
them differ radically from a mere "report on reality." They are often
devices for proceeding "as if" the ultimate reality were thus-and-so.
The "as if" is particularly evident in artistic truth, which is not make-
believe, but a means of remolding experience in order to learn about it
things not otherwise expressible. After James, one may say, the clear-
cut separation of the True, the Good, and the Beautiful and the simple
definition of each no longer satisfy. What we know about our sensibility
contradicts the three-fold division, and what we have come to discern
in art, ethics, and beliefs gives rise to more complex ideas.* Hence
James's conception of a single realm of experience, out of which the
mind pursues and fashions what it desires with the aid of many criteria—the 'jungle of concrete expediencies' that compete for our adoption.

This reinterpretation of truth and beauty as species of the good need
not keep us from using the three words in the old way, provided we
recognize that truth at large takes on diverse shapes, comes in different
layers of richness according to purpose. The common element throughout is the leading or guiding of action or potential action toward a desired goal. Truth is not 'an inert, static relation; the register of a standing
fixture. The truth of an idea is not a stagnant property in it; its verity is
an event, a process.' This way of thinking about truth may seem difficult, even though anyone would admit that "health," for example, is not
an inherent property of the body but a dynamic series of actions and

---

* The importance of esthetic feeling in the ethical desire to see poverty abolished is
one example of this complexity.

events. Likewise "I love you" is only shorthand for innumerable acts and feelings. Truth does not reside in a proposition any more than love in a proposal. In the activity of making truths our thought is not simply confirmed by what happens; we add something to experience; we re-shape reality. By virtue of this 'marriage function,' this engendering of truth upon the given, experience itself is modified; it is never the same again.

The advantage of conceiving truth as pragma is that it warns against asking for one sort of satisfaction, practical, theoretical, or esthetic, when another is offered.* Again, the pragmatist will not expect complete congruence between his truths and reality; most truths are approximate, indicative, in the literal sense of those words—"near" and "pointing to." For an idea to agree with reality, says James, 'can only mean to be guided straight up to it or into its surroundings, or to be put into such working touch with it as to handle either it or something connected with it better than if we disagreed. And often agreement will only mean the negative fact that nothing contradictory from that quarter of reality comes to interfere with the way in which our ideas guide us elsewhere.'

The demoting of truth from the image of perfection has lent color to what one may call the "charge of Americanism" against James. His appeal to experience evokes associations with the figure of the shrewd Yankee who "can't be bothered with theories" but "makes out well enough." It also recalls the unlovely streak in the character of Benjamin Franklin, the conscious operator who gloated over his little tricks in *Poor Richard* and his *Autobiography*. From there, it seems only a step to the books on how to win friends and influence people. Then, too, there is the old ambiguity about Success—the crude pioneers' make-shifts, the backyard inventors' knack, the robber barons' fraudulent schemes; and after them the organizers, all calculation and hypocrisy, who are bent on engineering every part of our lives. The success of the poet or scientist, the statesman or jurisprudent, is forgotten in the stereotype of the American way as synonymous with know-how, efficiency, results. Their aura, one feels, should not contaminate divine philosophy.**

But these traits, it turns out, were equally repellent to James and he knew very well that his psychological and philosophic analysis of truth

---

* At a recent board meeting that dealt with an important question straddling intellectual and financial matters, the chairman was heard to say: "A pragmatic compromise is our only course when no perfect solution is available." Who around the table had ever encountered a perfect solution to anything?

** Some readers of *Pragmatism* mistook, perhaps on purpose, James's use of the metaphor 'cash value' to express the fact that an idea is worthless if it cannot sooner or later be converted into the concreteness aimed at; theory being, as it were, a promissory note. He gave them no encouragement. He was the man who in his now classic phrase excoriated 'the bitch-goddess Success.' He had, from his earliest philosophizing, at the age of twenty-six, warned against 'an impatience of *results*. Inexperience of life is the cause of it, and I imagine it is generally an American characteristic. Results should not be too voluntarily aimed at or too busily thought of. They are sure to float up of their own accord from a long enough daily work at a given matter.'

Later, in a psychological essay entitled "The Gospel of Relaxation," he compared unfavorably the nervous tension, over-expressive faces, and stridency of Americans in daily life with the stolid British temper—he was describing the outward signs of "stress"—and he showed how needless and destructive it was. Like Henry, he found American voices a particularly unpleasant symptom of this hurly-burly and he subsequently made voice abatement an item in his recommendations to teachers of the young. As for practicality in the vulgar sense, James had some harsh words: 'The common foe of thought is the practical, conventionally thinking man to whom nothing has true seriousness but personal interests, and whose dry earnestness in those is only exceeded by that of the brute, which takes everything for granted and never laughs.'

In an interview given to the *New York Times* after the publication of *Pragmatism*—a remarkable piece of improvisation, by the way—James reasserted the total divergence between *practical* in that "American" sense and *pragmatic* in his: 'Instead of being a "practical" substitute for philosophy, good for engineers, doctors, sewage experts, and vigorous untaught minds in general to feed upon, pragmatism has proved so over-subtle that even academic critics have failed to catch its question, to say nothing of their misunderstanding of its answer.'

On this point of subtlety, James would shortly receive Bergson's confirmation: "people picture pragmatism *a priori* (I do not know why) as something that must necessarily be simple, something that it should be possible to sum up in a formula. I ceaselessly repeat, on the contrary, that pragmatism is one of the most subtle and *nuancées* doctrines that have ever appeared in philosophy." James became increasingly aware of 'the verbal mess: my own experience with "pragmatism" makes me

---

was not thinking of money returns, but of the "claim" made on experience by a truth, parallel to the claim made by a check or other form of credit upon solid value. This figure drawn from trade was interpreted as showing that pragmatism was business-inspired. It is interesting to compare some wordings used by Henry James (whom nobody would accuse of coarse mercantile thoughts) two years before *Pragmatism*. In *The Lesson of Balzac*, he speaks of "a really paying acquaintance with a writer." And, to repay his own debt to Balzac, "one could never have at once all the required cash in hand." And again, economy in a writer "proceeds from the consciousness of a limited capital." (Pp. 66, 70, 102.) Henry uses a few more commercial tropes, but one need not be a member of the James family to speak of "paying somebody in his own coin" or of "the competition in the free market of ideas."

shrink from the dangers that lie in the word "practical."'

The verbal mess shows again the power of concepts over the course of thought. What would have happened if James had not tried to honor Peirce's questionable priority and had called his own analysis of truth Functionalism? That name, popular in twentieth-century art talk, might have saved a lot of fruitless debate. I have at times used Perspectivism to stress purpose and point of departure in the search for truth; Functionalism would draw attention to the role truth has to play. But in truthmaking there is also action: truth is what acts or enables us to act. We rightly say "it's actually there, he actually believes it, in actuality it's very different." So Actualism might have served, even if by its very aptness it seemed to beg the question. In any case, the need to explain the Greek *pragma* by linking it with *practical* made Peirce and James's choice deplorable. It is a warning about meddling with Greek and Latin before the vernacular adopts them. Just imagine the result if *method*—now so glorious—had shown on its face the Greek connotation *trick, artifice, imposture*? Or yet again, if it were noticed that our vaunted *reality* embodies the Latin *res*, meaning nothing nobler than *thing*?

The pragmatic theory of truth contains still other elements. It makes the point that truth is known by signs and recorded in signs; it is symbolic first and last. Finally, the theory reminds us that truth is not a product of "pure thought" in the ordinary sense. The mind is impelled by desire—curiosity, doubt, "wanting to be shown." What could be more demanding, what better guaranty of truth being indeed truth? The call for proof expresses the pragmatic impulse which is a universal trait, even in times we call superstitious. All proposers of novelty, all prophets false and true, have to meet the challenge. In religion they are forced to give manifestations of their "powers"—healing or miracles. These satisfy, however crudely, the instinct for getting evidence. The sound belief that truth and the tangible must be connected presides over the most spiritual and contemplative concerns of mankind.

Plato himself, whom Chapman calls "the patron saint of those who sit in armchairs," could not wholly retreat into the geometrical life of pure concepts. His Socrates, the plain man, was ever digging into opinion and the material grounds for it. In his dialogues the deepest questions are argued with the aid of examples drawn from common life, which is why we read them still: Plato was an artist. One readily agrees with him when he says that "the unexamined life is not worth living." But we part company with him when he wants to soar above *this* life, and as we leave him we add that the unanchored vision—all dogma and no pragma—is not a boon but a menace to all. It brings blasted hopes to some and oppression by conceptual absolutes to the rest.

# The Varieties of Experience

In watching James pursuing truth we have taken it for granted that Experience as its guarantor is a plain and simple thing. "Everybody knows what is meant by experience." But do we? To think about it is to face a barrage of questions: How does experience come to us and where from? Is there anything behind it causing it to be as it is? Common sense tells us that we are in the universe, but common sense also puts experience of the universe inside us. We recall that James in his *Psychology* made it clear that our minds are directly aware of reality; they do not handle offprints of something out there, beyond reach, though objects are mainly perceived as independent of our thoughts about them. These various notions do not hang together. Common sense is a philosophy in disguise and one not quite well knit from end to end. It cannot explain, for instance, how the Empire State building, when you and I look at it, can be in your mind and also in my mind and also "where it is," besides being in the mind of anybody in San Francisco who happens to think of it.

It is to resolve such difficulties that philosophers spend sleepless nights, and James had something to show for his midnight meditations. As usual, what he said was new and therefore strange, despite its connections with past thought. But as he observed, 'philosophers are only men thinking about things in the most comprehensive possible way.' What goes by the forbidding name of metaphysics is 'nothing but an unusually obstinate effort to think clearly.' Philosophy is essentially second thoughts, and we must be ready to follow them with athletic fortitude.

James's first point of attack was Consciousness itself. The stream we are familiar with, but what kind of thing is it—is it in fact a thing? 'For twenty years past,' he wrote in 1904, 'I have mistrusted "consciousness" as an entity; for seven or eight years past I have suggested its non-existence to my students and tried to give them its pragmatic equivalent in realities of experience. It seems to me that the hour is ripe for it to be openly and universally discarded.'

This unhedging declaration takes James's revolution one step farther. In the *Psychology* he had pointed out that for things to be known no other knower is needed than the passing thought. But that might hold true only for the purposes of a naturalist psychology; now it was meant to hold without limitation. What strange world would it lead to? 'To deny plumply that "consciousness" exists seems so absurd on the face of it—for undeniably "thoughts" do exist—that I fear some readers will follow me no farther. Let me then immediately explain that I mean only to deny that the word stands for an entity, but to insist that it does stand for a function.'

That function occurs in experience, of course, but to say so does not resolve the puzzling impression we all have of things known by a knower who is oneself. 'Things not only are, but get reported, are known.' So there must be two entities in contact; philosophy has long called them subject (the knower) and object (the thing known). Our terms of praise, *objective, objectivity,* and of doubt, *subjective,* come from the common assumption that experience is made up of two parts, one of which is consciousness, the knower, and the other is what it knows. But it is also obvious that we never catch consciousness by itself; we infer its presence by subtracting the objects from the experience and supposing a container for them. Experience, James argues, 'has no such inner duplicity; the separation of it into consciousness and content comes, not by way of subtraction, but by way of addition—the addition, to a given concrete piece of it, of other sets of experiences. In one context a given piece will act as knower and in another as a thing known: in one group it figures as a thought, in another as a thing. And since it can figure in both groups simultaneously we have every right to speak of it as subjective and objective both at once.'

Interesting, if true. But why get rid of so intimate a companion as our consciousness in its familiar state of imagined separateness? Because it makes certain things hard to reconcile; it creates a "problem of knowledge"—the puzzle of how things outside the mind get inside. Not only is that gap or bifurcation in nature hard to jump, but there is a further split, engineered in the 1600s by Descartes. According to him, when we know objects outside, their only reality is their "extension," their shape. Their other qualities—color, touch, sound, taste, smell—are not "in" them at all, but in the mind.

This view of knowing disposed of the uncertain, variable impressions we get of these "secondary qualities"—they must be our doing; whereas extension is independent of us, reliable and permanent: it is "matter," homogeneous, measurable, and hence the substratum of the universe that science can study with confidence. To be sure, Berkeley in the century after Descartes showed that this "matter" was pure supposition since it is by definition hidden from the senses; it serves only as an assumed support for the real and direct sensations of color, taste, and so on. By what logic should these be demoted in favor of a verbal entity? But Berkeley was generally misunderstood to mean that physical objects did not exist, and the role he ascribed to God as sustainer of things made him suspect to the men of science; so it was not until James that experience was put forth as the sole shape and presence of whatever there is to talk about.

But what is it made of, if not our old matter plus consciousness? What is this stuff whose character is neither one nor the other but neutral or general? 'There is no general stuff of which experience at large is made. There are as many stuffs as there are "natures" in the things experienced. If you ask what any bit of pure experience is made of, the answer is always the same: "It is made of *that*, of just what appears—of space, of intensity, of flatness, brownness, heaviness, or what not." Experience is only a collective name for all these sensible natures, and save for time and space (and, if you like, for "being"), there appears no universal element of which all things are made.'

This unaccustomed view of what happens is what James calls "radical empiricism." An empiricist (as against a rationalist) is one whose philosophy explains the mystery of being by giving primacy to the part, the element, the individual, rather than the universal or the whole; 'it is a philosophy of plural facts,' which are not referred to Substance (matter) or to an Absolute Mind of which they are the emanation. To be "radical," this empiricism 'must neither admit into its constructions any element that is not directly experienced, nor exclude from them any element that is directly experienced.' What is more, 'the relations that connect experiences must themselves be experienced relations and any kind of relation experienced must be accounted as real as anything else.'

One clear merit of this hospitable outlook, this 'taking everything that comes without disfavor,' is that it gets rid of the hide-and-seek of Appearance and Reality and the quarrels among their various classifiers. It puts ideas, feelings, sensations, perceptions, concepts, art, science, faith, conscious, unconscious, objects, and so-called illusions on a footing of equality as regards being real. There is of course the task of getting each "real" accurately described and its functions and relations charted. But 'a real place must be found for every kind of thing experienced.' Radical empiricism is, to begin with, a mind stretcher.

That merit is to some a demerit, because this openness confronts philosophy and the individual with a great deal more work than other schemes. Under it, all these bits of experience have to be examined and re-examined to ascertain how they hang together and what they may do or mean; there is no grand rule for grouping, subordinating, or throwing out. How can such an exceedingly loose-jointed and windswept abode constitute a universe? It does to the extent that experience offers us relations (including functions) already *there*. The philosophers' universes have 'always turned on grammatical particles. With, near, next, like, from, towards, against, because, for, through, my—these words designate types of conjunctive relation arranged in a roughly ascending order of intimacy and inclusiveness. We can imagine a universe of withness but no nextness; or one of nextness but no likeness, or of likeness but no activity, or of activity with no purpose, or of purpose with no ego. These would be universes each with its own grade of unity.'

Whatever anybody may mean by experience, it is clear that it comes well provided with all these conjunctions, or as they are often called, categories of thought. As we saw before, 'the organization of the Self as a system of memories, purposes, strivings, fulfilments or disappointments, is incidental to the most intimate of all relations, those of activity, change, tendency, resistance and the causal order generally.' So there is some order and system in the view of radical empiricism, even though it is not the perfect order and system that rationalists desire; like truth, it is not unity ready made but, when worked at, progressively achieved. The incompleteness of both universe and truth is in fact one and the same incompleteness, which a certain type of mind finds intolerably chaotic.

But there it is: 'No one single type of connection runs through all the experiences that compose it. If we take space relations, they fail to connect minds into a regular system. Causes and purposes obtain only among special series of facts. The self relation seems extremely limited and does not link two different minds together.' Anybody who wants to overcome these discouraging realities—discouraging to the beholder bent on finding the cosmos a grand, perfected system—must seek an Absolute that takes care of all the gaps and imperfections.

As we noted in passing, one such absolute is matter; it is assumed to be the only real thing in things and thus it connects them all perfectly. By definition it excludes from the real: mind, purpose, faith, and all moral and spiritual perceptions—art, for instance, is harmless illusion, as the materialist Freud believed. Materialism offers the simplest absolute and a convenient philosophy for science, which loses its footing when it is not possible to measure by reducing the mixed or variable to the homogeneous.

The opposite absolute is naturally Mind. Thinkers who choose Mind as the unifying substance start from the conviction that their own mind is not an illusion; it knows things and is very different from a piece of matter, which by definition knows nothing, least of all itself. So they posit an all-powerful thinker who by knowing all things makes them be and be real. Such a mind has traditionally been called God, but in James's time the strength of materialistic science had damaged all ideas that were anthropomorphic: God seemed too much like the enlarged figure of Man. Hence the substitution, by the philosophers called Idealists, of an entity called the Absolute Idea, or simply the Absolute.

The Absolute has no man-like features and it does not reside outside the universe like the creator-deity; it is the sum total of mind, which includes our minds as constituent parts. It is thus the perfect unifier for the devotees of unity. For them, 'the world is no collection, but one great all-inclusive fact' which, being mind, 'makes the partial facts by thinking them, just as we make objects in a dream by dreaming them, or personages in a story by imagining them.'

The ultimate unity thus assumed takes care of the discontinuities mentioned earlier—the gap between human minds and the disconnected clusters among things. The Absolute also explains the presence of evil: it is a form of good—good elsewhere, of which our narrow vision cannot see the point. Idealism thereby makes things tidy. The helter-skelter of history and human lives disappears as an illusion due to our inability to see the whole in its full purpose.

All these explanations show the universe as rational through and through, which in turn validates moral conduct, as well as faith in the singleness and eternity of truth and the natural yearning for the transcendent. It also encourages one of the doctrines of art, that which calls it akin to the mystical experience in giving glimpses of the ideal world. Emerson and Whitman, among others, reveled in their intimations of this totality, this Oversoul, which could be made to say:

> If the red slayer think he slays,
> Or if the slain think he is slain,
> They know not well the subtle ways
> I keep, and pass, and turn again.*

* Emerson's "Brahma," in the first number of The Atlantic Monthly (1857). The principle in the quatrain owes much to the reading of Hindu scriptures which, newly translated in the early nineteenth century, influenced many western thinkers and artists. It must have been congenial to educated Americans if the new magazine offered them a cryptic poem about it.

We learn what the "subtle ways" are from a later line: "When me they fly, I am the wings"; its clear sense is that there is no real difference between the mugger and the mugged of the first two lines. To James, this was false in fact and logic. The Absolute became his chief philosophical enemy, for Idealism was the dominant school in England and America. His close friend and respected colleague at Harvard, Josiah Royce, was a brilliant expounder of the doctrine; James's admiring and admired opponent, the subtle dialectician F. H. Bradley, led the Idealists at Oxford. The Absolute filled not only the cracks in the cosmos, but also the journals and the universities.

The factual objection to it is that if an abstract All-Knower is the sole reality, the cosmos loses its palpable massiveness. 'All the thickness, concreteness, and individuality of experience exists in the immediate and relatively unnamed stages of it.' Concepts about experience are real, too; they have consequences, but 'thought deals solely with surfaces. It can name the thickness or reality, but it cannot fathom it.' The only way to know it is to experience or imagine it.

The further flaw, in logic, says James, is this: Idealism rightly maintains that things exist as given to our minds in experience; mind is real and takes in the real. But then we are asked to believe in contradictory realities: 'As the absolute takes me, I appear *with* everything else in its field of perfect knowledge. As I take myself, I appear *without* most other things in my field of relative ignorance. And practical differences result from its knowledge and my ignorance. Ignorance breeds mistake, curiosity, misfortune, pain, for me. I suffer these consequences. The absolute knows of those things, of course, for it knows me and my suffering, but it doesn't itself suffer. It can't be ignorant, for simultaneous with its knowledge of each question goes its knowledge of each answer. It can't be patient, for it has to wait for nothing, having everything at once in its possession. It can't be surprised; it can't be guilty. Things true of the world in its finite aspects, then, are not true of it in its infinite capacity. "Let us imitate the All" said the prospectus of that admirable Chicago quarterly, *The Monist*. As if we could, either in thought or conduct! We are invincibly parts, let us talk as we will.'*

One may pause here to note the relevance of this critique to the cults of oriental and pseudo-oriental thought that in our day are enjoying a fresh vogue. The All is so vast that it cannot bestow the hoped-for warmth of kinship on imperfect mortals unless the latter give up being what they are; they cannot individually become the All, so they must

---

* Besides, it is hard to see how the perfect whole of absolute mind can be made up of imperfect parts—our minds. There is a slippage here from "complete" (which can be the sum of incompletes) to "perfect," which needs its own quality throughout.

individually lose or forget their actual existence, call their normal self an illusion, play what I have called the hide-and-seek of Appearance and Reality. Self-forgetting may be a pleasure, but the philosophic unity is achieved by whisking away half the data. The one comfort that an All-Knower provides is a world with 'something clean and intellectual in the way of inner structure. As compared with it, pluralistic empiricism offers but a sorry appearance. It is a turbid, muddled, gothic sort of an affair, without a sweeping outline and with little pictorial nobility.'

To abide by fact and logic, then, James turns his back on the absolutes of Matter and Idea and takes his stand in pure experience. In this phrase "pure" does not mean purified or distilled; it means sheer experience, raw experience. Nothing else is so unmistakably given—and given to everyone. Actually, 'only new-born babes or men in semi-coma from sleep, drugs, illnesses, or blows may be assumed to have an experience pure in the literal sense of a *that* which is not yet any definite *what,* tho' ready to be all sorts of *whats.* Pure experience in this state is but another name for sensation. But the flux of it no sooner comes than it tends to fill itself with emphases, and these salient parts become identified and fixed and abstracted.'

This activity explains how experience, which is not any single stuff but is whatever comes, serves the familiar functions called subject and object, consciousness and "world outside." James offers an analogy with ordinary paint: 'In a pot in a paint shop, it serves in its entirety as so much salable matter. Spread on a canvas, with other paints around it, it represents on the contrary a feature in a picture and performs a spiritual function. Just so, I maintain, does a given undivided portion of experience, taken in one context of associates, play the part of a knower, of a state of mind, of consciousness; while in a different context the same undivided bit of experience plays the part of a thing known. In one group it figures as a thought, in another group as a thing.'

As he did with the copy theory of truth, James here preserves the outline of the dualism that we express in the words of common sense but, by specifying its contents, 'instead of being mysterious and elusive it becomes verifiable and concrete.' Knowing is then 'an affair of relations, it falls outside, not inside the single bit of experience.' By this account we are able to solve the riddle of reality "out there" as well as in the mind. The old theory that things shoot off a representation of themselves into each mind did not square with the many different and distorted pictures of those things and it violated the sense of life, the conviction of immediate seeing and believing.

If the reader is skeptical, let him 'begin with a perceptual experience of a physical object, his actual field of vision, the room he sits in, with the book he is reading as its centre; and let him for the present treat this complex object in the commonsense way as being "really" what it seems to be, namely, a collection of physical things cut out from an environing world of other physical things with which these physical things have actual or potential relations. Now at the same time it is just those self-same things which his mind, as we say, perceives. The puzzle is at bottom just the puzzle of how one identical point can be on two lines. It can, if it be situated at their intersection; and similarly, if the "pure experience" of the room were a place of intersection of two processes, which connected it with different groups of associates respectively, it could be counted twice over as belonging to either group, and spoken of loosely as existing in two places, although it would remain a single thing. What are the two processes? One of them is the reader's personal biography, the other is the history of the house of which the room is part.'

So we are not spectators watching the film Reality as it unrolls; we are participants of events, confluences, conjunctions that divide themselves into ideas tinged with feelings, on the one hand, and objects endowed with qualities on the other, depending upon the connections of each. These we discover pragmatically. We find, for example, a kind of fire that burns and we call it "real"; and again, a fire that does not burn, which we call the idea of fire. For the infant there is no distinction; for the adult both are in fact equally real, though practical interests have given us through language, a bias in favor of objects.*

It may at first seem odd that objects and ideas should be of one species, but it is less surprising if both are "extracts" from a single continuum. "Nature" and the "the mind" thereby possess—in Whitehead's phrase—"mutual immanence." And in its wayward fashion language has recorded this other characteristic too: 'Experiences of painful objects, for example are painful experiences; perceptions of loveliness, of ugliness, tend to pass muster as lovely or ugly perceptions. Sometimes the adjective wanders as if uncertain where to fix itself. Shall we speak of seductive visions or of visions of seductive things? Of wicked desires or of desires for wickedness? Of good impulses, or of impulses toward the good?' Such relations of feeling to object seem 'not quite inner nor quite outer, as if a diremption had begun but had not made itself complete.'

The seamless web of experience is even more apparent if we look at

---

* It is plausible to suppose that the memory of our earliest years vanishes because the later distinctions between these two series of experiences shut out the original feeling of the single flux. And its contents, of course, lacked words by which to remember how it felt.

our hand resting flat on top of the table. Is there any way to distinguish the physical hand "out there," an object like the teapot, from the "inner" feelings which make it "our hand"—its warmth and pressure on the cool surface? Whichever detail we single out by attention is of the same texture as every other; no line separates thought and object as if we were looking through bifocals. 'Sometimes I treat my body purely as part of outer nature. Sometimes I think of it as "mine." If I sort it with the "me," then certain local changes in it pass for mental happenings. Its sensorial adjustments are my "attention," its kinesthetic alterations are my "efforts," its visceral perturbations are my "emotions." ' About the body, in short, we literally do a "double take" that shows the experiential identity of subject and object.

Nor is this ambiguity or neutrality of experience limited to our sentient parts. In the larger scene objects do not act in a single-track way either. 'Take a mass of carrion, for example, and the "disgustingness" which for us is part of the experience. The sun caresses it and the zephyr woos it as if it were a bed of roses. So the disgustingness fails to operate within the realm of suns and breezes. But the carrion turns our stomach by what seems a direct operation—it does function physically in that limited sphere of physics. We can treat it as physical or non-physical according as we take it in the narrower or in the wider context, and conversely, of course, we must treat it as non-mental or as mental.'*

Another feature of Jamesian empiricism is its ability to answer the question how two minds can know one thing. If an experience is assumed to be "pure"—raw—until it gets added to, linked with other experiences that make it part of your consciousness or mine, there is no reason why it cannot belong to two or more minds. For raw experience, having no context, is itself not conscious at all; 'it is "mine" only as it is felt as mine, and "yours" only as it is felt as yours. It is felt as neither by itself, but only when "owned" by our two several remembering experiences, just as one undivided estate is owned by several heirs.'

It is on this point that James quotes Kierkegaard's observation on thought: "We live forward but we understand backward"; that is, the looking back upon what *has* happened is the experience we call being conscious, aware not of *now* but of *then*; for the present moment is—well, try and grasp it: the stream does not permit.

But what is experience as a whole? James has already told us: it is no one thing but all things—"natures"—as they come. If an abstraction is wanted, 'it is a process in time whereby innumerable particular terms

---

* The details of this example recall so vividly those of Baudelaire's "*Une charogne*" that it is quite likely James remembered the poem, consciously or unconsciously. He was an early and a great admirer of *Les fleurs du mal.*

lapse and are superseded by others. In such a world transitions and arrivals (or terminations) are the only events that happen, though they happen by so many sorts of path.' The notable fact, which causes dismay to some temperaments, is that there is nothing behind experience to pull it together or make it mean some one thing. It is not irrational, but nonrational.* 'How the experiences ever get themselves made or why their relations are just such as appear, we cannot begin to understand.' And 'though one part of our experience may lean upon another part to make it what it is [such as knowing, making concepts, making objects], experience as a whole is self-containing and leans on nothing.'

Here it is appropriate to refer to the last chapter of the *Psychology*, "Necessary Truths and the Effects of Experience," a topic which was postponed for the sake of connecting it with this radical empiricism. James begins there by pointing out the ambiguity of the word *experience* in ordinary speech and in the writings of most empiricist philosophers. Both take it to mean "that which comes through the senses." For naturalist and evolutionist thinkers such experience is the sole agency that supplies and shapes whatever the mind knows. But as early as 1881, in an essay on reflex action, James had shown that the mind has other kinds of experiences—say, the ringing in the ears from taking quinine: no bell is there for the senses to report on. Experience as a whole is therefore broader than the tidings brought in by sensation.

Besides such feelings, there are also ideas that are 'born in the house': for example, those of resemblance and difference or the identities of mathematics. Lastly, experience includes—and this is all-important—those "emphases" James so often alludes to—interest, purpose, conception, attention. These seem to work upon what the senses bring as well as upon the inner feelings and ideas. In fact, all forms of thought called higher or rational consist of breaking up the mass of sense impressions in accordance with those wants: 'we break them into histories and we break them into arts and we break them into sciences, and then we feel at home. We discover among its parts relations that were never given to sense at all—mathematical relations, logarithmic functions, etc., and out of an infinite number we call certain ones essential and ignore the rest.'

It is these discoveries and inventions that lead rationalists to invest their worshipful trust in ideas and to despise the world of sense. They see all that is interesting and valuable in life as the result of inner expe-

---

* Irrationalism has such a terrible sound that in some quarters it is still used as a bugbear to frighten the innocent. "Irrationalists" seem like candidates for the strait jacket with whom it is impossible to reason. "Nonrational" is the proper description of a cosmos that is seen and felt as progressively made rational, instead of previously organized to suit the expectations of our reason.

rience and conceptual effort. The rest is common stuff, most of which is ignored, any of which could be replaced by more of the same. Hence the plausibility of a Great Mind, whose perfect workings our smaller minds haltingly recapitulate as we discover what has been flawlessly arranged.

James's acknowledgment of an inner activity is no departure from his naturalist description of mind, but on the contrary an extension of it so as to cover what obviously occurs; after which, radical empiricism with its redefinition of consciousness as a function is confirmed: experience is protean: one part of it can act on another—know it, own it, share it, abstract from it, link it to make now a fact, now an idea. In these ways is the universe fashioned, a universe that changes independently of our thought and also changes in accordance with it, that exists outside us and inside too. We can follow all its doings if we posit experience raw and all-embracing in the Jamesian manner.

This interpretation of the world we know, the life we live, may not be easy to keep in clear view and make into a habit of thought. There is perhaps no need to. Common sense serves well enough for most purposes. But the implications of James's empiricism are important and not difficult to make one's own. I have mentioned the reassembling of "nature," which should be of concern to the scientists at least, particularly those who see around the narrow limits of materialism and cannot accept the All-Knower Absolute. Already in James's time, "matter" was losing its primary qualities as it had earlier lost the secondary ones: electrons and charges, fields and waves are neither hard nor soft, neither solid nor liquid. So the world of science comes down to interactions, "events" in the sense defined above.

More generally, radical empiricism confers equality of status on all the intellectual and spiritual activities of man. It shows up the superstition that science alone is in touch with the real and can say anything useful about it. It disposes of the thought-cliché that "the sciences of nature have progressed but the sciences of man are in their infancy." It settles the question of art—is it illusion or a path to reality? Does beauty, emotion, meaning, sublimity reside in the object or in the beholder? The empiricist critic or connoisseur understands that qualities are relational yet genuine. As for the artist, if he sees his work as done within and upon experience—the endlessly malleable medium—he is freed from the tyranny of previous "rules" and of contemporary dogmas; he can create the taste by which he is to be judged and live to see nature imitating *his* art. The moralist also, or the mystic, or the simple believer is entitled to treat his experience as a reality when he comes upon it, instead of being bound to discount it at once as illusory.

Indeed, not only the artist and the seer, but everybody else is from the outset "unbound," perhaps uncomfortably so. For the world of experiences 'as they are immediately given presents itself as a quasi chaos. There is vastly more discontinuity in the sum total of experience than we commonly suppose. The distant parts of the physical world are at all times absent from us and form conceptual objects merely. The objective nucleus of every man's experience, his own body, is, it is true, a continuous percept and so is the material environment of that body, changing by gradual transition when the body moves.' Parts of this physical world are held in common, others not; and around the centers of shared "reality" 'floats the vast cloud of experiences that find not even an eventual ending for themselves in the perceptual world—the mere daydreams and joys and sufferings and wishes of the individual mind. These exist *with* one another, indeed, and with the objective nuclei, but out of them it is probable that to all eternity no interrelated system of any kind will ever be made.'

Experience, then, is a vast inflowing sea charted only in spots. The single word by which we call it for convenience is but a collective name for a miscellany, a pluralism. Experience comes in countless varieties; 'Nature is but another name for excess,' and in it novelty continually appears. When it does, it is tagged on the chart, incorporated in one or another of the unities already won. For 'as fast as verifications come, trains of experience once separate run into one another; the unity of the world is on the whole undergoing increase. The universe grows in quantity by new experiences that graft themselves upon the older mass.'

Even so, viewed as a whole, the world of being is no 'block universe'; it remains 'a federal republic.' And rightly taken, this conclusion should afford *some* comfort. The nature of things evidently has room for the efforts that enhance life through greater order; it encourages the play of mind by which all unities are forged; it gives no support to those who claim exclusive truth and try to enforce it as a finality; it enables us to withstand more calmly the drama of existence, in which the characters all have some raison d'être and seem to themselves entitled to live. In short, the empiricist universe keeps democratically open and is genuine through and through: 'Everything real must be experienceable somewhere, and every kind of thing experienced must somewhere be real.'

James having surveyed in detail the difficulties, the critiques, and the ramifications of his philosophy of pure experience in the dazzling pages of his *Essays in Radical Empiricism* (1904-1905), he next took up its corollaries, which may be summed up as the pluralistic universe. He chose to discuss them under that name in the Hibbert lectures that he was invited to give in 1908 at Oxford, the very stronghold of philosophical Idealism and its "block universe." As it is not my purpose to follow the technical arguments supporting James's thought, but only to uncover its bearing for present uses, so the historic siege of the Absolute at Oxford matters here only for its applicable results. James predicted that the battle over the One and the Many would be the great issue of the century; and in one sense pluralism and its adjective have indeed become commonplace, largely under the pressure of democracy and a world population increasingly mixed. Multiplied contacts and conflicts are a fact that takes getting used to as an idea. Before it could be appealed to as a principle, the idea needed a name.

But the link between philosophic pluralism and the familiar kind—social, political, cultural, and religious—is not merely verbal; it is not a metaphor or even a parallel; it is a single conception dealing with one phenomenon and its consequences. The diversities and incoherences that reveal to us the character of experience are plain to anybody who ponders his inner life. Unity or partial order is made there by effort; to organize what happens is the unending task. The only unity that is not worked for is that which we feel as the continuity of oneself. Hence the desire to reinforce this oneness (itself shaky at times) and hence the philosophic vision of the Absolute, a One beyond the self strong enough to overcome all conceivable disunion. It is a piece of Transcendental Egotism.

On earth, where action is inescapable, the practical need of unity seems equally great. Other people's wants, deeds, purposes, prejudices, hostilities, conquering creeds, and imbecile plans produce a chaos matching that of native experience—whence the creation of the traditional onenesses—monarchy, monogamy, the law—and the perpetual urge toward monopoly: enforcing orthodoxy, asserting one truth, finding one cause at work in history, one element basic to all things.

Even so, western civilization has by now become officially pluralist. Constitutions and laws allow a wide diversity of sects, opinions, associations, forms of art, choice of careers, medical theories, educational methods and contents. Latterly they even forbid uniformities of sex, age, or race. This state of affairs in society took a long time in the making. For millennia the ideal of unity prevailed, as it still does in two-thirds of the world. Pluralism could not succeed before the invention of social arrangements that would allow needs and desires to be satisfied in more than one way; and it had to wait for a re-education of the feelings that would enable the individual to accept some, at least, of his neighbor's differences in politics, religion, pigmentation, and taste.

This re-education is obviously more difficult or less, depending on the individual's philosophic outlook and moral training. Everybody is by nature an absolutist and imperialist: my view is right and shall be yours. Perspectivism must be taught in the teeth of this simple animal faith, and that teaching is still rudimentary. It does not yet include the art of finding the right words for stating rival truths in mutually accept-able ways. Such an art would bring about not simply a higher degree of tolerance but a new kind. At present, toleration means indifference be-tween the parties, or a division of territory, actual or intellectual, among absolutists none of whom is strong enough to impose his rule any far-ther. That is our present pluralism. Despite the billions of novels that have been read for "psychological insight," it still comes easiest to im-agine those who differ from us as lost in a fog of illusion, perhaps dan-gerously so for us. We create monsters of error and indeed enjoy doing it. A pragmatic search for opposite truths made acceptable by being more exactly delimited would create both a new kind of peace and a new kind of pleasure.

It is clear from James's letters and his friendships that this sort of pleasure was native to him. The very large circle of those with whom he corresponded about ideas was made up of vehement opponents as well as of partial followers—no intellectual agreement is ever com-plete.* The secret of his magnanimity was his power of concentration on the particular. Individuality, uniqueness were traits he discerned in-stantly where others only saw types or attitudes. 'The obstinate insisting that tweedledum is *not* tweedledee is the bone and marrow of life' (at least for James). This conviction, in turn, brought forth from others the peculiar genius hidden beneath the social oddities. 'The memory of Da-

---

* As in youth he argued with Chauncey Wright and Wendell Holmes, so to the end he relished every degree of "otherness." James Ward, G. Stanley Hall, Shadworth Hodgson, Croom Robertson, Carl Stumpf, George Santayana, F. H. Bradley, George Howison, James Sully, John Dewey, F. C. S. Schiller, Hugo Münsterberg, Mary W. Calkins, Sarah Whitman, Thomas Davidson, Benjamin Paul Blood, John Jay Chapman, Josiah Royce, F. W. H. Myers, Henry Sidgwick, Theodore Flournoy, J. M. Baldwin, Wincenty Lutoslawski, C. S. Peirce, Dickinson Miller, H. R. Marshall, L. T. Hobhouse, Charles Ritter, Henri Bergson, Rudyard Kipling, H. G. Wells, J. R. L. Delboeuf, E. L. Godkin, G. H. Palmer, Borden P. Bowne, James Leuba, Charles Eliot Norton, C. A. Strong, Frederick Pollock, T. S. Perry, A. O. Lovejoy, Emile Boutroux, Giovanni Papini—these names, once equal in intellectual importance, are representative of the company James kept, through all their deep differences with him and with one another. He also willingly endured the vagaries of the many lame dogs who repeatedly came to him for help.

vidson,' said James of one eccentric friend, 'will always strengthen my faith in personal freedom and its spontaneities, and make me less unqualifiedly respectful than ever of "civilization," with its herding and branding, licensing and degree-giving, authorizing and appointing, and in general regulating and administering by system the lives of human beings. Surely the individual, the person in the singular number is the more fundamental phenomenon.'

This remark shows how existentially James took his pluralist empirical philosophy. With him the given always comes first, the person or fact whose reality is complete and "thick" in comparison with concepts. But as by concepts and empirical search unities do get made, pluralism itself is not absolute. James is even willing to grant the Idealist his belief in the Absolute if he cannot live without it; for evidently some natures feel that even an abstract resolution of the apparent chaos will shield them from despair. Others, weary of the struggle to sort out and unify experience piecemeal, find in the Absolute a chance to take what James called a 'moral holiday.'

In society, to be sure, an unchecked pluralism can be disastrous. When everybody has to be listened to, or has a veto or usurps one through solitary or group obstruction, the quasi chaos returns. Time passes, angers mount, nothing gets done, and with each bout of paralysis the necessary faith in private and public institutions is breached. That is how, by a progressive failure of nerve, civilizations come to an end. Once again, the refusal to limit and qualify truths, because doing so would tarnish "principle," incurs its own punishment.

Self-defeat by stubborn abstraction occurs also in the opposite absolute of totalitarianism, which presupposes an All-Knower in charge who is also a flawless executive of what he knows. The results in our time have shown the lethal futility of the program. No comparisons with the past or promises about the future can counter the simple pragmatic test: you pretended to establish and maintain a society—indeed an improved society; on the facts, what you have is a badly kept prison.

In this light, it is not hard to state the merit of a so-called free economy—so-called, because it is in many ways not free. It is liable to endless abuses; those loudest in praise of it often subvert it for their private ends; the free entrepreneur works to capture the whole market. But the prime virtue of this non-system is that it provides for An Other—and more than one. In theory and also largely in practice, there is another shop, another outlet, another school, another church, another party, another publishing house, another place to live, another career, and another possibility to create more of each, as unlike as may be. And where any of these plural efforts is suppressed, it can appeal against the denial of otherness.

The right balance between diversity and unifying authority cannot be struck by rule. Since the success of pluralism depends on minds trained first to tolerate and then to live and work with the dissenters, heretics, and other menaces next door (as we do in accepting an electoral defeat instead of taking to arms), it follows that until pluralism becomes a sentiment and a habit among a whole people, the government cannot be free and democratic. On pain of anarchy—the return to quasi chaos—it must remain more or less autocratic, dictatorial.* Therefore it is not assured that states all over the world shall ever adopt what would be a curious paradox: a uniform degree of pluralism. Clearly, if we ever have "one world" it will be only after agreeing to be many—though not too many.

The rationalist-absolutist, then, may be for or against democracy, but he pines for a clearer-cut system. It does not follow that the other bent, toward Jamesian empiricism, indicates the impatient mind of the rebel. Rather, it could be best described as the *mind possessing a sense of history*, or at least a taste for it. That affinity (as I said earlier) is without doubt the reason of my early attachment to James: he is the historian among philosophers. In everything he wrote—letters, books, lectures, jottings—his habit is to introduce his theme by sketching what has led to its present state, in his mind or in the world. In developing his ideas, he cites cases, illustrates with historical events and persons, reports recent views and public facts; and he often finds in a philosophic position of the past a prop for his new one.

In the writings about James this practice has not received much attention, for it is unusual among philosophers. They tend to think as Coleridge did after reading the historians: "I do not *like* history. Metaphysics and poetry and 'facts of mind' . . . are my darling studies." Such a temperament has no use for "facts of time," whereas the radical empiricist logically regards history as the crystallized remains of experience. James's being alive to its double reality, then and now, shows once again that the common image of the pragmatist as narrowly subjective and looking only to future benefits is a travesty: 'Pent in, as the pragmatist more than anyone else sees himself to be, between the whole body of funded truths squeezed from the past and the coercions of the world of sense about him, who so well as he feels the immense pressure of objective control under which our minds perform their operations?'

---

* Not "authoritarian," as some like to say, for all governments are that; government *is* authority to rule.

Characteristically, in the chapter dealing with "Hegel and His Method," which riddles that method for its 'intolerable ambiguity, verbosity, and the unscrupulousness of the master's way of deducing things,' James praises Hegel's genius for history, for the feel of human events. 'Great injustice is done to Hegel by treating him as primarily a reasoner. He is in reality a naïvely observant man, only beset with a perverse preference for the use of technical and logical jargon. He plants himself in the empirical flux of things and gets the impression of what happens.'*

That same intuition of "what happens" James himself displays to the full in a pair of essays entitled "The Energies of Men" and "Great Men and Their Environment."** The first deals with humankind's moral and mental resources, some brought to light only by crises, others used more steadily by leaders and geniuses. The second describes the interplay between men and circumstances that permits or prevents changes on the world stage. The temper and substance of both essays are those of the historian. Indeed, the second amounts to a radical-empiricist theory of history. The spectacle of the past is inevitably a reflection of the quasi chaos of experience itself. In truth, we can know the past only because experience has a way of linking its parts from next to next across time and space till deeds and thoughts reach living knowers. 'That past time itself was, is guaranteed by its coherence with everything that's present.' The other features of experience are: novelty, accident, reversal, perpetual risk. Man does put some order in the given disorder, but what emerges is only the partial victory of some partial unity. In another context, purely philosophical, James concludes: 'Confusion may be a category of the Real itself, and "ever not quite" a permanent result of our attempts at thinking it out straighter.'

What James says and I subscribe to is of course the opposite of what is called a "philosophy of history." That name is reserved for the schemes, the systems, the "laws of history" such as are found in the works of Toynbee or Spengler, Buckle or Karl Marx. Hegel, too, had a philosophy of history, which Marx took and reconditioned, but his narrative imagination quite eclipses the system, the scaffolding he built around the facts. The reason he put up the structure, the reason Marx

---

* Naïf and naïvely in James's usage do not connote simple-mindedness, but lack of preconceptions or prejudices that would distort observation. Nowadays we might use "natural" and "natively" for the same purpose.

** Originally and significantly, the essay was called "Great Men, Great Thoughts, etc." "Men" in the title means "human beings," in keeping with etymology. James devotes a long passage to the superiority of women in sustaining moral intensity, and he describes with his usual vividness the full significance for psychology and society of the millions of women whose exertions in the world maintain a family under adverse conditions.

borrowed it, the reason all philosophers of history work at such a thing is the same reason that makes the Idealists want an Absolute: to house and hide the chaos.*

The philosophers of history want the confusion to have meaning, and only one. Every chance event and every active being must conspire and converge toward a single end as in the plot of a well-made play. The meaning, said Hegel, is the progress of freedom, and so did Croce. For Marx it was the evolution of class struggles toward the classless, stateless, happy society. Then history would stop, necessarily, since history to him *meant* class struggle and nothing else.

Such is the spell cast by the love of unity. As James remarked, it is a passion which is insatiate. Even truer historians than those I have cited fell victim to it. Henry Adams, dismayed by diversity in his own time, found unity in the thirteenth century, which was in fact a period of ferocious contentions. Other historians, in their search for unity, have been obsessed with the "single cause." They have attributed vast changes, such as the fall of the Roman Empire, to some one namable condition: Christianity, the falling birthrate, the advent of the malaria-bearing mosquito. Others have found the clue to all of history in climate or geography or racial "blood." Most lately, the devotees of depth psychology have invoked group or individual neurosis or fixation as determinants of lives and thus of events. To prove these causes, clues, meanings, or laws, the historian's facts have to be stuffed into prepared cubbyholes. They do not always fit, but system compels: for Toynbee's purpose, the Thirty Years' War had to be a small local war.

The historian who likes history for what it is—once living men's experiences—and not as raw material for a conclusion, takes the empiricist path. He deals with stubborn facts as every mind deals with the flux of experience—attending, comparing, making distinctions, finding likenesses, and perhaps arriving at modest unities, rather than starting and ending with one large one. That different historians give divergent accounts of the "same" past also corresponds with the experience of life—it is taken differently. Only an All-Knower could see it whole and "right," and access to his mind is not easy. Fortunately, in actual knowers the several perspectives affect meanings more than brute facts, so

---

* Marx thought he had upended Hegel and put his feet on the ground by substituting for the Hegelian "Idea" solid earthly things. But all Marx substituted was conceptual *talk* of such things—the "class struggle," the "means of production." These concepts are so empty of details and remote from the conditions of various nations that they have occasioned all the bloody debates of the Marxist sect and the failure of its predictions. The two abstractions above should have "caused" the Communist revolution to take place in Germany, not in Russia and Third World countries, all unindustrialized and lacking the right class to struggle against. In that vacuum of Marxist elements a mere Hegel-like idea has taken root.

that after reading several histories of the same events the scene be-comes clear, the truth grows by repeated takings. At that point it is most unlikely that the childish, colorless idea of a single cause will convince. The business and pleasure of history is to recapture an intuition of by-gone events by imaging their (plural) conditions.

Though the urge toward system-making is deep, one must ask what per-mits learned and intelligent men to indulge the desire so recklessly. Why is it not held in check by the empiricist's difficulties? The answer takes us back to the role and the prestige of concepts. 'The intellectual life of man consists almost wholly in his substitution of a conceptual order for the perceptual order in which his experience usually comes. Every book verbalizes some new concept, which becomes important in proportion to the use that can be made of it. Different universes of thought thus arise.' The highly trained mind is accordingly attracted to the framing of ever-more-inclusive concepts. This point was made earli-er and illustrated by the achievements of science, and scientific inten-tion undoubtedly inspires the would-be systematizer in any field.

By tradition, too, as was also noted, rationalist writers have always believed that 'conceptual knowledge was not only the more noble knowledge, but it originated independently of all perceptual particu-lars. Conceptual knowledge must thus be called a self-sufficing revela-tion admitting us to a world of universals rather than that of perishable facts; of essential qualities, immutable relations, eternal principles of truth and right.' Hence the appeal to the intellectually ambitious.

Apart from misplaced abstraction, one may absolve the great system builders from the common "fallacies through concepts" that we noticed earlier—empty verbalizing, overextension, and sheer name-calling. But there is a further misuse of concepts not so far mentioned. Concepts can be so handled as to suggest that they positively exclude what they do not positively affirm. This is their "privative use." James, who had to combat it in his campaign against the Absolute, called it 'vicious intel-lectualism.'

It has an ancient history. 'Intellectualism in the vicious sense began when Socrates and Plato taught that what a thing really is is told us by its definition. Ever since Socrates we have been taught that reality con-sists of essences, not of appearances, and that the essences of things are known whenever we know their definitions.' In Socrates' little game of quizzing his young, well-born, and docile pupils, a pilot is defined as one who has the skill to handle a ship. Therefore a pilot can never steer on the rocks and wreck his ship, for that is the act of an unskilful man.

Or again, to quote James's own example, 'a person whom you have once named an equestrian is thereby forever unable to walk on his own feet.' Greek science was hindered by this absolutism. It prevented, for instance, the conceiving of momentum, which makes one concept of speed and weight, two utterly disparate concepts.

The Greeks had some excuse for their failing. Knowing only their own language, they assumed that its terms denoted the true nature of the things named.* They lacked the perspective that the different takings by various tongues develop. Even in modern times philosophers have often overlooked the astute Lichtenberg's aphorism: "Language originated before philosophy; that's what's wrong with philosophy."**

Meantime, of course, common sense rebels at the notion that the essence of a horseman is to be always astride, and so develops the device of "insofar"—insofar as a man is a pilot he is wreckproof; all one has to worry about is the leftover portion which can steer wrong. Whole philosophies—Spinoza's being the most illustrious—have hinged on the "insofar" (quatenus) which, with the rest of scholastic Latin, makes the privative use of concepts seem the way to truth. The practice soon breeds in the mind the conviction that what it can *distinguish* is thereby *divided*. But this space put between things by an abstract notion of what they are violates experience, which always 'exceeds, surrounds, and overflows' the abstraction.

A very common example of this false division is the biographer's statement that the subject he is writing about was "a bundle of contradictions." The facts show, let us say, that though stingy toward his family, he was generous to strangers; open to new ideas of social reform but old-fashioned in his taste for clothing or art; trustworthy in love and business, but an unscrupulous gossip. These are made into contradictions by abstracting and dividing: "stinginess" contradicts "generosity." At that rate everybody is a "bundle" too, though there is no logical or psychological reason why a man's "generosity" should be total and invariable as the concept is—any more than his horsemanship should keep him at all times in the saddle.

This thought-cliché is perhaps of small consequence. More damaging is the political use of privative concepts by which a modern citizen thinks of himself as a liberal, a conservative, or a socialist. Anyone liv-

---

* I suspect that the prejudice against puns, the reason they are called "outrageous," is that they violate something like the Grecian respect for concepts. Puns in effect suddenly mix two ideas, felt as spatially far apart, through the trivial link of a sound—mere sensation rudely breaking in on delicate structures of thought.

** From his *Aphorisms* (1799). Georg Christoph Lichtenberg (1742–1799) was an amazing genius whose work in physics anticipated twentieth-century methods and conclusions. In his philosophizing one finds elements of Jamesian pragmatism, empiricism, and theory of emotion. See below, Epilogue-Anthology, p. 306.

ing in the free world today is necessarily all three: he or she supports and appreciates the established freedoms—hence a liberal. Freedoms being guaranteed by constitutions and laws, that same voter wants these kept inviolate, together with other established things—hence a conservative. Beyond the fixed and the free lies the socialism of institutions owned and run by governments, from roads, schools, and national parks to public utilities, food reserves, and armed forces; not to mention the use of the state's resources in social security, welfare, business and industry, the arts, scientific research, and what not else. Only total overthrowers want to abolish any of these three coexisting realms. And since the leeway left either for liberating or for wholly controlling activities is small, and nobody desires to keep everything just as it is, the three conceptual tags of politics that fitted the conditions of nineteenth-century Europe now only serve to obscure a complex reality, including the stubborn muddle in those who so label themselves.

Privative concepts also serve the ends of our dominant intellectual tendency—specialism. They help to reduce multiplicity and confusion—at first. That is no doubt the reason why we turn thinkers into isms. The original ideas are boiled down and congealed into something smaller, more portable—one man, one thought. It turns false by deprivation of its context, after which the followers and opponents start debating what nobody ever said. Pragmatism is a case in point; "Keynesianism" is another. The battle goes on among Keynesians, post-K.'s, and anti-K.'s quite as if K. himself had not defined the conditions under which one of his ideas—deficit spending—was appropriate. His revolution in economics was in fact to show that the concepts of the dismal science were not absolutes.

Right now (1982) it looks as if "economic man," carved out like the Greek pilot from the whole citizen, had rebelled against behaving just "insofar" and had resumed the right to be a whole wayward man. Economic actions are, after all, pieces of psychology; and at the best of times, as studies have shown, businessmen do not necessarily follow the cagey ways that theory requires. Hunch and impulse continue to exist and, with anxiety added, the canceling out of opposite economic choices fails to take place. This emancipation from prophecy is seen in the failure of such economic concepts as inflation, taxation, investment, unemployment, money supply to swing as they should, one up, one down, or two in tandem, for our greater good.

Meanwhile deductive theorists wrangle amid disorder. In some, faith in the power of the "single cause" falters—for instance, the belief that controlling the money supply will manipulate the behavior of a huge mass of individuals. Others point out that the usual indices on which theory relies are far from actual, owing to the tangle of definitions used to obtain the figures.* The best-qualified judges affirm contrary conclusions like the blind sages describing the elephant. If this spectacle of concepts doing a jig did not affect millions of human beings, one would be tempted to rename the whole subject "the comic science."

Quite apart from their subject matter, the modern specialisms (particularly the proliferating social studies) answer to the intellectualist, concept-loving temperament. They are avenues to detachment and protection from the buzzing confusion of life, the bewildering multiplicity of people and things. How is this refuge secured by concepts? If we liken the particulars of life to the plain numbers of arithmetic, then concepts are an algebra. With 5's and 7's you face at once the size or quantity of things; with $a$ and $b$, things are remote; you are in the dark until the equation is solved—and it may have several solutions. This anonymity of algebra is a great advantage; it saves thinking about details and it can ferret out unknowns—besides being a fascinating game.**

But the advantage turns into a loss unless the $a$'s and $b$'s—the concepts—'merge themselves again in the particulars of our present and future perceptions.' That is the hitch. How do we return to the world of tangibles—and why should we? 'We are so subject to the philosophic tradition which treats discursive thought as the sole avenue to truth, that to fall back on raw unverbalized life as more of a revealer comes very hard. But difficult as such a revolution is, there is no other way, I believe, to the possession of reality.'

James is speaking at large and thinking, as we have done, of temperaments. He finds the rationalist depicting the world as 'a universe in many editions—the real one, the infinite folio or *édition de luxe*, eternally complete; and then the various finite editions, full of false readings, distorted and mutilated each in its own way.' The other temperament accepts and even prefers the finite and imperfect. James called the two types 'tough-minded' and 'tender-minded'; and like several of his pregnant phrases this one has entered the language, but changed in meaning. James's designations have nothing to do with outward attitude

---

* This is no new discovery. To quote but one example, an English economist wrote twenty years ago: "There has been much theoretical examination of what we measure . . . and most of it leads to the conclusion that, except in very special and unusual circumstances, it is not possible to give any significant meaning to index numbers of real national income, production, or price." (Ely Devons, *Essays in Economics*, London, 1961, p. 112.)

** One of the most amazing instances of "algebraic" game, which is also "vicious intellectualism," has held sway in music theory for over half a century. It is the so-called "Schenker-analysis," named after the German Heinrich Schenker (1868–1935). With his *Urlinie* and other concepts one can reduce any piece of music to a formula of the utmost simplicity. The method takes no account of melody, rhythm, meter, timbre, or register. These aside, the formula yields "the essential music."

or learned profession. A hectoring lawyer is not necessarily tough-minded or a gentle scholar tender-minded. The scientist is not tough and the artist tender—more often it is the reverse. The tough empiricist temper we have been discovering in James himself. The tender mind is known by its wanting the security of a settled order. It wears 'a doctrinaire and authoritative complexion. The phrase "*must be*" is ever on its lips. The belly band of its universe must be tight. It wants something unexposed to accident, eternal and unalterable. The mutable in experience must be founded on immutability.'

But while the tough are flexing their muscles, it is only fair to add that the tender minds' ideal structure serves a need that both the tender and the tough may well desire: an object of contemplation. When science in the nineteenth century seemed to require that God be displaced from the center of life, nothing was left as a fit spectacle for the desire to behold with reverence, let alone for worship. The "edifice of science" is a mere verbalism; science comprises specialties without end, mostly inaccessible to outsiders; it is a cultural pluralism if ever there was one. And so is art, for although it has inherited some of the functions and all the fervor of religion, the feelings it inspires are necessarily scattered among many objects.

This dearth leaves two possibilities: religion somehow redefined (as it has been, repeatedly, in our time) and philosophy. But this last, overawed by science, has become so specialized, analytic, verbally obsessed, and arcane, that in effect it has declared itself unavailable for most human purposes. James was prescient once again when in his latter years he observed that 'the overtechnicality and consequent dreariness of the younger disciples at our American university is appalling. It comes from too much following of German models and manners. Let me fervently express the hope that there will be a return to the more humane English tradition.' As a master of language and a reader of journals, James knew that one can make distinctions indefinitely, and thereby "refute" all other positions, and still not advance the cause of philosophy or of *a* philosophy.

He was sure also that there would never be *the* philosophy, verified in all its parts and so convincing to all the world that it would end all debate. From the very relation of finite minds to a multifarious universe 'no philosophy can ever be anything but a summary sketch, a picture of the world in abridgement, a foreshortened bird's eye view of the perspective of events.' Inevitably that sketch is drawn from the sight we have of the pieces of the world we know. 'We can invent no new forms of conception applicable to the whole exclusively, and not suggested originally by the parts.'

These pictures of the world given by philosophy James also called visions. They spring from temperament in answer to need, as the historian of culture can show. 'All follow one analogy or another; and all analogies are with some one or another of the universe's subdivisions. Everyone is nevertheless prone to claim that his conclusions are the only logical ones, that they are necessities of universal reason, they being all the while, at bottom, accidents more or less of personal vision, which had better be avowed as such; for one man's vision may be much more valuable than another's, and our visions are usually not only our most interesting but our most respectable contributions to the world in which we play our part. One man may care for finality and security more than the other. Or their tastes in language may be different. One may like a universe that lends itself to lofty and exalted characterization. To another this may seem sentimental and rhetorical. The theists take their cue from manufacture, the pantheists from growth. For one man, the world is like a thought or a grammatical sentence in which a thought is expressed: the whole must logically be prior to the parts, for letters would never have been invented without syllables to spell, or syllables without words to utter.'

The analogy that fits James's empiricism is, as we might expect, the artistic: 'there is no really inherent order; it is we who project order into the world by selecting objects and tracing relations so as to gratify our intellectual interests. We carve out order by leaving the disorderly parts out; and the world is conceived thus after the analogy of a forest or a block of marble from which parks or statues may be produced by eliminating irrelevant trees or chips of stone.'

One proof that this pluralistic interpretation of the history of thought is truer than that which sees it as progress toward a future unified truth is that in history these visions do not come single file; they are simultaneous, they clash or overlap, and yet they satisfy the creators and their adherents. 'No one of them is the wholly perverse demon which another often imagines him to be. Both are loyal to the world that bears them; neither wishes to spoil it; neither wishes to regard it as an insane incoherence; both want to keep it as a universe of some kind; and their differences are all secondary to this deep agreement. All the parties are human beings with the same essential interests.'

In other words, philosophies are neither willful nor lacking in general significance. Let us not forget: one man's vision may be more valuable than another's, and James believed that human beings singly and collectively need as comprehensive a vision as can be fashioned, to guide their thoughts and acts and especially to give them what I have called an object of contemplation. It was on these grounds that he criticized systematic pessimism, skepticism, and nihilism: their guidance and the things they ask us to contemplate undermine "the energies of men." They give satisfaction only to minds that have come to enjoy dwelling on the badness of things and wish to share the pleasure of their grievance. It is just because evil is real that the empiricist philosopher wants to discern it in the flux; not escape it by a formula, but by taking thought help to lessen the strangeness and uncertainty of the world.

The rationalist Hegel himself conceded that such is the purpose of knowledge, though his writings—his prose—can only be said to have *added* to the amount of strangeness and uncertainty in the world. James, who considered philosophic visions important not to specialists only but to all mankind, was bound to regard the failure to write intelligibly a fundamental flaw in any vision. Jargon beclouds meaning and makes philosophy a debatable secret even for the few. Though admiring Hegel for his sense of history and giving him credit for the suggestive idea of a dialectical logic, James denounced 'his abominable habits of speech, his passion for the slipshod in the way of sentences, his unprincipled playing fast and loose with terms; his dreadful vocabulary, his systematic refusal to let you know whether he is talking logic or physics or psychology, his whole deliberately adopted policy of ambiguity, in short. For my own part, there seems something grotesque in the pretension of a style so disobedient to the first rules of sound communication between minds to be the authentic mother-tongue of reason and the Absolute's own ways of thinking.'

This failure of prose is not a monopoly of the philosophers; it is now endemic in science and scholarship. The German academic tradition, imported into nearly every country in the nineteenth century, is largely responsible, which does not mean that all German thinkers wrote like Hegel. Schopenhauer, Fechner, Paulsen, Nietzsche are stylists in the great tradition of lucidity and grace. But now even more than in James's time there is a marked advantage, a vested interest, in *not* writing well: what is clear is not profound; what is clear may be more easily challenged; what is clear gives itself away when it is a truism or a platitude.

James knew that he disconcerted his colleagues and sometimes even his popular audiences by his manner of exposition—his straightforward speech, his many concrete illustrations, alien to lofty thought, and his vivid renderings of the listener's unspoken objections. He would utter the strong image that came into his mind; he would let the man show through the words instead of presenting a smooth façade of impersonal abstractions.* For example: 'I fear that few of you will sympathize with the attempt to limit the role of concepts. It is too much like looking

* As occurs, for example, in Santayana, where assertion follows assertion without a shadow of argument. It has passed muster as philosophy as much for its "seriousness" as for its merits.

downward and not up. Philosophy, you will say, doesn't lie down on its belly in the middle of experience, in the very thick of its sand and gravel, never getting a peep at anything from above.' James's learned audience was doubtless embarrassed. 'They are so brought up on technical ways of handling things that when a man handles them bare, they are non-plussed, can neither understand, agree, nor reply.'

But besides being the preference of a true writer, this choice of style was also the natural application of his intellectual method. Pragmatism asks: What does your statement come down to? What is this truth 'known-as'? "Handling things bare" is not intended for others' convenience or admiration, it is the best way to sift out the truth for oneself and to get it confirmed or revised by those others. Unlike the majority of philosophers, 'whose besetting sin has always been the absolutism of their intellects,' James wanted criticism and believed that candor and the revelation of biases were the best way of ascertaining truth; wrangling over small points left all parties sniping from their trenches and stuck there. 'I know very well that in talking of dislikes to those who never mention them, I am doing a very coarse thing. But for the life of me I cannot help it, because I feel sure that likes and dislikes must be among the ultimate factors of their philosophy as well as of mine. Would they but admit it! How sweetly we then could hold converse together!'

Acknowledging that philosophies are visions does not mean that answers to the great philosophic questions may be strung together anyhow. They must fit present facts as well as recorded truths. These operations call for logic, subtle discriminations, and a strong imagination. James did not ignore the necessity of professional skill in philosophic discussion; he filled hundreds of pages of notes that show him at the task. But he considered technical solutions preliminary, not the final substance. He was ready, even in his popular lectures, to take a mixed group of listeners quite far into the reasoning behind his concerns.* But he also made them see how his conclusion and his opponents' could enter into the lives of men and the difference each might make there.

Philosophy, in short, was not to him a profession or any sort of specialism. It was "man thinking," and 'a man with no philosophy in him is the most inauspicious and unprofitable of all possible social mates.' Whoever thinks about man's destiny and conduct in a detached way philosophizes. Take a haphazard group of people in a stalled commuter train and start the question "How did the world come to be?" and not one person within earshot—as I have experienced more than once—

---

* Such reasoning in support of the assertions I have brought together are too many and elaborate to give here even in brief. See his *Essays in Radical Empiricism*, Chs. VI and VII, and *Some Problems of Philosophy*, Ch. XIII.

will remain uninvolved. God, science, and immortality will soon be the subject of the impromptu seminar. Philosophy has 'no method peculiar to itself; it observes, discriminates, generalizes, classifies, looks for causes, traces analogies, and makes hypotheses.' In these last three words James implies the hope that philosophy will present views *as* hypotheses and 'end by forswearing all dogmatism whatever,' in which event 'philosophers may get into as close contact as realistic novelists with the facts of life.'

What else could philosophy be for? The original cause of man's wonder—how came the cosmos to be and why anything should be at all—eludes our grasp. But one need only 'shut oneself in a closet and begin to think of the fact of one's being there, of one's queer bodily shape in the darkness, of one's fantastic character and all, to have the wonder steal over the detail as much as over the general fact of being, and to see that it is only familiarity that blunts it. Not only that *anything* should be, but that *this* very thing should be, is mysterious. Whether the original nothing burst into God and vanished, as night vanishes into day, while God thereupon became the creative principle of all lesser beings; or whether all things have foisted or shaped themselves imperceptibly into existence, the same amount of existence has in the end to be assumed and begged. If you are a rationalist you beg a kilogram of being at once; if you are an empiricist you beg a thousand successive grams; but you beg the same amount in each case and you are the same beggar whatever you may pretend.'

Nor can science add a single helpful word. It ignores purpose and first cause; as the Nobel physicist Steven Weinberg has said: "The more the universe becomes comprehensible, the more it also seems pointless." He meant: comprehensible scientifically. What science leaves for philosophy to do is to examine 'the extreme diversity of aspects under which reality undoubtedly exists'; to 'see the familiar as if it were strange and the strange as if it were familiar' and thus 'rouse us from our native dogmatic slumber and break up our caked prejudices.' Historically, philosophy has pursued and coordinated four human interests—science, art, religion, and logic. 'It has sought by hard reasoning for results emotionally valuable. To have some contact with it, to catch its influence, is thus good for both literary and scientific students. Both types of student ought to get from philosophy a livelier spirit, more air, more mental background.'

And what students can derive from philosophy any thoughtful person can get, with the same benefit. "*More* mental background" is a diplomatic way of suggesting the shallowness, the automatic conceptual simplicity, with which most of us respond to the vicissitudes of life. To possess a philosophic vision gives the perspective on oneself that comes from seeing things in their universal aspect and thereby come back strengthened for dealing with their particular reality, "knowledge about" ministering to "knowledge of."

For this gymnastic use of thought it is obviously necessary that live philosophers should not only address themselves to philosophic questions in their current form but should also address the public about them. Philosophy, as I have said, must be understandable by more than the dogged few. But on this ecumenical function James was at odds with his friend Peirce and their little rift is instructive. In 1897 once more, James had arranged for him a series of paid lectures. Peirce made up a syllabus dealing exclusively with logic and involving mathematics. Since the lectures were intended for Harvard students and others not specially prepared, James wrote: 'Now be a good boy and think a more popular plan out. I don't want the audience to dwindle to three or four. Separate topics of a vitally important character would do perfectly well.' Peirce was annoyed. He entitled his lectures "Detached Ideas on Vitally Important Topics," but devoted the first to a harsh repudiation of the idea that philosophy should concern itself with topics of vital importance. By the phrase that Peirce adopted ironically, James did not mean topics of current or local interest; he said what he had in mind: 'anti-nominalism, categories, hypothesis, tychism, and synechism,' which are not exactly kindergarten subjects. They would suit the group he would invite to the house of Mrs. Ole Bull, the widow of the famous Norwegian violinist.

But Peirce was actuated by the analogy with science, not by a vision: "My philosophy . . . is not an 'idea' with which I 'brim over'; it is a serious research. . . . People who cannot reason exactly (which alone is reasoning) simply cannot understand my philosophy." * And this high task of research absolved him from moral and intellectual obligation to his hearers. In science it is indeed true that findings which seem peripheral or obscure at first can later lead to great central results. But the analogy is lame. Science is carried on in laboratories among peers and its results are published in specialist journals, not in public halls or living rooms peopled by the laity. Nor does science touch human beings directly through affirmations about ethics, religion, art, politics, history, and the cosmos—affirmations that must be believed and felt before they can affect life.

* Note here the privative concept Reason (the pilot cannot go wrong) and the forgetting of Lichtenberg's warning about words. No philosophy can hope to be exact like mathematics. One has only to compare the two ways in which Whitehead was treated: as mathematical logician he was impeccable; as a philosopher of high merit his works aroused innumerable objections. This difference explains why to this day there are Aristotelians, Thomists, Kantians, and followers of other "refuted" philosophies.

Yet today the substance of philosophy is determined by just such attitudes toward science and language. Peirce's way has prevailed, with the curious result that although doctrines in vogue each owe something to James's work, they have long since rejected his notion of duty toward the common world of ideas; they have become specialisms occupying a much reduced terrain and dealing with narrow matters in language unintelligible to the educated.

Whether of the "logical positivist" school or that of the "language analysts," they are concerned primarily with definition and distinctions. The logicians seek to unify philosophy, science, and mathematics, dismissing as meaningless, "because empirically unprovable," statements about other human interests. The language men, an offshoot of the former, concentrate on speech to show that philosophical questions arise from mistaken ideas about the use of words. By taking the common-sense view of the world and common usage as a standard, they restrict philosophy to a purpose that has been called therapeutic: the therapy is to get rid of philosophic problems.

Existentialists and phenomenologists are more hospitable to the ancient riddles of human thought and existence, but their works too are opaque. After Kierkegaard, who can be read, Sartre, Heidegger, and their sources, Husserl, Simmel, and others show German academic discourse at its densest.* It could be argued that the barbed-wire prose is due to the intricacy of the subject, but the base on which these doctrines rests is the Jamesian view that we make our universe out of experience by acts of thought and will; and this idea he managed to convey and elaborate without torturing his readers. Existentialists differ from his radical empiricism in their view of objects, but as their view is that of common sense or materialism—"the alien world outside"—there is no enigma that should make the philosopher stammer.** But try to read Heidegger and then imagine James's comments. They are perhaps deducible from what he wrote to a colleague in 1905: 'I am getting impatient with the awful abstract rigmarole in which our philosophers obscure the truth. It will be fatal. It revives the palmy days of Hege-

---

* See "Analysts Win Battle in War of Philosophy." (*New York Times*, January 6, 1982.) Their opponents at the annual meeting of the American Philosophical Association, Eastern Division, were oddly named "Pluralists," to cover their various existential or phenomenological leanings.

** I have myself pragmatically tested this assertion by working with a friend and colleague in the close editing of several chapters of his ultra-modern philosophy. Under the pressure of my needs as reader, what I could understand with difficulty he made clearer, what was ambiguous he succeeded in making definite, what was impenetrable he had to rethink for rewriting. His good nature allowed him to admit that in the "finished text" with which we started, the process of thought had not gone far enough. Yet a learned journal would have published it as it stood.

lianism. It means utter relaxation of intellectual duty, and God will smite it. It there's anything he hates, it is that kind of oozy writing.'*

The important accusation in these words, applicable to all the newest visions (an ironic word for studies in obscurity), is 'utter relaxation of intellectual duty.' When on one side philosophers dismiss large questions as meaningless and, on the other, large questions receive answers akin to tongue-twisters, it is fair to say that philosophy has abdicated its public role. It remains only as a profession, an academic employment, a debating society of limited liability for usefulness. As in other academic disciplines—for example, literary criticism and art history—philosophy's taking refuge in Alexandrianism, in the Byzantine magnification of trifles, is the sign of a cultural terminus. Thus ended also, in verbalism, the originally powerful medieval philosophy of the scholastics. Its very name still retains the connotation of decline to futility. It may be that Wittgenstein himself, the master of linguistic philosophers, had an inkling of the danger when he admonished some overzealous students with a Jamesian-empiricist command: "Don't think, look!"

There may be hope in that last word "look!" It gives a hint of vision and might imply something to contemplate. If so, after the ground where philosophy once stood has been leveled flat by the diggers and the extinguishers, we may see the return of philosophizing for life in the place of using life to practice philosophy.


James's temperament we now know pretty well, or should know after hearing his voice on so many topics. He is as open as the universe—the pluriverse—that he depicted. His "likes" are the particulars, the flux taken as real and not as a false show. Plato's analogy of humankind as prisoners in a cave, with the light behind them, and seeing a vague shadow-play on the prison walls, found no echo in James's thought. His vision was almost in so many words the exact opposite. As Alice reports in her diary, a true image of his mind is found in his remark that he had now acquired in the country 'the most delightful house you ever saw; it has fourteen doors, all opening outwards.'**

* Periodically the question comes up, What is the proper style for philosophy? In James's own day, Taine in France and Grote in England castigated their colleagues for needless obscurity. In our century Brand Blanshard wrote an instructive essay, On Philosophical Style (Indianapolis, 1954), and a French critic made a survey of some fifty thinkers, including Bergson: Comment Doivent Ecrire les Philosophes? (Constant Bourquin, Paris, 1923.)

** The house in Chocorua, New Hampshire. It was there that by his wish he was carried back from Europe to die (August 26, 1910). The place takes its name from a peak in the Sandwich range which survived an effort to rename it Mt. Eisenhower in 1955. (New York Times, July 22, 1955.)

But on top of native bias, the events of James's early years were bound to magnify his scope. Travel and life abroad from childhood on, incessant family debate, the ability to think in five languages, addiction to literature and the arts, coupled with the professional study of chemistry, physiology, medicine, and psychology—all these pursued over a ground bass of philosophic reading—furnished his mind with a host of facts and ideas inescapably plural in kind, perspective, and significance. Compared with James and his experience of life by the age of twenty-five most philosophers have been men of the bookshelf and the lamp.

Of course, intensity of experience matters as much as extensiveness. But here also everything (including the episode of depression in youth) shows that James's powers of feeling and imagination were as deep and wide as the range of his takings. It is evident, too, that in the struggle to find himself, the strong esthetic tendency of his mind kept in balance the conceptual, enabling him to question the dominant Idealist thought and arrive at a vision of the world based on accepting all of the given as real. This called for a reconstruction in philosophy, in effecting which he became (as we shall see) one of the makers of the new culture of our century.

Radical empiricism never made doctrinaire disciples. Those belong only to certain kinds of system and only to the party-leader type of thinker. But it has done better. From its inception it swept like a strong wind, carrying with it different seeds over the landscape of thought and feeling. One may even see an ultimate and unwitting outgrowth of its temper in the modern artists who take, and compel us to take, sensation "as it comes." The random throwing-on of paint in Abstract Expressionism (a most inapt label) is an act of trust in experience and a lesson about it. In similarly random ("aleatory") music or poetry and in simply "found" art, the intention is to wean us from all ideas, moral or esthetic, and even from the concept of art itself.

It was certainly not a reading of James's philosophy that inspired the performances of these artists; they derive after much else from the first modernism, before 1914, which James did influence. He would himself be critical of pure sensation in art and of the makers of random works, not because they have gone too far, but because they have gone on too long. James's empiricism does not stop and stagnate in the raw particulars. It draws attention to them—as the artists do with their strictly sensory works—in order to re-engage and refresh perception. But James expects the freshly perceived to generate new concepts, and these to be incorporated in the body of previous truths.

It is by this means that the unities are formed within the cosmos.

They appear to our sight as a hierarchy of truths, of activities, of spheres of interest to which we give hollow academic names but which, as a body, possess our minds and attach our emotions and condition our actions: mathematics and the natural sciences, now almost beyond numbering; literature and the arts in their vastness; the ethical, religious and theological visions of man and his destiny; history and its sister disciplines falsely called social sciences; and philosophy in all its branches from epistemology to cosmology. These exhibit the triumph of the conceptual power, and largely make us what we are—human beings and deliberate thinkers. For concepts, no matter how often misused, or mistaken and revised, are as real as any perceptions; abstractions command as much feeling and action as the concretes with which they deal: that is why they are so dangerous and must be watched within us and without.

And though always changing, these unities also furnish us with the manifold object of contemplation that the philosophic mind looks for. But for it to be an object, a spectacle, it has to be explained and seen as (for me) James sees and explains it. Actually, its parts ought not to be called a hierarchy of truths and facts, which would imply higher and lower as well as set in compartments. Rather, they form a grid, a flexible net with innumerable intersections, at which points we meet them as mental or physical events in our own lives. We do not need to know, we cannot know them all. But where we are ignorant we have intimations of their bearing or influence and they command imagination—mine at least—more firmly than the single All, Whole, or One, be it matter or mind. For 'the worth and interest of the world consists not in its elements, be these elements things, or be they the conjunction of things; it exists rather in the dramatic outcome in the whole process and in the meaning of the successive stages which the elements work out.'

They "work out," and in dramatic fashion, because activity, our activity, is a genuine fact, not the result of a push or an "idea" from elsewhere. If we look at the mass of things in the midst of which the life of men is passed and ask, "How came they here?," the only broad answer is that man's desire preceded and produced most of them. 'Life'—and here James paraphrases the idealist Royce as if to show that they do not inhabit separate worlds but share partly congruent visions—'life is full of significance, of meaning, of success and of defeat, of hoping and striving, of longing, of desire, and of inner value. It is a total presence that embodies worth. To live our own lives better in this presence is the true reason why we wish to know the elements of things.'

The intense love of natural sights and sounds, which was part of James's emotional makeup, is the fit counterpart of this outlook on life and its elements, the radical empiricist outlook. For nature esthetically seen, without dissecting tools, exhibits growth and the glories of surface rather than structure and inner depths; and it is these outward features that give vividness to the "presence" that James felt when, as philosopher, he contemplated the variety, the unities, and the infinite possibilities of meaning in experience.

# Freedom and Risk

To have shown as a scientist and self-observer that the human mind is a stream running after some half-sensed goal, yet capable of attention, forming objects like an artist and concepts like a geometrician, while the whole organism, acting like a sounding-board, generates the emotions that reason is meant to serve; to regard the passing thought as the thinker, its objects as primary, and concepts as devices for unifying, simplifying, and remembering—experience being always richer and more complete than words and categories; to have redefined truth and described the signs and tests by which it is known, noting in this activity the role of Time, perspective, and past truths—all these governing both theory and practice; to relish opposition and difference, because minds do not take from experience the same realities, though as a whole experience is exactly what it seems and not a lying façade hiding a system of absolute truths—this genuine but plural reality and possible novelty therefore requiring the philosophic mind to enter into whatever is Other, like a dramatist ever attentive to the individual and the particular: these traits, attitudes, ideas, and powers we have found to be the chief characteristics, so far, of the thinker we chose to accompany.

There is much yet to discover, but this inventory is enough to show our guide as a complex nature. It is as if he had made his own the qualities of the medium he works in, the fluidity and iridescence of the stream and also its power to conceive and imagine. But after all, as a naturalist in psychology, he had undertaken to show us the widest possible ambit of mind, not just of his own mind.

Yet his own mind is not intoxicated by so much scope; it is *responsive* to the manyness of experience, not vulnerable, both because it is content to accept its own limitedness and because within its boundaries it is fastidious and demanding. This phrase, which I make into a leitmotif, points to the usual qualities of intellect—judgment, imagination, logic, hunger and respect for evidence. But when as in James fastidiousness becomes virtually a category of thought, it is seen to be a moral category as well, a quality of emotion which is perhaps best described as "schooled feeling."*

To appreciate the role of this trait in James's mind one should be familiar with the bulk of his writings, including the letters. But any reader of the novels of Henry James will know the virtue I am trying to describe, for the brothers shared it without naming or noticing it. In Henry's fiction the characters who work evil and cause harm do so not because of what they desire but because of their heedless way of gaining it. They are not demanding enough of themselves and do not sufficiently feel the horror of snatching. Even in his wonderful gallery of characters who are not evil but weak and shady, Henry shows that their need to deceive is a lack of power to feel the idea of decency.

In William, as we saw, part of his demand on himself was his striving for exhaustive literary expression. Beyond the search for evidence of the forgotten or the unexpected, James labored to give original or improved statements of things and relations that came under his scrutiny. The two notes of my leitmotif are thus the appropriate ones to sound as the introduction to James's moral philosophy, for its contents and its reception by critics present a little drama involving these same elements in conflict.

James's long discussions in youth with Wendell Holmes and the great essay-review of Spencer's *Psychology* in 1878 were his first attempts to vindicate the character of the moral life.** It had to be done because the phrase "in an age of science" was already taking on the implication that everything in human life had changed and must be re-examined before its license to exist could be renewed.

For James as a naturalist, the double question was: how to establish the reality of moral choice as part of nature; and how to show that this choice was a free individual act, not a resultant of extraneous "forces."

---

* That this mode of feeling-thought was in James both deep-rooted and subtle is shown by a diary note of his twenty-seventh year, when he was beginning to assess the philosophical meaning of experience under various afflictions. There were, he wrote to himself, 'three quantities to determine: (1) how much pain I'll stand; (2) how much other's pain I'll inflict (by existing); (3) how much other's pain I'll "accept" without ceasing to take pleasure in their existence.' (Perry, *op. cit.* I, p. 302.)

** See above, p. 22ff.

The evidence James begins with is the root phenomenon of the reflex arc with which we are familiar: a sensory stimulus affects the brain, and its result is some form of action. 'All action is re-action upon the outer world. The current of life which runs in at our eyes and ears is meant to run out at our hands, feet, or lips. The only use of the thoughts which it occasions while inside is to determine its direction to whichever of these organs shall, under the circumstances actually present, act in the way most propitious to our welfare.'

Evolutionists in the 1870s were content to go no further; and behaviorists today follow suit. One of them has earned a certain reputation by entrenching himself in this neurological base and arguing that we should give up the idea of moral responsibility in human beings. We should replace it by a system of rewards and punishments that will "condition" (i.e., determine) right action. How such conditioning will ensure proper behavior in the unpredictable occasions of daily life and who will have decided what is proper are apparently trifling details to be settled later.

What James saw and said a hundred years ago is that reflex action is not like stepping on one end of a see-saw and getting hit in the face by the other. Between stimulus and action comes response, and which response it is to be is by no means always automatic. Whatever may be the link between brain and mind, we experience the stimulus. Except in the simple cases of touching a hot stove or a sharp blade, response varies widely. The mind interposes at the midpoint of the arc its peculiar and complex individual characteristics.*

This interlude of response may seem a slender support for the moral world, but it is the same support that holds up and indeed constitutes the whole of our conscious life, with which moral judgment and choice are intertwined. The important point is to recognize preference as a given element and one that is inescapably individual. It is that taking which we have seen as central to the Jamesian conception of reality. In one of his most charming essays, "On a Certain Blindness in Human Beings," James relates a picturesque incident of his driving with a North Carolina farmer through a remote valley recently opened to cultivation. James was appalled at the devastation—beautiful trees felled, then charred stumps bearing witness to the struggle for level ground; great gashes in the greenery and patches of corn and other plantings

---

* Recent testimony by a sufferer from the Tourette syndrome of "uncontrollable" tics and blinks and twitches throws a sidelight on the topic. He says that over the years he came to recognize the signals preceding such movements and he found that although the "leap from impulse to movement" was almost uncontrollable, "the movements are actually voluntary. The intention is to relieve a sensation, as surely as the movement to scratch an itch is to relieve the itch." (New York Times, January 6, 1981.)

irregularly scattered, like the pigs and chickens, among the miserable log cabins, across what must have been an enchanted vale. 'The forest had been destroyed; and what had "improved" it out of existence was hideous, a sort of ulcer without a single element of artificial grace to make up for the loss of Nature's beauty.' James put a tactful question to his driver, whose reply changed the whole scene: '"Why, we ain't happy here, unless we're getting one of these coves under cultivation." I instantly felt,' James goes on, 'that I had been losing the whole inward significance of the situation. Because to me the clearings spoke of naught but denudation, I thought they could tell no other story. But when they looked on the hideous stumps, what they thought of was personal victory, of honest sweat, persistent toil, and final reward. The cabin was a warrant of safety for self and wife and babes. The clearing was a symbol redolent with moral memories of duty, struggle, and success.'

Preferences, then, the ends that we pursue, 'do not exist at all in the world of impressions we receive by way of our senses, but are set by our emotional and practical subjectivity altogether. Destroy the volitional nature, the definite subjective purposes, preferences, fondnesses for certain effects, forms, orders, and not the slightest motive would remain for the brute order of our experience to be remodelled at all.'

It is our desires, our "fondnesses" as James calls them, that underlie the state of mind in which we say "this is good, this is bad; that is better and this is worse." Or we imply these judgments by a taking or a rejecting, instinctive or deliberate. Desires are of course not limited to bodily need. Man has developed a want for the superfluous, which is infinite and includes those satisfactions termed moral satisfactions. The moral order, in other words, turns out to be the meaning attached to experience by every being who thinks while he feels.

But this conclusion is only the threshold of the higher moral questions. Thoughtful people wonder about the status of ethical ideas strictly so called, the meaning of the terms right and wrong, duty and conscience, and the standards that they comply with. In ordinary speech, "ethics" means not cheating or stealing, "morals" means sexual propriety; and the "decline of moral standards" so frequently discussed turns on how much there is of the one and how little of the other. "Wider moral issues" occupy writers and preachers and even politicians: What is a just society? Is equality of opportunity enough to ensure it? Is the criminal reared in poverty responsible for his acts? Does the right to life begin in the embryo? And in comparing groups or individuals, the question is asked, What "values" has she, he, they got? Tell us your "priorities." "Lifestyles" themselves, voguish and vaguish as the term is, embody the kind of judgment called moral, and the same estimating of worth comes into play in every realm of thought and action: art, science, philosophy, and religion are equally exposed to moral judgment; they form part of the moral life of man.

Its difficulty is that because it relies on estimates, because it arises from our different perspectives, certainty and agreement are not to be had, even with the aid of a particular religious revelation. And supposing that revelation did bring about unity, the multiplicity of creeds at variance on moral questions would still leave the philosopher having to choose among revelations. He wants a prescription to fit all mankind if he can discover it. What can he turn to?

In answering the challenge, James gives in passing some credit to the Utilitarians, who ascribe good and bad to associations with pleasure and pain. Association does train us morally, but only up to a point. As James's *Psychology* makes clear, there are tendencies of the human mind that are "born in the house" and not developed by utility. 'Take the love of drunkenness; take bashfulness, the terror of high places, the susceptibility to musical sounds; take the emotion of the comical, the passion for poetry, for mathematics, or for metaphysics—no one of these things can be wholly explained by either association or utility. A vast number of our moral perceptions deal with directly felt fitnesses between things and fly in the teeth of all the prepossessions of habit and presumptions of utility. The moment you get beyond the coarser moral maxims, the Decalogues and Poor Richard's Almanacs, you fall into schemes and positions which to the eye of common sense seem fantastic and overstrained. The sense for abstract justice, which some persons have, is as eccentric a variation as is the passion for music. The feeling of the inward dignity of certain spiritual attitudes, as peace, serenity, simplicity, veracity; and of the essential vulgarity of others, as querulousness, anxiety, egoistic fussiness are quite inexplicable except by an innate preference of the moral ideal attitude.'

Since these attitudes are individual facts and unevenly distributed among mankind, it follows that 'there is no such thing possible as an ethical philosophy dogmatically made up in advance. We all help to determine the content of ethical philosophy so far as we contribute to the race's moral life. In other words, there can be no final truth in ethics any more than in physics, until the last man has had his experience and said his say.' This is what we should expect in a universe that is inherently pluralistic and unfinished.

Are there no such things as moral principles? Is it meaningless to speak of principled action, of a man, a woman of principle? For if all these are empty words, how can moral behavior be taught and misbehavior reproved? The demand for a common standard is as strong a feeling as that of wanting justice in our special case. We ask incessantly, What is the law? the entrance requirements? the speed limit? We need yardsticks to set our minds at rest and bring others to book—the phrase is literal: the book is the record of accepted measures for ordinary thought and action. Hence the similar call for principles in the cloudier sphere of moral judgment.

But the word, with its aura of personal merit and firmness in a shaky world, is ambiguous. To the absolutist a principle is a teaching fixed for all time and good on all occasions, a dogma. One should not be afraid of the name, for it conveys the advantage that principles have when proclaimed with authority as "indelible moral truths, not mere opinion." In that guise principle seems to possess an inherent compelling force—no need of the police behind it. At the same time, dogma has acquired its unwelcome sound because it claims universal sway, while modern liberal constitutions require the peaceful coexistence of several conflicting dogmas. So the very general demand for principles and men of principle comes down to asking that everyone have "some principle or other" and diversity is back to plague us as before.

A further difficulty with principles is that they clash among themselves, even within the same system of morality. Albert Schweitzer, for instance, preached "Reverence for Life" and got the reputation of a saint. But what pragmatic contents does the formula cover? If it means no vivisection, more humane slaughter-houses, forbidding blood-sports—even if it means vegetarianism—Schweitzer's injunction can at least be debated. But as a universal rule it is mere concept-worship. Schweitzer must have daily flouted his own law. If his hospital at Lambaréné was even moderately aseptic, many living crawling creatures had to be denied reverence. The tapeworm and tsetse fly could bear witness to his unprincipled behavior, and he was ruthless to cancer cells, which are also a form of life. "Oh but that's not what he meant!" What then *did* he mean? An absolute rule is literal or it is nothing. Here the nothing is a pompous echo of a general tendency already well-rooted in our mores.

Schweitzer was too intelligent a man not to see the objection and he made some verbal gestures to gloss it over: good sense should govern the application of principle. That saving clause, expressed or not, seems to go with every ideal when one begins to analyze it. It enables the absolutist to pass for a moral champion and sensible as well: proclaim the principle inviolable, denounce as unprincipled—as pragmatists—

those who question the heroics of absolutes, then reserve the right to do quietly what the "unprincipled" say has to be done.*

In the last half-century the game has been played with this same "sanctity of life" to bring about the widespread abolition of capital punishment; it now goes on about legalized abortion. "The state should not commit—or abet—murder." The noble rhetoric blankets the varieties of experience and flouts the proper use of words: a judicial execution or a legal operation is not murder. And other considerations than the life of the criminal or the fetus have relevance. To name but two, the sanctity of life is hardly honored by incarceration for years in the prisons we have. Nor is it reasonable to prohibit abortion and permit all the persons and powers of society, whether through high literature or low advertising, to work upon the eye and the imagination with ubiquitous incitements to sexual activity.

In a word, principles are at best shorthand summaries of what civilized life requires in general, in ordinary relations, in open-and-shut situations: do not lie, steal, or kill. But the pure imperative gives no guidance whatever in difficult cases. Universal lying would be dreadful, but you do not tell the truth to the madman armed with a knife who asks which way his intended victim went. And even routinely, you lie to spare the feelings of the hostess who apologizes for her spoiled dinner or dull company. The police shoot in hot pursuit and sometimes kill the innocent bystanders, just as they would, and do, to quell a riot. The very right of self-defense works for *and against* the sanctity of life. And whether or not the unborn have a "right to life" from the moment of conception, it would be morally monstrous to force the victim of incest or rape (especially if accompanied by venereal disease) to bear her child. The child itself might come to wish it had never been born and curse the blinkered moralist.**

Every human situation being a tangle of facts and meanings and possible consequences, moral judgment consists in deciding how much evil may be averted and the good sustained or extracted. Sometimes the complication is tragic, as in the case that E. M. Forster discussed at the outbreak of the Second World War: "Should I betray my country or my

---

* The love of abstraction and hatred of usefulness go so far in certain moralists as to make them affirm that it would be better for morality if honesty were *not* the best policy. In other words, the right is what people ought to do, with no reason given—except that they ought to, because it is right. Imperatives satisfy, even vicariously, the imperial emotions.

** Awareness of the inadequacy of "principle" occasionally strikes even a religious leader. The archbishop of Canterbury said at the time of his enthronement that he feared "being a platitude-machine. The hollownesss of ringing declarations and general moralizing divorced from direct experience of the doubts and difficulties of ordinary people is only too evident." (*New York Times*, March 26, 1980.)

friend?" The dilemma may have seemed improbable at the time; it no longer looks it after the revelations of high-minded spying and treason. And the moralist is no nearer a solution than Antigone was two thousand years ago when she had to choose whether to obey the law of the gods commanding her to bury her brother or the law of the state forbidding her to do it because he was a rebel.

If these various degrees of uncertainty and horror do characterize the life of man precisely because he is a moral being, what help can thinking about it abstractly provide? James has but two generalities to offer, but they are comprehensive. The first is that 'there is but one unconditional commandment, which is that we should seek incessantly, with fear and trembling, so to act as to bring about the very largest total universe of good that we can see. Abstract rules indeed can help; but they help less in proportion as our intuitions are more piercing and our vocation the stronger for the moral life. For every dilemma is in literal strictness a unique situation; and the exact combination of ideals realized and ideals disappointed which each decision creates is always a universe without precedent and for which no adequate previous rule exists. The philosopher, then, qua philosopher, is no better able to determine the best universe in the concrete emergency than other men. He sees, indeed, somewhat better than most men what the question always is—not a question of this good or that good simply taken, but of the two universes with which these goods respectively belong.'

"Not this good, or that good"—it is the whole tangle that must be resolved, just as it is from the new emergencies that moral habits grow more delicate. If we no longer make fun of the insane, abuse the crippled, or beat the abc's into little children, it is because individuals with "piercing intuitions" have persuaded society that their sensibility to others' pain implied a moral duty to stop inflicting it. But short of such great reforms, what moral contribution can the morally alive person make? Start, as James always tells us to do, with the idea of a tangible result. 'If one ideal judgment be objectively better than another, that betterness must be made flesh by being lodged concretely in someone's actual perception. It cannot float in the atmosphere, for it is not a sort of meteorological phenomenon like the aurora borealis.'

The second general principle as to the question what ought to be done, what one's duty is in the circumstances, what the ground of our obligation is, brings us to the possibly surprising conclusion 'that without a claim actually made by some concrete person there can be no obligation, and that there is some obligation wherever there is a claim. Our ordinary attitude of regarding ourselves as subject to an overarching system of moral relations true "in themselves" is therefore either an out-and-out superstition, or else it must be treated as a merely provisional abstraction from that real Thinker in whose actual demand obligation must be ultimately based.' James, being a naturalist, does not posit such a Thinker; he is only showing those who do that their traditional religious morality implies a claimant. It follows that in a world which acknowledges no God—or not everywhere the same one—the claim must come from the beings whose existence we do acknowledge.

James knows the strangeness of thinking that every claim imposes a duty. With our habit of always wanting a backing to reality, we look for some sign of "validity" behind the claim to turn it into an obligation, something beyond, which 'rains down upon the claim from some sublime dimension of being which the moral law inhabits. But how can such an inorganic abstract character of imperativeness, additional to the imperativeness which is the concrete claim itself, exist? Take any demand, however slight, which any creature, however weak, may make. Ought it not, for its own sole sake, to be satisfied? If not, prove why not. The only possible kind of proof would be the exhibition of another creature who should make a demand that ran the other way.'

So here we are, each of us, at the center of the conflicting claims that assail us. They may come from animals or infants or strangers: the range of claims we are subjected to depends on the degree of our awareness; the extent of our moral effect on the world depends on our ability to sort and fulfill them. I confess that when I first read James on "The Moral Philosopher and the Moral Life," I was struck by a sense of helplessness about carrying out his injunction. But on reflecting, when I had grasped his extraordinary idea, I felt the sudden release from interminable shilly-shallying: X has asked me to do this for him. Perhaps I should. But I don't really like X, so why should I? But it's absurd to decide on mere dislike. Why not do what he asks if I can without too much trouble? Yes, but he probably won't return the favor. Surely that's no reason for not doing it—and so on. The amount of inner wear and tear saved by the Jamesian redefinition of duty can be very great. Our modern cant phrases—to sort out one's priorities, to stick to one's values—hardly help in comparison with James's simple idea that the burden of proof in our moral relations is always on the negative: given a claim concretely presented, why should I not satisfy it? The search for a "why should I" is futile see-sawing or a grudging surrender to the "superstitious abstraction."

The result of honoring as many claims as possible is to raise the amount of satisfaction in the world, increase the sum of good, and thereby "moralize" the universe more than it is already. For if reducing cruelty to animals makes for a universe better than it was before, so does giving our claimants more of what they assert to be their good. Superficially, the judgment may look like the Utilitarian's "greatest good of the greatest number"; actually, it differs in having nothing to do with legislating the good of society at large or with the wishes of a majority. It is a concrete relation between persons.

That relation may even be what is meant by the utopian commandment that we should love one another. At the same time, the requirement of an existing, live claim prevents intrusive do-goodism under the cloak of love. But what if the claimants misjudge and call good what is bad—ask for drugs or the means of harming others? In such cases there is obviously a counterclaim which nullifies theirs, the claim of their kindred or of the rest of society. Besides, claims of this sort fall within the circle of mores and laws about which the moral person has long since settled his doubts. One is not bound to be perplexed and imagine a dilemma every time a choice has to be made. A great deal of the present century's feelings of guilt are the result not so much of moral conscience as of the self-conscious ego. Its feelings are not insincere, but they are more about the status of the self in its own eyes than about the object of its concern. Thus Mrs. Jellyby in Dickens, who neglected her children in her zeal for the natives of Borrioboola-Gha.

To respond to all possible claims, one must begin looking for them in one's own immediate sphere of knowledge. One must recognize the limits of one's power, but with a resolve to act. Indignation about this bad world is cheaply come by and morally worthless. As Robert Frost once recounted, he gave up reading Lincoln Steffens on the plight of cities, because as a poet he knew he could not go and help.* Self-acceptance strengthens the moral judgment in an essential way, for in deciding which claims to fulfill there are times when the claims of the self must be heeded. The traditional self-sacrifice of a grown child to an aged parent, for example, must be weighed against its possibly immoral results—domestic tyranny and emotional blackmail, on one side, gradually creating embittered hostility toward the whole world, on the other.

As always, it is easier to dispose of such questions from the distance of the writer's desk or the philosopher's lectern. The merit of James's view of obligation is that its concreteness and perception of the unique warn us against the errors of casuistry. The word has acquired the sense of deviousness only because in the sixteenth and seventeenth centuries the religious casuists tried to foresee and rule on all conceivable predicaments in advance, in a "case book." On paper their solutions sounded

---

* More recently the distinguished publisher and writer William Jovanovich declared: "I've made up my mind not to complain about things if I'm not willing to try and reform them." (*New York Times*, December 26, 1980.)

contemptible. Moral dilemmas, like experience itself, can never be all told, as is shown by our innumerable books of casuistry—our novels. They lead us to admire or despise the same acts, doubtless because these only look the same, or because disparate moral truths are invoked.*

Imbued with the tragic view of life, James was certain that moral action often demands the sacrifice of self; duty is hard; it entails pain and sometimes death. For evil is real and must be fought, repeatedly, endlessly, at great risk. Not only is there no guaranty that one's moral decision is right; there is not even any assurance that the fulfilled claim will not turn from a good to an evil. James's knowledge of history brought enough instances to his mind to leave no doubt.**

To speak of moral decisions implies that human beings faced with a moral choice are free to do one thing or another. This privilege is denied by thinkers who believe in determinism. They may belong to either camp of James's opponents; they may be idealists or materialists. Both accept the fact of volition: you can raise your arm if so minded or refuse to if you choose. But that choice is not really yours nor is it decided on at the moment; everything in the past has been interlinked in a chain of causes and effects, of which your present act is but the latest link to the next. We see here the block universe of the Absolute or of blind matter, either of which locks all things in a tight network for all eternity.

The battle over free will is ancient and neither side can win, because satisfactory evidence on the subject can never be found. The definition of "free" is itself a source of disagreement. Those who say that man acts for a *reason* and not from a cause are told that reasons too are foregone. The thorny notion of cause and effect divides even scientists, though most prefer determinism as more convenient to work with. This state of affairs leaves belief in free will as itself something to choose or reject. James was brought to see this option by the French philosopher Renouvier and like him he chose free will, on moral grounds. He pointed out at the same time that the determinists also choose—the opposite. Let them have their way, says James, it then follows that 'you and I have been foredoomed to the error of continuing to believe in liberty. It is

---

* For a vivid contrast, take our modern scorn for the medieval trial by combat or by ordeal to determine guilt. In an age of belief in a divine providence that governs every event, it was a most moral and logical procedure, and our method of trusting in the doubtful word of mortal witnesses would have seemed reckless and absurd.

** A striking one has emerged since his death: the benevolent, liberal, highly moral treaty that Great Britain made after the Boer War saddled South Africa with a regime based on the continuance of race oppression.

fortunate for winding up the controversy that in every discussion with determinism this *argumentum ad hominem* can be its adversary's last word.'

But this debonair taunt and argument are not enough. In "The Dilemma of Determinism" James shows what follows his choosing and what he means by its moral grounds. Take any deplorable event (his example is a brutal murder, then recent) and see the difficulties that arise if a determinist regrets its occurrence. 'Are we to say, though it *couldn't be*, yet it *would have been* a better universe with something different from this Brockton murder in it? Calling a thing bad means that the thing ought not to be, that something else ought to be in its place. Determinism [thus] virtually defines the universe as a place in which what ought to be is impossible.' And 'what about the judgments of regret themselves? If they are wrong, other judgments, of approval presumably, ought to be in their place. But as they are necessitated, nothing else *can* be in their place; and the universe is what it was before—a place where what ought to be appears impossible. We have got one foot out of the pessimistic bog, but the other sinks all the deeper. We have rescued our actions from the bonds of evil, but our judgments are now held fast. When murders and treacheries cease to be sins, regrets are theoretic absurdities and errors.'

In other words, under determinism there can be no clear and consistent meaning in the terms moral life, moral judgment, moral action.

Freedom thus regained does not mean "deuces wild"—everybody free every instant to will what he or she pleases. There *are* networks of compulsion—instinct, habit, bodily makeup—and it is as clear to indeterminists as to others that one can predict fairly well what someone else will do when one knows the doer's character and the constraints he works under. Determinists seem to fear that the cosmos will fall apart if free will is permitted to exist. 'It is as likely (according to McTaggart) that a majority of Londoners will burn themselves tomorrow as that they will partake of food; as likely that I shall be hanged for brushing my hair as for committing murder, and so forth.' Clearly, the dispute itself is very free; it suffers no constraints from common sense. And in James's universe, as we know, things are not totally loose and disjointed. All kinds of unities and relations among things and among ideas coerce. The one permanent avenue of freedom, however narrow, is that 'in an activity situation, what happens is not pure repetition; novelty is perpetually entering the world.'*

One might have expected that James's large definition of duty and his

* The full technical argument is given in Chapter VI of *Essays in Radical Empiricism*, "The Experience of Activity," and again at greater length in the last five chapters of *Some Problems of Philosophy*.

solid reasoning in favor of free will would satisfy the moralist "in an age of science." But they do not, because James's maxim requires that an action for good shall be related to the entire present situation, which he says is new and cannot be judged by previous rule. Besides, morality is the *right* and James's precept looks like the expedient, the changeful. A moralist may admit the changing character of truth, because he has accommodated himself to "progress" in science, but this concession probably makes him all the more unbending about the "right." He is sure that the pragmatic imagination playing upon context and consequence can only make for uncertainty in human relations, set people adrift and helpless amid temptations, in short replace Right absolute by shifty Relativism.

In everyday life, relativism is a familiar adjustment to varied circumstances. It is the flexibility that enables us to understand how a large woman can sit in a small car or a tall man be too short to touch the ceiling. Conceptually, large and small, tall and short cannot apply to the same thing, but the mind fortunately disregards the rigidity of its own concepts and duly relates itself afresh to each purpose. Still, relativism at large has a bad name. There is an ancient tale of a traveler who lost his way and was given shelter by peasants in an isolated hut. As they watched over him they noticed that first he blew on his hands to warm them and later on his soup to cool it. Greatly frightened, in the night they killed him—a dangerous relativist.

In spite of all reasons and examples, the bugbear of relativism is so strong that the charge is often admitted by those against whom it is leveled—as if they lived indeed by a lower grade of ethics but could do no better. Nor is it noticed that the attack brings together two different sets of facts. One is the diversity of existing moralities, each of them absolute to some tribe or nation; the other the diversity of individuals within tribe or nation. When Europe discovered the new world in early modern times it was seen that peoples lived by different rules. Montaigne pointed out that cannibals were not immoral at home though they were abominable murderers in Europe. By the next century Pascal notes that even in Europe moral truth is one thing on this side of the Pyrenees and another on the other side.

This being the state of affairs from time immemorial, it seems rather egotistical to proclaim any one set of commandments the sole morality, and somewhat fanciful to speak of "indelible moral truths implanted in the human heart." Is it moral or immoral for the Mohammedan to have four wives? Or the African chief to have forty, each worth so many head of cattle? An otherwise worldly Pope recently declared that to look with lust upon one's wife was tantamount to adultery. If this is morality for Catholic believers, is it incumbent upon their neighbors on the same street? In many parts of the world, a gift of value for doing business, giving justice, or performing a helpful official act is only courtesy; in the West it is bribery, immoral and criminal. Murder in early medieval England was paid for by a fine—that is the original meaning of the word murder; later it was paid for by one's life; now, in this country, the penalty is a life sentence, and the meaning of that is seven years in jail. (If life is sacred, by the way, the Eskimos' law is the most moral: the murderer is told to go away and join another tribe.)

Like it or not, humanity is radically diverse. It is only by successive abstractions that we come to conceive of a single "human nature." If you take away one by one heredity, education, the social forces of the time and the place, you can arrive at the essential human being, the forked radish with four limbs, needing food and shelter, and who will surely die. But having defined him—or it, rather—no specimen of the kind can be found; like an average prescription for eyeglasses, the definition does not fit anybody.

It is with this point that we discern the second and different target of the foe of Relativism. Actual life is lived by a collection of somebodies who are no more alike among themselves than are the groups to which they belong. Ascetics and Lotharios, extroverts and introverts, the pensive and the gregarious, the poet and the athlete, and many other varieties and subvarieties breathe and move under the same customs and costume. If the moralist perforce tolerates different national and tribal ethics, why the indignation at internal diversity?—unless it is such as to disturb the peace, which is a political, not a moral matter. In advanced civilizations the idea occurs to very moral persons that different types of character are entitled to different treatment.* Since 1914, for example, we recognize the conscientious objector. As Shaw pointed out even earlier, to do unto others as we would have them do unto us may be unjust: they are not us and their tastes may differ. It is precisely the social behaviorist's mistake to suppose that the same lure and the same whip will work on all alike. It is also the error of the speculative reformer; Utopias are invariably made for one type.

The anti-relativist of today, with his high ideal of inflexibility, needs

* Contrary to common opinion, it is in governing and administering that rules should be rigid. If well drawn, they save time and preclude indecision. In the life of institutions good fixed rules are the prime producers of efficiency and fairness. To be sure, such grooves for sensible action must be redrawn as often as necessary. The complicated work of civilization today is chaotic because of antiquated procedures. Everybody "makes policy" and leaves action to chance or precedent. But this failure due to scarcity of administrative genius is aggravated by false notions of "flexibility," "compassion," and other forms of muddling inequity. In the struggle with the bureaucracies of business and government and education, what makes the public hate "the system" is that it is not a system.

to see that without the acceptance of different ethical norms we should never have got away from those of the caveman. The refinement of feeling and conduct that moralists pride themselves on comes from change, not fixity. The law of an eye for an eye, a tooth for a tooth gets outgrown, but at first its denial necessarily appears as a violation of principle. The fear that if one rule is altered, then "anything goes" is the fallacy of all or none. "Things" could hardly "go" farther than we see them doing at present, yet our age is extremely moralistic, if not moral; it lacks "morals" in the vulgar sense but it is full of moral scruples and it labors under innumerable codes aimed at giving equal treatment and protecting the helpless. We have come so far as to cherish even "endangered species"—small, unknown, speechless claimants such as the snail darter, which now arouse widespread moral passions.* Indeed, our moralism is one cause of the perpetual anger at society: why isn't it perfect?

In discussing the meaning of *pragmatic* earlier, it was shown that its supposed contrast with *moral* was a misusage. Since James's moral philosophy follows the pragmatic pattern of considering outcome as well as antecedents, it is clear that his relativism, far from being footloose, is held fast by as many demands and duties as the moral agent can think of. His relativism *relates*, which means many links to fixed points. It would be better named Relationism. In thus relating one's decision or conduct to several needs and ideals, one gives the observer as many chances to criticize, whereas the absolutist relates his act to only one thing: the fine abstraction that his God or his grandfather once uttered emphatically. In other words, James insists as usual that theory be given concrete, namable contents. *Those* are the "objective values" that moralists preach; what they rant about is but a formula, a form of words.**

The Jamesian obligation to connect the moral judgment not to 'this good or that good simply taken but to the universe with which they belong' also clears up the common confusion about morals in politics and foreign affairs. Lincoln's struggle with his followers' narrow absolutes may serve again to illustrate. In 1863, when summoned to change leaders in troubled Missouri, he gave a reply that should be read as a textbook case in political morality: "We are in Civil War. In such cases, there is always the main question; but in this case that question is a perplexing compound—Union and Slavery. It thus becomes a question

---

* UNESCO has adopted a Declaration of the Universal Rights of Animals, but it has not helped the goats of San Clemente Island, which were liquidated for endangering several species of plants and the habitats of other, less common creatures. Ah, principle! (*New York Times*, August 19, 1979.)

** Looking at the sum of moral ends achieved permits moralities and cultures—whatever anthropologists may say—to be adjudged better or worse.

not of two sides merely, but of at least four sides even among those who are for the Union. . . . Thus, those who are for the Union *with*, but not *without* slavery—those for it *with* or *without*, but prefer it *with*—and those for it *with* or *without*, but prefer it *without*. Among these again, is a subdivision of those who are for *immediate*, but not *gradual* extinction of slavery." To each party, each of the six choices was the only moral goal, as Lincoln knew: "all these shades of opinion and even more" are "entertained by honest and truthful men. . . . Yet all being for the Union, by reason of these differences each will prefer a different way of sustaining the Union. At once sincerity is questioned, and motives are assailed. Actual war coming, blood grows hot, and blood is spilled. Thought is forced from old channels into confusion. Deception breeds and thrives. Confidence dies, and universal suspicion reigns. Each man feels an impulse to kill his neighbor, lest he be first killed by him. Revenge and retaliation follow. And all this, as before said, may be among honest men only." It is as Dorothy Sayers told us: "the first thing a principle does is to kill somebody."

The statesman thus appears as something greater and wiser and more tragic than the image of "the man of principle," who follows the rule by rote and lets the heavens fall. He is actually one who says: "Gentlemen, I beg you to rise above principle" and who persuades the ever-warring factions of his party and his nation to give up their absolutes and be guided by his superior pragmatism. In the murderous battle of principles, he keeps in view the aim and end of moral action. The end is the test, justifying him when the story is over.

But even before, along the way, the end is the standard for judging which principle is to be followed and which must be waived. Hear Lincoln before his presidency, during the debates with Douglas: "Much as I hate slavery, I would consent to the extension of it rather than see the Union dissolved, just as I would consent to any great evil, to avoid a greater one. But when I go to Union saving, I must believe, at least, that the means I employ has some adaptation to the end. To my mind Nebraska has no such adaptation."

Here with the word *means* Lincoln introduces the last component of moral conduct: besides the variety of claims and ends to be weighed and combined, there is the mode of action to be chosen. No man was more dedicated to freedom than Lincoln, but as Chief Executive he restricted freedom of speech, suspended habeas corpus, and used the army to enforce the draft against rioters—with regret, no doubt, but without compunction.

Does this not mean that the end justifies the means? Yes. Horrors! No formula arouses greater indignation in moralists; it is the mark of the

Evil One; it is the reason given for regarding avowed pragmatists as suspect. Anybody who subscribes to the wicked notion in so many words has to explain himself, offer some excuse. Well, for a start, everyone without exception acts on it in ordinary life. For instance: a man takes a sharp knife and slashes a child. He is a brute, a monster. But just a minute! The man is Dr. X, about to remove the inflamed appendix. Immediately the cut in the abdomen becomes desirable, praiseworthy, highly paid. The end—and nothing else—has changed the moral standing of the violent act. The end justifies the means.

Again, we take that same child, we take all children, and, at an age when they are bundles of energy bent only on running and playing and shouting, we coop them up for four hours, six hours a day, and compel them without due process of law to struggle over tasks they do not care for and see no point in. It is called Education. We piously plead: the end justifies the means. Similarly, the ends justify monogamous marriage, imprisonment by law, monastic retreat from the world, and its seeming opposite: society itself. For as Rousseau and Freud pointed out, to live in society is a harsh, unnatural discipline justifiable only by the ends of relative safety for continuous toil.

The modern state particularly is built on the ends-and-means formula so hastily condemned. From compulsory vaccination and seizing land for public use to the control of a thousand normal acts—eating and drinking, teaching and learning, traveling and importing—our laws and administrative rules interfere hourly with harmless human purposes: we have not repealed Prohibition, only the Volstead Act.

We tell ourselves that the end—the common welfare—justifies. The same maxim is also blessed by one ancient church that guides the conduct of millions. It teaches, on the basis of scriptures even older than itself, that procreation in wedlock is the sole justification of sexual intercourse. The end apparently justifies the otherwise reprehensible means. On occasions less intimate and recurrent anybody would behave in the same spirit: we would not hesitate to knock down man, woman, or child to save any of them, on the instant, from being run over or burned to death by clothing on fire.

The bugbear phrase is evidently a misnomer for something else; and cleansing it of odium is not a merely verbal matter, for its present use is to distort the actual relation of ends to means and discredit pragmatic moral judgments. What needs to be embodied in a formula is a distinct situation, that in which *the means corrupt the end*—or destroy it, as would happen, for example, if one should drug a child to stop it from crying. Weak minds are often tempted to use such means, which in effect covertly substitute one end for another; the true end is a child at peace and not crying; the false is a child merely silenced by a dose of poison.

The habit of thinking about means-and-ends in linked form has intellectual as well as moral consequences. It helps, for instance, to settle the interminable debate about human equality, an issue that affects moral feeling and conduct. Though congenial to modern man since 1776, the statement that all men are equal has been disputed from the beginning. It has seemed easy to disprove: A is not equal to B in strength, wits, moral worth. Again, the concept "equal" implies interchangeable. If $3 + 2 = 5$, then wherever 5 occurs we can substitute $3 + 2$. But any three men joined to any other two will not, in nature or society, replace five other men.

Nobody, in fact, has ever supposed men to be equal in that sense. The counter-suggestion is then offered that the meaning is: all human souls are equal in the sight of God. But this hope, too, presents difficulties. God consigns one soul to eternal perdition, another to bliss, and moreover is said to prefer a repentant sinner to the steadily good. If it is only at the outset, "in principle," that souls are equal, then earthly inequalities can be rationalized in the same way: we all start equal as citizens, equal before the law, and native gifts or lacks produce the later inequalities we see.

Next comes the argument that all are equal in their humanity, qualitatively equal through their basic needs, fundamental traits, and ultimate fate. But as was suggested earlier, that is an abstraction which satisfies only the distant observer, not the claimant to some concrete good. If anything has to do with quantity and only quantity, it is the property of being equal. Thus when we say "equally tall" we assert a quantitative sameness, but only in one respect; and this does not satisfy the ideal of all men *thoroughly* equal to one another.

Yet by the same reasoning, to measure human differences in height, wealth, moral strength, or intellectual achievement shows *in*equality, again in the single feature chosen. Beyond such limited comparisons all is biased opinion. Who shall say whether an experienced guide through the Canadian north woods is or is not the equal of a brilliant head nurse in a Chicago hospital and of a ranking physicist in the Academy of Science? Even if some elaborate scheme of points were devised for each human attribute, the total would be meaningless, because traits are not static possessions and the measurement would be time-bound. Courage, for example, may lie dormant till fire or flood brings it out. The only tenable conclusion is: human beings concretely taken are neither equal nor unequal, they are incommensurable.

It follows that the idea of human equality is a social assumption made for its desirable consequences. The first example of that assumption—which is also a social necessity—is the relation of hosts and guests. A sociable evening run on lines of inequality is hard to imagine. Equal treatment at the festive board is what makes it festive. The individuals continue to differ—feed them all arsenic sandwiches and only some will die. But you feed them, talk to them, handshake them as equals without a second thought.

There has in fact always been equality in the world. In armies, clans, families, as today within offices or hierarchies, those of the same rank form enclaves of equality. Under the most rigid caste system, the members of each caste or class were and acted as equals among themselves, or life would have been unbearable. So true is this that in monarchies the king is pitied because he has no equals. He is isolated; nobody goes up to him and says, "See here!"

Modern egalitarian theory is thus a pragmatic moral assumption, which has largely created what it hoped for. It replaces by fiat the separate equalities of birth, fighting ability, religion, or whatever. The new assumption depends on the existence of a fairly stable society in which the principle of "careers open to talent" allows individual ability to find its role. This free-for-all is not possible in times of disorder—for instance in the late Roman Empire, when the fighting man was at a premium and he necessarily became the overlord protecting the serfs who grew the food. But once the nation-state has been formed and is at peace, it becomes evident that in three or four generations the hereditary ranks no longer earn their privilege, from idleness or enfeebled powers. Equality then gives a greater yield of competence, it enlarges the social sphere of each, while it also satisfies the intuitive sense of justice.


To speak of moral intuition and believe in free will on moral grounds argues the valuing of belief itself as a human activity. To accept equality or any other "moral truth" for its good consequences is an act of faith and therefore a risk. But as early as the 1870s and 80s, when James was discussing these questions, faith had become a privative concept which meant: unscientific, illusory, antiquated nonsense, probably of religious origin. Those who took this attitude generally called themselves Positivists, after the name given by Auguste Comte to his philosophy of knowledge. In effect, it admitted as knowledge only what science had certified—positive(ly) knowledge. Toward everything else these minds were skeptical; toward religion specifically, or anything called spiritual, they declared themselves "agnostic"—Huxley's bad coinage for one who says: "I don't know."*

The purpose embodied in this then new word is important; it was to teach the lesson of withholding belief. The agnostic does not deny divinity like the atheist; he waits for evidence one way or the other. Such a position sounds worthy beyond cavil, but its balancing act between Yea and Nay rarely proves stable. Most positivists were assertive materialists, and James found himself obliged to meet their hidden metaphysics head on. 'Science, these positivists say, has proved that personality, so far from being an elementary force in nature, is but a passive resultant of the really elementary forces, physical, chemical, physiological, and psycho-physical, which are all impersonal and general in character. Nothing individual accomplishes anything in the universe save insofar as it obeys and exemplifies some universal law.' Thus—and this was the analogy that Taine made famous in 1864 in the preface to his *History of English Literature*—"Vice and virtue are products like vitriol and sugar." James shows that the argument rests on the genetic fallacy. Treating moral facts like so many chemicals is 'as if the same breath which should succeed in explaining their origin would simultaneously explain away their significance.' And he adds that he feels 'impatience at the somewhat ridiculous swagger of the program, in view of what the authors are actually able to perform.'

Besides, this reductivism works both ways. If 'William's religious melancholy is due to bad digestion, scientific theories are organically conditioned just as much as religious emotions are.' James called such interpretations "medical materialism" and saw in it sheer intellectual arrogance. He resented the trick that transformed useful discoveries (his own included) about the dependence of mental upon bodily states into a gratuitous identification of the two. It is a permanent temptation, as the poet and scholar Joy Gresham, who became Mrs. C. S. Lewis, confessed about her youthful views: "'Men,' I said, 'are only apes. Love, art, altruism are only sex. The universe is only matter. Matter is only energy. I forget what I said energy was only.'"

By the time one does get to energy, amid the elementary particles of physics, which exist for us only as traces on film and which are identical within their kinds, it is evident that something must be added to

---

* The word is badly formed, because *gnosis* in Greek means "seeking to know, inquiry," and secondarily "wisdom"; with the privative prefix *a* it means the absence or refusal of those things. As for the Latin *agnosco*, which Huxley once used as his rejoinder to belief, it means not: "I do not know," but: "I recognize, I know it well." Rarely have these examples of unintended irony been surpassed.

them before they can become even the ape that we say we are.* Yet when one makes this simple reflection one is suspected of "smuggling" something illicit into the universe. The word "mysticism" is murmured and one is accused of being "against science," or just too stupid to see how, for the enlightened, science has become "a way of life."

Science can be no such thing, since it begins by excluding what it cannot measure or classify. No scientist has ever chosen a wife or bought a house by scientific methods, nor does he laugh or applaud a musical work on scientific grounds. Two-thirds of his life is totally remote from science. To speak of belief, free will, or faith of any kind as "smuggled in" would mean that natural science offered a complete account of experience. What it offers—too readily—is the promise to do so in future, coupled with the command to sit and wait. Huxley, again, gave the formula: "To rest in comfortable illusion when scientific truth is conceivably within reach is to desecrate oneself and the universe." Here it is the idea of illusion that is smuggled in. As for the feat of desecrating the universe, it seems a great temptation; I can imagine an amateur Satan taking the dare by indulging in a perfect orgy of belief.

Some writers of our time, though eager to vindicate the moral life, have accepted the Huxleyan premise that science legitimately occupies all the land, but with the hope that it might be induced to lease some untilled portion for non-scientific use. When James met the claim of total ownership he took a different and intellectually sounder line. The opportunity was given him by a statement in which the English mathematician W. K. Clifford, who was also James's friend and fellow psychologist, summed up the new orthodoxy: believe nothing without sufficient evidence—it is a sin: '"Whoso would deserve well of his fellows in this matter will guard the purity of his belief with a very fanaticism of jealous care.... If a belief has been accepted on insufficient evidence (even though the belief be true, as Clifford on the same page explains) the pleasure is a stolen one. It is sinful because it is stolen in defiance of our duty to mankind.... It is wrong, always, everywhere, and for everyone to believe anything upon insufficient evidence."'

On this text James wrote a closely reasoned essay which he called "The Will to Believe." The title has passed into common usage with (as usual) the erroneous meaning of "believe what you please." Seeing this, James regretted the phrase and thought he should have said "the right

---

* It is noteworthy that when men of science forgather periodically to observe some anniversary—Newton's or Darwin's or Einstein's—they profess to celebrate "great minds," who contributed *original* thoughts (i.e., novelty) to the world. The speeches do not refer to them as "chemical machines" as do some of the textbooks written by those same speech makers.

to believe." In fact, the demonstration is about the right *and* the will to believe, each restricted to precisely stated conditions.

Clifford's preachment 'with somewhat too much robustious pathos in the voice' is self-refuting on the face of it. Clifford, like everybody else, believed thousands of things on little or no evidence—for example, whatever he knew, or thought he knew, about his family and friends; and he acted on faith whenever he said with no quiver of doubt: "I'll see you next Monday."

It is such facts of belief and their source in experience that James begins by examining. 'We find ourselves believing, we hardly know how or why. We all of us believe in molecules and the conservation of energy, in democracy and necessary progress, in Protestant Christianity and the duty of fighting for "the doctrine of the immortal Monroe"—all for no reasons worthy of the name. We see into these matters with not more inner clearness, and probably with much less, than any disbeliever in them might possess. His unconventionality would probably have some grounds to show for its conclusions; but for us, not insight, but the prestige of the opinions, is what makes the spark shoot from them that lights up our sleeping magazines of faith. Our faith is faith in someone else's faith, and in the greatest matters this is most the case. Our belief in truth itself is that there is a truth and that our minds and it are made for each other.'

As we learned earlier, our thoughts are energized by feelings of all kinds, and it is the varied origins, character, and intensity of feeling that pose the problem of which ideas to trust. 'Our next duty, having recognized this mixed-up state of affairs, is to ask whether it be simply reprehensible and pathological, or whether, on the contrary, we must treat it as a normal element in making up our minds.'

To help settle the question James defines a few terms. Call *hypothesis* anything proposed to our belief and see if it seems to us *live* or *dead*. A live hypothesis is one that the individual finds believable. To an atheist, the reincarnation of souls is not a live hypothesis, but "medical materialism" might be. He could in the end reject it, but it was not "unthinkable" like the other. If one thinks one might take action there is "liveness" in the hypothesis: 'there is some believing tendency wherever there is willingness to act at all.' ("Act" here would include rearranging one's other opinions and altering one's vocabulary.)

The choice between hypotheses James calls an option and he classifies options as living or dead, forced or avoidable, momentous or trivial. What he goes on to state applies only to an option that is forced, living, and momentous. It is *only* within these narrow limits and *only* when no empirical evidence is to be had, that James finds the right and the will to believe legitimate. Belief under these conditions is no frolic when teacher's back is turned; it has a reason to exist, which is: that *not* deciding is a form of decision. Thus for most people free will is a tenable idea—it is live, which makes the option living, and it is certainly not trivial; it is forced, because there is no third possibility. So in the absence of evidence one has the right to believe in free will, for not deciding would be to decide against it.

These safeguards against credulity have been so regularly overlooked in discussions of James's essay that they bear restating in his own words:* 'Our passional nature not only may, but must, decide an option between propositions, whenever it is a genuine option that cannot by its nature be decided on intellectual grounds; for to say under such circumstances, "Do not decide but leave the question open," is itself a passional decision and is attended with the same risk of losing the truth.'

So much for the right to believe. The will to do so is a related subject, but its limiting conditions are different. First, willing is not mere wishing or "velleity," as it is called. "I wish I were a millionaire" and "Everybody falls in love with me" are not forms of the will to believe; they are commonplace fantasies. Not the superficial wish but the deep-seated will is a strenuous expression of the self. When Walter Scott, caught as partner in the bankruptcy of his publishing firm, decided for his honor to pay all its debts by writing novels, essays, biographies indefatigably, he noted in his journal: "I must not doubt. To doubt is to lose." That resolve was his will to believe—in his own powers, in his eventual success.

But belief is a far from simple thing. One often hears the strong beliefs of others explained away: "He thinks so because he wants to so much." But try, yourself, to believe that you are younger, or a better dancer, than you actually are; the probability is that you cannot, no matter how much you want to. Peter the apostle wanted to walk on the waters of the stormy lake; his life depended on it, but he could not will it. The test of willing, as usual, is action. Every great artist starts out unknown, uncalled for, but possessed of a belief in himself and of the will to make it true. His periods of discouragement show that it is will which is at work in periods of production.

These facts define the situation in which the will to believe is legiti-

* One exception must be noted: Edwin L. Clarke, in a modest textbook entitled *The Art of Straight Thinking* (New York, 1929), devotes half a page to explaining that James carefully limits the domain in which belief without evidence has its rights. Professor Clarke may have been annoyed by the ubiquitous will to misunderstand on the part of other scholars.

mate and, what is more, "creative": 'there are cases where a fact cannot come at all unless a preliminary faith exists in its coming. And where faith in a fact can help create the fact, that would be an insane logic which would say that faith running ahead of scientific evidence is "the lowest kind of immorality." Yet such is the logic by which our scientific absolutists pretend to regulate our lives!' James then gives a physical example to make vivid a type of predicament that one meets more often in social or emotional life: 'Suppose that you are climbing a mountain, and have worked yourself into a position from which the only escape is a terrible leap. Have faith that you can successfully make it, and your feet are nerved to its accomplishment. But mistrust yourself, and think of all the sweet things you have heard scientists say of *maybes*, and you will hesitate so long that, at last, all unstrung and trembling, and launching yourself in a moment of despair, you roll into the abyss.'

Life being full of "maybes," it forces every conscious being to act a thousand times on the strength of the will to believe. The will functions without our knowing it as such, or appreciating the philosophic and psychological reasons for its reality, as against the unlifelike view of the Cliffords and the Huxleys. But any initial doubt or faith has the aspect that everyone can prove himself right: 'Refuse to believe, and you shall indeed be right, for you shall irretrievably perish. But believe, and again you shall be right, for you shall save yourself. You make one or the other of two possible universes true by your trust or mistrust—both universes having been only *maybes* in this particular, before you con- tributed your act.'*

One very ordinary situation in which belief contributes to making itself true is that in which trust, candor, courtesy, or love produces the same pleasant attitudes in return. And so with their opposites; the grouchy and suspicious generally find their worst expectations come true. In bodily matters, the placebo effect, long used by physicians, is of the same kind; give a sugar pill to a patient with the will to cure himself and he may do as well as the one who is truly drugged. This peculiarity of the body-mind, though not uniform in its action, is so noticeable that it has inspired more than one cult of self-help: to double your energy and succeed in all things, repeat three cheerful slogans before break- fast. That is a caricature of the will to believe, but caricature implies a real original.

'Our willing nature,' as James calls it, is normally restrained; it needs favoring conditions before it can act to our benefit. The common belief

* Thanks to the currency of the phrase "self-fulfilling prophecy," the public is now familiar with the workings of the negative will: predict that your wedding will not take place and make it so by not showing up for it.

of those around us is one enabling cause. A vivid imagination is another, but it must summon emotional force behind its image and keep it at the forefront of consciousness. The will to believe is the will to attend; that is why we say of genius that it is obsessed. As Hemingway puts it somewhere: "It was not just something he believed. It was his belief."

The distinction points to a generally neglected fact—the gradations of belief, the varying quality of our several beliefs. Think of them in this light and the shadings appear indeed infinite. We believe the broadcast report of a catastrophe; we believe more strongly when the details are told in the next day's paper; we believe to the full when not merely a witness but a friend saw it happen.

There is even a step beyond, which is faith, or belief unconscious of itself. One senses the difference between believing *that* something exists and believing in the thing itself. People are chock-full of beliefs, but life is lived on faith—a buried assumption on which one acts; for example, that the shopkeeper will give you change for your ten-dollar bill and not say it was a five, as he could safely do if he were in *bad faith*. When any deep trust has to be put into words we discover that belief— its statement—is the interruption of faith. One used to have unthinking faith in the safety of the streets; now one at best *believes* that the stranger coming along will not assault one. Common speech records the shifting emphasis when it uses "I believe so" to mean "I am not sure."

If in order to leap the mountain chasm it was necessary to overcome "The fear that kills," it is no less important to remember the poet's next line: "And hope unwilling to be fed." For despite the derivation of the word, it is a mistake to suppose that everybody wants to believe what is agreeable.* Many prefer the worst; to them news or ideas feel true because they are gloomy. When Freud said that science was the conquest of will over the pleasure principle, he evidently felt that the truths of science robbed him of pleasure, and rejoiced. But it is just as reasonable to say that scientific work is the expression of man's free will invading the realm of necessity, in which case science is one form of the pursuit of happiness.

These opposed views are doubtless never to be reconciled, but they illustrate a main contradiction of our century. The age cries out for all the freedoms—the free will of individual self-determination, the free choice of social and cultural pluralism, the right to free beliefs and utterance, the free access to good things that the practice of equality

---

* "Belief" seems to have a two-pronged etymology: be-lief means be-glad, as in "I'd just as lief," lief being related to love; belief is also connected with leave in the sense of allow. Our belief is thus what we should be glad to think when it is allowable to do so: exactly James's position.

affords. But it also believes in the material, medical, subpsychical determinism of all acts and thoughts, and it turns its back upon risk, the
necessary companion of free will as well as of the right and will to
believe. So while half our energy goes to freeing, the other half is spent
on trying to make safe, to control, to predetermine by means akin to the
behaviorist's conditioning or the polltaker's way of freezing the future.
Our worship of science springs from the same passion for certainty
(plus the hold it gives on others' opinions) rather than from intellectual
pleasure and admiration. Similarly, because they are risky and disturbing, heroism and ambition are thought wrong and ridiculous; tests, statistics, diets, charts tell everybody, "This is what you ought to be—
indeed, whether you know it or not, this is what you are." And with that
denial of freedom and risk, anxious guilt replaces the sense of accomplishment.

What the world has a right to expect of moral philosophers is a nice
question. Some write doctrine, others preach. Of these last, some practice what they preach—it sets an encouraging example, although as Dr.
Johnson pointed out, the drunkard who warns against intemperance has
a great argument in himself. James, with his insistence on action as the
proper end of thought and a guaranty against sentimentalism, practiced
his morality of risk and faith in both private and public life. He showed
none of the common fear of being duped by strange new ideas or compromised by association with the odd fish that promoted them.* When
he took part in movements of protest and reform, he did not merely
huddle in indignation with his kind, but remained critical and practical,
and on several occasions stood alone with his belief. Were he alive
today, he would not come under the stricture uttered by the French
critic and novelist Romain Gary: "American liberals are great. They've
got a sense of injustice bigger than anyone else, but not much of a sense
of justice—that is, they don't want to face the consequences."
 Among the consequences, a reformer must reckon the effect of his
public acts on his private circle. James was a Cambridge academic and
university life predisposes to a superior kind of conformity, whether the
reigning prejudice be diehard or radical. But James believed that the
way to create the better of the two universes which results from our
moral choice is to begin close to home, where one knows the options
intimately, and, within the home circle, face friends' disapproval rather
than that of one's own conscience.

* Henry James thought William showed very poor taste in his choice of associates.
(Notes of a Son and Brother, pp. 323-28.)

This is what happened when the issue of licensing physicians came before the Massachusetts legislature and James was asked to testify; he spoke against the bill. He pointed out that medical knowledge was far from complete and changing rapidly; new ideas should get a hearing and be tested no matter whom they came from. He was ever suspicious of professional bodies and their prejudgment, which so often shuts out experience;* and he considered regulative laws 'mere abstract paper thunder, under which every ignorance and abuse can still go on.'

The increasing disenchantment with the professions in our time has proved James right on both counts. Complaints of abuses and incompetence have been directed from many sides not only against doctors and lawyers, but against licensed practitioners in general and schoolteachers in particular. With them it is not merely individual ignorance that is chargeable, but institutionalized obscurantism in the licensing requirements themselves. During the same period we have allowed many kinds of psychologists, counselors, and therapists to perform unlicensed, on the strength of their training and degrees, which is what James wanted the whole field kept open for.

His testimony scandalized his colleagues. He was said to have been gulled by the faith healers, because he had publicly recognized the natural basis of their occasional success. But he had equally publicly warned against their claims and their hocus-pocus. Besides, he rightly thought the patent-medicine racket much more dangerous. In any event, he took no adolescent pleasure in defiance and he was sorry to forfeit the esteem of the medical and other supporters of licensing. 'I never did anything that required as much moral courage in my life.'

Not long before, as chief speaker at the commemoration of Robert Gould Shaw, the young Civil War hero in command of the first black Massachusetts regiment, James had of course paid tribute to soldierly bravery; but he had in closing reminded the audience of the moral courage Shaw had displayed in giving up 'his warm commission in the glorious Second to head your dubious fortunes, Negroes of the Fifty-Fourth. That lonely kind of courage (civic courage, as we call it in times of peace) is the kind of valor to which the monuments of nations should most of all be reared. Of five hundred of us who could storm a battery side by side with others, perhaps not one would be found ready to risk his worldly fortunes all alone in resisting an enthroned abuse.'

---

* He may have had in mind what happened to young Dr. Oliver Wendell Holmes when he asserted the contagiousness of puerperal fever and its cause. This battle took place in Boston at the same time as Semmelweiss was waging his on the same subject in Vienna—1843-44. The outcome was not so tragic for Holmes as for Semmelweiss; but twenty years after his first paper, Holmes was still being attacked: he had said that the doctor's filthy hands and instruments killed the women after childbirth. (O. W. Holmes, *Medical Essays*, 3rd ed., Boston, 1897, pp. 103 ff.)

James knew that a nation always needs to be saved from its internal enemies. 'The civic genius of the people does the saving day by day, by acts without external picturesqueness.' And in the licensing issue as well as more "picturesque" ones, James was faithful to his idea of day-to-day moral affirmation. He joked about it to J. J. Chapman: 'Says I to myself, Shall civic virtue be confined entirely to Zola, J. J. C., and Colonel Picquart?' The allusion is to the heroes of the Dreyfus Affair, which moved James to many comments in his letters and digressions in his talks to students. The anti-semitism and chauvinist nationalism of half the French people were abhorrent to him. He saw in them the same bulldozer spirit that he loathed in the methods of the American business barons with their trusts and cartels.

This spectacle abroad and at home prompted an outburst to a friend that has often been quoted and anthologized. In it James declares himself 'against bigness and greatness in all their forms, and with the invisible molecular moral forces that work from individual to individual, stealing in through the crannies of the world like so many soft rootlets, or like the capillary oozing of water, and yet rending the hardest monuments of man's pride, if you give them time. The bigger the unit you deal with, the hollower, the more brutal, the more mendacious is the life displayed. So I am against all big organizations as such, national ones first and foremost; against all big success and big results; and in favor of the eternal forces of truth which always work in the individual and immediately unsuccessful way, under-dogs always, till history comes, after they are long dead, and puts them on top.'

He immediately adds: 'You need take no notice of these ebullitions of spleen,' probably aware that the unqualified phrasing of his rejections (e.g., "greatness") might mislead. But the tenor represents him fairly. In the Dreyfus case, the French army was the big unit where life was hollow and mendacious, and the new tag with which its supporters derided their opponents—les intellectuels—James adopted for himself and helped to popularize. He thought it an excellent name for the party he felt he belonged to. Intellect was the natural antagonist of blind bigness. But it must remain intellect taking part in public policy, not that very different thing, intellectuals taken in tow by partisanship. This apparently easy descent has been the choice of tens of thousands throughout the western world during the last half century, inducing them to love and forgive one set of police states if colored red, and hate another set, indistinguishable in their acts.

Between 1890 and 1910, the last decades of his life, James had—and took—more than one opportunity to show how he conceived civic duty, moral and intellectual. In rapid succession, the Venezuela crisis with England, the Spanish-American War, the Peace Movement, the annex-

ation of the Philippines, and the Roosevelt doctrine of the big stick presented thoughtful Americans with the choice of imperialism versus the
rights of small nations, war versus diplomacy and arbitration. On the
Venezuela affair, which had set off 'a fighting mob hysteria,' James
wrote a long letter to his congressman which was reproduced in the
Congressional Record, and he replied to Roosevelt in The Harvard
Crimson. To his friend of many years, E. L. Godkin, the editor of The
Nation, he outlined a policy that he hoped Godkin would adopt for the
'long, long campaign of education' that was needed. He repeated his
proposed diplomacy to his English friends; otherwise 'our countries will
soon be soaked in each other's gore. You will be disembowelling me
and Hodgson cleaving Lodge's skull.'

A little later, to Henry, also in England, he explained that the burst of
Anglophobia had subsided but that 'the really bad thing here is the silly
wave that has gone over the public mind—protection humbug, silver,
jingoism, etc. It is a case of mob psychology.' The wave rose higher in
the few months preceding the outbreak of war with Spain. It was then
that James "gave his class at the Jefferson Laboratory a speech concluding with a sentence they never forgot: 'Don't yelp with the pack!'"*

From then on, events kept James busy speaking and writing against
the new-born American imperialism. In the Boston Transcript, the New
York Evening Post, the Springfield (Mass.) Daily Republican, The Harvard Crimson, he published within less than five years a variety of
statements, letters, and translations from foreign witnesses in and about
the Philippines, together with an open letter to Roosevelt on the Strenuous Life in its application to international affairs. Learning of "Hell-
roaring Jake Smith's" policy in the Philippines—the destruction of entire villages, the shooting of prisoners, the use of dum-dum bullets, the
torture of civilians by the "water-cure"—in short, atrocity for atrocity
against the native insurgents and their leader Aguinaldo, James kept up
his polemic on the theme: "The infamy and iniquity of a war of conquest must stop."** He rallied and described public sentiment in New
England for the benefit of congressmen at a time when the anti-imperialist press seems to have been stunned into silence, and he explained
the imperialists to themselves: they were intoxicated with power and
bigness. But 'the worst of our imperialists is that they do not themselves
know where sincerity ends and insincerity begins. Their state of con-

* Charles Eliot Norton, James's friend and colleague in art history, speaking about the
same time, advised his students to consider carefully whether they served their country
by enlisting. He was abused, his dismissal demanded, and his resignation accepted.
** Smith (Brigadier-General Jacob) and other officers were finally court-martialed in
1902 for "conduct prejudicial to good order and military discipline." Found guilty and
publicly reprimanded by President Roosevelt, Smith was forced into early retirement.

sciousness is so new, so mixed of primitively human passions and, in political circles, of calculations; so at variance with their former mental habits; and so empty of definite data and contents that they face various ways at once. One reads the President's speech as if the very words were squinting on the page.'

Some of James's utterances on these topics were reprinted in the bulletin of the Anti-Imperialist League of New England, in which he began to take an interest in 1902. He lent his aid and became an officer, although he was 'saddened by the sight of what I knew already, that when you get a lot of prime idealists together they don't show up as strong as an equal lot of practical men.' The same conclusion applied to the Peace Movement. It had begun in the nineties, aided by the wealth of Nobel and Carnegie—cordite and steel—and graced by the patronage of the mild Tsar Nicholas II in 1899, but made intense and international by the repeated crises in four of the five continents. The threats, whether Teddy Roosevelt's or William II's, heightened the fear bred by industrial armaments and "the nation in arms," which were sure to replace the horse-mounted professional fighter waving a saber and clad in red and gold. In October 1904, a Universal Peace Congress was held in Boston and James addressed its opening banquet.* He had begun a systematic study of the psychology of the soldier and the theory and realities of war, and his remarks to the panelists were mainly a warning about 'the strength of our enemy, the rooted bellicosity of human nature.'

This fact forms the starting point of the two complementary essays "The Energies of Men" and "The Moral Equivalent of War." The title of the second is now famous in the Jamesian way, that is, widely used without understanding. It is the curse of the half-educated to seize upon something interesting and novel—a phrase, a title, an observation—and without further look or caution to fabricate out of their resources what *they* would make it mean. The White House under President Carter made a slogan of the Moral Equivalent at the beginning of the oil embargo that threatened our energy supply. Investigative reporters repeated the phrase without a second thought, and now it serves as a synonym for economizing fuel and power. What the voice from the White House hoped to say was that such self-restraint recalled the privations of wartime, which ought to be accepted with civilian fortitude. This meaning was the exact opposite of James's proposal, whose intention was the release of aggression through the useful *expenditure* of energy.**

* The other speakers were Booker T. Washington and Bliss Perry.
** The only public man I have heard using the phrase correctly is Senator Daniel Patrick Moynihan of New York.

James's subject is nevertheless what the title literally says: an equivalent of war that shall be moral, in the double sense of ethical and of virtual, as in "a moral victory," "a moral certainty." As he had told the peaceful banqueteers, to cry for peace was futile. The historical fact is that 'our actual civilization, good and bad, has had past wars for its determining condition.' Besides, though man 'lives by habit, what he lives for is thrills and excitements. The only relief from Habit's tediousness is periodical excitement,' which up to now war has helped to provide. Indeed, war is one of the humanities; it is an art and it has produced art, as Ruskin had shown; the Parthenon is a war memorial.

James no doubt remembered the frenzy of joining up in the North at the beginning of the Civil War, when he was nineteen. His conclusion therefore was: 'We do ill to talk much of universal peace or of a general disarmament. We must go in for preventive medicine, not for radical cure. Put peace-men in power; educate the editors and statesmen to responsiblity.' ("Editors" was an allusion to the raucous journalism that had precipitated the Spanish-American War.) But 'let the general possibility of war be left open, in Heaven's name, for the imagination to dally with,' and then: 'foster rival excitements and invent new outlets for heroic energy.'

Anyone who witnessed student uprisings here or abroad in the mid-1960s will recall how much joy there was in the banding together, the break-ins and sit-ins, the destruction of premises, and the imprisoning and humiliation of "enemies." On many a campus, after the excitement had quieted down, one could hear the once united students and instructors repeat that they had never felt so alive—"never had the university had such a common purpose."

Hence the aptness of James's sober opening: 'The war against war is going to be no holiday excursion or camping party.' Then follow some vivid pages on the tradition and literature of war since Homer ('War is the romance of history') and a discussion of contemporary pacifist arguments. But: 'So long as anti-militarists propose no substitute for war's disciplinary function, no *moral equivalent* of war, analogous—one might say—to the mechanical equivalent of heat, so long they fail to realize the full inwardness of the situation.' Utopias require *existing* motives, so James broaches his own: 'I devoutly believe in the reign of peace and in the gradual advent of some sort of socialistic equilibrium. The fatalistic view of the war function is to me nonsense, for I know that war-making is due to definite motives, and when the science of destruction vies with the sciences of production, I see that war becomes absurd and impossible from its own monstrosity.'

That is the spot at which we are still stuck in the 1980s, still without the emotional detergent that James proposed: 'a conscription of the whole youthful population to form for a certain number of years a part of the army enlisted against Nature';* in other words, constructive effort in a militant mood. The idea anticipates the Civilian Conservation Corps of the New Deal and the later Peace Corps. It is practicable so far as mustering and organizing "the troops" is concerned, though it would need highly capable administrators to keep the service from turning into a shambles and a bore.

Whether it would discharge aggression cannot be known till it is tried. For the passion at work is not a simple one; it is the urge to-kill-or-be-killed—not the popular "death wish," but the angry resolve not to live rather than accept the intolerable thing, l'infâme. It is the stern opposite of "Better Red than dead," a spineless prudence James would have abhorred: 'Anyone is ready to be savage in some cause. The difference between the good man and the bad man lies in the choice of the cause.'

So war, for James, is not to be "outlawed," which is a contradiction in terms—policing is making war—and the recourse to war must be expected to continue as long as organized evil, outrage, oppression, terrorism themselves continue; the world today is a demonstration of the need of war. What a moral equivalent is designed to abate is the stupid, the vainglorious, the hot-headed, and the "what fun" impulse to fight. With this sense of the complex reality, James was not likely to agree with the suggestion of his fellow-philosopher, Morris Cohen, that a sufficient moral equivalent might be—baseball. Professional sports today would come nearer the mark when they lead (as they frequently do all over the world) to postludic bloodshed among the contestants, spectators, referees, and police. But this edifying outlet provides no communal life and discipline.

More to the point, James saw in his proposal some beneficial by-products, to one of which he attached great importance: 'That so many men, by mere accidents of birth and opportunity, should have a life of nothing else but toil and pain and harshness and inferiority, is capable of arousing indignation in reflective minds. This injustice would tend to be evened out; no one would remain blind, as the luxurious classes are now blind, to man's relation to the globe he lives on and to the permanently sour and hard foundations of his higher life.'

Another "balancing factor," which James often referred to as "social-

---

* This statement has been taken by my friend René Dubos as meaning that "James perceived Nature as a villain," whereas "she" is a mother who deserves our loving care. (The Wooing of Earth, New York, 1980, p. 77.) This objection based on environmentalist sentiment misses the point. James used the personification of Nature, like the word army, as a shorthand way of indicating the kind of hard work he had in mind: digging a ditch for irrigation, clearing underbrush in the forestry service, and the like. Are these acts of hostility toward "nature" or of tenderness toward fruits and trees?

ism," was what we know as welfare legislation. He remembered his father's sympathy with the socialism of Fourier and the "colonies of equals" it had generated, mostly in this country. But what seemed more promising for 'a better equilibrium' in the distribution of wealth was the social security measures of Bismarck in Germany, soon to be imitated by the Liberal party in England, and accompanied by the acceptance of trade unions. James thought of himself as a liberal, but in quotation marks and with the reservation that 'the chronic fault of liberalism is its lack of speed and passion.' And though he argued for the economic improvement of the masses in response to the growing moral sense of the privileged, he doubted whether it would make 'any *vital* difference on a large scale to the lives of our descendants.' The human condition would always remain 'the marriage of some ideal with fidelity, courage, endurance, with some man's or woman's pains.'*

Sober thoughts did not prevent action. On various domestic issues, moral and political, James continued outspoken. At the age of twenty-seven he had reviewed together Mill's book on *The Subjection of Women* and an attack on feminism by a well-known American clergyman named Bushnell. James made short work of Bushnell's pieties about womanhood and gave his whole mind to the strong and weak points of Mill's 'smashing projectile.' He was among those who 'fully sympathize with his practical aims,' and he offered only two criticisms of the argument—one is that since a similar education could equalize capabilities in the sexes, Mill need not try to belittle their present disparity. The other is that while presenting an attractive picture of equal partners in marriage, Mill does not take up its 'necessary corollaries—divorce at will with all the tremendous changes such divorce must entail upon the relation of children to society.' In mature life James favored the extension of democratic rights to all who were denied them.** In a long letter, widely reprinted, he raised his voice against "the lynching epidemic." He joined in the demand for the control but not the outlawing of vivisection and in the propaganda for temperance. On this subject James as usual had unusual things to say: 'Sobriety diminishes, discriminates, and says no: drunkenness expands, unites, and

---

* A critic once seized on this psychological observation to assert that James was blind to the effects of material deprivation on the majority of men. (M. C. Otto, "On a Certain Blindness in William James," *Ethics*, April 1943, pp. 184–191.) James's words in the preceding paragraphs and in half-a-dozen other places disprove the charge; and now that unionization and the welfare state have vastly reduced poverty, the evidence is again on James's side that physical well-being is not equatable with contentment. The source of the "vital difference" between happy and unhappy lives lies elsewhere.

**He even expressed mingled wonder and sympathy—it was all he could do—about a couple who were braving jail to affirm the right to print dirty words in their little magazine, *The Voice*. (Perry, *op cit.*, II, 275.)

says Yes. It is in fact the great exciter of the *Yes* function in man. It brings its votary from the chill periphery of things to the radiant core. It makes him for the moment one with truth. Not through mere perversity do men run after it. To the poor and the unlettered it stands in the place of symphony concerts and of literature; and it is part of the tragedy of life that whiffs and gleams of something that we immediately recognize as excellent should be vouchsafed to so many of us only in the earlier phases of what in its totality is so degrading a poisoning.'

James also supported Clifford Beers in the formation of a national society for improving the conditions of the insane—James knew these at first hand and 'never ceased to believe that such improvement is one of the most "crying" needs of civilization.' Little has changed in seventy-five years, but another part of James's concern was fruitful and lasting. He gave time and money to help Beers start the first association for mental health, after finding a publisher for Beers's epoch-making book, *A Mind That Found Itself.* Forty letters to Beers show how James understood the word help, and this at a time when his health was failing and his burden of work enormous.*

Making these activities still more meritorious was that James intensely disliked committees and organizations. He had no taste for polemics and contradiction (very different from intellectual discussion) and he knew that his vocation was 'to treat of things in an all-round manner and not make ex parte pleas to influence a jury.' Nor did he relish victory and vindictiveness. That is why the remark quoted earlier about history putting underdogs on top, though accurate as to fact, may mislead about his feelings. Obviously, any triumph that went automatically to the weak and simply had them change places with the strong would leave things no better and would make moral judgment unnecessary. The point deserves attention in times of emancipation like ours. Made into a rule and enforced by law, the underdog principle brings on reverse discrimination and its insoluble problems. What is wanted is a method by which the two dogs become side-by-side dogs more or less at peace.

Seeing James in all these moods and phases one is not surprised at Chapman's retrospect on his friend: "I cannot think that anyone ever

---

* Even when the cause at stake was slight or nonexistent, an individual appeal to James was rarely resisted: 'A poor crank of a Russian Jew, a regular Spinosa, has been melting the heart out of me by his desire to get his magnum opus published. The stuff might have made some stir in 1650, but is hopeless now. Nevertheless, as a fellow crank I am moved to subscribe with the aid of friends $50 toward its publication.' (To Henry Holt, June 19, 1896, in Perry, *op. cit.*, II 287–88.)

met James without feeling that James was a better man than himself."
One might add that it was also a case, rare since Diogenes, of the man
and the philosopher being one. But James wore more clothes and had a
more balanced view of life.

For his estimate of life he has been accused of optimism, which
shows again the difficulty of getting heard correctly when one propounds a "third position," that is, an original one, other than the familiar pair of pro and con. Of course, the observer's eye also affects the
verdict, and in this characterization of James as optimistic it is hard to
tell whether doctrine or deportment is being judged. Face to face, James
was energetic and he conformed to the rule of manners that one owes a
cheerful countenance to one's fellow man. This could mislead the inat-
tentive; the more penetrating Chapman thought James a sad man underneath, like most persons who reflect and possess humor. But there is
no doubt that in his writings he attacked pessimism and that he answered Yes to the question he took as the title of a speech: "Is Life
Worth Living?"

The subject was topical, because the end of the nineteenth century
experienced a time of despair. After the great surge of industry and
science, self-distrust set in, at least for some of the detached onlookers.
Henry Adams was groaning in earnest over bewildering "multiplicity,"
and the old trumpet major, Huxley himself, in a lecture that shocked
Oxford, predicted doom for mankind if a purposive ethics was not
grafted upon mechanical evolution. Schopenhauer's essays urging resignation to perpetual evil came into vogue again, and the phrase fin de
siècle was taken as a sign of a final closing: life was absurd and uncalled for. James knew the appeal of despondency and suicide to the
young, and when he was invited to address the Harvard YMCA in
1896, he took the opportunity to discuss the worth of life.

The question, he said, could not be settled by abstract ideas. It is for
everyone a forced option and momentous; it is a challenge to faith
which everybody answers in action, whatever the accompanying words.
Yet words can contaminate, and it is important to think straight about
the issue: is evil fundamental and unconquerable, as Schopenhauer
taught, and only mitigated for the saint and the artist?—quite a modern
state of mind.* Pessimism says that good is an illusion to be got rid of.

---

* Consider, for example, the judgment seriously uttered by a distinguished critic and
novelist: "Anyone who doesn't feel that Chekhov is one of the relatively rare excuses for
the existence of the human race starts from a base ... different from my own." (Stanley
Kauffmann, World, July 17, 1973, p. 40.)

From the side of the scientists, Steven Weinberg asserts that the only thing that re-
deems the "farce" of human existence is the search for truth. (The First Three Minutes,
New York, 1977, p. 154.)

With materialism, it teaches the old game of appearance and reality, which James's empiricism will not play: 'If this life be not a real fight, it is no better than a game of private theatricals from which one may withdraw at will. But it *feels* like a real fight—as if there were something really wild in the universe which we, with all our idealities and faithfulnesses, are needed to redeem. For such a half-wild, half-saved universe our nature is adapted. The deepest thing in our nature is this dumb region of the heart in which we dwell alone with our willingness and unwillingness, our faiths and fears. Compared with these concrete movements of our soul all abstract statements and scientific arguments—the veto, for example, which the positivist pronounces upon our faith—sound to us like mere chattering of the teeth.' For the positivist's voice is not that of 'intellect against all passions; it is only intellect with one passion laying down the law.'

From his earliest writings, James had opposed—and, in his own toying with suicide, had overcome—Schopenhauer's reasoning about evil rendered bearable by anodynes. To begin with, art is not made to be used as a narcotic. Next, 'how is pessimism shown logically legitimate? By the assertion that there is no good upshot to the whole. Optimism, to be logical, must also refer to the general upshot and not to the details, part of which are empirically bad.' But this business of judging wholes is speculative, arbitrary, and it leaves out one element, which James put his finger on twenty years before "The Will to Believe." No proof can be given, he says, of either pessimism or optimism, but optimism as a hypothesis has this advantage, that we can make it *become* true. To refuse 'that hypothetical door and give oneself the benefit of its presence argues either a perfectly morbid appetite for dogmatic forms of thought, or an astounding lack of genuine sense for the tragic.'

The tragic is the opposite of the melancholy and it occurs only in action. 'This evil which we feel so deeply is something that we can also help to overthrow; for its sources, now that no "Substance" or "Spirit" is behind them, are finite, and we can deal with each of them in turn. The sovereign source of melancholy is repletion. Need and struggle are what excite and inspire us; our hour of triumph is what brings the void. Not the Jews of the captivity, but those of the days of Solomon's glory are those from whom the pessimistic utterances in our Bible come.'

These are also reasons why James could not endure the prefabricated good of would-be utopian arrangements. One taste of the thing was enough: 'A few summers ago I spent a happy week at the famous Assembly Grounds on the borders of Chautauqua Lake. The moment one treads that sacred enclosure, one feels oneself in an atmosphere of success. Sobriety and industry, intelligence and goodness, orderliness and ideality, prosperity and cheerfulness pervade the air. It is a serious and studious picnic on a gigantic scale. Here you have a town of many thousands of inhabitants, beautifully laid out in the forest and drained and equipped with means of satisfying all the necessary lower and most of the superfluous higher wants of man. You have a first-class college in full blast. You have magnificent music—a chorus of 700 voices, with possibly the most perfect open-air auditorium of the world. You have every sort of athletic exercise from sailing, rowing, swimming, bicycling, to the ballfield and the more artificial doings of the gymnasium. You have kindergartens and model secondary schools. You have general religious services and special club-houses for the several sects. You have perpetually running soda-water fountains and daily popular lectures by distinguished men. You have the best of company, and yet no effort. You have no zymotic diseases, no poverty, no drunkenness, no crime, no police. You have culture, you have kindness, you have cheapness, you have equality, you have the best fruits of what mankind has fought and bled and striven for under the name of civilization for centuries. You have, in short, a foretaste of what human society might be, were it all in the light, with no suffering and no dark corners.

'I went in curiosity for a day. I stayed a week, held spell-bound by the charm and ease of everything, by the middle-class paradise, without a sin, without a victim, without a blot, without a tear.

'And yet what was my own astonishment, on emerging into the dark and wicked world again, to catch myself quite unexpectedly and involuntarily saying: "Ouf, what a relief! Now for something primordial and savage, even though it were an Armenian massacre, to set the balance straight again. This order is too tame, this culture too second-rate, this goodness too uninspiring. This human drama without a villain or a pang; this community so refined that ice-cream soda is the utmost offering it can make to the brute animal in man; this city simmering in the tepid lakeside sun; this atrocious harmlessness in all things—I cannot abide with them. Let me take my chances again in the big outside worldly wilderness with all its sins and sufferings."'*

James had certainly not read Dostoevsky's fable of "The Grand Inquisitor"; it was not yet in English. But James's report on the ideal society, full of his irony and exaggeration, yet also fair to fair intentions, is a perfect counterpart to the grim fable of Ivan Karamazov, which contrasts the settled order of the sad inquisitor with the tragic chaos offered

---

* James's 'astonishment' at his response may have been a rhetorical device to make his point with the audience; there is no "surprise" in the account he wrote to his wife. He was simply 'glad to get into something less blameless and more admiration-worthy. The flash of a pistol, a dagger, or a devilish eye, anything to break the unlovely level of 10,000 good people.' (Letters, July 29, 1896, vol. II, p. 43.)

by Jesus. The one supplies bread, security, and miracles to the masses; the other freedom and risk, suffering and death. Both take James's "wilderness" or "wild element" as a permanent feature of this world, but Jesus and James see our individual natures adapted to wrestling with it, not needing it tamed.

James's dramatic morality (as it may be called) would have made him find self-centered and sniveling the modern attitude expressed in Eliot's lines "We are all guilty creatures/ But we can beg forgiveness." The tender conscience must look outward; there is plenty for it to do. And the question whether man is good or bad is a false issue, like literal equality. Assuming original badness as Eliot does and then carrying on as a sinner after getting forgiven is another self-fulfilling game that strains no moral fiber. James agreed with Shaw in *Major Barbara*, where the drunken lout must *change* after feeling guilty, not just seek through forgiveness a license to beat up his mother again with a free mind and a free hand. We expect reform of criminals in the worst possible environment, yet we who are still outside cherish guilt as the companion of all our misbehaviors, nursing the egotism of self-contempt as well as the false burden of responsibility for every outrage in the world, past and present.

It is perhaps fair to add that the generations since James have been browbeaten into this moaning passiveness by dogmatic science telling them that the vast universe is indifferent and hostile to man. Existentialist misery starts with that assumption and goes on to trace our nearer ills, errors, and crimes to the original absurdity of man's turning up in so unsuitable a place. The cosmos is plainly not Chautauqua. True, but—to begin with—there is no need to accept science's privative concept of Nature and, next, the reasoning from the assumption is flawed: if the scientific universe is but matter in motion, it has no feelings toward us. Indifference and hostility are human emotions, and as part of the universe *we* are its feelings. Besides, what is indifferent is not hostile; all we may say is that outer nature is strange and uncertain from the point of view of our wants.

But historically we have arrived at our sense of total alienation from nature only after thousands of years of shrewd and successful efforts to reduce its uncertainties. So the strangeness should be reduced too. Yet by a paradox of perspective, of sheer taking, it was in the earlier ages that men saw all around them the proofs of nature's bountifulness and manifold solicitude for human needs. They dwelt on the fitness of the environment and the many natural sources of pleasure and joy; nor did they so much ignore the rest as take it to be the price of the blessings. Today—is it the discontent of risen expectations, or is it because the fruits of the earth are picked green?—we feel only the bitter and the sour of life. We may of course be simply reacting against a former excess of praise for providence. At any rate, the new estimate seems neither factually nor logically sound. It substitutes the sorry for the tragic that James insisted on as needed for moral strength, and it turns undoubted sources of joy—art, love, literature, learning, religion, meditation into tidings of despair.

James's moral philosophy is thus a constant critique of our *Angst* and our "values." He himself applied its test in writing about Santayana's *Interpretations of Poetry and Religion*. After saying that he 'squealed with delight at the imperturbable perfection with which the position is laid down on page after page,' he goes on, 'What a fantastic philosophy!—as if "the world of values" were independent of existence. It is only as *being* that one thing is better than another.' So the hard question that James's demanding morality puts to us daily and hourly is a summons to creating that *being* when face to face with the evil at hand: 'Do we accept life on these terms; and if not, because honor forbids, what do we do about it?'

# The Reign of William and Henry

At our first glimpse of William James, he was crossing Harvard Yard in conversation with his students and the year was 1890. The choice of that year was not only to show him on the verge of publishing *The Principles of Psychology*; it was also to hint that we must think of him as a man of the nineties. His share in the reform struggles of that time is but a small part of his close relation to it. I am here using "The Nineties" in a special sense shortly to be explained, after which it will be clear why at this point it seems appropriate to give a rapid yet systematic glance at the intellectual and artistic scene of James's day.

In scanning the age, we should picture James as one who, like every outstanding talent, starts out in life from his own corner, working along his own line, and at the midpoint of his journey finds himself rather suddenly in a large and tumultuous company of his peers—the makers of culture for his era and the next. The newcomer to the group is cited, read, written to, agreed and argued with, visited, possibly honored, and he reciprocates those acts. This assimilation explains how these makers come in retrospect to wear a distinctive look, a family likeness. For James the process began, as we saw, during his European trip of 1882–83; it was completed after the publication of the *Principles* in 1890. It is thus no digression, much less a regression, to review the exploits of "the nineties."

That decade evokes its adjectives like many others—as if every ten years, punctually, civilization changed course and put on a new costume. This belief is a little too simple and what the nicknames leave in the memory is largely false. There was no doubt a "mauve decade," a "gay nineties," and a despairing mood properly called *fin de siècle*.

"Esthetes" could be found who shut out the sun with black curtains to brood by candlelight on the refining of their perceptions through art and poetry, while others saw visible change as final decadence. But the landscape should be surveyed from higher ground. Indeed, "the nineties" ought to mean, in the way of shorthand, the full turn of the century, the period stretching from the Paris Exhibition of 1889 with its Eiffel Tower and Galerie des Machines to the outbreak of war in 1914. So taken, with a ragged edge of years at each end, the epoch reveals a deep transformation: Victorian thought, art, and morals were disposed of and replaced by what must be called Modernism. This label, it is true, has had a footloose existence, applied here and there to several movements of different dates; but it rightly belongs to those twenty-five years in which nearly every idea of the twentieth century was hatched.

The mechanical inventions of the time are still the most familiar props of our daily life: the automobile, the airplane, the movies, the X-ray, the wireless. It was then that electricity began to mean "power" and helped to clean up, as well as light up, the factory and the home, while removing from the city (through the street car) the unsanitary horse and his threat to public health.

It was the time of other innovations that we tend to think much more recent and peculiarly ours: the popularity of appendicitis, emblem of the new abdominal (and even heart) surgery; organ transplants (in animals); experiments with mescaline and advocacy of the "drug experience"; "research and development" for and by industry; the data-processing machine (Hollerith punch card, still in use); radium treatment for breast cancer; the chlorinated water supply; color photography; and man-made fibers for textiles.

On the domestic scene, the novelties included: the vacuum cleaner; the electric elevator, refrigerator, motorcar, oven, toaster, iron, dishwasher, sewing machine, and central heating plant; stainless-steel utensils; the aluminum saucepan; the flashlight; rubber heels; the zip fastener; toothpaste in a tube; breakfast cereals, margarine, the ice-cream cone, Coca-Cola, chop suey, chewing gum, and book matches; the first printed crossword puzzle and the first fully automated device, the player piano.* As for inventions planned in that era and only actualized

---

* This list is far from exhaustive. During the first six years alone of this inventive period we find the first practical designs and often the bulk manufacture of: the dial and coin-operated phone with automatic central exchange; the pneumatic tire for cars, celluloid roll film, the automatic pistol, the Ferris wheel, the subway train, the electric chair, the baby incubator, the chain store, the shopping center (112 luxury shops under arcades in Cleveland in 1893), the public library with open shelves, travelers' checks, the newspaper banner headline, the coffee-vending machine, and the juke box.

later, they were numerous, among them the brilliant foreshadowing of the microcard that G. K. Chesterton gave in his first Father Brown story, "The Blue Cross" (1911).

New products and machines were not the cause but the concomitant of an extraordinary ferment in all departments of life. Many social and political ideas, devices and forces that we still reckon with were born or broke out then: sexual emancipation, the battle for women's rights;* the concentration camp; the assassination of heads of state and the planting of bombs in public places to advertise a cause; student riots; the hunger strike; black humor in print and sadism and bloodshed on stage; organized and motorized crime (*la bande à Bonnot*), as well as a host of lesser innovations such as the use of protest buttons (Anti-Imperialist), of acronyms, and of questionnaire surveys; hiring "stars" to advertise soap; the pinup girl (in the form of pocket cards and posters); the Homburg hat for real and gray eminences, Edward VII style; the creation of the Boy Scouts; the invention of musical comedy, the use of gloves in championship boxing, and the inauguration of the strip tease. That fecund period gave the thematic catalogue, as it were, of our achievements and our desires.

These facts are known in some fashion today, but hardly felt, which means that the significance of James's time for ours is not understood. We think we have got beyond "the turn," when except for technology we are scarcely up to it. Only in the last few years, for example, has awareness dawned that the "Cubist Decade" in art—1905–14—contains in essence and realizations nearly all that has come since. Because of this laggard state of mind, largely due to the blurring and dislocating effect of the First World War, we still hunt for solutions already found, we stumble over mental hurdles already removed, we rediscover naïvely and painfully. Our contribution, when we consciously build on those early foundations, is to refine and multiply. Our achievement—and it is no small one—has been to standardize and democratize; the car is a prime example, paralleled in hundreds of other machines, opinions, and attitudes. But intellectually, morally, and socially, much from the nineties that might have been used or surpassed has been lost.

Hence this glance at the work of the twenty-five years I call forma-

---

* "Battle" is not a metaphor, nor was sexual emancipation merely a program. The best souls gave lectures on birth control and practiced free love on principle, marriage and domesticity being evident forms of slavery. In pursuit of the vote, well-bred women turned into demonic street orators, stormed government buildings and initiated the sit-in, invaded Parliament, and after bloody scuffles with the police went triumphantly to jail. Poor Augustine Birrell, a literary man who was also an M.P., was knocked down and trampled by five women in St. James's Park. Other suffragettes took up revolver practice and one martyr threw herself under the racing horses at Ascot.

tive will indicate several further reasons for the present use—the urgent
need—of types of thought to which James's own is the best introduction.


To begin with, James was a true assessor of the intellectual and emotional revolution of his time. The mood he sensed in 1904 applies not
solely to the work of professional thinkers but to culture and society at
large: 'It is difficult not to notice a curious unrest in the philosophic
atmosphere of the time, a loosening of old landmarks, a softening of
oppositions, a mutual borrowing from one another on the part of systems anciently closed, and an interest in new suggestions, however
vague, as if the one thing sure were the inadequacy of the extant
school-solutions. The dissatisfaction with these seems due for the most
part to a feeling that they are too abstract and academic. Life is confused and superabundant, and what the younger generation appears to
crave is more of the temperament of life in its philosophy, even though
it were at some cost of logical rigor and of formal purity. I seem to read
the signs of a great unsettlement, as if the upheaval of more real conceptions and more fruitful methods were imminent, as if a truer landscape might result, less clipped, straight-edged, and artificial.'
    The main heads under which the 'unsettlement' may be considered
for review are those that our itinerary so far has made familiar: the
natural (or material) versus the ideal; science as one mode of thought
versus the world of feeling that it excludes; the permanence of truth
versus the evolution of all things (the permanence, rather, of perspectivism in truth); the claims of science versus those of religion and (just
as momentous) the claims of art versus those of religion.
    To use historical labels for these conflicts, the new consciousness of
the nineties had to deal with Positivism and Darwinism, with Industri-
alism and Democracy, with Realism in art and Populism in politics,
education, and taste. When movements that we know under their limited, topical names—for example, Symbolism and Naturalism—are taken
as parts of the larger wave of rebellion and reform, the coherence of
the myriad seemingly chaotic efforts becomes clear and their cultural
bearing obvious. The only thing that is hard to understand is why this
surge of novelty has not hitherto been treated as one whole and its
creators and promulgators as one group, regardless of doctrine and
sphere of action. The answer is probably, again, the excessive attention
to private concepts—individual ideas—and the neglect of results.
    The material setting in which the battle of ideas took place was
marked by many maladjustments. As a result of invention and organization, world trade was increasing at a dizzying rate and the common

man was suffering the side-effects of the power struggles and market upheavals that resulted. These, we recall, provoked James's suspicion of Bigness, in which he was not alone. The very success of industrial production, transportation, and high finance was forcing the public to count the human cost and try to deal with what was then called "the social question"—the poor, the old, the sick, the unemployed. Under this pressure, liberalism turned upside down. Calling for the economic uplift of the masses, it began to build up the welfare state, which is a network of political controls, the opposite of liberal theory and practice as it had been preached for a century before.* We can appreciate now, ninety years later, the difficulties of *both* systems. On the one hand, the poverty line in the western world has been lowered to a level unexampled in history. On the other, the tangle of controls is found to be crippling and corrupting. The debate on these very issues, proposals, and consequences is already in Chesterton, Belloc, and Shaw, the *Fabian Essays* of the late eighties and Belloc's *Servile State* of 1912. The American counterparts were the Muckrakers.

Their time like ours was determined to serve humanity, and as in ours, love of mankind was seasoned with violence. The anarchist's philosophy was brotherly cooperation, but the apostolic urge drove the most impatient to shooting and bombing. Henry James gives in *The Princess Casamassima* a clear view of the reasoning and the mood. Stimulated, no doubt, by the general excitement, professional criminals ceased to reside conveniently in a particular district and spread all over the rapidly growing cities. The police had to devise new means of control and with the aid of "science" (Hanss Gross) set up their archives of *portraits parlés* (Bertillon) and fingerprints (Galton).

Out from underground also in the nineties, the first well-organized Marxist parties won elections; but during this long incubation the original theory had been much refuted and diluted; which is why the new professional revolutionist—a disciplined soldier, in fact—was being defined and taught by Lenin through his newspaper *Iskra* (*The Spark*, 1900). Within the trade-union movement, encouraged by the great English dockers' strike of 1888, the syndicalists on the Continent were preaching "direct action" to the industrial workers: the general strike, sabotage, the boycott, and whatever might follow (Congress at Tours, 1896). Georges Sorel, the engineer turned social theorist, addressed the young intellectuals (including Mussolini) in his *Reflections on Violence*

---

* In the United States the corresponding movement created the Populist party, founded in 1891 and which polled 1.5 million votes in the Congressional elections of 1894. Thereafter its proposals were taken over and amplified by the Democratic party as Woodrow Wilson's New Freedom and later the New Deal.

(1908), to show them that reform was hopeless. A "myth" of revolution was needed to muster the shock troops of a new order: without believers led by conscious plotters, no socialist or communist state would ever be. Ten, twenty, thirty years later, Russia, Italy, and Germany put the lesson to use and proved that if anything is elitist it is a revolution.

But revolution was no monopoly of the working classes. Other intellectuals than the Marxist and Syndicalist leaders were laying down the goals and justification of what was later known as Fascism, or revolution against parliamentary government, its chaos and corruption. Unity was to be attained by exalting the bonds of nation and race. This doctrine, in France and Germany especially, was linked with the cult of art and a contempt for the taste and habits of the masses. The populace, now risen to influence as voters, consumers, and newspaper readers, was felt as a threat to culture, tradition, civilization itself.* In the sequel it turned out that the fascist movements found their strength in the lower middle class, the very group most despised by the leading theorists— Maurras, Daudet, Langbehn, Moeller van den Bruck.

In the peace movement (as to which we saw James's sympathy mixed with skepticism), no one contemplated bloodshed. It was to be persuasion, for which Björnson wrote the text of an oratorio, set to music by Grieg: Peace (1891/1899). The one hopeful innovation was the international conference of heads of state—now called "summits"—with working delegations to devise rules for settling disputes and plans for a league of nations and a world court. We have not got much farther after two postwar tries.

Even more hopeful was the great expansion of public education. In the United States the free public high school of 1900 was a bold departure that became the envy of all liberal minds abroad. The parallel "revolution in child rearing" and schooling (to be discussed later from James's point of view) was to be yet another liberation of the oppressed. The work of Maria Montessori and of John Dewey, like Ellen Key's proclamation of the coming "Century of the Child" (1900), were proofs of an enlarging moral sense.** How the mismanagement of these initiatives has brought us to schools that do not teach but foster violence, drug use, and promiscuity and inspire the hope of "deschooling society" is another story.

---

* For the first time in history, a private soldier (in the Boer War) recorded his impressions in the field and saw them published at once in a newspaper. Soon other sheets started printing extracts from letters, complaints, and corrections of official reports. (*The Anglo-Saxon Review*, March 1900, p. 255.)

** The first chapter of Ellen Key's book was well calculated to rouse the infant masses: "The Right of the Child to Choose His Parents."

In that effervescent time the philanthropic passions of western man seemed to have broken all the restraints of habit and prudence. It would take a book to enumerate the independent impulses struggling to make all things new. Primitivism (natural foods, the simplified life, nudism) was rife. It informed the admiration of Javanese art and of the African sculpture that inspired Picasso and Vlaminck. It spurred the youth movements—the "wandering birds," often of both sexes, in the German woods, English lanes, and French inns. It reinforced the passion for sports and a concern for hygiene. Sexuality benefited from this new cult of regarding the body with simplicity, and eugenics—mating with an eye to physical perfection and sterilizing the unfit—was coolly discussed. Among the signs of the open mind on such subjects were the publication for general readers of the specialist studies of sex that had for some time filled medical books and journals (Paolo Mantegazza, Magnus Hirschfeld, Krafft-Ebing, Havelock Ellis, Iwan Bloch). Fiction readmitted physical love as a subject worth treating at length (Hardy, H. G. Wells, Anatole France, Lafcadio Hearn), and not merely as a cause of disaster. Divorce became acceptable and through the stage (Oscar Wilde, Pinero) a woman's "past" ceased to seem just cause for heartless behavior. After the Wilde trials, too, there were whispers of the coming vindication of homosexuality, which Gide finally voiced and Proust seemed to exemplify.

It may seem strange that in the same decades when these moral convictions and ideal goals were creating new standards and new institutions, a full-scale attack on morality was being led by nearly all the forward-looking artists and publicists. That attack, we can now see, was but the intensification of the war opened at the beginning of the nineteenth century against the bourgeois and the philistine as embodiments of respectability and resistance to change. The clue to the paradox of an anti-moralist crusade accompanying an enlarged moral concern lies in an old association of ideas: "morality" meant hardened custom; "respectable" had become a term of reproach. The new motive to action was not moral: no, the reason for taking care of everybody, for cleaning up cities and rivers, for abolishing slums and their denizens, was esthetic. Liberating women, educating children with more tenderness, respecting the natives of India and Africa, salvaging the dignity of convicts, stamping out cruelty to animals, fulfilled the same beautifying, hygienic desire. It appealed to the sense of fitness and order, not charity or pity.

Thus Camillo Sitte, one of the creators of city-planning in Central Europe, and Patrick Geddes, the "social biologist," fought the engineers and rectilinear specialists who till then had ruled city planning.* The fresh eye saw the grim results of reliance on machinery and laisser-faire, and the new imagination designed town or regional rehabilitation in the spirit of the "total work of art." Those men did it on a scale and with a foresight not yet acted upon. They knew that art seconded by science could regenerate the city of man, because man now had the technical means to rebuild it new and fair—fair to its members and fair to behold. Art was in fact the power that overthrew the faith of two hundred years in automatic progress.

That art should act as a force in society strikes us as normal and reasonable, but it seems so only because the nineties made it so. The supreme importance of art was first expounded in the early 1800s; it was the Romanticist faith. But only toward the end of the century, when organized religion was losing its authority in the struggle with organized science, did the faith in art gain general acceptance. By then the long war of ridicule and hate against the philistine had finally converted him or sent him underground into hypocrisy.** Art had won in what Henry James called "the conflict between art and 'the world,'" which by paternal tradition he had always regarded as "one of the half-dozen great primary motives."

The religion of art has a short creed: the worship of masterpieces and of the company of geniuses; the conviction that art, being the highest expression of man's spirit, is superior to religion and the state, and for some superior to life itself. "Art," said Huysmans, "is the only clean thing on earth, except holiness." The artist accordingly has the right and the duty to judge, denounce, or reject every moral attitude and social institution, though he himself remains free from ordinary modes and rules of conduct.

This dogma may be read in all the artistic achievements of the period as well as in the sayings of the makers and commentators. The poet Mallarmé came to believe that the universe exists in order to be trans-muted into a poem *(Le livre)*. Yeats believed art opened the door to magical experiences buried in the memory of the race and without

---

* In 1896 the novelist Ouida (Louise de la Ramée) denounced—like Jane Jacobs in our time—the destruction of communities within the city through the multiplication of "long, high, blank spaces." (*Nineteenth Century Opinion*, Extracts from *The Nineteenth Century*, ed. Michael Goodwin, London, 1951, pp. 161–62.)

** For those who like emblematic dates, that of Puccini's *Vissi d'arte* in *Tosca* (1900) will suggest the victory of the long crusade. "I lived by—or through—art" (not "for art" as it is sometimes translated) was already the motto of Berlioz's *Benvenuto Cellini* in 1838, but it was meaningless to the general public until the end of the century. By coincidence, one month after the production of *Tosca*, Charpentier's *Louise* had its première, setting forth a young woman's "right" to leave home for love—love of an artist.

which nations cannot endure. Kandinsky discoursed "On the Spiritual in Art" as a first step in radically changing the esthetics of painting and enhancing the well-being of man. And the great artistic hero of the nineties, the newly popular Wagner, was idolized because he was thought to be the embodiment of artist power: at once the musician-poet and prophet-seer, the revolutionary feted by kings and the impresario of successful festivals.

To move the collective will toward the good society, the artistic fervor had to be linked to new ideas and slogans, which explains the presence of so many artists and devotees of art among the reformers of the nineties. Just as William Morris and his disciples of the arts-and-crafts movement worked to restore quality to common goods after the flood of shoddy manufacture, so Morris again, and Shaw, and Ruskin, and their followers campaigned to reintroduce quality into life itself. These men advocated guilds, cooperatives, and socialisms of various brands. Others preached the single tax, and still others (Belloc, Chesterton) the breakup of property into small holdings. H. G. Wells, the best-selling essayist, novelist, and pioneer of science fiction, is a good recorder of the great clamor, his own views being a curious blend of hope and apprehension about the march of social planning and technology. He predicted the improvement of the common lot and the liberation of the ruling classes from ignorant prejudices, together with the decline of culture into mediocrity and the collapse of Europe in war. Then would come totalitarian dictators breeding always further wars (*Anticipations*, 1901).

Meanwhile, the churches sought to justify their existence in an age when, in Nietzsche's words, God was dead. The "social gospel" therefore recruited strenuous volunteers who worked at bettering the life of the urban poor (Stewart Headlam, Albert de Mun). At the same time, large-scale statistics and "studies" (Booth, Rowntree), no less than the "naturalistic novel" and the "problem play" (Zola, Goncourt, Sudermann, Strindberg, George Moore, Brieux, Galsworthy, Arnold Bennett, Gerhart Hauptmann, Frank Norris, Jack London, Theodore Dreiser, Upton Sinclair) were making vivid to "the comfortable classes" how the other half lived. Every activity, it seemed, converged toward the same cosmetic end. What unites an age is not its warring "solutions" but its vision of common needs.

Given the facts, it was no epigram but a sober thought that Wilde offered to the readers of the *Saturday Review* in 1894, when he wrote that Art was the only serious thing in the world. Nietzsche, as yet hardly known, had said the same thing earlier, seeing in art the sole enhancer of life and a protection against having nothing to gaze at but the void created by science; and Tolstoy undertook his crusade to rehumanize mankind with the aid of a simplified and deeply moral art.

If these new principles were sound, then the existing ones, still powerful, were wrong. Hence the extraordinary unanimity of the attack on "ideals," on virtue, on truth with a capital T. Oscar Wilde's maxims, essays, and plays—and especially his masterpiece, *The Importance of Being Earnest*—carry the message: every established assumption about goodness and rightness is false. Virtues and vices must be revalued in opposite directions. The result was, on the surface, wit, but it is a mistake to regard Wilde as a brilliant trifler. His writings constitute a summary of the transformation of thought and attitudes, observed by a strong and ubiquitous intelligence.* Far from his leading a cult of art for art's sake, it was a cult of art for life's sake.

To be sure, others had prepared the ground and supplied cases: Ibsen teaching that it takes two to tell the truth and riddling the ideal of "ideals" ("Don't use that foreign word. We have that good native word: lies!"); Samuel Butler in his famous *Notebooks* turning "proper sentiments" upside down ("'Tis better to have loved and lost than never to have lost at all") and showing throughout *The Way of All Flesh* that self-sacrifice is egoism; Shaw pointing out (as we saw) that the golden rule disregards the variety of needs and tastes and that "Christian" repentance and forgiveness is a scheme for maintaining the moral status quo; Strindberg and Wedekind, also using the stage to teach, and telling the public what complex and ugly impulses moved heroes and heroines, especially in the sexual relation; Nietzsche calling for a Superman, not to conquer others but to be strong in solitude and honest with himself, since Christianity as practiced only produced respectable cowards and sensualists. For all these creator-destroyers one might say that the keynote was struck in 1889 in the inspired title of a book: Edward Carpenter's *Civilization: its Cause and Cure*. It was a program in itself.

The triumph of art as a cult meant another change that we also take for granted: it is no longer the work, the craft, that defines the species "artist," but the love of art. So the critic, too, is called an artist, and the connoisseur, and the bourgeois who has seen the light and who "collects" or "subscribes" or "follows." Every educated person must take or pretend an interest in art; he or she owes it to the social self, just as

---

* Read, for example, his remarkable essay "The Soul of Man Under Socialism" and you see the reasons for which some of Wilde's contemporaries and later artists espoused communist doctrine. To Wilde also belongs a fine anticipation of Sartre's "Hell is other people": "LORD GORING: Other people are quite dreadful. The only possible society is oneself. PHIPPS: Yes, my lord." (*An Ideal Husband*, 1895, Act III, sc. 1.)

formerly everyone must go to church and say family prayers. Listen to
our witness Henry James: "Art indeed has in our day taken on so many
honours and emoluments that the recognition of its importance is more
than a custom, has become on occasion almost a fury." Should there be
doubt that this is a remarkable change, consider whether we ask or care
what Dr. Johnson thought of Handel's music or if Matthew Arnold
spent much time in the Louvre. Their soul could be saved without submission to the grace of art. But since the turn of the century art has
become an object of dedicated pursuit for all those who, at that very
time, were first called "intellectuals." A fusion had taken place among
artists and men of ideas in all fields, including reform and revolution.

The resulting "party," though unorganized and never by any possibility acknowledging a single platform or a sole artist-god, nevertheless
tended to act like a vested interest. In France this attitude was strengthened by the Dreyfus Affair, which dramatized the issue of the individual against society and which elevated Zola and Anatole France as
artist-heroes of a national movement. And to many intellectuals duty
seemed to go beyond protest in a political affair. As William James told
a group of college women, there was a role for intellect in modern society. 'Cultivated minds,' he said, formed 'a permanent presence' within
an ever-shifting democracy: 'We have continuous traditions, we stand
for ideal interests solely, for we have no corporate selfishness and
wield no powers of corruption. We ought to have our own class-
consciousness. "Les Intellectuels!" What prouder club-name could
there be than this one, used ironically by the party of "red blood," the
party of every stupid prejudice and passion during the anti-Dreyfus
craze, to satirize the men in France who still retained some critical
sense and judgment!'

This part of the new consciousness of the nineties ushers in the now
familiar commitment of artists and intellectuals (even scientists) to
"causes." But the duty to be political or engagé, which seems at first a
logical outgrowth of democratic life, ends in paradox. For intellectual
politics is not political work—work with politicians inside the political
machinery. It is concept-work outside, men of ideas having little taste or
leisure for the full-time activity. And merely to speak as the voice of
enlightened conscience does not endear the speaker to those who carry
on the struggle day by day and know its conditions. Worse still, the
intellectual's choice of cause or party—often one faraway and ideal-
ized—commits him to loyal following: there cannot be hundreds of
leaders. But in this obedience, hardly congenial to the independent
thinker, what becomes of his priceless contribution of critical sense and
detachment?

Since some public affairs cannot leave the conscience unmoved—as we saw in William's case—the decision to take part (and what part to take) is an anxious one, not to be made solely on the grounds of being a man of art or of thought, but on that of special fitness for the task—influence, expertise, power—coupled with the will to become truly political. By the 1940s, when thousands of intellectuals everywhere had joined and left political parties, or been expelled by them or killed as partisans or traitors, it could be seen from the individual tragedies and collective helplessness that the high esthetic and critical movement of the nineties had deviated into self-defeat. Art and thought influence society in deeper, slower, longer-lasting ways than politics, which can never be more than hasty management under stress.

The class consciousness that James discerned among artists and intellectuals did not make their works any more unanimous than they have usually been. On the contrary, the numerous schools seemed more discordant than ever, but the confusion covered certain clear wants and needs. In literature, the two main tendencies, Naturalism and Symbolism, expressed a dissatisfaction with the commonplace, which had been the staple of mid-century Realism. Deliberately "average" and unemphatic and expressing the great discouragement following the aborted revolutions of 1848, Realist work rendered neither the "vehement and real life" as it surged anew nor the desire for spirituality, for the unseen and transcendent. The nineties believed that this "more real" other world could be reached only through symbols—hence the name Symbolists—while the Naturalists searched for the harsh clinical truths about those who lived in the lower depths and had also been unseen. Both contributed to that "great unsettlement" which James noted as characteristic of the age.

The two techniques might well seem incompatible, except that a good many writers found it easy to move from one mode to the other and even to mix them. What the feat suggests, beyond a common scorn for the ordinary, is the affinity we noted earlier between materialists and idealists in metaphysics. Out of their conflict of absolutes came modernism. Meanwhile, the religious mission of art animating all schools was to reshape man's whole being—not just his ideas. By esthetic arousal, the conventions—bare concepts—would be replaced by genuine experience. This Jamesian change would remake the world. Like every other, that generation was bent on exhibiting the really real.

On the Naturalist side, the effort to bring new truth took from sci-

ence, very crudely, the ideas of evolution, heredity, and "medical materialism." In the fiction of Zola and others, every kind of abnormality
and disease subdued the strong and the weak alike; aberrations served
the educational endeavor that the novel had become. That is its interest
for us. Naturalism and Symbolism as schools have been pronounced
dead for a good while; but they survive as purpose and method in all
the literature we produce. Present-day novels that are called disturbing,
shameless, psychiatric, proletarian, "black," "blue," or otherwise colored by sex, violence, madness, and high impossibility descend in a
straight line from Goncourt, Zola, Huysmans, and their earliest English
and American counterparts—George Moore, Gissing, Norris, Crane,
Dreiser, the Powys brothers. Arthur Morrison's *Tales of Mean Streets*
(1894) suggests a collective title for the whole output. No subject was
beneath notice. For example, the recent featuring of onanism in a best
seller by one of our most popular yet respected story-tellers was anticipated in a Naturalist novel that created a scandal and led to criminal
proceedings in 1883. The author was acquitted on his plea of "having
done a piece of scientific work."* Turning fiction into a "human document," a "slice of life," a "piece of science" ensured that by 1914 no
corner of social or private life had been left unscraped for materials.
Speaking more generally, what Naturalism, aided by "science," be-
queathed to our literature is an inquisitive enjoyment of factuality. It is
an acquired taste: though it be Naturalism, it is not natural.

In the Symbolist genre, it was the inner life, vague longings and fleeting intimations of another world, that were being "studied." This division of labor helps to explain how writers could shift from gross to
subtle realities. The second enterprise produced the "interior mono-
logue," the forerunner of stream-of-consciousness fiction. Symbolist
and Naturalist work alike were studies of "states" or "conditions," a
change from "story" that we are well inured to.

And in Symbolism there was the further attraction of the symbols
themselves, which created suspense until deciphered. We know all
about that also: what is said is surface only; the meaning lies below. In
addition, Symbolist language was new and strange, syntax distorted and
the vocabulary strained and amplified by a host of technical words,
while proper names contained clues to meanings congruent with the
whole.** Our education in these matters has been so thorough that we

---

* Paul Bonnetain, *Charlot s'amuse*, with a preface by Henry Céard, another Naturalist
and Zola's closest friend. See Léon Deffoux, *Le Naturalisme*, Paris, 1929, p. 111 and n.

** To these should be added the device, familiar since James Joyce's *Ulysses* (1922), of
fusing two or more words for a simultaneous meaning. It was first used by the poet Lafor-
gue, e.g., *violupté* (= *viol*: rape + *volupté*: pleasure) in *Complaintes* (1893).

now regularly apply the same perceptive skill to novels written earlier on a different plan.

Painting, in the quarter century under review, shows similar "timely" preoccupations and attitudes. The Impressionists, who may be seen as using Symbolist means in their various types of fluidity, were late in attaining recognition and it was the Naturalist Zola who helped to vindicate them; Manet seemed to him a Naturalist. Soon came the Post-Impressionists, pursuing the aim of restoring solidity to depicted objects, though not in the plain Realist way. Van Gogh, Gauguin, Cézanne produced what Zola had admitted all art was: "a corner of nature seen through a temperament." The strikingly unlike results ushered in stylistic pluralism, based on the unique perspectivism we now accept as the very definition of creative artist.

What is more, by ignoring the demand for the recognizable in scene or surface and by making shape, color, and even thickness—substance—emphatic, the new artists led the way to establishing the painting itself as self-sufficient. This thrusting of the object on the beholder is comparable to James's reminder in his radical empiricism that sensation, experience, comes before idea and generates it as may be.

Subsequent styles, from Cubism onward, presuppose that same refreshed perception. We call the works abstract or non-objective, which is perverse, since the painting is there primarily *as* an object, not a facsimile or rendering of something else; still less as a carrier of concepts or abstract ideas. This object, again, the viewer is free to take as he wishes or as he can; his freedom forces him to adopt a "point of view," à la William or Henry.

The changed sensibility that inspired the pictorial work of the period is well described by an unexpected witness—Thomas Hardy. He had begun life as a draftsman and architect and had not lost his graphic sense when he wrote in the late eighties: "I find that . . . the 'simply natural' is interesting no longer. The much decried, mad, late Turner rendering is now necessary to create my interest. . . . What he paints chiefly is light as modified by objects. . . . The exact truth as to material fact ceases to be of importance in art. . . . It is the style of a period when the mind . . . does not bring anything to the object that coalesces with and translates the qualities that are already there." "The mind" in this remark obviously means the same thing as "temperament" for Zola or "point of view" for either James.

With the change came a new terminology. "Picture" seemed to imply imitation. "Organization of lines on a flat surface," or "exploration of space," or "experiment in color" sounded more exact. Whistler had shown the way earlier when he called his works "arrangements" or (with a musical allusion) "nocturne in blue and silver." Battersea Bridge at night might trigger his vision, but it was not his "subject."* Portrait painting lost caste and was left to the photographers—rather, to some photographers, for this was the time when "art photography" developed its styles (Steichen, Stieglitz, and others), in keeping with the improved powers of the camera and the new doctrine of "arrangement" rather than "picture."

To justify to the public this steady flouting of its expectations required many words; the situation made it more than ever compulsory for every artist to find a striking label for his work and produce or borrow a theory to go with it. And as the ability to theorize well is rare and unconnected with the artistic gift, the world since then has been faced with a growing literature of explanation which it takes innumerable critics and scholars to explain in their turn. Babel was a unison compared to the result. Statements and counterstatements were often cobbled together by young artists more intent on feeding demand than taking thought. Thus Maurice Denis, one of the painters who called themselves Nabis, admitted later: "We made a singular mixture of Plotinus, Edgar Poe, Baudelaire, and Schopenhauer." Today the practice continues in shorter forms—the artist's page in the exhibition catalogue or program notes, or the solemn interview with the poet or novelist.

From the confusion one common dogma emerged and has survived: art is autonomous. Each work is "a world apart obeying its own laws" (E. M. Forster, A. H. Bradley at Oxford).** This maxim goes with the notion of "pure form" as the essence of art and with Pater's belief that all the arts tend toward the condition of music, the immaterial—as music is mistakenly thought to be. These assertions were necessary to differentiate an encounter with art from reading the newspapers or gazing about the world. Out of this distinction comes our belief in something unique called the esthetic experience. Art stands there, an object challenging perception; its complexity or obscurity is the means by which it overshadows its workaday surroundings and affirms its spirituality over the shapeless, ugly, indeed unreal world, whose essence is convention.

There is no inconsistency in expecting art to figure as object and asking that it be taken also as ideal, spiritual, ethereal, musical, nocturnal, symbolic, ineffable. It is the doubleness of James's empiricism, the bit of experience 'taken twice over,' as object and as idea. If in art the

* Even "Whistler's Mother" was only "an arrangement," as the artist pleaded in an open letter when someone criticized the canvas as a poor portrait. (T. Martin Wood, *Whistler*, London, n.d., p.62.)

** "A poem should not mean/But be." These lines by Archibald MacLeish in his "*Ars Poetica*" (1926) express the dogma as tersely as can be for all the arts; and show its paradox, too, since a meaning *is* conveyed. (*Collected Poems: 1917–1952*, Boston, 1952, p. 40.)

symbolic yields vagueness, it is a perfectly definite, intentional vagueness. In the conscious stream, as we know, James had thought it important to notice vagueness as a precise experience. Thus had Monet "taken" Rouen cathedral in twenty different lights and shown the solid stones as changeable masses of iridescence.

At any rate, the "autonomous art object" is what our culture has lived on ever since the idea was first propounded. It justifies every type of surprise—non-representational painting and sculpture; architecture that "plays" with space and materials regardless of human discomfort; poems and novels that do not "communicate"; music that is better read than heard, or that cannot be heard because it is measured silence. These applications of the Object Theory have ended logically in the schools of Found Art, Minimal Art, Disposable Art, and Anti-Art, which variously exclude both maker and purpose. Most lately, the computer has been enlisted to produce "randomized" poetry and music. The art object has turned scientific object.

Criticism has kept pace by codifying "methods" to pluck the mystery out of the "solutions" that creators give to their "artistic problems." Structure, thematic and mythic underpinning, the identification of symbols, the reduction of meanings to neuroses, the primacy of technique, sensation, and "material" (e.g., "language" seen as "the main character" in a Shakespeare play)—all these systems of analysis have sprouted in answer to the presence of art as object to be unriddled, like the objects of science. Interpretation has in fact changed the chief quality of art, and with it the beholder's commonest term of praise: the work is not "beautiful" but "interesting." The titles of the objects themselves seek the aura of technology or science ("Ionisation," "Invention 16"); the curious phrase "experimental art" has acquired a meaning, and in his promotional claims the artist speaks of "rigorous investigation of space" or "painstaking research in the rhythm and dynamics of movement." Inspiration is at a discount—"I too am a laboratory man."

Another face of art we owe to the turn of the century derives from the softening up of public resistance to the new by shock, outrage, and derision. Alfred Jarry with his play Ubu roi in 1896 gave a model of this type of intimidation by direct insult and crude parody. The spectator is afraid to associate himself with the object ridiculed, but he is being laughed at all the same—a sophomoric ploy.* Jarry was soon followed by Marinetti and the Futurists, who accustomed the new century to the jape or joke as the main weapon against moral and esthetic habits. No

---

* It is not irrelevant that the character Ubu is based on one of Jarry's unhappy lycée teachers and that the first sketches of the play and its wisecracks ("in Poland, which is to say nowhere") date from the author's early school years.

longer épater le bourgeois but paralyze or silence him by fear and invective. It was a case of Ring Lardner's "'Shut up,' he explained." But in attacking every belief, the debunker was bound to include the traditional value placed upon art; the tenet of Anti-Art is thus no invention of our day, nor even of the Dadaists and Surrealists of the 1920s; it was proclaimed a necessity in a Futurist manifesto of 1909. Destroy all preconceptions, call the paying customer names, feed the brutes raw sensation, and the whole culture will be propelled out of convention into reality: such was the Abolitionist strategy.

Not all modes of persuasion in the nineties were so drastic, but it is noteworthy that the theatre was a principal medium of propaganda. Being public in a collective way, the stage magnifies any shock administered. When Shaw used "bloody" in Pygmalion it stirred the town; in a novel it would only have irritated as a "lapse of taste." And the dramatic output of those years throughout Europe—in retrospect a renaissance—was a theatre of ideas. Nearly every capital gave birth to a "free theatre," that is, unconventional and at first for initiates only, but soon conquering the fashionable world.

In Stockholm, besides his radical simplification of staging (paralleled by Max Reinhardt's in Vienna), Strindberg was creating a new genre at his intime playhouse. Taking his oeuvre as a whole, he appears as the fountainhead of the modern drama and of much modern thought, his greatness and range of influence not yet fully acknowledged. In Ireland, the Abbey Theatre was combining high literature with nationalist politics. In Central Europe, the preferred themes were sexuality and the social question, Arthur Schnitzler in Vienna capturing a mode of life in tragicomedies whose worth is also undervalued now. In France, Naturalism and Symbolism again—Brieux, Renard, Maeterlinck—replaced the threadbare adultery play with acerb studies of individual and social psychology. In England, Shaw led a two-sided crusade—against social abuses and against the public's notion of personality as single-minded. Especially through his modernized historical plays, this double influence took effect on the unlike pair, Pirandello and Brecht. At home, Shaw with Galsworthy helped to undermine Victorian ideals and upperclass complacency. The latter's Justice and other works have lost their luster for us, but when Shaw's Misalliance (1910) was revived in New York in 1981, its presentment of the career woman, the generation gap, marital relations, business mores, and the citizen's ambiguous attitude toward crime appeared topical and fresh.

At the same time, another sort of theatre stressed ambiguity, too, but through the symbols of rigid movement and masks; I mean the circus and all puppet stages down to those of André Breton, Ionesco, and

Beckett. It was in the nineties that painters discovered the circus as a theme, while in the music of *Petrouchka* and *Pierrot lunaire* the clown became a philosophic hero. One meaning of these stiff comic figures may be found in Wilde's phrase "The Truth of Masks." This idea was part of the new uncertainty about truth and the belief that lying and pretence convey as much as sincerity. The Symbolists agreed and so did Nietzsche and Strindberg. A second meaning was supplied by Bergson in his theory of laughter (1900), which explains that we laugh when the spontaneity characteristic of human beings is abruptly stopped by the mechanical—automatism arresting free activity. We laugh, and we also wonder where reality is found, in the human or the mechanical. The artistic nineties never could forget the competitive proximity of science.

It would take us too far afield to point out other anticipations, from the Ballets Russes and Isadora Duncan, who created the modern dance, to jazz and atonality (Schönberg's *Harmonielehre*, 1911); simultaneity in poetry, later called concrete poetry (Barzun, 1908); the new architecture (Louis Sullivan, Tony Garnier, Auguste Perret, Walter Gropius, 1890–1913), and the non-fiction novel of Gide, in which the author moves in and out of the thin story to comment as an author on its telling while the characters are so spontaneous as to act from no motives, like our leading criminals today.*

A critical eye will note that in a sketch of events and ideas such as this, the coupling of names and bridging of countries disregards some important differences among artists, thinkers, and their achievements. It is also incomplete. But it should not mislead if one remembers that the purpose is not to study single figures or even groups, but to characterize an era and its role in history. Generalization is suggestive, not literal, and exceptions and qualifiers are not excluded by being omitted.

Suggestive generalization was in fact the reason why critics and historians have given this period of our concern the name Neo-Romanticism. The phrase is appropriate, because both the early Romanticists (1790–1850) and the late (1890–1914) took on the mission of rebuilding a moral and spiritual world after the decay or destruction of its predecessor. Such a reconstruction calls for a certain temperament and shows certain features in the product. For the right interpretation of "Roman-

---

* I use the epithet "non-fiction" in the original sense that I gave it in a number of book reviews. (*The Atlantic*, July 1946, *The Griffin*, April 1956.) I meant it to describe novels in which little or no attempt is made to create lifelikeness by strict plausibility—the fictional feel. Its place is taken by moral, psychological, and metaphysical ideas, which the story and the characters are manhandled to bring to the fore.

tic" in this context we can do no better than go to James when he applies it to his own work. Looking back in 1901 on the history of psychology, he says that he is struck by two tendencies running through it:

'Apart from the great contrast between minds that are teleological or
biological and minds that are mechanical, between the animists and the
associationists, there is the entirely different contrast between what I
will call the classic-academic and the romantic type of imagination. The
former has a fondness for clean pure lines and noble simplicity in its
constructions. The facts must lie in a neat assemblage and the psychologist must be enabled to cover them and tuck them in safely under his
system. Until quite recently all psychology was written on classic-
academic lines. The consequence was that the human mind, as it figured in this literature, was largely an abstraction. A sort of sunlit terrace
was exhibited on which it took its exercise. And where the terrace
stopped, the mind stopped. But of late years the terrace has been over-
run by romantic improvers, and to pass to their work is like going from
classic to gothic architecture, where few outlines are pure and where
uncouth forms lurk in the shadows.'

Elsewhere, this time about his pragmatism and empiricism, James recurs to the contrast: 'Just so when we condemn all noble, clean-cut,
fixed, eternal, temple-like systems of philosophy. These contradict the
*dramatic temperament* of our nature, as our dealings with nature and
our habits of thinking have so far brought us to conceive it. They seem
oddly personal and artificial, even when not bureaucratic and professional in an absurd degree. We turn from them to the great unpent and
unstayed wilderness of truth.'

'Romantic,' then, stands for the vision of a world *to be* organized, not
one found in tidy completeness. 'Bureaucratic and professional' mean a
solidly established order—in the nineties the Victorian. The new order
will be 'gothic' because irregular and because the mind exploring it is
itself full of dark recesses. Finally, the atmosphere of reconstruction is
dramatic, because a multitude on its way to creating a new order generates conflict.

Such is the serious and suggestive meaning of Romantic, whether applied to the men of 1800 or to those of 1890.* Unfortunately by 1890 and
often today, a different meaning, degraded by the connotations of "romance," is found side by side with the other. Shaw, for instance—and
at times James himself—uses *romantic* pejoratively to mean silly, un-

---

* This central meaning has implications that vary with the several facets of culture. For
example, in an essay of 1894, Hermann Bahr says: "In their arrogance toward common
tastes and all things commercial they resemble the Romantics, and in a sense they are the
'new-Romantics.'" (*Studien zur Kritik der Moderne*, Frankfurt A/M, 1894, p. 23.)

imaginative, deluded by weak or misplaced sentiment. Shaw does this on the same page as he holds up Shelley and Blake and other Romantics as intellectual models and as "masters of reality." So the reader must beware: like *realism* and *realistic*, "romantic" flung as an epithet in the heat of argument conveys little more than the debater's disapproval.

Being *Neo*-Romanticists did not, of course, mean repeating the past. Much was changed and much added to produce Modernism. Here we may turn to the other James, Henry, for an important aspect of what was new. In "The Lesson of Balzac," James at great length relates his work to that of the Romanticist fountainhead, Balzac: "Every road comes back to him."* But from what James criticizes in the master we can infer what the later time wanted and added: stricter form and a refined technique. In the "autonomous world" (at least until Gide complicated it) there must be perfect structure and the "point of view" must remain constant. Like the scientist, the observer in the story can achieve objectivity only if he stays outside the field of study. He "reports," while his presence is also skillfully made legitimate. Thus Zola, the theorist of Naturalism, worked up for each book a huge documentation but conceded that his "experimental novel" presupposed a "temperament," namely, the experimenter. Henry James put the position more subtly in one of his retrospective prefaces: "The house of fiction has ... not one window, but a million.... At each of them stands a figure with a pair of eyes ... which forms, for observation, a unique instrument." The very words "observation," "instrument" date the theory; they would have surprised Fielding or Jane Austen.

But note a distinction. Whereas Zola and his fellow-Naturalists offered their "experimental" results in the simple way of mid-nineteenth-century science, James is already a step ahead in his conception of truth. He is, as he told William, a practicing pragmatist—and had been one before William's book supplied the reasons for his intuition. In that same preface, Henry goes on after the words "a unique instrument": "ensuring to the person making use of it an impression distinct from any other. He and his neighbors are watching the same show, but one seeing more where the other sees less, one seeing black where the other sees white." Throughout the eighteen prefaces forming *The Art of the Novel* the word "consciousness" must recur one hundred times. As for "the same show," it is the world assumed to be "out there"; but for Henry as for William in his *Psychology*, the endless varieties of experi-

---

* By no possibility is Balzac anything but a Romantic. He shared the governing assumptions of his time and died in 1850. To call him a Realist is to deny the effort by which his successors, notably Flaubert, modified the novel.

ence are all we have to go by till we compare—compare reports with our fellows, contrast novels by different authors, compare the less with the more and the white with the black in the search for an ever-new "realism."

These matters of doctrine and practice show in what sense Henry James "represents" or is emblematic of the great quarter century. His work is "realistic" but he is not a Realist; it is full of symbols, but he is not a Symbolist. By the end of his career he was stretching syntax (without distortion) to achieve his unearthly effects, but his novels also form a summa of observations and of moral lessons that point always to ideal behavior—the fine flower of feeling expressed in action. These features taken together make of James's art a synthesis of Naturalism and Symbolism, marked by strong influences direct from the Romantics and colored by the unique perceptions and passions that show Henry and William brothers indeed. Neither took from the other; they shared and intermittently compared notes, doubtless aware of a common inheritance from Henry Sr.

But the literary labels I have used being notoriously inadequate, they need the supplement of the artist's own sayings; Henry James wrote theory to make the meanings of his art unmistakable. The strain of *philosophic* naturalism in him comes out—William-like—in what he calls "the terrible law of the artist . . . the law of the acceptance of *all* experience, of *all* suggestion and sensation and illumination."\* This radical pluralism keeps him from the Symbolists' desire for attenuation through distilling selected experiences in small drops. But James's mode of notation and expression certainly meets theirs more than halfway; it is the opposite of the *literary* Naturalists' rough, direct handling. Rather, it is to "reduce one's reader, 'artistically' inclined, to such a state of hallucination by the images one has evoked as doesn't permit him to rest till he has . . . set up some semblance of them in his own other medium, by his own other 'art.'"

The net effect of a fiction, in James, is that of a parable. The images of the observed world carry an idea, his real subject. He is not afraid to start from vague intimations of his most general subject, which is life: "I want,"

---

\* It was sheer critical acumen that made James appreciate Naturalist work; the subjects were not his meat at all. He was hard on the Goncourt brothers, of whom he said (justly) that "what they commemorate is the breakdown of joy"; and he had no liking for Hardy or Huysmans. But as early as 1881 he argued against a friend's hostile review of Zola and thirty years later he not only yielded the fullest admiration to three of the great works but credited Zola with having set a new standard of "handling" in collective scenes. (*Selected Literary Criticism*, New York, 1964, p. 120; V. Harlow, "T. S. Perry and Henry James," *Boston Public Library Quarterly*, July 1949, p. 50; Henry James, *Notes on Novelists*, New York, 1914, pp. 63-64; and Geoffrey Keynes, *Henry James in Cambridge*, Cambridge, Eng., 1967, p. 18.)

he notes in 1893, "to do something fine, a strong, large human episode . . . that brings into play character and sincerity and passion. . . .I feel again the multitudinous presence . . . the surge of *life*." And although by his method of induced "hallucination," he tends to show passionate conflicts from the inner side of the drama, he also keeps his eye on the usual outer objects—love, money, death, clumsy fears, vulgar ambition, emotional blackmail, and the rest. His observations of the current world move from outer to inner and back again as he sees in 1895 the approaching century: "The deluge of people, the insane movement for movement, the ruin of thought, of life, the negation of work, of literature, the swelling roaring crowds." He is so full of this spectacle that it inspires an occasional doubt as to technique: "I'm too afraid to be *banal*."

But he is altogether a man of the nineties: his art is his castle. Art presents him with "fearful difficulties," but also with "consolation and encouragements." Without it, "the world would be indeed a howling desert." As soon as he crosses the threshold of art, "I believe, I see, I *do*." Yet—it must be said again—this "1890" brand on the shoulder means, not art for art's sake, but art for life's sake. James loves his characters—especially his women—not alone for their delicacy and fastidiousness, but for their "acuteness and intensity, reflection and passion." The culminating statement of James's loyalty to life is given by Lambert Strether in a great scene of *The Ambassadors* and that statement is addressed not to artists only but to all men and women.

Like the Naturalists and the Symbolists, by the end of the century every conscious mind worked under what must be called the cultural pressure of science, and that, too, was something new. The word science was incessantly hammered into the public mind and its associated virtues conjured up—rigor, order, patience, skepticism, experiment, hypothesis, tested truth. These methods and virtues became what all decent minds must display, even when bored or baffled by science or simply wanting to restrain its imperialism. The trappings of science themselves figured as the lure in two new genres still abundantly flourishing: science fiction, which H. G. Wells first endowed with terror and a significance beyond mere wonder at mechanics; and detective fiction, which since then has taught the public most of what it knows of chemistry and pathology. Conan Doyle gave the impetus with Sherlock Holmes, who combines scientific "powers" with being a moody esthete and drug taker. Then R. Austin Freeman systematically made applied science the main interest of his stories from 1905 on, shortly before

E. C. Bentley established the form for the modern full-length tale with *Trent's Last Case* (1912), and rescued the genre from obesity, melodrama, and the French police.

In describing this haphazard interchange between art and science within what is obviously one culture, not two, the word science has been used as if it also was one thing from the time of its public triumph to the present. A doubt was indeed hinted at when I said that the Naturalists accepted the mid-nineteenth-century idea of science as clear and simple—matter charted by experiment. The Symbolists, though unsuspecting, were in fact closer to the spirit of the new science of the nineties, which was shedding "matter" and common sense and looking beyond them into an ideal world of symbols and "pure" relations. That kinship would have made many poets and intellectuals unhappy. All who thought of themselves as sensitive regarded science—booming and useful—as part of the enemy, the world. The crusade against this powerful coalition has continued into our times precisely because the bearing of the new science has not reached or convinced the crusaders. That is a pity, because the result has been to contaminate all the arts with the same unceasing complaints: "Down with bourgeois values—with commerce and calculation, technology and scientific reductivism, the factual mind murdering the poet." Never, perhaps, has there been so much repetition of social, moral, and esthetic teachings through art, despite its claim to be autonomous and above worldly thoughts. The public has swallowed the preachings in the theatre, the art gallery, and the bookroom with a quite Victorian obedience; it still responds as artists still reiterate. To anyone who, like myself, grew up in one center of innovation during the latter years of "the turn," the more than half-century since 1920 can only seem the Age of Déjà Vu.

The transformation of science which should have cut off the plaint began when the phenomena of electromagnetism and radiation failed to fit the equations for matter and motion that had been perfected since Newton. After the Michelson-Morley experiments of 1887 had failed to show the existence of an "ether" for light waves to be carried in, and when the Pierre Curies discovered radium—a substance 'paying heat away indefinitely out of its own pocket,' as James put it—it was evident that the accepted scheme of things was in trouble. Soon the work of Rutherford, Planck, Poincaré, Einstein, Minkowsky, and their colleagues produced a new version of the universe.

Well before their inspirations were confirmed, the very idea of "laws of nature" and of "exact science" had been reconsidered. As James remarked, the so-called laws were no longer thought of as inflexible commands but as pragmatically tested 'correspondences, approximations, [and] so numerous that there is no counting them; so many rival formulations are proposed in all the branches of science that investigators have become accustomed to the notion that no theory is absolutely a transcript of reality, but that any one of them may from some point of view be useful.' Said Poincaré: "Geometry is not true, it is convenient."

At the same time, the atom lost its primacy as the small, ultimate unit of matter and became a little planetary system made up of a core and circling electrons. But that was far from the end of the breakdown, as every newspaper reader now knows. He is perhaps less aware that the new facts changed not merely the contents of science but also its character. The exploration of the subatomic world had, in the words of a contemporary, "dematerialized matter" and shown to what extent scientific statements—says James again—are 'only man-made language, a conceptual shorthand.'

The upshot was that science could no longer be spoken of as "organized common sense"; the educated public could no longer "follow the progress of science" as it had done with awe and pleasure for two and a half centuries. It was not alone the mathematics of the subject that was abstruse, it was the ideas themselves that defied imagining—curved space, zero mass, a wave without a medium. The ways of the universe, recently so clear and simple, were now as obscure as the syntax and meaning of a Symbolist poem. Did either the science or the poem point to reality? And what does "real" mean at this late date? In what sense do the physicist's particles exist? By now some of them are called "virtual." Most are, quite literally, but a flash in the pan, seen only in their decay as traces on film.

And the language that goes with the fantasmagoria! Is it chance that has lately inspired sober men of science to borrow terms from James Joyce and name what they find as if they were poets or humorists: *quark, charm, strangeness;* and also: *anti-matter, nuclear democracy?* As to the facts, can it take so many fugitive impalpables to make up what we experience in our normal state? It is ridiculous for popularizers to keep talking about the "building blocks of the universe." Anything less like blocks could not be imagined. And why do our plain senses and our learned minds contradict each other so violently while engaged in the same inquiry? The universe more and more resembles an infinite onion without a core, which ingenious man goes on peeling forever.

Physical objects and scientific objects are clearly different kinds of things—perspectivism at work, as James's *Psychology* had explained before the atom came apart: 'The order of scientific thought is quite incongruent with the way in which reality exists or with the way in which it comes before us. We break the solid plenitude of fact into separate essences, conceive generally what exists only particularly. The reality exists as a *plenum*. All its parts are contemporaneous, each is as real as any other. But we can neither experience nor think this *plenum*. What we experience is a chaos of fragmentary impressions; what we *think* is an abstract system of hypothetical data and laws.'

In the earlier science, moreover, the observer and his point of view were left out on purpose; science was "objective" precisely because it ignored his presence in the cosmos. The new science found that it had to take account of the observer's position. It had to conceive of space-time as a continuum, to accept *dis*continuity in the quantum emission of radiation, to admit the impossibility of ascertaining at once the speed and the position of a particle, and to consider light as waves or as particles according to the convenience of the moment.

The anticipation and explanation of what occurred—by James or anybody else—had a meager influence on common thought and speech. The educated may be aware of the general drift in non-technical form, but they continue to talk and reason in mechanical terms like Spencer and Huxley. True, since the twenties some philosophers and religious thinkers have argued from the so-called indeterminacy principle that there is now a basis in science for religion, free will, and the soul. The books on this topic are always sure of wide acclaim; but they misconceive physics and do not convert materialists. Trying to use science to prove that nonscience is after all "scientific" is the recurrent mistake. It is indeed pathetic to see an advanced civilization expecting physical science—itself now at grips with the impalpable and the virtual—to validate, to "authorize" realities that mankind has experienced for thousands of years.* The desire to get the approving nod from science before feeling or thinking as one feels or thinks only shows how superstitiously science is taken, and how little the wisdom of the nineties has been let into our intellectual life.**

Yet there is nothing obscure or remote about that wisdom. Nietzsche, Ernst Mach, Samuel Butler, Poincaré, and others are accessible and highly readable; and of course William James, who shows how science has always worked, not by copying reality bit by bit till the map is

* Whitehead wittily remarks: "Scientists animated by the purpose of proving that they are purposeless constitute an interesting subject for study." (The *Function of Reason*, Princeton, 1929, p. 12.)

** A Swiss physicist, Marcus Fierz, makes the same point somewhat differently: "The scientific insights of our age shed such glaring light on certain aspects of experience that they leave the rest in even greater darkness." (Quoted by Victor F. Weisskopf in "The Frontiers and Limits of Science," *Bulletin of the American Academy of Arts and Sciences*, March 1975, p. 25.)

complete, but by framing concepts which will connect phenomena by "taking as"—light *as* waves, gravitation *as* the curvature of space. None of this can be done without 'ignoring conditions which are always present. The elementary laws of mechanics, physics, and chemistry are all of this sort. The principle of the uniformity of nature is of this sort; it has to be sought under and in spite of the most rebellious appearances; and our conviction of its truth is far more like a religious faith than like assent to a demonstration.'

In short, what happened in the nineties is not that science finally encompassed all of life; on the contrary, it fled from every tangible part of it, and like an absentee prince issued from a distance laws that the natives cannot understand. But the laws can be applied, by technology, and their effect readily felt. So we may say that science is one domain, its boundaries fixed by its assumptions, and the world of experience is the entire limitless territory. But owing to the cultural lag, the world still thinks of science as gradually colonizing the whole; people see what falls under its rule as real at last, and expect that the rest will shortly be brought there.

The results of this self-enslavement to authority are beyond calculation. In private life it undermines self-confidence and encourages superstition. James called science when taken so 'an idol of the den, or rather, of the shop,' and he warned that 'if the religion of exclusive scientificism should ever succeed in suffocating all other appetites out of a nation's mind, that nation will surely fall a prey to its more richly constituted neighbors.' Certainly, in most important matters "science" has nothing to urge and pseudo-science pronounces fifty-six different ways. But the faith reinforces our commonest mode of thought: reductivism. Nothing is what it seems; it is something else, hidden, below, and smaller but potent.* This "it" explains actions, opinions, tastes, loves, mistakes, and their opposites. What happens is not the result of an act by a person but of a process due to some component that science has found. If we were thoroughgoing in our reductivism we would say that some nuclear particles are radical and others conservative or that quarks and quirks are causally related.

The real joke is that in its own work science has got rid of this crude linear thought: 'The activity and the causal efficacy which lingered in physics long after secondary qualities [color, taste, and the like] were banished are now treated as illusory projections outwards of our own

---

* From the "Editorial Notebook" of the *New York Times*, June 29, 1981: ". . . but generally I believe it is not the tragic sweep of human history and the whips and scorns of time that bring on depression. Rather, it is some internal disposition of the glands."

consciousness. There are no activities or effects in nature. Nature only exhibits changes which habitually coincide with one another so that their habits are describable.'

The pattern of our scientism is from physics, and for laboratory purposes it does physicists no harm if they are tacit materialists. One cannot always be examining premises and implications. But among biologists doubts have arisen again and again. Since the nineties it has been astonishing how many leading ones have been brought up short by the inadequacy of the mechanical-material principle and have registered the evidence against it.* James did not take part in the debate, though his knowledge of physiology (which he taught) entitled him to an opinion. But his position may be inferred from a remark to a colleague on what pragmatism does not mean: 'Of course, everything can be expressed—after a fashion and theoretically—in terms of chemistry, that is, everything except the vital principle of the whole; and that, they say, there is no pragmatic use in trying to express; it has no bearings—for them.' Chemistry does shed light on life, but life evidently takes in something more than chemistry, or there would be no additional sciences to pursue, such as biology, physiology, and psychology. True, in biology the hypothesis of a "vital force" proves as untenable as mechanism. It is this deadlock that has led to the view which one of its adherents has called "resignation";** that is, doubting mechanism, denying vitalism—and keeping on with research.

After the recent triumphs of molecular biology, description in the life sciences has adopted the language of information theory; everybody speaks of a genetic "code," the RNA "messenger" and what a molecule "dictates." The revigorated faith in heredity even speaks of genes as if they were carriers of knowledge and attitudes, which then burst like blossoms in the developing mind. But the famed geneticist Dobzhansky objected that the gene held only potential characters and needed many favoring circumstances outside itself.*** And Waddington opposed "the strait-jacket of information theory." In any case the whole "code" and "information" imagery sounds culpably anthropomorphic, a 'projection outward of our consciousness,' if ever there was one.

* Notably Hans Driesch, J. S. Haldane, Giard, de Haan, McDougall, and Woodger.
** See Nordenskiöld, *History of Biology*. (New York, 1936, p. 612.) See also "The Limitations of Mechanistic Methods in the Biological Sciences," by Adrian G. Moulyn in *The Scientific Monthly*, July 1950, pp. 44–49: "If one wants to study biological phenomena that can be isolated from the rest of the organism, mechanistic methods . . . are eminently successful. . . . If, however, one seeks to understand the organism as a whole, mechanistic methods fail" (p. 44).
*** For example, the gene required for breeding the giant fruit fly will not bring about giantism in the absence of the necessary food.

To sidestep this difficulty, some scientists make of it a general condition of science. Science, they say, cannot give a description of reality; it can only create "metaphors" for what it finds. We seem to hear the Symbolist poet again. But metaphor will not do; it implies a four-term relation. "A babe in the woods" is a metaphor; it says that an innocent person is to the world of intrigue as an infant would be to exposure in the woods. But in scientific utterance there are only two terms: the theory and the perceptions that test it. So the mystery remains why concepts and their equations happen to fit observed relations among things.

A modern mathematical physicist, E. P. Wigner, says this accident must not be forgotten, because it is as likely as not that "the unifying idea, the ultimate truth that science seeks for harmonizing all phenomena" will be forever out of our reach, especially if "a theory of consciousness or even of biology should be formulated, for it might well be in conflict with the principles of physics, and abstract theorizing on this issue would be by definition beyond the reach of experiment." In other words, none of the doubts and difficulties raised so widely and acutely at the turn of the century have been resolved; but the failure since then to make them common knowledge is hardly excusable.

Nothing in all this robs science of any of its glory. Its achievement is all the more stupendous that it has been fashioned in defiance of both logic and common sense.* At the same time, its paradoxical character as verified but unstable propositions should be acknowledged and its place in human experience understood: it can no longer be that of absolute monarch; it does not say the last word on everything. One of its friendliest interpreters, Karl Popper, sums up the case: "Science is not a system of certain or well-established statements, nor is it a system which steadily advances toward finality. Our science is not knowledge (episteme): it can never claim to have attained truth or even a substitute for it such as probability.... We do not know: we can only guess. And our guesses are guided by the unscientific, and metaphysical, though biologically explicable faith in laws, in regularities.... Like Bacon, we might describe our own contemporary science as consisting of 'anticipations, rash and premature' and of 'prejudices.' But these . . . are carefully and soberly controlled by systematic tests. Once put forward, none of our anticipations are dogmatically upheld.... On the contrary, we try to overthrow them.... Every scientific statement remains tentative forever."

---

* An exception must be made for the contribution of technology to science. Historically, mechanical inventions, themselves the fruit of common sense, came before (and spurred) the scientific explanation of their working. Modern historians of science should not read back the idea of paradigms and intellectual models into the days of plain trial and error, classifying, and measuring.

A good example of this perpetual revision and uncertainty is occurring right now in the enlarging debate about evolution. I do not refer to the political struggle between creationists and scientists over what to teach in schools. Nor, in the debate that I mean, is evolution itself in question. It is the extent of the evidence for evolution as well as the means by which it proceeds. These were burning issues in the 1890s, after appearing to have been settled at long last by Darwin in 1859. James's pitching into Spencer at every turn was part of the scientific critique of the Darwinian orthodoxy—the orthodoxy that had blocked recognition of Gregor Mendel's work and delayed the rise of genetics by forty years.

The means of evolutionary change proposed by Darwin and Alfred Russel Wallace in 1859, and before them by Spencer, Naudin, Charles Wells, and Patrick Matthew, was Natural Selection. "Nature"—a personification of the environment—was conceived as "selecting" from among living forms those fitted to survive. This fitness might be enhanced by any new variation in form that was useful in escaping enemies or leaving offspring. By the gradual addition of one small feature after another over eons of time, it was thought that entirely new species would arise—the origin of *species*, not of life. And the whole process would explain the present profusion of living forms on earth.

This hypothesis has been the sole doctrine in modern biology, because it fits the scientific assumption that mechanisms, automatic and purposeless, account for change—any change. Earlier doctrines were less automatic, but had been widely accepted after long debate. In 1750 Buffon was almost the only evolutionist, but by 1800 many "natural philosophers" believed firmly in evolution, among them Lamarck, Goethe, and Charles's grandfather Erasmus Darwin, who wrote on the subject an important work in two volumes.* To complicate the story, Charles Darwin was not a true Darwinist. By the sixth and last edition of the *Origin of Species* (1876), he had come to believe that natural selection was aided by direct environmental effects and by the use and disuse of organs, which implies the inheritance of acquired characteristics. The former was Buffon's contribution and the latter was Lamarck's a generation later.

In the nineties, strict, single-cause Darwinism was losing ground. First, the rehabilitation of Mendel's work spurred the study of heredity and showed how stable and distinct species were. Then studies of the

---

* *Zoonomia* (1796). For a short history of the evolution of evolution, see my *Darwin, Marx, Wagner* (1941; 3rd ed., Chicago, 1981); and for a full account, Samuel Butler's *Evolution Old and New* (1879–1882).

environment changed the picture of "Nature red in tooth and claw." "Weak" forms seemed to survive, "mutual assistance" took place, and biologists began to speak of "the fitness of the environment." A new hypothesis of "emergent evolution"—that is, self-propelled—gained adherents. To save pure Darwinism, Weismann argued that the survival of the fittest occurred not in the external world but in the "germ plasm": chance determined only whose genes got transmitted with what variation. Others stressed the role of the large mutations (De Vries), while the specialists in classification and in fossil remains brought up factual objections to the idea of a graduated series of animal forms with only occasional gaps.

Besides, Darwin had not stuck to his last; in several large works he had made detailed applications of his ideas to morals and society; so had Huxley and Spencer, making evolution part of an ism, a doctrine, and thus vulnerable on many fronts. James, a convinced evolutionist, had frequent occasion to deplore the 'fatal effect of Darwinian ideas in letting loose the springs of irresponsible theorizing. Survival of the fittest, sexual selection, cross-fertilization, are phrases [that encourage] a sort of a priori philosophizing which to a truly scientific mind is disheartening.' Again and again in his scientific work, James felt he must rebuke the 'ordinary' or the 'cock-sure' or the 'simple-minded' evolutionist. Their error came in part from the tendency 'to make one single principle do duty for the explanation of every possible case—the vice which is the curse of the Spencerian school: an illusory simplicity gained only by leaving out essential data.' Darwin's biology itself, which James studied and even reviewed while still in medical school, he found guilty of circular reasoning: 'these marks are facts of reversion to the wild form X, because circumstances make it likely that X is the common ancestor; then X is all the more certainly the common ancestor, because these marks of reversion are all found in X.' Certainly, during the last hundred years the magic word Evolution has been a mind-stopper as overworked as the earlier syllable "God."

As to the means of evolution, James did invoke natural selection in dealing with the rise and influence of leaders, ideas, and inventions in society; there, surely, selection has the literal meaning of choice by conscious beings. But he kept an open mind about what the late nineteenth century called Neo-Lamarckism—a return to the hypothesis ultimately shared by Darwin himself that characteristics acquired by a creature during its life might be inherited by offspring. Most important, James kept in view what almost all his contemporaries except Samuel Butler forgot, namely, that the real means of change, and hence the origin of species, were those "accidental variations" presumed to be useful. 'Darwin never professed to explain the original variations, but only to account for their accumulation and survival.' Forgetting this gap in the theory was so usual among "enlightened" intellectuals that James wondered whether readers who needed to be reminded of the fact 'were worth writing for at all.' He added that 'accidental' meant only 'belonging to a cycle of causation inaccessible to the present order of research' and that a whole range of inborn traits and powers in man—illustrated by the familiar pair, music and mathematics—could never have had survival value.

It was Samuel Butler, like James a firm believer in evolution, who just before 1890 drew up the full indictment of Natural Selection. The term, he said, begged the question by imputing a choice like an animal breeder's to a personified Nature. And no deliberate breeder had ever produced a species. Darwinism moreover assumed that every change that made a species evolve was necessary for survival; but each variation being small, it needed many additions and long ages to *make* it useful. Darwin himself was bothered by the eye, which needs so many separate parts neatly put together before it can see. How could it evolve out of fragments none of which sufficed to help live and procreate? The eye kept him awake at nights and he did not even know what has only recently been discovered, which is that tears, besides lubricating, supply an antiseptic substance. When one thinks of the myriad elaborate schemes and devices by which animals and plants maintain and reproduce themselves, the hypothesis of a chance assembly line seems hard to accept.*

That was why Huxley himself during the nineties admitted that natural selection was only a hypothesis and that Darwin's *Origin* was difficult to follow on the main issue. He was accurately reflecting the new uncertainties. Soon, Henry Adams was to sum up the public's state of mind: "Forty years ago, our friends always explained things and had the cosmos down to a point, *teste* Darwin and Charles Lyell. Now they say that they don't believe there is any explanation, or that you can choose between half a dozen, all correct. . . . Every generalization that

---

* For example, it is hard to conceive how a single selective pressure could produce a different external appearance and behavior with each season in butterflies that belong to one and the same species throughout the year. And as for "strange devices," one may instance those butterflies' development of "shivering for warmth" to make up for the inadequacy of their wings.

Or again, what of the aye-aye, a lemur from Madagascar with remarkable hands, complete with claws, an opposable thumb, and a very thin third finger that enables the creature to pull out tree-boring insects from their holes? Did that single finger attenuate itself gradually? If so, what was its survival value before it got to the right size? If it got thin by sudden mutation, how did the one or two lemurs so gifted outrival the rest, who up to then had managed to survive quite well?

we settled on forty years ago is abandoned. The one most completely thrown over is gentle Darwin's survival of the fittest, which no longer has a leg to stand on."

How—on what leg—do things stand today? What is one to believe? Between the ferment of the ante-bellum period up to 1914 and the current requestionings, the views of the leading authorities made up the so-called Modern Synthesis. It was a working agreement rather than a common conclusion from independent findings. It was no longer the fantasy that is still taught in many schools and colleges with charts or "trees of descent," dates of "great changes on the way to Man," and the assurance that the proofs of evolution by natural selection are all in hand. "Old Darwinism," with its erroneous teaching that Charles Darwin discovered evolution and the origin of *life*, has survived—not fittingly—but it forms no part of the Modern Synthesis.

That synthetic effort left Darwinism rather to one side and concentrated on genetics guided by mathematics. It also gave up many details of the "story" of evolution and acknowledged the great difficulties that go with it. Besides these general and local retreats, it appeared that the dozen or more scientists who led the advances of the last half-century were apt to contradict each other and themselves on main points, as Darwin did. One must conclude that the data are resistant to clear theorizing.*

The latest news on the tangled subject is that experimenters have reported cases supporting the inheritance of acquired characteristics. It is not the first time such an announcement has been made. Previous cases have periodically been discounted as irregular or fraudulent.** The importance of the issue is this: if traits acquired during life can be inherited, then the purposive behavior of the creature becomes a possible cause of evolution—as Darwin (but not the Darwinists) believed to the end. It may be said that James, like Darwin, accepted the inheritance of acquired characteristics. It seems required for two of James's important suggestions: one, that our inborn ideas have become such over the course of human evolution; and two, that some of the unconscious motor responses of the organism were once conscious and then delegated to the cerebellum. Both acquisitions imply use and purpose. And of course, if purpose is introduced into biology, there is a breach in the basic tenets of science.

---

* Anyone interested will find a dispassionate comparison of authoritative works in a short and lucid book by Norman Macbeth, *Darwin Retried*. (Boston, 1971.)

** The Russian Lysenko was declared fraudulent quasi-universally, but Brown-Séquard, at one time at Harvard and working in Paris in the eighties and nineties, was a respected and indeed famous physiologist.

Further questions about evolution were aired at a conference held in the Chicago Field Museum of Natural History in November 1980 and again that same winter in Toronto. While some of the assembled scientists—two hundred or more—brought out perplexing facts inconsistent with the Modern Synthesis, they also pointed to the "myths" embedded in the wider, older doctrine. Others defended it, and still others expressed fears that the belief in *evolution* would suffer from the renewed doubts about *Darwinism*. They probably wish—a little late—that their predecessors had not religiously falsified history for so long and made the two terms synonymous.

The present discontent is still too recent to assess. The unfortunate resurgence of a "Creationist" movement of opinion adds to the confusion by rekindling the scientists' fears and crusading ardors, especially since Bible believers have seized on the "Big Bang theory" of neighboring physics to use as proof of an act of creation. No situation could better illustrate the general failure to understand science: not the sciences in their multitudinous detail, but what science is and does. A better understanding of our formative period, a wider diffusion of even such brief extracts from James as I have reproduced, could have become part of common knowledge in the ordinary way of cultural transmission, and by supplying a background for debates and revisions made them less bewildering.

For my part, I am an evolutionist, perhaps of a unique sort. I am not a Darwin*ist* but until further notice I am a complete Darwinian: I believe in the grandfather and the grandson and the holy spirit of their inquiries. On the one hand, the thought of innumerable separate creations by a Master bio-engineer defies probability and many facts. On the other, the story of protoplasmic blobs shooting off little changes in all directions until, by piling up useful accidents of shape, they wind up as a profusion of complex creatures overlooks the presence of coordinated arrangements—of design. Poor Charles Darwin worried over the complicated eye; but what of the simple buttocks of mankind, the distinctive feature that led to representative government by making committee work possible? It—they—developed no matter how gradually after the erect posture: we had to stand in order to want to sit. But why the decision to stand up? Chance works in mysterious ways its wonders to perform. But if it should be proved that acquired traits can be inherited, the suppressed side of Darwinism will reappear and perhaps the ideas of grandfather Erasmus also.

His hypothesis was that the creature itself developed changed characteristics, from use and need. He distributed, so to speak, the task of design among many striving individuals and species. This account may be as hard to imagine as the other two stories, but at least we can see birds and beavers and spiders and pilot fish doing amazing things in ways nobody taught them, ways so complex as to seem beyond buildup by chance—for example, the deposit of a drop of poison at the end of each tentacle of the Portuguese man-of-war. The visible power in living things to exploit and adapt would then explain the variety of lifestyles as "home grown," a pluralism only part-conscious and often doomed to perish by natural selection, but also fostered by the "fitness of the environment," which mostly means other forms of life.

In the several "revolutions" of the nineties, from the new physics to the new psychology, the role of ideas was paramount; it was philosophical criticism that set off the redefinition of space, time, matter, energy, and mind. The ideas themselves arose from the perception of facts that previous schemes could not accommodate. Whether the target was Victorianism, Positivism, or Darwinism, the general assault was against past rigidities and in the name of the Jamesian truth that reality overflows all attempts to capture and bottle it. The new consciousness embraced intellectual novelty and change of method, recognizing as it did that life, truth, morals, the law, religion, mathematics, science, logic itself contain an irreducible psychological ingredient. This reinstatement of the human element widened the fields of inquiry and brought a sense of depths unexplored.

For the individual, it meant the release of much repressed thought and feeling. Moral standards were not given up, as the depreciating of morality had seemed to presage at first, but judgment was made more humane. Not only practical and scientific but also spiritual renovation could be felt as something electrical in the air. Perhaps even the mournful decadents felt it and were only posing, to seem accursed and interesting. At any rate, boundaries were being crossed, remote ideas were being joined, "impossible" notions were being entertained—not just about time or geometry but about emotion, sex, and personality, single or double, conscious and unconscious. The "transvaluation of all values" which Nietzsche had called for was under way. The ambition of the age is suggested by a sardonic jotting of Strindberg's: "The multiplication table is in need of examination and reform."

In his own domain we saw James acutely aware of the turn; its works vindicated the stand he had taken against Spencer and Hegel and the "medical materialists." In 1908 at Oxford he could express confidence that 'our age seems to be growing philosophical again. Even non-philosophers have begun to take an interest in a controversy over what is known as pluralism or humanism. It looks a little as if the ancient English empiricism, so long put out of fashion here by nobler-sounding German formulas, might be repluming itself and getting ready for a stronger flight than ever. It looks as if foundations were being sounded and examined afresh.'

In speculative thought the output was indeed enormous. I have mentioned Bergson and Butler and Nietzsche, who belong to the "wide public" category. But theirs was also the time of C. S. Peirce, Ernst Mach, Samuel Alexander, Arthur Balfour, and the brothers Haldane; of G. E. Moore employing linguistic analysis in philosophy; of Hans Vaihinger and his "Philosophy of 'As If'"; of Croce the demolisher of Marx's dialectical materialism in Italy; of Unamuno in Spain, and with him the somewhat younger Ortega y Gasset, both fighting Positivism; of the German (existential) phenomenologists Husserl, Simmel, Scheler, and Dilthey; of Ostwald the great chemist-philosopher, of J. B. Stallo, the Cincinnati judge who trenchantly criticized the assumptions of physics; of Emile Boutroux, who showed the "laws of nature" to be contingent, statistical, and hence not "exact," and who later wrote an admiring study of James.

These and other thinkers diverged on many points and will be found classed in different schools—some were still partly in the German idealist camp—but all responded to the new presence of the human mind as adventurer on earth prior to the scheme, the system, the classical order. Everywhere, fixed notions of Reason and Truth were yielding to what Karl Mannheim called relational thought. It was these more complex, less fated conclusions that aroused Lenin to fight a rearguard action for Marxist determinism in his onslaught on Ernst Mach and on the movement at large that Lenin in 1909 dubbed "empirio-criticism."

This orchestral burst of thought was felt and heard in all realms at once. History and the ologies started afresh in new shapes. They liked more than ever to call themselves sciences, beginning with history; but the label meant only high seriousness. For Lamprecht in 1904—to take but one example—the "new science of history" denoted its fusion with psychology and sociology. Our latest psycho- and quanto-historians have added nothing to his theoretical base. For the more philosophical Dilthey, history was the rethinking of past cultural forms and events—much later Collingwood (and Spengler in a slanted way) adopted this fruitful formula. And the now glorified French school of "Annalistes" (with Fernand Braudel as its present hero) adopted the "anti-bureaucratic" view that all the activities of mankind should figure on the historian's canvas.

This was also the premise of the new anthropology, which Franz

Boas turned away from measuring skulls and classifying by skin pigment to studying whole cultures, on the spot, and with no preconceptions about any "primitive mind." Emile Durkheim similarly defined a "social fact" as an entity not derived from anything else and capable of being studied apart from economics or psychology. Like "a culture" for the anthropologist, "society" acquired a life of its own—the way "the crowd" does, as was shown in 1896 by Gustave Le Bon in the classic that bears his name. To such conceptions we owe the flood of studies that tell us how we behave, how "our culture" works upon us, and how "his society"—the artist's—warps his soul.

These reports were not at first intended to be deterministic, as is shown in the autonomy claimed by each sector. But just as James's naturalist psychology was twisted thirty years later into a mindless Behaviorism, so the rejuvenated ologies of the turn of the century, by following the path of least cultural resistance, have seen their ideas baked hard into ideology or neo-materialism. The most conspicuous case is that of Freud who, in his desire to be a true scientist and recognized as such, espoused determinism while offering a therapy based on immaterial means: a true feeling, a correct memory, a new perspective formed the essence of his cure. On these points more will be said shortly when James's work on the Unconscious comes to be discussed.

New knowledge in other fields was likewise a recasting of the subject, not a mere addition to it. With Henry Sidgwick and Saussure, linguistics entered new realms of research and speculation of which we see the outcome today. Alfred Sidgwick gave logic a new aspect by studying the use of words in reasoning. Pitt-Rivers and Flinders Petrie developed new techniques for archeologists. Frazer, by his first volumes of The Golden Bough (1890), reawakened writers and readers to a mode of thought long-neglected: the mythic. With its aid, Gilbert Murray reinterpreted ancient Greece. Other ventures, perhaps not to be classed as knowledge—faith healing, hypnotism, psychical research, occultism, theosophy—contributed to the ferment and were sometimes productive, as we saw in Yeats's case. Nor should one overlook the revival of the encyclopedic Thomist philosophy, well adapted to the temper of science and hospitable to the claims of human reason in living this life and apprehending the next. But these could not match the influence of Frazer's work. In his view myth involved magic, and magic was a primitive form of science. These conclusions have been discarded and some of them again readmitted, but whatever their status, they served to reunite man to his past. And Frazer's great collection of tales remains, a source of fictional patterns and poetic images exploited throughout modern literature.

That linguistics has tried to supplant history and that myth-and-symbol-hunting has debauched criticism are consequences Frazer would have disowned. He shared James's root conviction about the locus of reality. As he put it near the end of *The Golden Bough:* "the history of thought should warn us against concluding that because the scientific theory of the world is the best that has yet been formulated, it is necessarily complete and final.... the generalisations of science, or in common parlance, the laws of nature, are merely hypotheses devised to explain that ever-shifting phantasmagoria of thought which we dignify with the high-sounding names of the world and the universe. In the last analysis magic, religion, and science are nothing but theories of thought."

So if one had to find a single intention that underlay all this reconstruction of the western mind, it might be stated as the reuniting of elements hitherto divided by analysis. For doing so meant rediscovering the role of the observer within the whole, restoring what James called personality, what Samuel Butler called mind, to its place in the universe. This aim is what prompted James's followers to rename his empiricism and pragmatism a humanism.*

Such are the facts and considerations that justify (I hope) the exaggeration by which I have ventured to refer to this pregnant quarter-century as the reign of William and Henry. The two Jameses obviously did not lead or outtop the galaxy of geniuses who reshaped the western mind from 1890 to 1914. But William and Henry were part of the vanguard and may in this sketch of the times serve as representatives—Henry of the tone and temper of art and its new moral tendencies, William of the new premises of science and the new conceptions of truth, mind, and social life.

And as we saw earlier, in moral outlook William and Henry were at one. The pragmatism that Henry avowed to William taught that ethics, honor, virtue were the matching of promises or pretensions with conformable conduct. Moral excellence consisted in being fastidious about the means employed to satisfy desires. This criterion is the one William saw as governing the search for truth—truth by results: not *any* results, not careless neglect of other truths; and similarly in the moral life, not neglect of rival claims, for every claim creates an obligation.

When conventional opinion serves up its contrast between William, "typically American," and Henry, so innately civilized that he could

---

* Humanism is by now a poor name for any set of ideas or beliefs. Since the Renaissance it has been applied to half a dozen different views, and its connotations of atheism are confusing and unfortunate.

enjoy life only abroad, it is well to remember a letter culminating in a famous phrase that William wrote to H. G. Wells in 1906: 'Exactly that callousness to abstract justice is *the* sinister feature and, to me as well as to you, the incomprehensible feature, of our U.S. civilization. When the ordinary American hears of cases of injustice he begins to pooh-pooh and minimize and tone down the thing, and breed excuses from his general fund of optimism and respect for expediency. "It's under-standable from the point of view of the parties interested"—but under-standable in onlooking citizens only as a symptom of the moral flabbi-ness born of the exclusive worship of the bitch-goddess SUCCESS. That—with the squalid cash interpretation put on the word success—is our national disease.'

The imaginary divergence in temper and delicacy between the broth-ers leads me to discuss a further discord that some have found within their mutual affection and admiration. Henry evidently adored William from childhood, as his words to the end of his life testify.* But William has been represented by some devotees of Henry as having repaid this warmth with a nagging hoity-toity condescension. This elder-brother stance is attributed to William's lack of esthetic sensibilities, to his ener-getic, coarse-grained practicality, which resented the other's fineness and thus prolonged "sibling rivalry" into maturity.

In this account of the philistine badgering the artist the pièce de résis-tance is a letter that William wrote to Henry about *The Golden Bowl* and *The Wings of the Dove*. It begins, let it be noted in passing, with a remark about *The American Scene*, which William says seems to him 'in its peculiar way *supremely* great.' He goes on: 'you know how op-posed your whole "third manner" of execution is to the literary ideals which animate my crude and Orson-like breast, mine being to say a thing in one sentence as straight and explicit as it can be made, and then to drop it forever; yours being to avoid naming it straight, but by dint of breathing and sighing all round and round it, to arouse in the reader who may have had a similar perception already (Heaven help him if he hasn't) the illusion of a solid object, made (like the "ghost" at the Polytechnic) wholly out of impalpable materials, air, and the pris-matic interferences of light, ingeniously focused by mirrors upon empty space. But you *do* it, that's the queerness! and the complication of innu-endo and associative reference on the enormous scale to which you give way to it does so *build out* the matter for the reader that the result is to solidify, by the mere bulk of the process, the like perception from

---

* Henry wrote to Edith Wharton on August 26, 1910: "My beloved brother's death has cut into me, deep down, as an absolute mutilation." The loss of William's "beautiful gen-ius and noble intellect" made Henry feel "stricken and old and ended." (*Edith Wharton, a biography,* by R. W. B. Lewis, New York, 1975, p. 292.)

which *he* has to start. As air, by dint of its volume, will weigh like a corporeal body; so his own poor little initial perception, swathed in this gigantic envelopment of suggestive atmosphere grows like a germ into something vastly bigger and more substantial.'

Now that is superb criticism—the rare kind which, while objecting to the manner or method or substance of a work of art, nonetheless describes these exactly, vividly, and appreciates the effect without relishing it. William admired without enjoying and said so fairly—not a word here of sarcasm or denigration or belittlement, which indeed no student of William's character would think possible about *any* subject of discourse, much less the work of the "Dearest Henry," "Beloved H.," whom he salutes at the head of every letter.

True, from the very intensity of that affection, and no doubt from habit as the elder and leader since boyhood, William goes on to warn, not hectoring, only pleading with the solicitude of love: 'But it's the rummest method for one to employ systematically as you do nowadays; and you employ it at your peril. In this crowded and hurried reading age, pages that require such close attention remain unread and neglected. You can't skip a word if you are to get the effect, and 19 out of 20 worthy readers grow intolerant. The method seems perverse: "Say it *out*, for God's sake," they cry, "and have done with it." And so I say now, give us *one* thing in your older, directer manner, just to show that, in spite of your paradoxical success in this unheard-of method, you *can* still write according to accepted canons.'

The "paradoxical success" William refers to is that which he himself so fully perceives, not any success Henry had with readers and critics. Henry in his final period lost them, bewildering them as he did *not* bewilder William. Except for a little band of faithful, it took some forty years for the third manner to justify itself and become fodder for academic dissertations. And to this day there are (and will continue to be) objectors, armed with tenable arguments against it.* Those put by William imply no obtuseness or philistinism: 'For gleams and innuendos and felicitous verbal insinuations, you are unapproachable, but the *core* of literature is solid. Give it to us *once* again!'**

* Having been among the earliest few to help turn the tide in Henry's favor during the 1930s, I may acknowledge the force of these arguments without endorsing them and without losing an ounce of my enjoyment and admiration of the later novels. Their rightness or wrongness must be established, like all artistic merits and demerits, on the exactest pragmatic judgment.

** Mrs. Henry Adams, a person of true sensibility, spoke for many when she said of Henry in his third manner: "He chews more than he can bite off." The English poet Francis Thompson, reviewing *The Golden Bowl*, wrote: "The intellectuality overpowers the sensuous and objective traits proper to a novel until one has the impression of reading an abstruse treatise of psychology rather than a tale." (*Literary Criticisms*, ed. T. L. Connolly, New York, 1948, p. 299.) It was left for Van Wyck Brooks to characterize the third manner a regrettable aberration.

In so urging, William was inspired by unmixed devotion. He wanted for Henry the widest renown, the fulfillment of his manifest destiny as the greatest living American novelist. Henry was unmoved, quite properly. He had retorted in strong words to earlier hints of the same sort.* The brothers knew how to take each other better than their biographers do: 'your last was your delightful reply to my remarks about your "third manner," wherein you said you would consider your bald head dishonored if you ever came to pleasing me by what you wrote, so shocking was my taste. Well! write only for me, and leave the question of pleasing open!' And William reiterates his clear perception of Henry's achievement: 'I have to admit that in The Golden Bowl and The Wings of the Dove you have succeeded in getting there after a fashion, in spite of the perversity of the method and its longness.' And after the critiques comes a due disclaimer of their authority: 'For God's sake don't answer these remarks, which (as Uncle Howard used to say of Father's writings) are but the peristaltic belchings of my own crabbed organism.'

These brotherly exchanges are exemplary. It is remarkable, to begin with, when members of a family read the books it produces—it is almost unheard of—and still more remarkable that literary artists with different aims should so far sympathize with each other's productions. William saw his own task as discerning, transfixing, and reproducing in concrete language the multiplicities of experience, in order to have it seen as the fundamental reality that we take in endless ways for as many purposes. Henry, out to slay the very same conventions of life and thought, wanted to go beneath them into the ramifications of feeling, fantasy, and will that are concealed from ordinary sight. So his exhibiting could not be done through direct exposition like William's, but only through the presentation of the stuff itself: he must not tell, but show—and hence their divergent methods.

That both writers acquired from their father and the home circle a comparable gift of language, a genius for imagery and similitudes, and the power to disentangle and describe the motions of the human mind, is what inspired the anonymous epigram that Henry wrote novels like a psychologist and William wrote psychology like a novelist. But the range of their tastes was not the same, as we just saw, and the "con-

---

* "I mean (in response to what you write me of your having read the Golden B.) to try to produce some uncanny form of thing, in fiction, that will gratify you, as Brother—but let me say, dear William, that I shall be greatly humiliated if you do like it, and thereby lump it, in your affection, with things of the current age, that I have heard you express admiration for and that I would sooner descend to a dishonored grave than have written." (Letters of Henry James, 1920, II, p. 43.)

temporary productions" that William admired and Henry dismissed showed William as the more inclusive appreciator. He found merit and pleasure in the works of Shaw, Wells, and Chesterton when these were still dubious newcomers. He read Tolstoy soon after French translations appeared and thought *War and Peace* the greatest novel ever written.* He relished Hardy and William Dean Howells, and he fell—like the rest of the western world—under the spell of the young Kipling ('Much of his present coarseness and jerkiness is youth only, divine youth') though his admiration for some of the later works grew less.

Despite his own disclaimer that he was deaf to poetry, William's prose is studded with quotations and allusions to the English poets from Crashaw to Francis Thompson, as well as to Homer, Dante, the Greek Anthology, and the great French and German writers. He felt the power and the vision in Zola's 'truly magnificent' *Germinal,* and in *Madame Bovary* 'the persistent euphony, a rich river that never foamed or ran thin.' As for Renan, then a demigod to the French, James quite early detected in him, behind the music of the prose, foppish vagueness, insincerity, and pretension. He was moved by the "art and spirituality" of Baudelaire at a time when Henry found little in *Les fleurs du mal* but "weeds plucked from the swamps of evil." William knew his Whitman thoroughly, taught his students to enjoy him, and quoted him repeatedly and at length, though rejecting his voracious Oneness engulfing all things. He perceived, moreover, the difference between that poetic transcendentalism and Emerson's. He enjoyed reading Shakespeare through in chronological order—not just reading about him—and the upshot was equal surprise at the playwright's power and the amount of ranting and bombast, due no doubt to his 'intolerable fluency.' Independently of Shaw and Tolstoy, William was also puzzled by Shakespeare's lack of moral, cosmic, or other convictions; for he was close reader enough to see that in a work of fiction without a perceptible tendency, the characters' utterances cancel each other out and produce a species of nihilism. These judgments, like his objection to the monotony of Palgrave's *Golden Treasury* ('too much of an aviary') were not the conventional ones acquired in college: William had never gone to college; his humanistic education was foreign and we may be sure that his opinions owed nothing to low,

---

* 'Life indeed seems less real than his tale of it, and now I feel as if I knew *perfection* in the representation of human life. The impressions haunt me as nothing literary has ever haunted me before.' (*The Letters of William James and Theodore Flournoy,* ed. Robert C. LeClair, Madison, Wis., 1966, p. 56.)

middle, or high fashion: they were his own, formed without aid from literary cliques.*

To William, then, art was an extension and clarification of the fluid, fugitive deliverances of experience. It was a special, deliberate mode of "taking." It was creation also in the sense in which the mind creates all objects, but with inner and outer relationships offered in a form that gives the impression of complete novelty and a heightened reality. It satisfies a need not satisfied by work, play, thought, or worship.

From such a sensibility one might expect a corresponding subtlety of perception and behavior in personal relations. The link is not logically necessary but empirically likely. And indeed we find James acute in thought and feeling about others, alive to their pain or distress in an almost pathological degree—William's sister, Alice, is here the best witness—and we have seen him large-spirited in judgment. There would be no need to say more if the gratuitous partisanship I have mentioned as blinding some of Henry's admirers did not couple with the imputation of insensitivity to Henry's art the charge that his brother treated him in a bullying way that concealed an unconscious jealousy.

The allegation raises large questions about the craft of biography and the application of therapeutic psychologies to documentary evidence. These questions I have discussed elsewhere.** William and Henry's exchanges—and they were full and frequent for men moving mostly in different circles and different countries—are in the conversational tone of perfect equality. On the point of William's "bullying" and apropos of literary disagreements, here is one of his messages to Henry:

'Last Sunday I dined with Howells and was much delighted to hear him say that you were both a friend and admirer of Rudyard Kipling. I am ashamed to say that I have been ashamed to write of my adoration of that infant phenomenon, not knowing, with your exquisitely refined taste, how you might be affected by him and fearing to *jar*.'

Not one letter to Henry, incidentally, makes use of the raillery and

---

* Henry notes in his diary for 1905: "William's inspired transcript, on the exquisite little urn of Alice's ashes, William's divine gift to us and to *her*, of the Dantean lines:

> Dopo lungo exilio e martiro
> Viene a questa pace."
> [After her long exile and torturing pain
> she has come to peaceful rest.]

(*The Notebooks of Henry James*, New York, 1947, p. 321.) Henry's adjective "Dantean" correctly indicates "in the manner of Dante," for the lines do not occur in the poet's works. William was probably inspired by the neighboring ideas expressed in *Paradiso, X*, 129 and *XV*, 148 and he relied on his memory, since *Exilio* should have read *esilio* or *essilio*. Another partial model occurs in *Epistolae*, III, 24, but it is not likely that James read Dante's Latin works.

** *Clio and the Doctors*, Chicago, 1974.

comradely banter that William occasionally indulged in with friends whom he knew to be ready to reply in kind. Times change, mores also, and the verbal vehemence that obtained at the James Sr.s' table is doubtless a thing of the past. It was never common in America. Indeed, one may wonder how Henry Sr. fared after writing to an editor about "the slipslop ladled out in your journal," this being said not in anger but in friendly rallying.*

To be gentlemanly without being genteel, free and blunt in expression in the manner of European intellectuals, was and is a style at the opposite extreme from the foam-rubber, public-relations language that we nowadays adapt to all occasions. Try to imagine an academic of the 1980s writing to a colleague as William did to John Jay Chapman after reading an article in manuscript: 'Wonderful! wonderful! Shallow, incoherent, obnoxious to its own criticism of Chesterton and Shaw, off its balance, accidental, whimsical, false; but with central fires of truth "blazing fuliginous mid murkiest confusion," telling the reader nothing of the Comic except that it's smaller than the Tragic, but readable and splendid. Pray patch some kind of finale to it and send it to the *Atlantic*—Yours ever fondly, W. J. (Membre de l'Institut).'**

To understand William properly one must grasp at once why the last phrase was tacked on: he disliked titles and honors and pushed away as many as he could, but membership in the French Academy of Moral Sciences had descended upon him and it could not be shuffled off without churlishness. So, once Chapman has been raked appreciatively over the coals, it occurs to James that his closing instructions sound schoolteacherish and he puts down his "qualification" to make fun of himself, knowing that Chapman will be amused.

A period when it was possible to enjoy receiving such a missive and replying in kind was one which bred strong personalities, while manners permitted strength and individuality to be admired. What met with contempt was vulgar feelings—suspicion, envy, self-pity: they were not to be given room in heart or mind; indeed, they were to be chased out if

---

* Or again, the recipient's fellow believers are "like dried Cod on Boston wharf" compared with the live fish. The critic adds: "Pardon my freedom. I was impressed by your friendliness towards me and speak to you therefore in return with all the frankness of friendship." (Quoted in *The Letters of William James*, London, 1920, pp. 15–16.)

** In our time the correspondence between Nabokov and Edmund Wilson might be cited as belonging to that tradition, but one should note that Nabokov was a European, Wilson a crabbed temperament, and their verbal scrimmage was interrupted by periods during which offense was felt and resented.

More to the point are such records as Harold Nicolson's diary, where one finds quoted the hard-hitting words of his friends about his work, with no change in their mutual affection and regard. As for the abuse in the letters of Ezra Pound, it shows an American writer's misconception of how the thing is done. The model of the true manner is found in the letters of Bernard Shaw—and William James.

they crept in, and conduct must be in keeping. I use "conduct," and not our social-science term "behavior," to stress the primacy of responsibility and control. Whether that "inner direction" (in modern technicalese) was better for man and society than the open-heart self-surgery we consider more honest and unassuming is not a question to thrash out here. The fact of the difference is the point, and its bearing on biographical judgment.

The present-day tendency is for biography to tell us not about character—that is, conduct—but about its conditions. The mode is scientism and concept-work; the famous man or woman is a congeries of troubles who collapses into a case. That is how the relations of William and Henry (which we cannot leave yet, for this very reason) have been traced back by some to a lifelong conflict due to their parents' partiality: William, the bright youth, occupied center stage while Henry sat in a corner reading. Hence arrogant superiority in the older, mixed with an envious hostility to the younger's finer clay. Elsewhere, by the same method, both brothers have been shown as culpably victimizing sister Alice: they blandly suppressed her literary talents, which in turn aggravated her illness and ended her life prematurely. The parents were guilty of injustice, it seems, and as for William and Henry, they wanted no competition in their domain—charming motives all around.

This depiction is made up of anachronisms. American and British society in the later nineteenth century was certainly not hostile to women writers. Hundreds of them achieved success with very slender gifts, just like the men, and Alice James in the nineties could have done as much had she willed so. Unfortunately she was an Elizabeth Barrett without a Prince Browning. To require now that her family should have given "encouragement" is to ask that the habits of today should have obtained a century ago. Not until education and the cult of art became fully democratized, after the First World War, did it become usual to "encourage" everybody on little or no provocation. Earlier, man, woman, or child had to signalize his or her ambition by an overt performance, before someone—usually a practitioner—gave encouragement. No one yet knows whether our less selective way has brought gain or loss.

What is certain is that the real objection to turning biography into diagnosis is not that it bemeans those subjected to it. Rather, the issue is: what does the public want to hear about? Some readers think the discussion of art and ideas more interesting than the retrospective gossip that is often substituted for it and they find character blurred, not highlighted, by clinical analysis, since such analysis rests on seeing different *persons* as similar *patients*. How inapplicable to the James family! With a resident father of no trade or profession, yet full of stillborn ideas and much traveled, the clan of seven was singular in its own day. Its uncommon complexion, its European tincture, its intense affection, its private language prone to exaggeration, the tone and mores of its time*—these are the true objects of a legitimate biographical curiosity. And these traits and habits make it risky to judge Jamesian actions unless we modify our standards to reflect the family "culture." We do as much for the natives of Borneo.

Accordingly, when we read William's letter to his father at the news of his approaching death, we should not think it strange or unfeeling but perfect for them both.** We should similarly read aright a passing phrase that has been interpreted as the culminating "proof" of William's lording it over Henry. It occurs in a letter to the head of the American Academy of Arts and Letters declining the honor of membership in the Academy, after having been for some years at the lower level of member of the Institute. James gave as his main reason his dislike of inactive bodies, whose only purpose seemed to be to announce: '"we are in and you are out."' He then goes on for half a dozen lines ironically playing with the idea that as an austere philosopher he should by precept and example '"refrain, renounce, abstain"' from the vanities of this world, including this new title, 'even though it seems a sour and ungenial act.' He adds that he is encouraged in this course by the fact that 'my younger and shallower and vainer brother' has accepted membership, and the pair of them would overpopulate the Academy with Jameses. Henry is thus tagged in comparison with William's high-minded abstention and in keeping with the irony of the whole fantasia.

Those are the words that have been seized on to clinch the charge of antagonism repressed and bursting out. One might more plausibly say that this version of the incident shows us up. The Jameses sustained a feeling of family oneness in a fashion quite forgotten today, when to be alive is to be invidious first, and loving—if at all—second. The nineteenth was, after all, the century of love. It had its rules of the heart-and-mind. To record Henry's lifelong devotion to William and also to represent this "beloved brother" as in essence a brute, unappreciative and jealous, is to turn Henry into a thick-skinned brute himself, or else into a man lacking in pride and courage, who could endure repeated

---

* Exaggeration to William and Henry alike was in part a relief from the exactitude of conscious art and thought. As a sample, here is Henry's acceptance of an invitation: "'COME!'" he cried, "I would walk across London with bare feet on the snow to meet George Santayana. At what time? One thirty! I will come. At one thirty I shall inevitably, inexorably make my appearance." (The Legend of the Master, New York, 1948, p. 83.)

** See below, pp. 260-61.

slights and call the inflicter a "noble intellect." This is rather much to ask of our faith in arcane psychology.

And the historical facts suggest something further. William wrote his letter to the Academy from Cambridge (Mass.) on June 17, 1905, having just arrived there from London on the 11th. Henry, in the United States for the first time in twenty years, was returning from California and arrived east on the 16th to stay a few days with Will at 95 Irving Street. When one knows the two men as persons, not cases, it is beyond the bounds of imagination that the day after their reunion William vented his secret spleen behind Henry's visible back in two derogatory adjectives.

What one should see in them, on the contrary, is a sign of William's exuberant joy when absorbed in the thought of those he loved. Mock insults to express strong affection are nothing new between men, and the reason for their presence in a letter to a stranger is that they were in effect addressed to Henry: the likelihood is that William showed or read the letter aloud to him as they discussed, inevitably, the instant decision not to accept the empty title of academician. What Henry himself recorded in his diary of that time and place was this: "Whenever one is with William one receives such an immense accession of suggestion and impresssion that the memory of the episode remains bathed for one in the very liquidity of his extraordinary play of mind." On neither side any hint of woundings intended or suppressed. Deep psychologizing on this frail topic is itself shallow and vain. A knowledge of the depths, as we are about to see, calls for much study and reflection on a greater mass of collective evidence, together with a scientist's modesty as to any results obtained.

# Beyond the
# Conscious Mind

The reader will remember that after James had given up medicine, his career embraced psychology and philosophy jointly, not in succession.* This important fact strikes us again as we approach the birth of James's second masterpiece, *The Varieties of Religious Experience*. Delivered as the Gifford lectures in Edinburgh in 1901–1902, the book appeared in June of the latter year—those were the happy days of rapid publishing. The work is manifestly one of psychology; its subtitle is "A Study in Human Nature," and its subject matter and naturalistic method are in no way compromised by the application of James's three philosophic principles: radical empiricism, pluralism, and pragmatism. The first formal exposition of pragmatism, we remember, took place in 1898, and the first accounts of the other two doctrines also appeared in the late nineties, just preceding the systematic preparation of these lectures.

But besides philosophy, *The Varieties of Religious Experience* contains much that comes from James's studies in psychopathology. These were extensive and formed the basis of a set of Lowell lectures delivered in Boston in 1896 under the title of *Exceptional Mental States*. The phrase indicates the position: James sees no sharp distinction between the healthy and the morbid mind. 'Much comes from our attitude

---

* By a not unusual fluke of academic administration James was successively: assistant professor of physiology after teaching psychology for two years; assistant professor of philosophy two years after undertaking to write *The Principles of Psychology* and establishing the first psychological laboratory in the country; and full professor of philosophy five years before the *Psychology* appeared and seven before he handed over the direction of the laboratory. But of course he had begun teaching Philosophy 3 thirteen years earlier, while still in the department of physiology!

toward it. No one symptom is by itself morbid: it's the role that it plays.' Melancholy, for example, occurs in every life. The eight lectures on: Dreams and Hypnotism, Automatism, Hysteria, Multiple Personality, Demoniacal Possession, Witchcraft, Degeneration, and Genius were never published or written up from the notes that survive, no doubt because the invitation to give the lectures on religion came during the same year and the subjects overlapped.* But James had yet to do an enormous amount of research in the records and the scholarship of the specifically religious experiences.

As the reader will surmise, those experiences can be exceptional without being pathological. For exceptional states include sleep, which would be 'a dreadful disease but for its familiarity.' As for dreams, which no one takes for an illness, they should be 'a subject of medical wonder': dreams enlarge our knowledge of waking life, like intoxicants, both generating partial states that 'look like all of reality.' James then ushers in the unconscious: 'waking experience may also be but a fragment of the whole. Who says that ordinary experience is the only one possible?'

With a foreshortened vision of the past, modern opinion tends to think that the unconscious was discovered by Freud. It's a case of Darwin and evolution over again. The fact is that, like Darwin, Freud was the great summarizer and propounder who applied to a vast array of preceding research a system apparently justified by success. As Freud's scheme was meant for therapy, it spread among the people and supplied our age with widely applicable ideas and a set of phrases for lay psychologizing. But in the definitive work on *The Discovery of the Unconscious*,** one has to read some 420 large pages and cover a century and a quarter of medicine and psychology before reaching Freud.

What broke open the unitary, single-minded mind—if one may so put it—was the evidence arising from two phenomena finally accepted as genuine: hypnotism and hysteria, together with the kindred manifestations of double personality. By the same token, these facts made impossible the mechanical view of mind. James in the nineties was one of many researchers in physiology, psychology, and medicine who were grappling with what seemed an "epidemic" of mental disorders. Was it the result of an accelerated industrial and urban life? Or was it only the result of closer attention to troubled people, in keeping with the new humanitarian impulse? James's early work, especially in hypnotism, of

---

* Mr. Eugene R. Taylor, a scholar from Cambridge, Mass., has been working on a reconstruction of the Lowell lectures from reports in the press and from references in the notes to cases and authorities James used. When published, the work should form an important addition to the James corpus.
** Henri F. Ellenberger, New York, 1970.

which he gave a brilliant summary in a chapter of the *Psychology*, influenced Pierre Janet (who coined the word subconscious) and Janet's work led direct to Freud's. Others—James's friend Flournoy in Geneva; Josef Breuer, Moritz Benedikt, Eugen Bleuler, Krafft-Ebing in Austria; Liébeault, Bernheim, Forel, Dubois, Adolf Meyer in Switzerland; Richet, Ribot, Binet, Charcot in France; Frederic Myers, Edmund Gurney, Havelock Ellis in England; and many more whose names live only in the pages of learned journals now unread—were bending their minds on new enigmas of the mind.

Hypnotic trance had at long last (more than a century after the Mesmer of mesmerism) been found readily producible—almost commonplace; and so had the strange working of post-hypnotic suggestion—the patient's acting out after the trance a command given during its course.* There was even the possibility of cure by hypnosis. The pioneer in this therapy was the American Dr. John Kearsley Mitchell of Philadelphia, whose work James noted in the *Psychology*. If a mind could thus be manipulated by someone other than its owner, what became of the familiar oneself-hood? James's contemporaries read in Du Maurier's novel the sad story of Trilby and her hypnotist Svengali. Stevenson's "Dr. Jekyll and Mr. Hyde" popularized the drama of the split personality, then deemed abnormal, now the cherished state of every educated being. James conducted many hypnotic experiments with his students in the psychology laboratory, where he had built apparatus for the purpose, and he published the results in a statistical study (1887). He saw opportunities for systematic therapy and recommended to his ailing sister Alice in England that she try a practitioner there. A hundred years later, the medical use of hypnosis is enjoying a new vogue; it is even being used in criminal investigation by the FBI and Scotland Yard.

James saw in hypnotism the sign that the mind is a 'confederation of psychic entities,' not a monarchy. Everybody, he notes, experiences a hypnotic situation twice a day, when going to and from sleep; which shows further that the so-called trance is not sleep. Variability everpresent in the waking mind becomes dissociation under the "magnetism" of a leader or the irresistible suggestion of a mob.

The further manifestations of the split mind in automatism, hysteria, and unconscious whispering confirmed the fact that the conscious self does not hold the field alone. 'A sound mind is in gear, integrated with every other idea and having a field, a focus, and a margin. What is on the margin, however, *controls*.' In automatic writing, in cases of double

---

* In the 1780s Benjamin Franklin and Lavoisier were the leading minds of a committee that investigated Mesmer for five months and reported that cures by hypnosis were coincidences; the "fluid" could not be grasped by the senses—and his activities should be suppressed by law.

or triple personality, the control has slipped, and rival steersmen alternate at the helm. Since the *brain* is not split or damaged, the inference is that the entities involved are mental. Among the hypotheses then current, James adopted the idea proposed by Frederic W. H. Myers in 1892, of a "subliminal self."* It is presumably the container of the buried memories of the human race, for the conscious mind is able to delegate what it has learned to other centers, as in habit and instinct. The idea was in the air: Samuel Butler in *Unconscious Memory* (1880) and Ewald Hering in a lecture of the previous decade had suggested it independently. It was an aspect of vitalism: all organized matter has memory, conscious and unconscious, or it could not "behave"; it would only be pushed and pulled.

To James, the subliminal self forms with the conscious mind a continuous spectrum, not distinct layers with a corridor between. Observing this, he posed what he called the Myers Problem: how elements from either end of the spectrum can come into consciousness through the same channel—for example in playing the piano while conversing, automatism and consciousness cooperating. For there is no such thing as an "unconscious idea." Only what is conscious can be part of consciousness, but other mental systems can and do operate simultaneously with consciousness. The casual use in post-Freudian times of phrases like *unconscious idea* and *unconscious motive* has led the public to see the mind as a condominium with several floors below ground, its tenants on each struggling to dictate to those above and the top one having no role but to obey. The conscious mind we carry above ground thus becomes once again an epiphenomenon, as in old Huxley's automaton theory of 1872.

James respected the rich contents of the subliminal self. The flights of genius are 'uprisings from below' and so are the highest religious visions. The archaic ones represent our past and the transcendent our future. This state of things suggests that a cure for hysteria and other mental disorders must be found in ideas, for the origin of the morbidity is psychic. In discussing hysteria, James quoted Janet, Breuer, and Freud, who were just then creating a stir throughout the learned world; and when reviewing four related works in the *Psychological Review* for 1894, James lent his authority to the Breuer-Freud position: the ob-

---

* With his usual generosity, James made this acknowledgment without qualification. But two years before Myers, he had written an article on "The Hidden Self," using some hints from Janet and his own experimental observations. The Romantics, moreover, had recorded the existence of a second self in their tales of the *Doppelgänger* and were convinced that true art was the expression of an unconscious force over which reason and rules had little control. Nor should we forget Dr. Oliver Wendell Holmes's notion of the mind as multi-chambered and his three "psychiatric" novels (1861, '67, '85) in which the instincts account for the schizophrenia, phobia, and split personality of his representative characters.

served weakness of hysterics was the result and not the cause of the split mind.*

That notice marks a date: by this earliest mention of the principle in the United States, mental healing was established as proved fact and legitimate. James reports and concurs in the hypothesis that the memory of a shock can become 'subconscious and parasitic.' He quotes the now commonplace expression *trauma(ta)* |*wound(s)]* used by Breuer-Freud, and he amplifies it as 'thorns of the spirit, so to speak.' He knew something about thorns at first hand, since he attributed his own self-cure, twenty-five years earlier, to the recognition (helped by reading Renouvier) that ideas and the will were involved in mental disorder; it was not invariably caused by a physical lesion. Not being exclusively a book psychologist, James moreover had the intuition of others' mental states as much as of his own, and he pointed out in the essay on "The Energies of Men" that 'There are in every one potential forms of activity that actually are shunted out from use.' Social conventions, over-critical rearing, and other repressions account for 'part of the imperfect vitality under which we labor. One part of our mind dams up—even *damns* up!—the other parts.' James had previously quoted to his students 'a Viennese neurologist of considerable reputation' [Freud] as saying that no doctor can be fully effective until he acquires a sense of the "buried life" in the patient. So it was no new attitude for James to describe in his review the method proposed for 'handling the buried idea' and 'making a new connection with the principal consciousness, whose breach is restored.'

The notion of the mind healing itself by its own action, of "mind cure" as it was then vulgarly called, required courage in any scientist who adopted it, and for more than one reason. Scientific materialism still reigned in spite of all informed objections, and medicine was visibly making strides by adhering to it. The age, moreover, saw the mushrooming of new religions by the score, from Theosophy (Mme. Blavatsky) and Christian Science (Mary Baker Eddy) to various styles of New Thought, Raja Yoga (Swami Vivekananda), Esoteric Buddhism, and other occultisms and orientalisms that professed to enlarge or restore the true self. Amid the lot flourished other groups touting secular formulas explicitly for "mind cures." All these gave mental healing a bad name. James, ever-inquiring and truly scientific in that he formed no *a priori* judgments, had been interested in the facts where available. He quite recognized that the movement had 'reached the stage when the demand

---

* Perhaps it still needs to be said that in technical usage "hysterics" are not patients who scream and gesticulate; on the contrary, they are apathetic, incapable of action or decision, often unable to feel the pricking or cutting of the skin, without memory or sense of self, and sometimes split into two or more selves.

for its literature is great enough for insincere stuff, mechanically produced for the market, to be supplied by publishers.' But that there were
authentic cures was to him evident. Observant physicians had long
since noticed that their patients' "mental set" played a part in the success or failure of physical treatment, and James, having also studied the
psychology of belief, was in all ways prepared to credit the claims of
Breuer and Freud.

Twenty to twenty-five years later, our century was ready to accept
the most elaborately scaffolded mind cure of them all: psychoanalysis.
It dawned on the first postwar world as a true science. For Freud always insisted that he had charted the workings of a material force,
"psychic energy," and that the entities he named Id, Ego, and Superego
were organs of the mind.

James did not live to see the doctrine in its full-blown state. One year
before his death, when Freud came to Clark University in Worcester to
deliver five lectures on his work and receive the first and only honor-
ary degree of his career, James journeyed over to hear him. He was
impressed by Freud's sincerity and painstaking, but not convinced that
the libido or sexual drive was an all-sufficient agency, as Freud and his
Vienna group affirmed: 'They can't fail to throw light on human nature,' he wrote to Flournoy (another student of the unconscious), 'but I
confess he made on me personally the impression of a man obsessed
with a fixed idea. I can make nothing in my own case with his dream
theories, and obviously "symbolism" is a most dangerous method.' A
report of the Worcester conference said that Freud had 'condemned the
American religious therapy (which has such extensive results) as "very
dangerous" and "unscientific." Bah!' But, James went on, 'I hope that
he and his pupils will push his dream theory to its limits, as undoubtedly it covers some facts and will add to our understanding of "functional" psychology, which is the real psychology.'

At the conference, James also met Jung, who made 'a very pleasant
impression.' On his side, Freud was invigorated by being "received by
the foremost men as an equal"; and James made on him "a lasting impression." To those words in his autobiography written twenty-five
years afterward, Freud adds an anecdote: "I shall never forget one little
scene that occurred as we were on a walk together. He stopped suddenly, handed me a bag he was carrying and asked me to walk on, saying
he would catch up as soon as he had got through an attack of angina
pectoris which was just coming on. He died of that disease a year later;
and I have always wished that I might be as fearless as he was in the
face of approaching death."

James's skepticism about interpretation by symbols was matched by
Freud's about truth as pragma. As a positivist, Freud felt he must deny

to religion and philosophy any valid insights into the mind. No two men more vividly illustrate the pluralism of temperaments than James and Freud. Calling the pragmatists "anarchists," Freud repeats the usual misconception that if truths "are products of our own needs and desires . . . we find only what we need to find and see only what we desire to see; so that it is absolutely immaterial what views we accept." When we reflect that Freud's system contains not a scrap of empirical observation but is all inference, fashioned into constructs and analogies so as to fit situations inherently confused, we see that his sole method is pragmatic and depends for its chief verification on success in curing. This his scientism would not let him see—the scientism that arose from his "need and desire" to be taken seriously, as he deserved.

Again, Freud's view of art was the opposite of James's. The esthetic interest, for James, is native to the mind, and in him it was acute and intense. To Freud, clinging to "reality" in its narrowest sense, art was, like sleep and dreams, an escape from the real: art "does not seek to be anything else but illusion. Save in the case of a few people who are, one might say, obsessed with art, it never dares to make any attacks on the realm of reality." He concludes that it may be judged "harmless"— except perhaps to those who, like Freud, find music irritating. Elsewhere, Freud dismisses the whole world of art with the remark that artists exploit their daydreams commercially to satisfy their desire for money, fame, and women. One might well think this an imputation that deserves analysis.

In reporting the Breuer-Freud mode of cure, which by recalling the trauma makes its meaning conscious and manageable, James had pointed out a happy consequence: 'The awful becomes relatively trivial.' Later, in a presidential address to the American Philosophical Association, he again recommended the study of "dynamogenesis": 'Here is a program of concrete individual psychology, at which anyone in some measure may work. It is replete with interesting facts, and points to practical issues superior in importance to anything we know. I urge it therefore upon your consideration.' Laboratory psychology could describe within a small range, as James knew; dynamic psychology could explain both the normal and the abnormal in the mind.

He could not suspect that as it gained ground, the new psychology would become another device for reductivism and a public mode of discourse which effectually replaces—not to say destroys—the fullness and inwardness of any subject at issue. To take an early and Freudian example: James's colleague Dr. Putnam, of the Harvard Medical School, had been the prime mover in getting Freud to New England and he remained his advocate and promoter in this country. Freud was grateful but also annoyed at some of Putnam's views that diverged from his own and were tinged with "optimism" and "altruism." After Putnam's death, Freud permitted himself to judge those views by calling the man "one of those happily compensated people of the obsessional type for whom what is noble is second nature and . . . unworthiness an impossibility." So much for the role of character.

To depreciate an idea or explain it away by finding (i.e., guessing) the reason why it is held is the prevailing form of polemics in the twentieth century. We owe it to the popularity of Freud and Marx, whose systems imply that any resistance to them proves how right they are. Agree or disagree, it is all one: dispute a Freudian interpretation of Nietzsche and the act shows your "defense mechanism" at work.* Similarly, any opinion contrary to Marxism-Leninism reveals only the fraudulent bourgeois thought. This perversion of the sense in which ideas are instrumental is the new obscurantism in the garb of high theory. It ignores the central point James made about the mind, that all its "takings" are individual, as is the working of each unconscious.

Freud's unconscious as it soon came to be exploited outside the doctor's office and as it has been understood by the public is on the contrary standardized. It presents a "physics situation" (so the *Encyclopedia of Psychoanalysis* puts it), where compound movements among the forces of the id, ego, and superego yield such products as the dreams and parapraxes (slips of the tongue) that we register. The mind functions according to a Freudian mechanics as the cosmos does to a Newtonian, and the machine is set once for all in childhood. No real change between ten and eighty. The psychoanalysis that renders featureless so much modern biography under an appearance of making it more profound is in effect a return to the simple idea that every character is moved by a "ruling passion," or as Ben Jonson and the Elizabethans called it, a "humor." It dictates—and thus gets rid of all our explaining.** The practice is a retreat from the complexity of the vast, multiform unconscious first studied so fruitfully in the Jamesian era.


After meeting and chatting at Worcester, James and Jung had no further exchanges, but Jung continued to read and reflect on James. Unlike

---

* E.g., the argumentation in the late Professor Walter Kaufmann's *Discovering the Mind.* (New York, 1980.)

** That "dictation" is no metaphor is shown in a typical account of his own work by a modern writer: "The same task that could not be done because unknown emotional powers had forbidden it, now had to be done because other unconscious tendencies ordered it." (Preface to *Myth and Guilt* by Theodor Reik, New York, 1957, p. xii.) Yet in the Postscript to the same book, the discovery it contains is ascribed to "a stroke of luck like finding a neglected object in the street." (P. 431.) What had happened to the executive in the unconscious?

Freud, he regarded pragmatism as a valuable "transitional" philosophy, because it pointed to the importance of efficacy in judging between intellectual formations. But he believed that a deeper source of knowledge must be tapped if conflicts about truth were to be resolved. While making this objection, he was trying to establish his theory of types—introvert and extrovert—and this brought him to study James's distinction between tough- and tender-minded. Again, Jung found encouragement in the doctrine that temperaments play a role in the choice of philosophies; but he devoted a long chapter to disputing James's typology in the light of German philosophy.

Jung honestly misunderstood James's terms. He did not even see that they do not amount to a through-and-through division of mankind, but only indicate tendencies. To Jung's haggling over each of the traits that James listed, one need only quote James on a cognate topic: 'We should not treat our classifications with too much respect'; the reason being that individuals are not standard units. Jung also misstates pragmatism when he says that it restricts the value of truth to its utility. Now Jung in his so-called "fallow period" (1913–18) was bent on devising a system which would reconcile opposites in philosophy. James was on the contrary intent on giving each of them room to differ and to possess part of the truth without mutual cavil. Unifying was left to individual effort, the largest unity being the truest truth. For Jung, the collective unconscious—Butler's "race memories"—was to supply the unification, because these memories are presumably universal.

Jung's contribution, apart from therapy, has been to supply terms and notions particularly congenial to literary men. I remember J. B. Priestley's trying to persuade me, during one of his visits to this country in the early sixties, that no one concerned with art or literature, no one who wrote history or other works of intellect, could know what he was doing without familiarity with Jungian doctrine. But I had read *Dreams, Memories, Reflections*, and as a writer of history I could not swallow Jung's lumping of dreams, legends, and hearsay with recorded fact as if they were equal in evidential strength. Even among facts some are more equal than others.*

James, too, as a good historian objected to the method of symbol and myth; we heard him calling it in Freud's hands 'very dangerous.' Its essence being allusion, indefiniteness, it cannot help adding to the already vast morass of gossip and conjecture. It blandly ignores the pragmatic test, and the result is to bring down lives or works to a common

---

* This telling phrase was used, but not for the first time, by George Orwell in *Animal Farm* (1946). It belongs originally to Philip Guedalla, the historian and wit, who is also caricaturing Soviet reality in "A Russian Fairy Tale." (*The Missing Muse*, 1927, p. 308.)

likeness; symptoms and "elements," being concepts, are universal. Besides, by showing how easily worked such a system is, these proctologists of the mind encourage all the other schemes for decoding literature and art. Anything can be seen as a symbol replacing something else; any event or tale can be construed as a piece of myth or an ancestral archetype, any paired ideas as a metaphor. The imaginative perception of art, preferably wordless, thus gives way to perpetual verbalizing and the resolve to account for all features and details. This practice has degraded academic teaching and scholarship into a machine industry. Its workers neither believe in the myths nor take them as good stories but use them mechanically as interchangeable parts for the contents of the work of art. As one would expect, it was an American professor who sent C. S. Lewis (himself fond of veiling his thought in fantasy) a long questionnaire about the novel *Till We Have Faces*. Part of Lewis's answer was: "The children made mud pies not for symbolic purposes, but because children do."

How much more fruitful for our symptom-wearied day is the theme that runs through James's exposition of exceptional states of mind, that they are but aggravations and complications of ordinary ones 'by way of the menagerie and the mad house, the nursery, the prison, and the hospital.' Recent writers who have proclaimed "the death of psychiatry,"* because it patterns itself on medicine and oldtime science, would gain from a study of James's post-positivist naturalism. Its rule is to start from experience unreduced to something else and to reject no evidence, wherever it comes from. Was it not fortunate for Breuer and Freud that James's scientific openness led to his looking sympathetically into all accounts of mental healing? On their own authoritarian principles, the paper of theirs that James reported on in a respectable American journal should never have got a hearing.

What distinguishes James's view of the unconscious, then, is: that the line of demarcation from the conscious is dim and shifting; that the unconscious is at once individual, collective, and possibly wider still; and that it includes ancestral ideas and various responses formerly conscious and now inherited. It is not fixed in early years but capable of development and accessible to conscious thought. During life, habit and training produce unconscious modes of action that can be consciously summoned up and employed at will.

As the free investigator par excellence, James also looked into the claims of those interested in what we now call "consciousness raisers"—nitrous oxide, mescal, and other drugs producing what was then

---

* See the book of that title by Dr. E. F. Torrey (Radnor, Pa., 1974) and the writings of Thomas Szasz and Robert Coles, among others.

termed "anesthetic revelation." He tried them on himself with a fine recklessness, and his medical colleague in Philadelphia, the novelist S. Weir Mitchell, son of the doctor previously cited, urged him on.* But although James was interested enough to conduct a "census of hallucinations," he himself did not prove a good subject for such pleasures: 'It gives the most curious visions of color—every object of thought appears in a jeweled splendor unknown to the natural world. It disturbs the stomach somewhat, but that according to W. was a cheap price, etc. I will take the visions on trust!' He did not recommend the "drug experience" as a means of enlarging the mind, knowing that it can be enlarged only by tapping and *organizing* what is there.

Meanwhile, he was giving attention to mediums and other "psychic" manifestations and acting as a reporter for the American branch of the Society for Psychical Research, which he had helped to establish. It was through correspondence with the English founders Edmund Gurney and Frederic Myers that James had been confirmed in his view of the subliminal mind. In James's account, the medium's trance figures as a benign form of demonic possession; it is of course an aspect of the divisible self and in some ways resembles 'nerve shock in the American Civil War.' Similarly, the evidence of witchcraft often discloses a case of hysteria though not always. As for the effects grouped under the then current term Degeneration—phobias, compulsions, manias, and even more severe types of insanity—psychology had not yet come to grips with it. But James was sure that the mind is much more complex than the term degeneration implies. One slight comfort: 'one-idea'ed social reformers are apparently normal.'**

This happy thought leads James to the discussion of genius. Neither divine nor pathological, the genius is not normal in the sense of ordinary, but what the term really points to is a social conception, a function pragmatically fulfilled. Besides, such terms are relative—genius, health, normality have no essence or measure: 'the normal man is a nullity.' All we know, then, should induce tolerance of the morbid and further study, for it has much to teach us.

It has once or twice been said of James that to one subject alone he did not give due attention, the subject of sex. If by due attention is meant investigation or a chapter in the *Psychology*, the statement may stand. But if it means unawareness, or resistance to the facts, the com-

---

* In the spring of 1896, finding himself alone with his wife and youngest child in their house at Chocorua, N.H., without a telephone or transport or doctor within twenty miles, James considered the situation ideal for trying an unknown drug on himself: there would be no interruptions. (*Letters*, II, p. 35.)

** Accordingly today we must tolerate the propaganda of those who have the arrogance to call themselves "Citizens for a Sane World."

plaint is without foundation. There is a section on Love in the chapter on Instincts and throughout his writings, in illustration or analogy, James freely mentions 'the sexual passion.' In the *Psychology* he also refers to homosexuality, though regretting the need to advert to an unpleasant subject. To expect James or any of his contemporaries to have found it pleasant; or again, to imagine that in the very years when such facts were being marshalled and discussed for the first time, the author of a college textbook (which the *Psychology* was) could have aired them with our late-acquired (and incomplete) nonchalance, is to show oneself devoid of historical sense. The Victorian generations (William was born five years after the Queen's accession) were too alive to 'the animal potency of sex' (James's words) to refer to it in our debonair language. They never guessed that its explosive force could be defused, as we have done it, by simple publicity; that is, through ubiquitous quasi pornography, aided by talk in terms sterilized by science.

When James and his fellow scientists were dealing with hysteria they acknowledged through the very name of the disorder (*hyster* = womb) that it was somehow linked with sex. In the eighties and nineties the medical profession as a whole was observing sexuality with minute attention.* It knew, for instance, from many reports before Freud's, of sexual feeling and activity in children, as well as of the role of sex in art.** No, James did not shy away from what we absurdly call "the facts of life," as if life consisted only of genital facts. Early in the *Psychology*, in discussing Darwin's theory of sexual selection, James gives a vivid account of mating in frogs and toads, which takes place in 'an almost total exclusion of the power of choice. Copulation occurs *per fas aut nefas*, occasionally between males, often with dead females, in puddles exposed on the highway, and the male may be cut in two without letting go his hold.' One detects no shrinking prudery here nor elsewhere in James.

In declining to accept Freud's Libidinous Prime Mover, James was certainly not influenced by any distaste for the idea of sex. His reason,

---

* Ever since the mid-century, physicians had carried on research on the subject, among them: Clifford Allbutt, W. L. Distant, Balls-Headley, Schrenk-Notzing, Laycock, Playfair, Näcke, Krafft-Ebing, and the courageous American Denslow Lewis, whose "Gynecologic Consideration of the Sexual Act" was read in 1899 before the American Medical Association but denied publication in its *Journal*. Lewis made an issue of it and continued his researches and propaganda till his death in 1913.

** Nietzsche, Karl Just, Wilhelm Stekel, Colin Scott, Leo Berg, among others, contributed to this awareness. Zola has an episode of child sex in *Germinal* (1895); and ten years earlier, Mantegazza had surveyed *The Sexual Relations of Mankind*. See Stephen Kern, "Freud and the Discovery of Child Sexuality," *The History of Childhood Quarterly*, Summer 1973.

obvious to anyone familiar with his thought, was his mistrust of any all-purpose Single Cause. His perception of complexity and his freedom from the love of oneness saved him from that ever-recurring temptation.


James worked with "psychics" because he had no preconceived ideas about what the mind could or could not do;* and also because the purpose of the Society for Psychical Research was scientific. It meant to find out whether telepathy, poltergeist effects, hauntings, spirit return and spirit messages were facts or frauds. This effort was but another aspect of the urge to discover that animated the latter years of the nineteenth century. Science was not being flouted but enlarged. If hypnotic trance had turned out genuine after long skepticism and denunciation, it was rational to suppose that other impossible things in the lexicon of scientism might prove factual.

The difficulty was to devise tests under the conditions imposed by mediums and to keep away those who had already made up their minds pro or con. James devoted many hours and took many trips in the investigation and assessment of the "manifestations" selected by the Society.** His chief contribution was the study of a widely touted medium, Mrs. E. L. Piper. She convinced James and his wife that she possessed information that could not have been acquired in the ordinary way, but how she managed it was never resolved. When her "control" died, it fell to James to sum up all the recorded evidence about the man and Mrs. Piper. The strong and the weak points of the case are set forth with critical care. The verdict is Not Proven, though James 'finds himself doubting that Mrs. Piper's dream life, even equipped with "telepathic" powers, explains all the data.' His last word was: 'I remain uncertain and await more facts, facts which may not point clearly to a conclusion for fifty or a hundred years.'

The Jamesian writings on mediumship, as one would expect, are studded with typical word-sketches: 'Mrs. Piper's control "Rector" is a most impressive personage, who discerns in an extraordinary degree his sitter's inner needs and is capable of giving elevated counsel to fastidious and critical minds. Yet in many respects he is an arrant humbug.' There is no sign here of the gullibility that has sometimes been

* For example, the mind feels pain in a limb long since amputated, a phenomenon on which James gathered evidence and reported statistical findings.
** His written accounts, including letters, have been gathered into a volume edited by Gardner Murphy; *William James on Psychical Research.* (New York, 1960.)

imputed to James, on the ground that he "went in for" this forbidden subject.* What is valuable in his research is that he came to understand why in the psychics' performances there was so much fraud. As he pointed out, the same often occurs in the teaching of science—to save the demonstration from failure and with it the credit of the enterprise. But, he added, there has to be something to imitate, and in the repetitious manifestations, which show a species likeness through many ages and regions of the world, he surmised that there was a residue of fact.

It is worth noting that James did not enjoy this kind of inquiry. He pursued it in part to maintain a critical pressure on what he called Scientific Sectarianism—the people who were sure beforehand. But the work itself James found tedious, undignified, often disgusting—'a human rathole life.' He reflected that there was no reason why spirit messages—or "counterfeits" either—should be entertaining or dramatic, any more than ordinary backyard conversation. And he never forgot that 'what mankind at large most lacks is criticism and caution, especially when the conception has instinctive liking at its back. Were I addressing the Salvation Army, it would be a misuse of opportunity to preach the liberty of believing.'

His final impressions of psychical exhibits, a few months before his death, reinforced his surmise that 'our subconscious constitution' must be involved. For as soon as it is acknowledged that the conscious mind is not the sole keeper of feelings and images, that it can cut itself in half and each half can come and go, then any claim involving "mind"—floating or submerged or fitful—must be examined with an eye on the subconscious. Until further objective attention is given in that direction 'the judgments: "spirits" or: "bosh" are the one as silly as the other. "Bosh" is no more an ultimate element in nature or a really explanatory category in human life than "dirt" is in chemistry.'

He ends on a truly inspired hypothesis. Invoking evolution as an organizing principle and applying it to the genesis of the cosmos itself, James wonders whether there may not have been a time when all the elements of nature were in a chaotic state; regularities formed only slowly, and 'inconstant variations disappeared from being, wandered off as unrelated vagrants, only to manifest their existence by occasional lawless intrusions, like those which "psychic" phenomena now make into our scientifically organized world. On such a view, these phenomena ought to remain "pure bosh" forever, that is, they ought to be forever intractable to intellectual methods.'

* It should be added that Mrs. Piper denied that she was a spiritualist or had proof of "spirit return." She engaged in the work with James "because of my desire to learn if I were possessed or obsessed." (New York Herald, October 20, 1901, quoted in C. B. M. Hansel, ESP, New York, 1966, p. 231.)

For myself, that is where I am content to let the subject rest. I am confirmed by the latest impartial survey of all the experimental work done during the last eighty-five years.* It has found no reproducible regularities—which is what one should expect if the events are intrinsically irregular. It has never seemed likely to me that ESP tests with five cards would prove anything, quite apart from the disagreement as to the significance of scoring better than probability. If telepathy or second sight occurs, what reason is there to suppose it would turn up in a guessing game in which emotional interest is nil and repetition dulls even the ordinary senses? The scientific way of splitting phenomena into small bits for a closer look does not apply where the "power" to be studied is said from the start to violate the performer's own ordinary behavior: that power is not on tap. Nor am I sure that we can even analyze ordinary understanding—I mean the instant comprehension of another person's meaning over and beyond his words. Perhaps telepathy is at work every time we have true conversation, the kind we call heart-to-heart. Certainly, without words there is a magical yet visible communion between a mother and her infant. How then determine, analyze, similarly subtle, unformed intuitions and premonitions?

James, though also tempted to give up, chose to doubt his own hypothesis as 'going against too many intellectual prepossessions to be adopted save as a last resort of despair.' His scientific temper made him urge further work on these "lawless intrusions." 'For although I am baffled as to spirit return and as to many other problems, as to there being such real natural types of phenomena I am not baffled at all. I think there is "something in" these never-ending reports of physical phenomena, although I haven't yet the least positive notion of the something. It becomes to my mind a very worthy problem for investigation. Either I or the [dismissive] scientist is of course a fool, with our opposite views of probability; I only wish he might feel the liability, as cordially as I do, to pertain to both of us.' But James's ultimate word is : 'theoretically, I am no further than I was at the beginning.'

In facing the seasoned audiences of the Edinburgh elite with his Gifford lectures, presumably on "natural religion," James knew he was risking a peculiar sort of disaster. Lord Gifford, the founder of the lectureship, was a deeply religious man, brought up in the United Secession Church (its name must have delighted James if he happened to know it), but he was also an enlightened judge at the Court of Sessions and his will set no restrictions as to those who could be invited to lec-

* Hansel, *ESP, op. cit.*

ture. They must only treat of religion as "the science of Infinite Being, without reference to ... any supposed miraculous revelation." They might be freethinkers, "of no religion," but must be "able, reverent men and earnest inquirers after truth." Still, the town and university people probably numbered many doctrinaire believers, who had been soothed the year before by the idealist pieties of Josiah Royce, James's fellow-philosopher at Harvard. In any case, Natural Religion was an Enlightenment creed also called Deism, which asserted the presence in Everyman of innate religious truths: God created the world, he must be worshipped, and his moral law, inscribed in the individual conscience, must be obeyed. This rational faith distrusted all "enthusiasm" and intolerance, and if called upon it proved the existence of God by the wonderful design of the universe, which Newton had finally demonstrated. That Newton's own religious beliefs were nothing so calm and cool was ignored.

Now James, as an evolutionist, certainly did not believe in the design argument, whose elimination had wrecked Natural Religion. Besides, he was about to discuss and show the worth of "enthusiasm" in religion; and his naturalist psychology, despite sharing the word nature with the Deists, was not the "science of Infinite Being." The chances were great that he would disappoint or offend the faithful, warm or cool, who assembled to hear him. Indeed, when his plan, which was to classify religious experiences and extract their meaning, took him outside Christendom and brought in evidence from India, China, and the Moslem world (to say nothing of the newest occultisms and mind cures) he might well precipitate a protest or, subtler reproof, a boycott.

But nothing dramatic happened during or after the delivery of the twenty lectures, unless it was their resounding success from the very start.* And that too was a sign of the times. Not everybody had heard that God was dead, but traditional religion had suffered in the thirty years' war with the Darwinists. In our century, until the recent resurgence of theologies and faiths, James's work was more likely to be suspect for the opposite reason. The notion was afloat that James was a believer and *The Varieties of Religious Experience* a work of apologetics under guise of analysis. It is not, of course, anything masquerading as something else. It is in effect Volume 3 of *The Principles of Psychology*: it has the requisite bulk (over 200,000 words); it is explicitly subtitled "A Study in Human Nature"; it deals extensively with the subconscious and the pathological; it adheres to the naturalistic tone; it is a piece of stupendous research; and like the pair of volumes that I call its

---

* In the ten years following their publication, twenty-one reimpressions were called for and fifteen more during the next twenty years.

thematic predecessor, it ranges freely over the world of human affairs and puts James's whole philosophy to work.

The seeming digressions about poverty and the social system, the quotations from Whitman and other poets, the literary and moral criticism, the uses of biological evolution and social history, the refutations of crude scientism and shallow philosophy, the fine discrimination among the nuances of emotion and their expressions—these and the sinewy, lucid, vernacular prose, full of its own varieties to match the varying subjects, make the work a fit sequel and conclusion to The Masterpiece.

The candor of James's opening remarks at once pacified the suspicious and forecast an engrossing investigation. His 'purely existential point of view,' says James, does not imply a devaluing of what it describes. He gives as his first example George Fox (an "enthusiast" if ever there was one) whose 'Quaker religion it is impossible to overpraise. In a day of shams, it was a religion of veracity rooted in spiritual inwardness. No one can pretend that in point of spiritual sagacity and capacity, Fox's mind was unsound. Yet from the point of view of his nervous constitution, Fox was a psychopath or détraqué of the deepest dye.' And James quotes evidence from Fox's *Journal*.

But—and this is the originality of the handling—James knows that the mere act of classifying facts to which affection is attached makes the feeling mind recoil, often justly. 'Probably a crab would be filled with a sense of personal outrage if it could hear us class it as a crustacean. "I am no such thing," it would say, "I am MYSELF, MYSELF alone."' The classifiers' search for essences threatens or negates worth; in explaining, they explain away—and incite others to do so: 'Fanny's extraordinary conscientiousness is merely a matter of over-instigated nerves. William's melancholy about the universe is due to bad digestion—probably his liver is torpid. Eliza's delight in her church is a symptom of her hysterical constitution. A more fully developed example of reasoning is the fashion quite common nowadays among certain writers, of criticizing the religious emotions by showing a connection between them and the sexual life.' All this medical materialism, the busy 'discrediting of states of mind for which we have an antipathy,' he calls 'a too simple-minded system of thought.'

It is true that modern psychology—James's own brand—does 'assume as a convenient hypothesis that the dependence of mental states upon bodily conditions must be thorough-going and complete. St. Paul certainly had once an epileptoid, if not an epileptic, seizure. But now, I ask you, how can such an existential account of facts of mental history decide one way or another upon their spiritual significance?' The same

psychologizing would require that every state of mind be similarly regarded: 'Scientific theories are organically conditioned just as much as
religious emotions are. When we think superior states of mind superior
to others, is it ever because of what we know concerning their organic
antecedents? No! it is always for two entirely different reasons. It is
either because we take an immediate delight in them; or else it is because we believe them to bring us good consequential fruits for life.'

With reductivism set aside as unintelligent, James can go on to survey
the vast intricacy of the religious record. He is interested only in individual testimony. Churches and theologies are not the subject matter of
the psychologist and they themselves are by-products of the primary
religious impulse. To the first question, What is the religious sentiment?
the answer must be pluralistic and indefinite: it is a collective name for
the many sentiments aroused in the religious life. This in turn consists
of the experiences and acts of individuals when they feel themselves in
some relation to whatever they deem the divine. And the illustrative
case to single out here is James's incomparable treatment of Tolstoy's
conversion and new life.*

The mass of testimony, direct or from qualified observers, that James
culled from the literatures of the West and East is marshaled around six
great topics: the religion of healthy-mindedness; the sick soul; the divided self and its unification; conversion; saintliness; and mysticism. Nothing short of reading these chapters with their extracts and Jamesian
sidelights will give an idea of the total effect. It is a revelation, in its
palpitating reality, of mankind as a whole communing with the unseen;
fearing, doubting, hoping, worshiping, sacrificing, praying. The Golden
Bough yields something akin to this panorama, but its contents are necessarily without proportion, and the magical beliefs and practices that it
recounts are too remote from ours to move us. Through James's eyes we
see what the churches and sects themselves keep us from seeing—the
religious spectacle as such, universal, yet not by virtue of an abstraction, as it was for the Deists, but by virtue of the feeling that the word
enthusiasm records: the god at work within.

Supplementing the six main subjects are detailed discussions of the
social value of saintliness, the bearing of philosophy on religion, the
relations of religion and art, the psychology of prayer, the place of religious movements in the modern world, and James's own religious position. Although these final commentaries on the formative 1890s are the

---

* Though of utterly different character and genius, James and Tolstoy each experienced within a few months of each other a remarkably similar crisis. "Suddenly," as
Tolstoy wrote to his wife, "there came over me such a depression, fear, and horror as I
have never felt before and such as God grant no one to experience." But whereas James
suffered his ordeal at the age of twenty-eight, Tolstoy in 1869 was past forty. (Letters of
Tolstoy, ed. R. F. Christian, New York, 1978, vol. I, p. 222.)

portions of the book that one is likely to return to, the descriptive-analytic chapters are also chock-full of uncommon wisdom and deserve more than a single reading. Everybody will choose for himself what comes home to him most strongly after each perusal; what I take up now barely samples the feast.

I have spoken of James's genius for noting nuances of feeling. It is in fact an extraordinary capacity for speaking like an evangelist in behalf of each view; it is a Shakespearian ability to impersonate opposite temperaments. Here is, condensed, the equivalent of a dramatic dialogue:

'Much of what we call evil is due entirely to the way men take the phenomenon. It can so often be converted into a bracing and tonic good by a simple change of the sufferer's inner attitude from one of fear to one of fight. Refuse to admit the badness of the facts; despise their power; ignore their presence; turn your attention the other way; and so far as you yourself are concerned, though the facts may still exist, their evil character exists no longer. Hurrah for the Universe!—God's in his Heaven, all's right with the world.'

But 'how *can* things so insecure as the successful experiences of this world afford a stable anchorage? Unsuspectedly from the bottom of every fountain of pleasure, as the old poet said, something bitter rises up. The healthy-minded consciousness is left with an irremediable sense of precariousness. It is a bell with a crack. It draws its breath on sufferance and by an accident. Failure, then, failure! So the world stamps us at every turn. We strew it with our blunders, our misdeeds, our lost opportunities, with all the memorials of our inadequacy to our vocation. And with what a damning emphasis does it then blot us out! No easy fine, no mere apology or formal expiation will satisfy the world's demands, but every pound of flesh exacted is soaked with all its blood.'

Or again, a nuance in asceticism: 'All these sources of sin, pride, and sensuality must be resisted; and discipline and austerities are a most efficacious mode of meeting them. Hence there are always chapters on self-mortification. But whenever a procedure is codified, the more delicate spirit of it evaporates, and if we wish the undiluted ascetic spirit, the passion of self-contempt wreaking itself on the poor flesh, the divine irrationality of devotion making a sacrificial fight of all it has, we must go to autobiographies. Saint John of the Cross, a Spanish mystic who flourished—or rather who existed, for there was little that suggested flourishing about him—in the sixteenth century, will supply a passage.'

Finally, a contrast in saintliness: 'What with science, idealism, and democracy, our own imagination has grown to need a God of an entirely different temperament from that Being interested exclusively in dealing out personal favors. Smitten as we are with the vision of social righteousness, a God indifferent to everything but adulation, and full of partiality for his favorites, lacks an element of largeness; and even the best professional sainthood of former centuries, pent in as it is to such a conception, seems to us curiously shallow and unedifying.

'Take St. Teresa, for example, one of the ablest women, in many respects, of whose life we have the record. She had a powerful intellect of the practical order. She wrote admirable descriptive psychology, possessed a will equal to any emergency, great talent for politics and business, a buoyant disposition, and a first-rate literary style. She was tenaciously aspiring and put her whole life at the service of her ideas. Yet so paltry were these, according to our present way of thinking that (although I know that others have been moved differently), I confess that my only feeling in reading her has been pity that so much vitality of soul should have found such poor employment.'

After giving the religious life its several voices, James faces the question whether the sense of a divine presence is objectively true. The "reality of the unseen" and the mystic's communion with God being private unrepeatable events, how can they be brought into the class of objective experience? Theologians themselves have tended to disallow mystical experience as dangerously variable and deceptive. Ever the historian, James begins by pointing out that very few spiritual facts receive universal assent. He might have instanced the permanent dissensus about art; he contents himself with the state of philosophy: 'it does not banish differences; it founds schools and sects just as feeling does. I believe, in fact, that the logical reason of man operates in divinity exactly as it has always operated in love, or in patriotism, or in politics, or in any other of the wider affairs of life, in which our passions or our mystical intuitions fix our beliefs beforehand. It finds arguments for our conviction, for indeed it *has* to find them. It amplifies and defines our faith, and dignifies it, and lends it words and plausibility. It hardly ever engenders it; it cannot now secure it.'

But there is more to say. The intimation of something beyond our consciousness, the sense of a controlling force in our destiny, the feeling of transcendence, in short, James can say is objectively true. The reason is that it springs from the subliminal as 'the sense of a "more" operative outside the conscious self, continuous with it and of the same quality.' That the evidence for its existence is as personal as the evidence for the phenomena themselves has no bearing on the genuineness of either: 'The axis of reality runs solely through the egotistic places—they are strung upon it like so many beads.'

With this conclusion we are ready for James's own religious views, on which his father's influence is notable. Henry James, Sr., had died in 1882 and with filial regard William had brought out in 1884 a thick

volume, *The Literary Remains of Henry James*. A hundred-page introduction supplied the reader with facts about the scarcely known author
and with clues to his difficult writings. Such a task compelled William
to put in order his own ideas on the subject of the *Remains*, religion-
and-society. Two passages of that essay contain, all unsuspected by the
writer, the core of *The Varieties* as to method and conclusion.

With the highest regard for "Father's ideas," which he considered
'among the few truly original theological works,' he believed that his
father had been too little aware of other men's difficulties, emotional
and intellectual. William, as we know, grew up to be his complete antithesis. By temperament, Henry Sr. was a monist and mystic who could
not distill his thought to his own satisfaction and was often opaque and
always overabundant. Yet it was probably in him that William found
his most direct witness of religious experience; he called his father 'one
of that band of saints and mystics whose rare privilege it has been, by
the mere example and recital of their own bosom-experience, to prevent religion from becoming a fossil conventionalism.' Certainly father
and son agreed on two main matters: the radical conflict between religion and morality and the preference for an imperfect God. "I have no
belief," says Henry Sr. "in God's absolute or irrelative and unconditional perfection. That style of deity exerts no attraction either upon my
heart or my understanding. . . . What I crave—what my very flesh and
bones cry out for—is no longer a Sunday but a weekday God, grimy
with the dust and sweat of our most carnal appetites and passions, and
bent not for an instant upon inflating our worthless pietistic righteousness, but upon . . . the thorough cleansing of our physical and moral existence."

When William, twenty years later, came to set down his conception
of God, he first declared his 'inability to accept either popular Christianity or scholastic theism' and contented himself with acknowledging
the presence of 'a wider world of being than that of our everyday consciousness.' These 'transmundane energies' he is willing to call God, but
he separates that idea from the belief in an infinite power, which he
says is not unequivocally supported by the experiences recorded in his
study. '*Something* larger than ourselves, perhaps only a larger and
more godlike self,' but at any rate 'beyond each man a larger power
which is friendly to him—only so much is needed to give the individual
comfort and spur him to bend his energies in that same ideal direction.
For most men do require a centering purpose and for many it must be
transcendent.'

These tentative words hardly amount to a confession of faith; but
before noting the reason, a point of historical interest is that the two
Jameses' "partial divinity" finds its parallel in the religious declarations

of Nietzsche, Butler, and Bernard Shaw. William's tentativeness has two causes. First, he had but the merest "germ" (as he called it) of religious sentiment—just enough to imagine others' true fever. And second, he recognized that too little is known about the ground of his particular belief in transcendence—the unconscious. As for evidence of the "higher power" at work, James found it in many of his religious figures, from Mohammed to Joseph Smith, and earlier in the Hebrew prophets: all are inspired and write under dictation. Modern men and women also, though skeptical under the pressure of science, nevertheless say they feel the reality of a wider world. 'If the word "subliminal" is offensive to any of you, call it by any other name you please to distinguish it from the level of full sunlit consciousness. Call this latter the A-region of personality and call the other the B-region. The B-region, then is obviously the larger part of each of us, for it is the abode of everything that is latent and the reservoir of everything that passes unrecorded or unobserved. It contains such things as our momentarily inactive memories and it harbors the springs of all our obscurely motived passions, impulses, likes, dislikes, and prejudices; in general all our non-rational operations come from it. It is the source of our dreams and apparently they may return to it.'

These diverse feelings produce what James called "over-beliefs," that is, images or ideas in which the feeling of beyond is crystallized for permanence. The deeper the root of the feeling, the stronger the force of the image. He observed how revivals of religion also revived heresies and absurdities. If one wonders why James was so bent on explaining the source and validating the worth of over-beliefs, why he was eager to show his opponents, the philosophical idealists, that their religiosity could be reconciled functionally with the empiricism he espoused, the answer is not that he was kindly and preferred harmony. It is that he perceived as psychologist and historian that human life never had been possible without ideas of this species and never could be: 'Over-beliefs in various directions are absolutely indispensable.'*

When some over-belief is foolish or harmful or when we simply dislike it, we call it a superstition, which is just the Latin for what "stands over" the fact or feeling—hence over-belief. Think of your acquaintances one by one and you will not find any capable mind among them that does not harbor some rooted faith that qualifies as superstitious. In the biography of every forceful mind—artist, statesman, scientist—we find reference to some unprovable, unlikely proposition to which the

---

* In further proof of its naturalness, James had noted earlier, in the *Psychology*, that 'the emotion of belief is perfectly distinct and perfectly indescribable in words. This goes to a fully unutterable extreme in the nitrous oxide intoxication, in which a man's very soul will sweat with conviction and he will be all the while unable to tell what he is convinced of.' (*Principles*, II, p. 284.)

subject held as to a life line. Among scientists, the usual belief in the "edifice of science" which will someday be completed by the addition of the final brick of research; among scholars, the faith in their *contribution*—to what?—are respectably functional over-beliefs. These two in particular show a certain structural kinship with God's perfect realm, which others hope to enter as honored guests on the last day. The still more common ideal of Truth, one and indivisible, springs from the same need to direct our effort by the vision of a noble end, an end for which the only warrant is our feeling.

As philosopher, then, James invokes the pragmatic test for over-beliefs and sees that their variety is in keeping with the pluralism not merely of the religious passion, but of all experience. Over-beliefs that make a difference in conduct are real at least to the extent of that difference; they are a force in nature; and where no other means of gauging reality exist—as is true in most of "the serious affairs of life"—the effective belief must be held valid for the believer. That does not make the particular over-belief compulsory for others. If a poet thinks eating raw carrots strengthens his metrical skill, no other poet need follow his lead and the dietician may laugh: "No connection!" But if you somehow destroy the faith and this destroys the skill, what philosopher can deny *a* connection?*

Certain tribes have dwindled and perished after contact with others, from the undermining of the faith in their own traditions.** It won't do to say "the power of illusion." The philosopher or scientist is the last person who, faced with a phenomenon, can evade responsibility by saying "illusion." The experience of the Peace Corps has shown that western medicines work more surely on African patients if combined with native over-beliefs. Recently, this country has been made aware, in connection with the death of eighteen Laotians, of the Oriental nightmare-death syndrome; the evil dream is held as at least a conceivable cause by physicians at the Federal Disease Center in Atlanta. In the results of over-beliefs, the philosopher may suggest a different formulation of the event, point to a different linkage among elements, but most often he has nothing to offer.

Surveying the vast panorama of religion, James is certain that the existence of so many creeds and sects and rites is anything but regrettable.

* The example is not fanciful: Schiller wrote best when an open drawer of his desk was full of rotting apples, and Wagner needed a silk dressing gown for composing about his armor-clad heroes and heroines.

** Every experienced teacher has witnessed more than one case of the shattering effect of loss of faith in a student suddenly plunged into disbelief by a book or a thoughtless instructor.

'I do not see how it is possible that creatures in such different positions and with such different powers as human individuals are should have exactly the same functions and the same duties. No two have identical difficulties. Each takes in a certain sphere of fact and trouble, which each must deal with in a unique way. One must soften himself; another must harden himself. If an Emerson were forced to be a Wesley, or a Moody forced to be a Whitman, the total human consciousness of the divine would suffer. The divine can mean no single quality.'* On his last page, or nearly, James connects this pluralism with the possibility that the transcendent or subliminal, which seems to contain the "larger self" that for brevity he has called God, might in fact be 'a collection of selves, of different degrees of inclusiveness, with no absolute unity realized in it at all. Thus would a sort of polytheism return upon us.'

This is another juncture where my own feelings and over-beliefs gain support from my mentor's. I, too, lack the full-blown intuition, for in my time of crisis (if that is the right name for the devastation of a child's richly peopled world during the war of 1914) death superabundant and the rest of life endlessly disordered induced at last a suicidal state and swept away all but the verbalisms of the creed trustingly learned earlier. But having thus become "twice born" in the Jamesian sense and gained self-acceptance 'through altered powers of action,' I found with it the germ of an affinity with a multiple, unorganized transcendence. I am to this extent a Nietzsche-Shaw-James kind of believer; that is, persuaded of the manifold divine. I feel myself obedient to "spirit," knowing that from it alone come the things that justify life—things, in Nietzsche's words, "transfiguring, exquisite, mad, and divine."

Polytheism (which this is) has always been, as James points out, 'the real religion of common people'; it was also that of the heads of the old church when they were not theologians. In the rural districts of western Europe, moreover, the pagan gods and spirits live a veiled existence behind local customs and celebrations, including religious ones. By contrast, the single, all-powerful God, founder and efficient executive of the universe, has for me the thinness of abstraction. And when its faint outline is partly filled with liturgy and prayer, it seems to me the mirror-image of monarchy, calling for servility and praise too fulsome to be sincere. Still worse, the courtier's begging and receiving favors from his sovereign, which James notes in discussing St. Teresa, is coupled with

* Besides individual differences, there are those of surroundings and the ideas they generate. It is not only science that has forced a modification of religious beliefs but such practical things as the reversal of expectation about infant mortality and a longer life span than the former average of thirty-nine years; or again the change, affecting the impressionable in childhood, from nighttime darkness to our electric lighting instantly turned on and almost as pervasive as daylight.

the unedifying morality of a stockbroker, who denies himself on earth so as to invest in heavenly options.

In any case, the glaring contradiction between morality and religion makes "scholastic theism" and "popular Christianity" as unacceptable to me as to James. In practice, religion supports morality. The weekly sermon, the sacraments, prayer, confession, promised rewards and punishments—the whole church apparatus—works to arouse, sustain, and appease the believer's conscience. But originally and most worthily, the faith exists to forgive and unite, while morality divides and punishes. If there is more rejoicing in heaven at the repentance of one sinner than at the reception of any number of good people, the scheme is clearly not *pour encourager les autres*. From childhood I have responded to the parable of the prodigal son with emotions appropriate to a sentimental tale that is also a picture of life: it gives both the glow of a happy ending for the bad boy and the bitter truth that merit is overlooked when a charmer-scoundrel comes along.

But it so happens that the parable is meant as homily, as instruction about spiritual facts. And on that view it shows that morality is a poor, worldly, negligible thing compared to the pure fire of religion. 'The twice born,' says James, 'look down upon the rectilinear consciousness of life of the once-born as being "mere morality" and not properly religion.' And quoting Luther he shows how the properly religious emotion should sound: "That pernicious and pestilent opinion of man's righteousness, which will not be a sinner, unclean, miserable, and damnable, but righteous and holy, suffereth not God to come to his own natural and proper work." James's father, too, 'always made morality the target of his hottest attack, and pitted religion and it against each other as enemies, of whom one must die utterly if the other is to live in genuine form.'

It requires no more than a vague sense of this enmity to bring about social consequences. In our time few read Luther and fewer read Henry James, Sr.; but many read Dostoevsky, whose genius has made love of the sinner a cardinal trait of our ethos.* If *tout comprendre c'est tout pardonner*, then the more we understand, the more we must let others' evil take its course. This seems to be one great and conscious purpose of society at present. The criminal is more pitied and helped than the victim; the careless or selfish violator of the moral and social code commands the warm attentions of numerous agencies for his rescue and reform; in schools of every grade, for many decades past, it is not only

* The Russian critic Ilya Ehrenburg has said that Dostoevsky "told the whole truth about human nature" and many westerners agree with him. (*New York Times*, February 15, 1981.)

for mathematics and composition that "remedial" is the apt word: *all* deficiencies from idleness to cheating invite interested care—so much, that none is left to bestow on those who perversely perform and stay out of trouble. And generally in the presentative arts, health and integrity of character are suspect as contrary to the well-known signs of true merit. All this is in keeping with the original attitude of the 1890s toward bourgeois behavior and respectability: they are but moral and, as Luther taught, damnable. Only one little question remains: how long can endearing sinfulness and the soul's fulfillment by crime be endured in a crowded world?

James saw our modern impulse already at work and raised the same question: 'Love your enemies! Can there in general be a level of emotion so unifying, so obliterative of differences between man and man, that even enmity may come to be an irrelevant circumstance and fail to inhibit the friendlier interest aroused?' His answer could not be single-minded. Part of him knew that 'the whole history of constitutional government is a commentary on the excellence of resisting evil, and when one cheek is smitten, of smiting back and not turning the other cheek also. You will agree to this in general, and in spite of the Gospel, in spite of Quakerism, in spite of Tolstoy, you believe in fighting fire with fire. And yet you are sure, as I am sure, that were the world confined to the hard-headed, hard-hearted, and hard-fisted methods exclusively, the world would be an infinitely worse place to live in than it is now.'

True. The value of saintliness, which he is discussing, like the worth of all the utopias, consists in raising by unique or imagined examples the level of brutal, self-centered behavior. But the religious brotherhood of man and the efficacy of turning the other cheek depend on a strong teaching—to everybody, beforehand—of these same principles. The thief in *Les Misérables* was melted into contrition when the bishop whose silver candlestick he had stolen gave him the matching one while telling the police that the first was indeed a gift. And this was an historical, not a made-up incident.

But if the untutored thief thinks the old man a fool and despises him as our muggers do when they maim or kill those who do not resist, the moral equation is changed and every yielding becomes an encouragement to immorality. This is true in domestic life as well, when the loving ones give in to the browbeating of some tyrant, young or old. The public world today presents the ensuing spectacle: the most refined and active regard for the rights and needs of others, side by side with heartless violence and contemptuous death-dealing to enemies and innocents.* One reluctantly concludes that in a sophisticated age the saints and would-be saints should not be so numerous as to weaken the habits that moralize and the institutions that repress. If religion then says that it has no use for "mere morality," the answer will be: "Its use is to permit your saints to survive and bestow their grace."

James himself strongly believed in the reality of evil and the duty to resist it. Those who share his pluralism are in consistency bound to concur, for they do not believe in a sphere of absolute good where evil is somehow transmuted and all accounts are finally balanced. Polytheism finds it difficult not to posit Satan, and when his existence is denied, to wonder why wickedness is so energetic and successful.** Ignoring the facts if one happens to be fortunate resolves nothing. 'Pain and death and wrong must be fairly met and overcome in higher excitement, or else their sting remains essentially unbroken. If one has ever taken the fact of the prevalence of tragic death in this world's history fairly into his mind—freezing, drowning, entombment alive, wild beasts, worse men, and hideous diseases—he can with difficulty, it seems to me, continue his own career of worldly prosperity without suspecting that he may all the while not be really inside the game, that he may lack the great initiation.'

That "higher excitement" and the tragic sense of life should come from art, presumably, modern churches having lost their intelligent believers by going either literal or liberal and thus offending heart-and-mind. Nor can the reflections that keep a William James or a Bernard Shaw from religious practice be disposed of by saying that divinity is ineffable Being, mysterious and not to be probed. The mystery in things remains overwhelming enough without extending it to what is offered as explanation. The clearest Christian theology, the Thomism recognized as orthodox in the 1890s, affirms that reason is the right path toward religious truth; so it is not impious to think.

Art, then, is all that is left for direct solace and uplift. But as we saw, when art took up the task of denouncing the world in the old religious way it carried on its mission by preaching not hope and joy, or even resignation, but despair. It is thus useless for lives lived as most are today, at the mercy of forces that disintegrate the self; some means is

---

* We have coined the phrase "senseless murder" in recognition, apparently, of the good sense there is in killing your declared enemy or rival. The notion ought to be turned around, into a recognition that the so-called senseless murder means that anybody at random is rival and enemy, stands in one's way and begs to be removed.

** On the *Reality of the Devil*, see the first-rate study so titled, by Ruth Nanda Anshen (New York, 1974), and on the same personification in the various religions of the world, the classic work by Paul Carus, *The History of the Devil and the Idea of Evil* (reprint, New York, 1969).

needed of re-collecting that self in the manner Shaw describes in his remarkable essay "On Going to Church." But the means are wanting; neither solitary nor social rededication of the spiritual energies is provided for; churches and churchmen are largely given over to an amateurish sort of political journalism, while the few theologians work to one side, their influence not institutionalized but limited to readers of their books. It is not surprising in these conditions that Transcendental Meditation, Sufism, Yoga, and other cults and practices (down to the soundless cabin and tank of warm water for shutting out all stimuli) thrive on the religious need and the religious dearth.

With this situation in mind, the reader of *The Varieties* who turns to the Postscript telling James's own belief may well be astonished to find the statement that 'so far as I understand the Buddhist doctrine of Karma, I agree with it in principle.' One may be forgiven if reading this, one has a fleeting vision of William on a Cambridge street corner, shaved bald and chanting nasally under his tuft. But James had not lost his grip.* By the doctrine of Karma, he meant explicitly that 'facts are under the judgment of higher law'; in other words, the perceived object as we commonly think of it does not account for all that experience is known to contain. From a rock in a stream to Beethoven there are gradations, and to limit the idea of Beethoven to the minerals and water that make up his body is to hold an inadequate idea. If such a reduction is called naturalistic, then James the Buddhist is a supernaturalist.

I suspect that his reference to Karma was pure provocative mischief directed after twenty sessions at the solemn Scottish audience. He could have made his point some other way, for he takes care to explain that the higher law by which facts are "judged" is not some thinker or thought outside nature; 'it operates "causally" as a partial factor in the total fact.' Besides, he wants belief to produce "works" and not remain a mere gnostic attitude. What all this apparent shuttling between nature and something else points to is an assumption long embedded in our vocabulary: spirit is "above" nature. But for James and his acquiescing readers, nothing is supernatural. The word to use for our beliefs, our affections, our thrills in the presence of art, our philosophic and scientific visions, our admiration of nature itself, and all else that belongs to the realm of the unseen is the word *spiritual*. It describes a quality perceived as other than physical or strictly intellectual. Thus puberty is a physical change in the body; adolescence is a spiritual state; it is in-

---

* It is noteworthy that writers on Buddhist philosophy describe it as—among other things—empirical, pragmatic, psychological, democratic, and therapeutic. (Adjectives culled from various sources.)

separable from puberty but infinitely more complex and, of course, impalpable.

This rearrangement of terms is important especially "in an age of science." For it makes it unnecessary to hold incompatible convictions cached in distant parts of the mind. This keeping a double set of books is technically called Fideism. Pomponazzi, who named it in the sixteenth century, argued that he was not a heretic, because "I believe as a Christian what I cannot believe as a philosopher." Many fine minds—Montaigne, Pico della Mirandola, Pascal, Sir Thomas Browne—have been fideists, and James knew many a scientist 'who nourishes a religion in his irresponsible hours.'* He himself had no wish to be irresponsible, no need to be a fideist, because his view of nature was inclusive; it did not stop at "facts" but embraced the perfectly natural experience of "spirit."

When that experience takes the form of religious longing and questioning, it is apparent that purely intellectual answers and over-beliefs do not suffice. The Deism of the Enlightenment showed once for all that rational abstractions, however lofty, end in faint, perfunctory lip-service to transcendence. That condition may be a relief to some; to the majority it is a deprivation. And so we find the Romanticists, beginning with Rousseau, turning to the spectacle of nature as inspirer and object of religious feeling. The greatest artists of the period that follows are worshipers, regardless of their theology—Wordsworth, Byron, Goethe, Berlioz, Keats, Thoreau, Shelley, Beethoven, Emerson, and many others "sing" their cult of nature. Some call themselves atheists, others pantheists, others Christians of one denomination or another, but they all feel transcendence and lodge divinity either in the human breast or in visible nature; all of them would echo Landor's

Nature I loved; and next to Nature, Art.

Nothing shows more clearly William James's kinship with these men of the Romantic period than his passionate love of nature and the powerful attraction exerted on his mind by the religious philosophy of Gustav Theodor Fechner. Half a dozen years after *The Varieties*, in *A Pluralis-*

* In 1915, James's colleague Leuba conducted a survey to ascertain the beliefs in God and in immortality held by various categories of professional thinkers. Among physical scientists 43.9% believed in God—the largest percentage of any scientific group. Biologists showed only 30.5% and psychologists 24.2%. Sociologists and historians were close together with 46.3% and 48.3%. All but one of the corresponding percentages were higher for the belief in immortality, reaching 50% for the physical scientists. The philosophers, living up to their reputation for independence, turned in answers that permitted no statistical tabulation. (James H. Leuba, *The Belief in God and Immortality: A Psychological, Anthropological, and Statistical Study*, Boston, 1916, pp. 221–81.)

*tic Universe*, James has a long chapter "Concerning Fechner" to exemplify what could replace the abstract Absolute of the Idealist philosophy. James first came across Fechner's work as that of a fellow psychologist to whom the world owes "Fechner's law," the mathematical ratio between the force of a stimulus and the intensity of the sensation. With this finding Fechner started experimental psychology, and somewhat like James he had progressed to this new science from the older established ones. Like James also he was all the while a philosopher and the survivor of an emotional crisis. Add to these 'an admirable literary style of the vernacular sort,' and his appeal to James's imagination is readily conceived.

Fechner's religion was rooted in a mystical vision, though it was not a private mysticism. On the contrary, he called it "the daylight view of the world." James paraphrases it as the conviction 'that the whole universe in its different spans and wave-lengths, exclusions and envelopments, is everywhere alive and conscious.' The modern error of both science and common sense, according to Fechner, is 'our habit of regarding the spiritual not as the rule but as an exception in the midst of nature; or if we believe in a Divine Spirit, we fancy him on the one side as bodiless, and nature as soulless on the other. The book of nature turns into a volume on mechanics in which whatever has life is treated as an anomaly.'

To this last objection James would heartily subscribe. His sensitivity to the life force in human bodies, wills, and minds was matched by the same acute sympathy with the natural world. He reveled in the sights and sounds to be found away from cities. 'I am sorry,' he wrote, 'for the boy or girl, or man or woman who has never been touched by the spell of this mysterious sensorial life, with its irrationality—if you so like to call it—but its vigilance and its supreme felicity.' In his rambles through the Adirondacks, or New Hampshire, or Rhode Island, he was forever becoming enamored of some new-discovered spot, some hilltop he must buy, so as to be sure to return to it. The only trouble was that he must also have a brook to sit by or bathe in, and hill and brook were of necessity distant from each other. In the end, it was excessive climbing in the Adirondacks, spending several hours a day alone in the mountains and once getting lost and suffering long exposure, that overtaxed his heart and hastened his end.

Yet this vibrant response to nature could not carry James as far as Fechner's vision of the "earth soul"—the earth conscious in all its parts, we ourselves being so many of the earth's sense organs. James had cause to admire in Fechner the logical argumentation premised on a system of analogies and differences, coupled with the 'unexampled richness of his imagination of details.' The result was a vision that had for James the requisite 'thickness,' whereas by the end of the nineteenth century the standard religions 'ran thin.' Yet Fechner's system also winds up thin, at the top: his God is 'only a sort of limit of enclosure of the worlds above man.' For James, therefore, Fechner only shows a possible direction in the search for divinity.

But why undertake the search at all? Because the religious emotion goes with the feeling that we can act with some power in the universe to support and enhance the worthier and seemlier, we can transcend animal existence and oppose its evils. When Coriolanus exclaims, "There is a world elsewhere," it is in contempt of worldly baseness, and he need not be thinking of the hereafter to be sure that he aspires to a higher mode of being than that of the mob he addresses. *That* is the world elsewhere. For James the possibility existed that 'we may be in the universe as dogs and cats are in our libraries, seeing the books and hearing the conversation, but having no inkling of the meaning of it all. The outlines of the superhuman consciousness thus made probable must remain, however, very vague, and the number of functionally distinct "selves" it comports and carries has to be left entirely problematic.'

Here one must remember James's critique of the Absolute, idealist or materialist, with its block universe, its "fall" from reality into appearance, its total determinism and denial of history. If all these are unacceptable and one still wants but one God, then that God must be 'finite either in power or in knowledge, or in both at once; the monistic perfections that make him so paradoxical practically and morally' are but concept work.

It is remarkable on how many points James's position anticipated the intellectual requirements and the types of solution offered by the leading theologies of today. But one need not linger on still another example of his formative influence.* What must be noted is that the objection sometimes urged (e.g., by Collingwood) against *The Varieties of Religious Experience*—it is interesting but tells us nothing about religion— is a statement of distrust in the naturalistic method; the contents of the

---

* These solutions are conveniently summed up in *Twentieth-Century Religious Thought* by the Oxford theologian John Macquarrie (New York, 1981). He enumerates: "a certain degree of relativism"; dependence on social and historical conditions or "the *mood* of the culture"; the impossibility of absolute answers *or* questions, in which "everything would be noticed at once"; religion is "a practical matter, an attitude of the whole personality"; "to suspend judgment, as William James pointed out, is to act as if religion were untrue"; there is no "final truth on the matter"; finite man must face "the leap to be made"; religion should not call for the sacrifice of intellect; no conflict with science or common sense in their contemporary forms; religion must be comprehensive, that is: cognitive *and* affective; and it can only be "*on the way*," meaning capable of further developments. (Pp. 372–75.)

work and the use of its findings in current theology sufficiently refute the charge.

There is, to be sure, one kind of current "over-belief" that is as existential as James's—indeed, it calls itself Existentialism, as if nothing else were—and, as was mentioned earlier, it reaches the conclusion that man's place in the universe, man and the universe, are absurd.* When one asks why, the answer is that the creed, starting properly enough with man, does not see beyond him a "more" of the same character as our consciousness and continuous with it. Instead, it finds a "more" hostile or indifferent to our powers and of a nature we can never know. Existentialists also speak of risk, but they do not mean by it what James had in mind in the last sentences of The Varieties: 'a willingness to live on a chance,' meaning open chance, not one sure to end badly.

In their way, Existentialists re-espouse Schopenhauer's pessimism, through failing to judge science accurately; they are ever deploring—in Robert Lowell's words—that "We are but poor passing facts." Freud gives a clue to this pairing of ideas when he says that "science is after all the most complete renunciation of the pleasure principle our mental activity is capable of."** There is inverted pride in that belief—pride in the knowledge about the "pointless" aeons of geologic time and myriads of light-years, the whole cosmic show heading for the heat-death of the sun. James in the last months of his life encountered this argument in a privately printed paper that Henry Adams sent him for comment. Adams's thesis, later expanded in his theory of history, was that the running down of energy in the universe involved a parallel decay in human affairs.*** James disputed the analogy: 'Certain arrangements of matter on the same energy level are from the point of view of man superior while others are inferior. A dinosaur's brain may show as much intensity of energy exchange as a man's, but as a force it can only unlock the dinosaur's muscles, while the man's brain, by unlocking far feebler muscles, can by their means issue proclamations, write books, describe Chartres cathedral [Adams's own work] and guide the energies of the shrinking sun into channels which never would have been entered otherwise—in short, make history.' It is a lovely piece of judging by "the thing done" and it winds up: 'There is nothing in physics to

* There are existentialisms that embrace Christianity—Kierkegaard's, to begin with, and Gabriel Marcel's; but they have found admirers rather than adherents. The atheist-absurdist camp has been by far the more influential on literature and public opinion.

** The Romanticist Leopardi, in his beautiful poems of the 1830s, gives voice to the same shattering effect of knowledge upon human desires, but he also records the persistence of those desires and shows that they are right to utter a "Nevertheless!"

*** With Brooks Adams as co-author the work was published under the title of The Degradation of the Democratic Dogma (1919).

interfere with the hypothesis that the penultimate state [before extinction] might be the millennium.'* In this light the Existentialists' overbelief might be thought a device to deaden the fear of one's own extinction by belittling life and refusing to see its possibilities—such as being willing to become Einstein or Beethoven or William James.


Only after more than five hundred pages overflowing with religious experience, does James mention immortality. Freud told us that James was not afraid of death, and this trait is perhaps the reason why in *The Varieties* he calls the subject a 'secondary point,' all the while recognizing that 'for the great majority of our own race, religion *means* immortality and nothing else.' His own view was magnanimous: 'if our ideals are only cared for in "eternity," I do not see why we might not be willing to resign their care to other hands than ours. Yet I sympathize with the urgent impulse to be present ourselves, and in the conflict of impulses, both of them so vague yet both of them noble, I know not how to decide.'

Four years earlier, in 1898, James had given at Harvard the Ingersoll Lecture on Human Immortality, soon after published as a small book that elicited a good many objections. His opening remarks were an apology; he had been appointed lecturer 'not because he is known as an enthusiastic messenger of the future life, but because he is a university official.' And he adds, 'I have to confess that my own personal feeling about immortality has never been of the keenest order.'

All he intended to do was to show that immortality was not ruled out by the brain-function theory of ordinary consciousness and that the subliminal extended possibility even further. During his suicidal year 1868, when he was twenty-six, James had written in his diary: 'God is dead or at least irrelevant, ditto everything pertaining to the beyond.' Now, thanks to the growing disclosure of the Unconscious, the beyond was being defined for his eager listeners as a 'continuum of cosmic consciousness, against which our individuality builds up but accidental fences.' It was 'a hypothesis,' that is: 'eminently a case for facts to testify.' The public desire for personal survival after death could hardly feel satisfied—hence the objections.

What is of special interest to the student of James is the bearing of the phrase "consciousness against which we build fences." For it alludes to

---

* Not that James expected the millennium. On the contrary: one 'may fear that the being of man may be crushed by his own powers, his organism not adequate to stand the strain of [what] his intellect will more and more enable him to wield.' (*Pragmatism*, p. 187.)

a hypothesis about the mind that James at the end of his life thought plausible and worth investigating. He had come to suppose that the mysterious relation of brain to mind might be that of a triggering or screening arrangement. The subliminal and any other mind beyond the conscious was kept out, most of the time, by this barrier, screen, or trigger—the physical brain, which thereby set the pattern of our individual minds.* If it were true, it would explain many otherwise puzzling paradoxes, from double personality to the relocating of functions after brain damage.

From all these speculations some readers, including the late Julius Bixler in his excellent book on *Religion in the Philosophy of William James,* have found in James a true believer. I doubt the conclusion. I am confident that his considered statements go no further than what we have just heard. Santayana was right to say of him: "He did not really believe. He merely believed in the right of believing that you might be right if you believed." A man who says as James did that the best argument he knows for immortality is the existence of his friend Francis Child is not what I would call a shining example of Christian faith. On the three related questions of God and immortality, psychic phenomena, and the realm beyond conscious mind, James suspends judgment to the last. He says over and over that he wants more facts. The unconscious is actual and potent, but it is not an entity—how could it be when consciousness itself is not one? So the reality of the unconscious is not a positive answer to the three great questions. It is only a domain to explore, on the chance that the wanted facts will fill out the outline of a beginning science.

When James's casual statements contradict the considered ones, as they sometimes do, they seem to express only love in response to the needs and wants of others, with whom he always vividly identified himself. In the letter he wrote in his fortieth year to his father as the old sage lay dying, the clashing notes are struck, the deeper one being that which links "spirit" with a mission of the mind.** This farewell of William's is so much a single pulse of his feeling-thought that it is vandalism to abridge the words, as must be done:

'Darling Old Father: . . . We have been so long accustomed to the hy-

---

* Compare Shaw's *Back to Methuselah,* where the serpent says to Adam: "The voice in the garden is your own voice." Adam replies: "It is and it is not. It is something greater than me. I am only part of it." (Act I, middle.)

** Henry was similarly of divided feelings when he visited his parents' grave and read aloud on the spot William's letter to their father, "which I am sure he heard somewhere out of the depths of the still, bright winter air. He lies extraordinarily close to Mother, and . . . it was difficult not to believe that they were not united again in some consciousness of my belief." (Henry to William, January, 1883. F. O. Matthiessen, *The James Family,* New York, 1947, p. 133.)

pothesis of your being taken away from us, especially during the past ten months, that the thought that this may be your last illness conveys no very sudden shock. You are old enough, you've given your message to the world in many ways and will not be forgotten; you are here left alone, and on the other side, let us hope and pray, dear, dear old Mother is waiting for you to join her. If you go, it will not be an inharmonious thing. Only, if you are still in possession of your normal consciousness, I should like to see you once again before we part.

'... Meanwhile, my blessed old father, I scribble this line just to tell you how full of the tenderest memories and feelings about you my heart has for the last few days been filled.... Yours is still for me the central figure. All my intellectual life I derive from you; and though we have often seemed at odds in the expression thereof, I'm sure there's a harmony somewhere and that our strivings will combine. What my debt to you is goes beyond all my power of estimating—so early, so penetrating, and so constant has been the influence. You need be in no anxiety about your literary remains. I will see them well taken care of, and that your words shall not suffer for being concealed.

'... As for us, we shall live on each in his way—feeling somewhat unprotected, old as we are, for the absence of the parental bosoms as a refuge, but holding fast together in that common sacred memory. We shall stand by each other and by Alice, try to transmit the torch in our offspring as you did in us.... As for myself, I know what trouble I've given you at various times through my peculiarities; and as my own boys grow up I shall learn more of the kind of trial you had to overcome in superintending the development of a creature different from yourself, for whom you felt responsible. I say this merely to show how my *sympathy* with you is likely to grow much livelier rather than to fade— and not for the sake of regrets.

'As for the other side, and Mother, and our all possibly meeting, I *can't* say anything. More than ever at this moment do I feel that if that *were* true, all would be solved and justified. And it comes strangely over me in bidding you goodbye how a life is but a day and expresses mainly but a single note. It is so much like the act of bidding an ordinary good-night. Good-night, my sacred old Father! If I don't see you again—Farewell! a blessed farewell! Your—William.'

# The Genius

Whitehead on page one introduced us, as it were, to our guide by saying: "That adorable genius, William James." Prolonged acquaintance with almost anyone but the unregenerate is likely to bring liking, sympathy, enthusiastic admiration, as the case may be. But to arouse love without direct living acquaintance is unusual and to make one think genius adorable is very rare. On one occasion in the mid-1930s I asked Whitehead what traits in James he had most in mind when he wrote the phrase in *Science and the Modern World*. He said: "Greatness with simplicity"; and he added: "I mean by greatness the absence of smallness in *any* respect."

As words and incidents in this account have shown, James was warmly generous, intuitive in human encounters, and passionate in friendship; he was great-souled in the conduct of his intellectual and material interests, fastidious and demanding of himself. But one can think of other geniuses who in various ways answer to the same description. James belongs to the very small number who showed these traits with the final grace Whitehead mentioned: simplicity is the last perfection—it is there or it isn't; one cannot work for it. James would be the despair of modern sociology: he acted out no role, played no game, put on no "side." He had a professional conscience without resembling a professional man. In public and private he won trust and liking without a thought of "charming."* For Santayana, indeed, he was *too* natural. One did not know what "line" to take in order to deal with him.**

* —which does not mean that he lacked charm. Logan Pearsall Smith thought him "the most charming man he had ever met." (Gay Wilson Allen, *William James*, New York, 1967, p. 309.)

** See his actual words, p. 7 above.

"Dealing" was unnecessary. "Line" and "side" are social handles for steadying oneself during first approaches and, too often, throughout an acquaintance or even a friendship. So their absence disconcerts those used to relying on them. But how do they come to be missing? Samuel Butler once said that every man labors under a sense of wrong and he thought it important for judging anyone to know the kind of wrong suffered or imagined: "If only I had—this; if only I were—thus." The conspicuous fact about James is that he harbored no sense of wrong. After much self-distrust and self-disgust he had accepted himself. His occasional "envying" of one or another's powers expressed hearty admiration, without resentment at his own fate, or his schooling—or his mother.

In fact, William belongs to the group of geniuses for whom a remarkable father was the model and mentor. Others about whom we know through their sons' recollections include Montaigne, Berlioz, and John Stuart Mill. They did not seem to suffer from the tyranny or rivalry that popular psychology has led one to expect. Whatever the cause, James's freedom—from father, mother, and sense of wrong—was the source of his peculiar grace. The surprise is that a façade-free personality should also be sensitive and possessed of genius. Long habit makes us want our geniuses scarred. The sign of their authenticity is their affliction. They must be disagreeable, self-centered, dissolute, unscrupulous, maniacal, enslaved to alcohol or drugs. The festering wound, like Philoctetes', must be there or they can't draw the bow.

There is, of course, another model in stock—the vague, helpless, childlike genius, who suffers with angelic patience until rescued and pedestaled by a consortium of strong paternal hands. Either way, it seems as if in recent generations the vigorous and self-sustaining, socially capable and morally responsible geniuses of the first rank had been too few to stamp their type on the public mind; they lack the fascination of the abnormal. And of those strong ones, there are but a handful free of "side." James is the nearest to us; one thinks again of Berlioz, then of Diderot, Fielding, Byron, Blake, and one or two more on the *accessit* list and that is all. They are so singular they hardly seem to be geniuses—witness the way they admire and promote other geniuses, even in their own line of work.* As sister Alice wrote in her diary about William: "All that there is to be said of him, of course, is that he is simply himself; a creature who speaks another language, as Henry

---

* It is remarkable how often James referred to 'that whole seething life of private jealousy and exclusion which is the bane of this world's estate.' And again: 'The vice of ordinary Jack and Jill affection is not its intensity but its exclusions and jealousies.' (*Literary Remains of Henry James*, p. 88; "On a Certain Blindness. . . . ," *Talks to Teachers*, p. 267.)

says, from the rest of mankind, and who would lend charm to a tread-mill."

Of the several species of genius, James belongs to the hot kind, the kind we are warmed by in Balzac, Rubens, or Beethoven. The cool ones (Kant, Ingres, Debussy) doubtless work with a like amount of passion, but it is bottled up. James's heat-in-light has been plain enough along the way, but it needs interpreting, for nowadays cool is our preferred style—cool and sick. Thus in startled response to his radiating self, some have been quick to say that James was "greater as a man than as a philosopher." It is a convenient thought-cliché, of which I am more than tired. In my earlier studies it was "Berlioz a greater artist than musician; Delacroix a greater dramatist than painter; Diderot a greater disseminator than creator." Recent minute studies have shown up these absurd judgments as products of simple bewilderment, caused by extreme heat. To his contemporaries James seemed an extraordinary force. John Jay Chapman found it "hard to state what it was that penetrated and influenced us, what it is that we lack and feel the need of, now that he has so unexpectedly and incredibly died. I relied upon his sanctity as if it were sunlight."

It must always seem astonishing that anyone (and a philosopher at that) should have understood and enjoyed so many diverse people, ideas, and attitudes. Chapman thought James "liked everyone and everything too well." But of course this "liking" was not common gregariousness; it was an act of imagination. James saw others and their actions from within, and for the time being felt the same partiality for their world as they themselves did. It was, according to Peirce, "most wonderful. Who, for example, could be of a nature so different from his than I? He so concrete, so living; I a mere table of contents, so abstract. ... Yet in all my life I found scarce a soul that seemed to comprehend naturally ... the mainspring of my life better than he did. He was even greater in the practice than in the theory of psychology."

With such an imagination, new perceptions sprouted naturally wherever he turned his power. He himself thought genius a simple thing—'little more than the faculty of perceiving in an unhabitual way.' No doubt true, and many these days hope to show genius by doing or saying the opposite of the usual. But that is cleverness, not imagination. Besides, 'to do anything with one's genius requires passion; to do much requires doggedness. Hence the intense sensibility of the psychopathic temperament, when it adds itself to a first-rate intellect, greatly increases the chances that it will bear fruits.' James was not thinking of himself when writing those sentences but, short of psychopathic, they describe his makeup and mode of work. Note in his argumentative essays the fervor with which he states his opponents' case (imagination); then the equal warmth with which he affirms the counterarguments that temperamentally weigh with him (passion); finally the conclusion, chosen because *more* good reasons, not *all* good reasons are on that side (intellect, not cool, but judicious).

For this balance of forces, as James knew, tension is required. Just as a limb cannot move smoothly by the use of one muscle alone, but is held firm by pulling one while stretching another, so the best thought holds opposites simultaneously in view. There is thus no warrant for the critic's favorite trick of discovering "two strands," presumably ill-matched, in a thinker's work. In James the strands are intertwined and form a cable.

Since these tastes and powers struck observers as strange and disconcerting, it may be wondered how James's personality could also appear simple and accessible. There is no explanation except that his common impulses must have been unencumbered by his uncommon ones. While accepting himself he also felt the obligation to work on himself and resist the temptations that Perry chose to list as morbid traits—a tendency toward brooding melancholy; a susceptibility to abnormal mental states (he not only studied but experienced them more than once); an extreme variability—witness his own words: 'My *flux*-philosophy may well have to do with my extremely impatient temperament. I am a motor, need change, and get very quickly bored.'* Still, this motor energy was not excitement but zest, as he casually lets us see after the nostalgic passage already quoted from the *Psychology,* where he recalls the divine girls and books of his youthful time: 'Instead of all this, more zestful than ever, the work, the work, and fuller and deeper the import of common duties and common goods.'

But zest and impatience also meant being vulnerable to what Perry calls "the mirage of distant joys," which goes with a revulsion for what one is doing or has just done. For instance, poor James loathed proofreading: 'Send me no proofs! I will return them unopened and never speak to you again. I am of the eagle's race and free!' In larger matters, an absence of possessiveness about his own productions doubtless explains his brand of modesty. He went out of his way to credit others for things he had done independently or first—Peirce and Hodgson for the pragmatic test, Myers for the role of the unconscious, Bergson for that of concepts, Davidson, Royce, B. P. Blood and others for ideas which did not so much inspire as confirm his own thoughts.

That James had obsessive traits as well, is clear from one of his ironic

---

* Is a reminder necessary that "motor" in that sentence is not a metaphor but the technical term for a psycho-physiological type?

self-sketches, sent to Henry and Alice in London when James was enjoying a breathing spell of rural domesticity: 'I think even Alice [who
sometimes complained of William's exhausting presence] would feel
compunction if she could see me, the idol of the group of relatives and
dependents, dignified and serene, never worrying or "wishing," never
depreciating present possessions, never contradicting others' opinions
or pinning them down, never discussing personal anecdotes from the
point of view of abstract reasoning and absolute truth, never seeking a
second metaphor, or a third, when the first or second were good
enough, breathing, in short, an atmosphere of peace and rest wherever
I go. But enough of this: since you can't see it, it is well that you should
*hear* of it at least; and my Alice is, I fear, too shy to write such things.'

Unquestionably, William, though ever lovable and for posterity
"adorable," was not a bland, easy-going presence in the home and "my
Alice," with her ability to make him content, grateful, and able to work,
was the remarkable woman that he knew her to be. The lives of most
men who are impatient, energetic, and articulate are a succession of
quarrels, misunderstandings, and short-lived reconciliations. James's, as
we have seen, was the exact opposite—it moved among a perfect galaxy
of long, unbroken friendships, yet not because of a desire to be sociable. James enjoyed human society, but deep down he did not want or
need it. It was as much a curse as a desire that made him enter into the
lives of those he met, after which he could not help loving them "regardless." A pair of anecdotes throws light on this complex feeling. Devoted to his students, he would invite them to his house in groups. At
one such gathering, where all the young were having a good time under
Mrs. James's motherly eye, James took one student aside and said:
"Here, Smith, you want to get out of this *Hell*, don't you? I'll show you
how." And as the student told Mrs. James when he came in again by
the front door to get his hat, "Before I could answer he'd popped me out
through a back door. But really, I don't want to go!" On another occasion, when a shy youth, obviously miserable at tea in James's house,
murmured something about his discomfort, James said: 'Yes, I know,
when I see these people who know exactly what to do and say, I feel
like smashing their heads with a paving stone.' The student later reported: "The sympathetic understanding of my feelings and his characteristically forcible language gave me great satisfaction."

Endowed with capacities stretching over so wide a range of feeling,
James was clearly born to be a psychologist and to evolve a philosophy
rooted in that science. His unique fusion of the introspective power
with that of seeing into others, and with a "motor" temperament that
enabled him to value action, led to his seeing how mind and truth were

linked with doing—the concrete activities to which theory herself must be handmaiden. Abstract thought must be beautiful enough to delight the esthetic in us, but it is justified only by the *pragmata* of morals, art, and science, plus those needed for the business of living.

In that last domain, imagination, sympathy, and right reason enabled James to carry on long and close philosophical debates—fifteen years of public and private war with Bradley, for instance—without wounded feelings on either side. The record shows only two polemic incidents of the sort common enough in professional lives. One, with his publisher and rather irritable friend Henry Holt about competitive bidding and marketing, topped by an error in the firm's bookkeeping, brought an apology from Holt, some intransigence and a matching apology from James.* A second, with his fellow psychologist G. Stanley Hall, president of Clark University, is the only instance when James claimed priority for anything he had said or done. Hall was a prolific and much-respected writer, who in his own *American Journal of Psychology* published in 1895 an editorial giving a wholly self-centered view of the recent history of the subject. Half a dozen of those named in the piece published letters of protest in *Science*. James wrote direct to Hall: 'I frankly admit my great inferiority as a laboratory-teacher and investigator. But some little regard should be paid to the good will with which I have tried to force my nature, and to the actual things I have done. One of them, for example, was inducting YOU into experimental investigation, with very naïve methods, it is true, but you may remember that there was no other place but Harvard where during those years you could get even that. I well recognize how contemptible these beginnings were, and that you and your pupils have in these latter years left them far behind. But you are now professing to state history; beginnings are a part thereof and should not be written down in inverted order. If only my own person was concerned I should let you say what you like. In this case, however, the misstatement concerns the credit of my university.'**

One further trait deserving mention is one that is never popular with family and friends—the disregard of conventions in their presence. William's misbehavior once provoked Henry to unwonted fury in the presence of H. G. Wells. During a stay with Henry in southern England,

---

* See Charles A. Madison, *The Owl Among the Colophons* (New York, 1966, pp. 44 ff.)

** It would appear that James started not merely the first psychological laboratory in the United States but the first in the world. James's dates from 1875-76 and Wundt's at Leipzig, usually credited with being first, opened in 1879. Of course, several psychologists, including James and Wundt, began their work as physiologists and experimented in laboratories as such. (See Robert S. Harper, "The Laboratory of William James," *Harvard Alumni Bulletin*, 1949, pp. 169-73.)

William heard that G. K. Chesterton was in the garden next door. As a great admirer and curious also about Chesterton's well-known Falstaffian outline, William wanted to get a sight of him and took the readiest means. He put a ladder against the party wall and looked over. No doubt reports of similar breaches of decorum circulated around that other Yard, in Cambridge, and contributed to the official lip-pursing. James could have pleaded an "unfortunate background": his father was like that and his brother as well: the same anti-ladder Henry, when he went to a play he thought stupid, would embarrass his companion by repeatedly striking the floor with his gold-headed cane and then stomping out with loud ejaculations of "Rot! Imbecile rot!" One thing to note about such behavior among geniuses is that, unlike their vices and ailments, it is not said to "make them more human."

That question of humanity I believe ought to be settled by the simple fact that the subject is a man or a woman. But the current feeling is that only our imperfections establish our humanity and fundamental equality. This opinion has affected standards of judgment, so that it seemed a bold estimate when, fifteen years ago, Elizabeth Hardwick—a writer who always knows exactly what she means—published an essay on "William James—an American Hero." Her portrait naturally differs from mine—it is a poor sitter who looks the same to every draftsman— but she and I agree about the title of hero. And from conversations with a good many private persons over the years I have gathered that James is to them at least an American "figure." Their eyes light up when I speak of him with fervor. His aura has reached them, though it is only as a warm legend sustained by a few telling quotations that he lives in the public mind. But in what sharper sense is "hero" justified?

Speaking for myself, I find heroism from the very start of William's odyssey. His recovery from near-mindless depression and disease was an act of heroic will against the insidious pull of apathy and horror.* Thereafter he had to fight the demon again and again to accomplish what he deemed his mission. For three years before the Gifford lectures he went through a bout of neurasthenia, partly the result of being kept from his proper work by the financial need to teach and lecture.** To produce *The Varieties* in that period meant heroic work, but as Perry says: "He was very highly charged and his body was in a peculiar mea-

* For those gifted with sensibility and high powers each age seems to have its appointed disease: in the early nineteenth century it was tuberculosis, at the end, neurasthenia. In the twentieth century it is cancer and coronary thrombosis—at least for those who manage to avoid the mechanized options of death in war or on the road.

** There has been a rumor that James was once a patient under an assumed name at the McLean mental hospital in Watertown. No evidence for the story has been produced. It is not said whether the false name was used with or without the connivance of the

sure the instrument of his will." The mission was what great minds have always taken as their duty: 'to spend life for something which outlasts it. I live in apprehension lest the Avenger should cut me off before I get my message out. It is an esthetic tragedy to have begun a bridge and be stopped in the middle of an arch.'

James's pluralistic universe requires heroism and so does the tragic view of life. Its native conditions spell risk, challenge, disaster; and the will must overcome the common feelings these inspire. 'To the heroic mind, too, the objects are sinister and dreadful, unwelcome, incompatible with wished-for things. But it can face them if necessary, without for that losing its hold upon the rest of life.' That seems a fair description of the way James "took" the angina attack that came when he was walking in Worcester with Freud.*

An earthquake might also be considered "unwelcome," and when James encountered one on the morning of April 18, 1906, outside San Francisco—it was the San Francisco earthquake—he met it with a very firm hold upon the rest of life. After being thrown out of bed, dodging furniture, and feeling the room shaken 'as a terrier shakes a rat,' he observed himself and others with the naturalist's trained eye. Then, as one inured to the rough kiss of experience, he began to feel 'glee and admiration; glee at the vividness which such an abstract idea or verbal term as "earthquake" could put on when translated into sensible reality and verified concretely. [Heroic pragmatism, this "verification"!] "Go it!" I almost cried aloud, "and go it stronger!" I felt no trace whatever of fear; it was pure delight and welcome. As soon as I could think, I discerned retrospectively certain peculiar ways in which my consciousness had taken in the phenomenon, ways quite spontaneous, inevitable, and irresistible. First, I personified the earthquake as a permanent individual entity. It came, moreover, directly to me. It stole in behind my back, and once inside the room had me all to itself. Animus and intent were never more present in any human action. All whom I consulted on the point agree: "It was vicious." "It was bent upon destruction. It wanted to show its power."'**

---

authorities or for what reason. No dates for the stay are given nor does the correspondence of the family show absence or a gap in his activities. The cause, too, is not specified; was it depression as in youth—or a wish to experience at first hand the conditions of patient care, about which James felt grave concern and wrote professionally? If he needed such care it would, in the eyes of some, lift from him the onus of having been a genius tainted with lifelong sanity.

* See above, p. 232.

** Compare Henry's description of the fire in his house at Rye (England) in 1899: "We put him out, we made him stop, with soaked sponges." (Letters of Henry James, New York, 1920, I, p. 313.)

The historian of the unconscious interprets William's report as "a wonderful picture of how a man experiences the emergence of an archetype." (Henri F. Ellenberger, The Discovery of the Unconscious, New York, 1970, p. 706.)

A force of nature was a more congenial enemy than the evil or stubborn agencies of society, but we saw him taking on the latter with resolve and often solitary courage. He could not shrug off individual cases of injustice or distress. They haunted him till he was ready to approve the dictum that "pity is a vice to be exterminated along with its object," but he added 'I know that to be a lie, but I admit the canalization of pity to be a difficult engineering problem.' James's heroism, then, was both of the public and the quotidian kind, which is not spectacular, barely describable, except perhaps in the admirable words of William's sister Alice: "the only thing which survives is the resistance we bring to life and not the strain life brings to us." In William, the last record of fortitude is the remark of his final days that his death 'had come to seem a very trifling incident.'

On the heroism of others (including animals*) he speculated often and described the details vividly. We heard his main utterance on the subject when he dedicated the monument to Robert Gould Shaw, and wound up his praise of martial and social valor with a description of the lonely hero or prophet standing out against the errors or prejudices of the mass. In others of his tributes—to Emerson, Agassiz, Francis Boott, Thomas Davidson, Frederic Myers, Benjamin Paul Blood—James always singled out as chiefly memorable the precious 'victory gained in a brief critical hour.'

In using the phrase "an American hero," Elizabeth Hardwick was of course thinking of James under more aspects than the heroic. She had in mind the "outstanding figure" or "leading character," the hero as in fiction. There he is larger than life and since he is supposed to engage our interest as a model, his particular powers and defects are closely scanned. Until a while ago it was taken for granted that the former were genuine and at least as interesting as the latter. But the age of the anti-hero dawned in overreaction to earlier idolatries, and both fiction and biography began to prove at more than requisite length that heroes are among the exploded myths of an ignorant past.**

It had always been said than no man is a hero to his valet, because near-to the hero is full of faults. Now there are no valets, but first they got rid of all the heroes, by assimilation with themselves. So the praise is quite properly for those with whom our souls have an affinity, and since we view ourselves with deep disfavor, we prefer such figures as

---

* See the account he wrote to his young son from Yosemite about the death of a coyote 'without any clothes or house or books or anything, risking his life so cheerfully just to see if he could pick up a meal near the hotel.' (*Letters*, II, p. 81.)

** James himself had objected to the Germans' lack of judgment: 'The gumboil or the deficient teeth of a hero are thought of with the same romantic affection as his more strictly heroic "points."' (Perry, *op. cit.*, I, p. 280.)

the pitiable Baudelaire, the deplorable Thackeray, and the insufferable D. H. Lawrence. We feel warmer in their presence than in the presence of characters theoretically and formerly more admirable.

The hero we have lost and the anti-hero we have gained—I am speaking of historical, not fictional characters—seem to me on reflection to be always the same person. It is only the arithmetic we perform about them that differs. As we can see in William's numerous laudatory estimates of his friends and acquaintances, he is anything but gullible; his geese are not swans; he has noted their shortcomings, sometimes down to small particulars; but he doesn't subtract these from the high qualities: they coexist. It could have been predicted that as soon as one starts on the other system, of balancing the books, the qualities disappear under the load of trivialities and the greatest man is left with a minus account, in debt to the Treasury of Virtue and Wisdom. One wonders, why read about such a person at all? And in that same system, no tally of comforting faults really brings us nearer to greatness. At times, in conversation, I have been accused of hero-worship apropos of this or that writer, artist, or statesman, and I have been reminded that "after all, he was a man like us." No idea of worship was in my mind—just an estimate of height, and I could only answer: "He may have been a man like you, but he was certainly not one like me."

One result of this new habit, now almost a tradition, has not been noticed by those who, in the United States, watch over our moral and social heritage. It is this: In spite of the careful studies that keep appearing about our outstanding figures, they never gain in the public eye a well-labeled niche; they never form a company of worthies. James may be called a hero, a great man, a powerful intellectual influence, but no collective sense among those who know will assign and remember the corner he should occupy in the American pantheon, supposing there were one.

I mean by pantheon a comprehensive group of notables known to all who can read, and whose place in the firmament of fame is clear on merely naming them. Instead, we pursue our national destiny with no later symbols and myths than those of the Founding Fathers. After them we have only the haphazard products of publicity, accidental or fostered by special interests: the lawyers have canonized Judge Holmes; Audubon hangs on because he pleases the bird fanciers; assassination has secured Lincoln's glory. Academic toil has moreover put under the spotlight and the microscope a short list of writers, into which Melville was promoted culpably late. But surely there are two or three dozen more great Americans—men and women—who were as fruitful and amazing as those we have caught in our ill-mended net. For example,

Oliver Wendell Holmes, Sr.—not as poet, though he wrote some charming lines, but as thinker and prose writer, medical pioneer, and psychiatric novelist. We have produced very few great critics, but John Jay Chapman equals any of his foreign contemporaries. In George Perkins Marsh, we had a second all-round man comparable to Jefferson—inventor, diplomat, linguist, architect, art collector, and scholar (perhaps the first in the country), and certainly the first scientific ecologist and diagnostician of our ruinous treatment of nature. One would also think that in this the third wave of women's emancipation the name of Lucretia Mott would arise again, especially since she was remarkable as a preacher and social worker and not solely as a politician.

But we content ourselves with postage stamps. A postage stamp with us is the moral equivalent of a knighthood. It discharges a debt at small expense; the honor is posthumous, anonymous, and capricious. We have had Judge Holmes (15¢) and John Dewey (30¢), Carl Sandburg (13¢), Eugene O'Neill ($1), Lucy Stone (50¢), George M. Cohan (15¢), Will Rogers (15¢), John Steinbeck (15¢), Einstein (15¢), Babe Zaharias (18¢), Frank Lloyd Wright (2¢), Horatio Alger (20¢). Kudos is not measured by the denomination as such, but by its being the first-class rate at the time of issue, so that one dollar for Eugene O'Neill amounts to a thinly veiled insult—up to now. But seriously, where are Prescott and Ives, Willard Gibbs and Louis Sullivan and Mary Cassatt—all outstanding in their domains?* And where are the Jameses?

Not that William and Henry need to be stamped as great. The "honor" is not an indication about the recipient but about the culture. And to return to William, his present position in this peculiar realm of repute has all the advantages and drawbacks of ambiguity. He has not yet been fully assimilated academically or popularly. He is widely known but still a puzzle; he has won respect and genuine liking but not complete confidence—all of which, in an artist or a philosopher, is a sign of persisting contemporaneousness.

I have been calling names—and in copycat fashion, too—"genius" after Whitehead, "hero" after Hardwick. I must add another, which requires as much comment if not more: it is the explosive term "gentleman." And its application to James also originates with an earlier student than myself, the late Horace Kallen.**

* Since those words were written, Louis Sullivan's name and dates have appeared in microscopic print on an eighteen-cent stamp entitled in large letters "Architecture U.S.A." and showing a building that Sullivan undeniably built. I am reliably informed by someone with access to the committee in charge that William James was proposed and turned down three times. The criteria implied by the list above are fairly clear; it is the grounds of ineligibility that must be subtle.

** On May 14, 1944, Dr. Kallen was on the panel of the CBS program Invitation to Learning that discussed James's Varieties of Religious Experience. The other members

"Gentleman" nowadays is a grossly ambiguous, perhaps obsolescent word. The compulsory show of democratic feeling requires of everybody a lowlier-than-thou attitude, a negation of better and worse in manners and habits. As a consequence, one's response to the word is the surprise that I felt on hearing Kallen use it seriously and philosophically. A sense of history makes his meaning clearer. In his generation and James's too, "gentleman" no longer signified only birth and wealth; it implied genuine merits—gentlemanliness. The egalitarian socialist Bernard Shaw continually uses the term to mean a man of honor who in his dealings never loses sight of others' rights. His very definition of gentleman is: one who strives to give more to the community than he takes from it. And in their religion, says Shaw, "ladies and gentlemen cannot as such possibly allow anyone else to expiate their sins by suffering a cruel death."

Gentlemanliness is a social and intellectual code of ethics, unwritten but perfectly clear. For instance, James's contemporary Andrew Lang points out that "no gentleman ever *consciously* misrepresents the ideas of an opponent." As for James, he repeatedly associates the gentleman with a certain formation of the mind: 'At a technical school a man may grow into a first-rate instrument for doing a certain job, but he may miss all the graciousness of mind suggested by the term liberal culture. He may remain a cad, and not a gentleman, intellectually pinned down to his one narrow subject, literal, unable to suppose anything different from what he has seen, without imagination, atmosphere, or mental perspective.' In the *Psychology*, another contrast is drawn apropos of reasoning: 'the essence of plebeianism, that which separates vulgarity from aristocracy, is perhaps less a defect than an excess. To ignore, to disdain to consider, to overlook are the essence of the "gentleman."'

---

were Houston Peterson, the first biographer of Havelock Ellis, and I, who at the time was a frequent chairman of that talk show. After the live broadcast, Kallen and I went uptown together and he pleased me by "talking James" while I listened. He had studied under James at Harvard and was now critical of Perry's two-volume *Thought and Character* of the philosopher. Kallen, himself a teacher of philosophy, maintained that Perry had failed to understand his subject through insensitivity to everything in James that derived from his being a gentleman—most of all, the rapidity of his insights and neglect of the vulgarian's wish to have every *t* crossed and every *i* dotted before he will consent to catch your drift.

As I knew Kallen to be an unassuming man of plain democratic bearing and outlook, his words struck me as remarkable and I wrote them down on reaching home, pasting the sheet inside my copy of Perry's book. One might impute something of Kallen's animus to his being passed over as James's official biographer, but imputations are ugly and valueless. My only demurrer to Kallen's view (silent but noted at the time) is that it was fortunate to have the first full-scale survey of James's thought from a sympathetic but pedestrian mind, whose quibbles and bias in producing a source book can be ignored by all fit readers. Cultural history shows the need for step-down transformers. But the moral and intellectual significance of "gentleman" remains.

Often most provokingly so; for the things ignored may be of the deepest moral consequence. But in the very midst of our indignation with the gentleman, we have a consciousness that his preposterous inertia and negativeness is somehow or other allied with his general superiority to ourselves. It is not only that the gentleman ignores considerations relative to conduct, sordid suspicions, fears, calculations, etc., which the vulgarian is fated to entertain; it is that he is silent where the vulgarian talks; that he gives nothing but results where the vulgarian is profuse of reasons; that he uses one sentence instead of twenty; that, in a word, there is an amount of *interstitial* thinking, so to call it, which it is quite impossible to get him to perform. All this suppression of the secondary leaves the field clear—for higher flights, should they choose to come.'

Among these flights is conversation. 'When two minds of a high order, interested in kindred subjects, come together, their conversation is chiefly remarkable for the summariness of its allusions and the rapidity of its transitions.' The opposite is the subject of a complaint in a private letter: 'I've been meeting minds so earnest and helpless that it takes them half an hour to get from one idea to its immediately adjacent next neighbor. And then they lie down on it with their whole weight and can get no farther, like a cow on a doormat, so that you can get neither in nor out with them. Still, glibness is not all. Weight is something, even cow weight.'

Much of this difference James explains by upbringing, that of the child of poor parents being termed "unnatural," because it lacks the means of developing his instincts in more than a few directions: 'the timely age goes by in a sort of starvation of objects and the individual grows up with gaps in his psychic constitution which future experiences can never fill. Compare the accomplished gentleman with the poor artisan or tradesman of a city: during the adolescence of the former, objects appropriate to his growing interests, bodily and mental, were offered as fast as the interests awoke. Sport came to the rescue and completed his education where real things were lacking. He had tasted the essence of every side of human life, being sailor, hunter, athlete, scholar, fighter, talker, dandy, man of affairs all in one.'

This sort of gentleman was a nineteenth-century invention.* It merged the merits of four classes—the active interests of the old aristocrat, who was usually rude and unlettered; the moral responsibility of the bourgeois, possibly a philistine; the heady concerns of the intellec-

---

* Mark Twain's conception of a gentleman is given in the description of the county judge, York Driscoll, as "fine, just, and generous. To be a gentleman—without a stain or blemish—was his only religion and to it he was always faithful." (*Pudd'nhead Wilson*, 1894, p. 3.)

tual, who is not necessarily a polished citizen; and the lack of "side" of truly simple folk. For the amalgam to be an ideal it required an infusion of the chivalric sentiments: noblesse oblige—but eccentricities might go with it. Now none of these ingredients fit one for life in a modern urban or suburban setting, or even for a career in a professional or academic enclave, where "the narrow subject" will serve to describe both the man and his job. That this state of affairs already obtained in James's day is shown by his views on higher education, shortly to be sampled, as well as by Santayana's observation that James was always suspect to official Harvard—by 1890 a gentleman had begun to be an anomaly.* James himself once or twice, in letters to friends, would ask about an unknown whose work he found simpatico: 'Who and what is he? Gentleman? Professor? What?'

Whether we like it or not, then, James was a gentleman in that lost nineteenth-century sense.** Mrs. Agassiz made a point of saying so when William was a youth; Alice Boughton, the famous photographer, used the word to sum up her impressions of him toward the end of his life. These ladies should know. James had certainly had most of the needed advantages—absence of struggle for a living till he had found his way; travel, art, acquaintance with fine and great minds; and the requisite "objects," though not sport or "affairs," however defined. But to make the designation adequate, one must amplify it. Certain emotional conditions must be fulfilled before gentlemanliness becomes something other than a mark of caste: the human being must accept himself for what he is and forget about it. In the words of La Rochefoucauld, the well-bred man must not "make a point" of being or doing anything that redounds to the credit of the self (il ne se pique de rien).

The nuance is subtle, and difficult to explain if we remind ourselves that manners are "little morals" and morals often require conscious effort. To be free of self-consciousness while going about one's business among those afflicted with it presupposes a kind of innocence very rare in adults. When found, it usually goes with the virtue that Nietzsche preached without achieving—gaiety, the Italian sprezzatura or courteous veiling of seriousness. Since James's time the social grace of poise has been replaced by the greater obligation to journey into one's interi-

* Writing about Harvard a generation later, a scholar calls James the "Creative Undisciplinable" and confesses that "the passing of thirty years made a vast difference in one's estimate of William James." (R. W. Brown, Harvard Yard in the Golden Age, New York, 1948, p. 74.)

** A letter from H. G. Wells to the London Times may fortuitously supply an approximate date when the change went into effect. He was supporting the men in the coal strike of 1912 and pointed out that they "behave no longer as though they believe that our political leaders are in the last resort gentlemen, but ... in the worst sense of the words, lawyers and exploiters." (Your Obedient Servant, London, 1974, p. 84.)

or, where the darkness, more often than not, adds to the outer gloom. For this and other reasons, our models act as if they were spiritually allergic to themselves. One sometimes suspects a confusion between "Know thyself" and the rumination about oneself which, in all but the incurably vain, breeds perpetual self-consciousness and self-contempt.* Like Montaigne, James was in the habit of "haunting and frequenting" himself, but the psychologizing that he did not permit himself toward his opponents he also refrained from turning inward. In both directions he was properly fastidious, as I have so often had occasion to remark.

Cheerfulness, gaiety, the habit not so much of repressing as of resisting gloomy thoughts—all this may be dismissed as marks of the shallow optimist, but we learned earlier that James was precisely not that. Indeed, to Chapman's discerning glance, a deep sadness lay behind James's playfulness.** His humor "always three parts poetry" came, if not from, then with, his reasoned view that "better" is not fated but possible. Such an attitude proved its worth by being contagious. To quote Mrs. Agassiz again, after she had heard James speak at a college function in 1902: "his closing address sent the audience off in the best of humors by his wit and light touch which have a certain elegance in the turn of phrase, while it is also perfectly spontaneous and natural." In short, it was not modern humor, self-derisive, as a prophylactic.

It may be said that gentlemanliness in attitude and action is but the desire to please. True, and that desire is deeply moral compared with the wish to be loved. For the attitudes have to do, ultimately, with the respect for the individual's human dignity which is so often on our lips. One would suppose that this essential of a free democracy would enhance in each human being the sense of his separateness, bounded by, mingled with, the sense of a common humanity; and that common humanity should embrace something besides our animal functions and commonplace defects.***

* The only palliative (other than drugs) that moderns have found for self-consciousness seems to be speed. The rush of air, the rapid blurring of objects and persons by motion, the pleasure of danger, the irresponsibility—because responsibility is out of the question—form a sure remedy for self-consciousness; hence its appeal to the young.

** "You felt that he had just stepped out of this sadness in order to meet you and was to go back into it the moment you left him." (Memories and Milestones, New York, 1915, p. 26.)

*** Perhaps because an urban life, by crowding and anonymity, makes it hard to keep the self dignified and distinct—say in a subway crush—there is a tendency to make a democratic virtue of relishing the sensation of being animals in a litter. A comment involving James is instructive on this point. In a study by the same brilliant scholar who reviewed the pre-Freudian literature on infant sexuality, one reads that the germ theory of disease was very alarming at first and that "William James made an extraordinary confession of this general fear when describing 'what might be called the anti-sexual instinct, the instinct of personal isolation, the actual repulsiveness to us of the idea of intimate contact with most of the persons we meet.'" James's footnote to his own remark

A fitter subject for amazement is how James, a wild spirit (though dwelling in a well-bred and superconscious soul), came to occupy an academic cage. Campuses are no habitat for geniuses. And being a professor at the end of the last century still meant one had to teach. James took the duty seriously, as his students, from Gertrude and Leo Stein to Walter Lippmann and W. E. B. DuBois testified.* When in good form he held his hearers by lively words and motions and blackboard uses; and when not, he was easily roused to original thought by question and challenge. No one who sat under him ever forgot his dignified expression, his low-pitched voice—or his Norfolk jacket, no longer fashionable. "Except for a slight halting in his delivery"—the penalty of thinking, no doubt—"a perfect lecturer." The testimonials he received from his students twice in 1896 and again on his retirement in 1907 were the fruit of their gratitude, not his longevity, and the tribute would have been appropriate at almost any time after his apprenticeship; for without acting the friend, the father, or the psychiatrist, he regarded his students as persons with many claims upon him, including medical and social ones.**

An innocent person might therefore suppose that James liked to teach. On the contrary, he thought it an unnatural activity. He observed, as others have done, that every September he would return to the classroom in trepidation and with his mind a blank. Like other born teachers—persons whose grasp of the subject is matched by an intuitive knowledge of the individual minds before them—he doubtless felt that teaching is an invasion of privacy, a meddling with a stranger's self-development. But born teachers—who are fewer perhaps than born poets—when the demand comes, and despite their reluctance and disapproval, cannot help explaining, coaching, tutoring, enlightening.

---

is also called "amazing": 'To most of us it is unpleasant to sit in a chair still warm from occupancy by another person's body. To many, handshaking is disagreeable.'

This "exposure" of James's "lack of humanity" rather distorts the facts. His words occur in the chapter on Instinct in his *Psychology*, under the subhead Love and right after the mention of shyness, which also avoids close contacts. So it has nothing to do with the germ theory of disease and it is a report, not "a confession." Whether it is "extraordinary" or not, each one is free to judge; tolerance for warmed seats and handshakes varies like other traits. But if one does think of germs, one may wonder why in public places the common towel is prohibited by law and the common hand allowed to pass—from hand to hand. At any rate, James did not suffer from squeamishness and he was the first to say 'the art of being wise is the art of knowing what to overlook.' (Perry, *op. cit.*, II, 369.)

* "It [reading a certain book] eventually landed me squarely in the arms of William James at Harvard, for which God be praised." (DuBois, *Dusk of Dawn, Autobiography of a Race Concept*, New York, 1940, p. 33.)

** See above, p. 6 and n.

The ways of accomplishing this are endless. James's was the spontaneous—after long preparation. Each hour might bring forth a new perception, a new formulation. Woodbridge, himself a philosopher of note, has recorded how James would startle the group: "I recall a remark of William James's to the effect that we do not see out of the palms of our hands or from the middle of our backs. Such obvious remarks were characteristic of him and often more instructive than pages of forced reasoning. This one halted my own reading.... What is Nature from the middle of our backs? Take her with the palm of the hand but without vision! One may now meditate for hours, for days." At other times, the point was made by a grotesque exaggeration. The lawyer and author Arthur Train says in his autobiography: "I took philosophy because of my admiration for William James. How could you help listening to a college professor who denied that this could be the best of all possible worlds so long as there was 'a single cockroach suffering the pangs of unrequited love.'"

As for the managerial side of teaching, there is the incident of Gertrude Stein's finding herself mentally vacant in front of the final in James's course: too much opera-going was the cause. She addressed James on the blue book, saying she did not feel like writing philosophy that day. As she remembered it after thirty years, the next day, she had from James a postal card: 'I understand perfectly how you feel. I often feel like that myself.' He passed her then, but his sense of justice to others exacted an "exit" examination later.

The one conspicuous failure of rapport in James's teaching career occurred with George Santayana. James, like a magnet acting through both its poles on one iron filing, drew and repelled him simultaneously. During all his long life, Santayana kept bringing up James in his own writings, now praising, now damning with arrogance and malice. The men were temperamental opposites but only James could stand it. He praised Santayana's early book *The Sense of Beauty*. The rest struck James as overripe, nostalgic, and eclectic—'the perfection of rottenness,' as he told Santayana direct. The younger man tried to argue that their views were not so far apart, but the passage from student to colleague is often thorny, and Santayana's proudly-nurtured sense of wrong— against the world, America, and Cambridge, Mass.—never got over the spectacle of James's having conquered as deep a grievance in himself.

In 1907 James at last won his release. 'For thirty five years,' he wrote, 'I have been suffering from the exigencies of being a teacher, the pretension and the duty, namely, of meeting the mental needs and difficulties of other persons, needs that I couldn't possibly imagine and difficulties that I couldn't possibly understand; and now that I have shuffled off the professorial coil, the sense of freedom that comes to me is as surprising as it is exquisite. I wake up every morning with it: "What! not to have to accommodate myself to this mass of alien and recalcitrant humanity, not to think under resistance, not to have to square myself with others at every step I make—hurrah, it is too good to be true!"'

The conclusion to draw from this hymn of joy is not that James was miscast in his profession: we know he excelled in it. Rather, we should reflect on what his kind of teaching implies—all this squaring and divining and removing of ignorance through vocal exchanges with others. The worst of such a strain is that it is to be begun over and over again with each new batch of stubborn young minds; for though they desire, they resist—rightly, since learning will not stick without resistance. Then, the unsatisfactory enterprise once over, with all its holes and ragged edges remembered, it shows to neither party any clear and tangible result.

Being a teacher, and a well-known lecturer, and a psychologist, James was inevitably drawn into the contemporary movement of educational reform. The child had just been widely rediscovered and the twentieth century dedicated to him.* Science was expected to second the humanitarian impulse that would abolish school drudgery and punishment and transform learning into a perpetual delight. It was Harvard itself that asked James in 1892 to give a course of lectures to the teachers of Cambridge. Later, by request, he repeated a number of them elsewhere. When he published them in 1899, he added to the fifteen chapters three talks to students that deal with themes no less useful to the pedagogue,** though to him 'the teacher part' of the book was 'incarnate boredom.'

That teacher part naturally recapitulates relevant facts from the *Psychology*—on the stream of consciousness, the link between mind and action, the association of ideas, the will, the laws of habit, and so on. But the great originality of the book is James's reasoned skepticism about the "new psychology of education." 'In my humble opinion there *is* no "new psychology" worthy of the name. There is nothing but the old psychology plus a little physiology of the brain and sense and theory of evolution, and a few refinements of introspective detail, for the most part without adaptation to the teacher's use.'

The fundamentals that he recited in order to acquaint teachers with the ordinary workings of the mind *were* important, but he warned against newly raised hopes from "research": 'No elementary measurement capable of being performed in a laboratory can throw any light on the actual efficiency of the subject; for the vital thing about him, his

* See above, p. 186 and n..
** *Talks to Teachers on Psychology and to Students on Some of Life's Ideals.* (New York, Henry Holt and Company, 1899.)

emotional and moral energy, becomes known only by the total results in the long run.' Since James, talking and writing about education—the parody of thought—has swallowed billions of dollars and man-hours and has misled more than it has enlightened.* "Studies" by the hundreds have promised wonders and fed faddishness while contradicting one another, for they assume a sort of human mind which it was James's great contribution to have shown up as contrary to fact.

James's view of the child was as usual concrete. The 'little sensitive, impulsive, associative, and reactive organism, partly fated and partly free' calls for the kind of teaching that respects freedom *and* compulsion, individuality *and* the claims of common reason and common action. Such a view in 1890 was enlightened, and not widespread; nor was it what came to be called progressive. James knew that a child-centered school would be as bad as a teacher-centered or a book-centered one. He did not fall into the trap of supposing that a child's needs are the same as his wants. He pointed out on the contrary that there is no possibility of making schoolwork always easy and "natural." Much of it is repulsive till it has become habitual, and doing it requires a voluntary jerking back of attention, for voluntary attention comes in "beats." Certain subjects must borrow their interest from extraneous ideas, such as gaining rank, avoiding punishment, not being balked by difficulty, and the like. Even what becomes interesting enough to hold the attention is not thereby attended to without effort. Effort is always needed, and the teacher's utmost skill in supplying interest is 'to let loose the effort.'

Together with concentrated advice of this kind, James uttered two warnings that nowadays teachers in training never hear. One is about what he called 'the softer pedagogies,' that 'have taken the place of the old steep and rocky path to learning. From this lukewarm air the bracing oxygen of effort is left out. It is nonsense to suppose that every step in education *can* be interesting.' But James did not leave Difficulty hanging over teacher and pupil: 'The fighting impulse must be appealed to. Make the pupil ashamed of being scared at fractions, of being downed by the law of falling bodies; rouse his pugnacity and pride, and he will rush at the difficult places with a sort of inner wrath at himself that is one of the best moral faculties.' But he or she will respond so only if not previously demoralized. Today, many teachers know that they must avoid giving hard work if they want to escape

---

* The "research" by James McKeen Cattell, a pupil of Wundt's, which imposed "Look-and-say, Dick-and-Jane" on reading instruction half a century ago, and has only recently been proved false in theory as it was in practice, typifies the menace James apprehended. It has since been called "the corruption of education by psychology."

sullen or rebellious behavior by the students, sometimes backed up by physical threats.

The second warning was that the small child will grow up and that the mental diet appropriate to early years will cause harm if prolonged. Tender solicitude must be replaced by appeals to ambition and competition and the sense of accomplishment. Accordingly, 'pupils should know their marks. The child's eagerness to know how well he does is in the line of his normal completeness of function and should never be balked except for very definite reasons indeed—though here as elsewhere, concrete experience must prevail over psychological deduction.'

This wisdom is flouted almost universally today. Instead, the jargon of psychiatry replaces the direct judgment of what a pupil has done, while his performance itself is short-circuited by so-called objective multiple-choice tests—checking little boxes as vague recognition dawns under the stimulus of prefabricated statements of fact. In other things to be learned—reading, writing, speaking—little care is given to fluency and precision, which means that the operation of habit is ignored. James conceived of all education as the making of useful habits and he gave maxims for the purpose, winding up with: 'Don't preach to your pupils or abound in good talk in the abstract.' Only the thing done has a chance of becoming a power acquired. 'Every smallest stroke of virtue or of vice leaves its never-so-little scar.'

James had no reason to imagine that schools would turn into places where death by violence, the drug habit, rape, and teenage pregnancy would count as educational problems. He and his hearers were prepared for what was then childish misbehavior and thus to accept his advice: 'Respect always the original reactions, even when you are seeking to overcome their connection with certain objects. Bad behavior, from the point of view of the teacher's art, is as good a starting point as good behavior—in fact, often a better one.'

In that last maxim we find again James's analytic mode: we start with what is natural; it is the material to work upon; but it does not set the goal, for more than one is possible and desirable. Here lies the great difference between James's pedagogy and that derived from John Dewey, which has prevailed in American schools for most of this century and in its degraded forms brought them to their present instructional paralysis.* Dewey's effect on schooling was to dethrone subject matter and replace it by techniques, the main one being aimed at teaching "problem solving" regardless of subject. On the surface, this sounds like a fulfillment of Jamesian ideas. James, too, says that the uneducated

---

* I say "degraded forms," because Dewey has been abused enough—too much—and he should be read in the original, not in his followers' gloss.

person is 'one who is nonplussed by all but the most habitual situations,' whereas the educated can 'extricate himself from circumstances in which he never was placed before.' It looks as if we had in James the "life adjustment" idea full blown. He certainly thought that education should be democratic and 'fit the human being to his social and physical world.' But two great differences destroy this apparent similarity. One is the role that Dewey assigned to the mind, the other is the sense of Before and After.

To begin with the second, Dewey's doctrine allowed his interpreters to commit the mistake of "preposterism." Because a person who has been educated is able to cope with the unknown or unfamiliar, it does not follow that one who *is being* educated should be asked to do the same. That expectation is *pre-post-erous*, the cart before the horse. Adaptation to "life" is not to be engineered in the classroom. The contrived situations fool only the teachers and undermine their authority by silly make-believe. James never wanted to abolish school subjects, though he said that their division was *in some measure* arbitrary. Even so, the learner must be given the advantage of seeing and remembering the welter of new facts in a grouping that is more logical and consecutive than made-up situations permit.

This and the next difference from Dewey are related. In setting the child to problem solving, Dewey assigns intelligence but a single track, that of analysis on "scientific" lines. James, as one can see on every page of his *Talks to Teachers*, understands the child's mind (and the adult's, for that matter) as quite other. It is not an engine chugging away in regular five-stroke motion;* it is an artist mind; it works by jumps of association and memory, by yielding to esthetic lures and indulging private tastes—all in irregular beats of attention, in apparent wanderings out of which some deep sense of rationality rises to consciousness. There is no formula, for the trained or the untrained. 'The total mental efficiency of a man is the resultant of the working together of all his faculties. He is too complex a being for any one of them to have the casting vote. If any one of them do have the casting vote, it is more likely to be the strength of his desire and passion, the strength of the interest he takes in what is proposed.' Dewey's plan is thus another piece of preposterism. When a good mind has done its work, idiosyn-

---

* In *How We Think* (1910) Dewey described for the use of teachers the five steps in the thought of a trained mind: coming upon a puzzling fact or situation; diagnosing the difficulty; searching for explanations or solutions; testing each of these in turn; verifying or corroborating the one selected as most useful. As a stylized picture of the way the scientist goes to work, this may pass, though we know that scientific results are not arrived at in this way at all. At the very end of the book, Dewey does bring up the "artistic attitude" as applicable to all activities (pp. 219–21), but it is a perfunctory word—and too late to modify the thesis.

cratically, it will no doubt submit the results to others in Dewey form. But that is no warrant for believing or requiring that the end serve as a prescription of the means.

Dewey, I repeat, is not to be charged with the culpable vagaries of high progressivisim in education. His ideas, good and bad, were exploited by ignorant and irresponsible people—veritable Smerdiakovs—and imposed upon children, parents, and teachers alike. Anything less "pragmatic" than the present ineffectiveness of public schooling would be hard to imagine. And the permissive, "relaxed," "at your own pace" mode of instruction has generated an atmosphere notably tense, anxious, and straining for "achievements," themselves indefinite. James could already note the advancing wave of nonsense: 'It does seem as if there were a certainly fatality of mystification laid upon the teachers of our day. The matter of their profession, compact enough in itself, has to be frothed up for them in journals, and institutes, till its outlines threaten to be lost in a kind of vast uncertainty. And I think that if you teachers in the earlier grades have any defect—the slightest touch of a defect in the world—it is that you are a mite too docile.'

Higher education in James's day had changed its spots even more completely. The American college had been topped, if not crowned, by the graduate and professional schools. The physical sciences had taken over a large slice of the undergraduate curriculum and forced a new standard upon intellect everywhere—specialization. Out of the bits and pieces of the college "electives" a student was supposed to educate himself and acquire or prepare for a specialty. Only two men raised their voices against the onward rush of the bandwagon: Woodrow Wilson, then president of Princeton, who maintained that the duty of a college was to "re-generalize every generation"; and William James, who in lectures and articles defined cultivation in contrast to training and opposed "the Ph.D. Octopus."*

James was not battling to preserve a genteel mode of life. When he spoke on "The Social Value of the College-Bred," he wanted democratic society to avoid becoming a mass of money-grubbers and single-track professionals. Education should imply an awareness of the human odyssey and its achievements—the humanities, which include science. I quoted James on their nature at our starting out: they are what they are, not through their substance but through their handling; remember: "art a catalogue" when it is wrongly taught.** James missed no chance to

* John Jay Chapman was at one with James in these matters but carried no weight, his remarkable essays in cultural criticism being little read, considered eccentric, and felt as lacking authority.

** See Prologue, p. 5. The whole passage amounts to the program for the new way of teaching science to undergraduates that James B. Conant introduced at Harvard. (See On Understanding Science, An Historical Approach, New Haven, 1947.)

decry "catalogues"—for example 'the American textbook Moloch, in whose belly living children's minds are turned to ashes, and in which the science is pre-digested for the teacher and for the pupil comminuted into small print and large print and paragraph headings and cross references and examination questions, and every up to date device for frustrating the natural movement of the mind when reading and preventing that irresponsible rumination of the material in one's own way which is the soul of culture.' In short, let 'virgin-minded youth' read the great books. Textbooks grew out of the specialist attitude, akin to that of the feudal lord behind his moat; its indifference negates culture, because 'real culture lives by sympathies and admirations, not by dislikes and disdains.'

James also met a perennial question with an answer that is often quoted as if it were only a witticism struck off in conversation. It is actually a considered statement of deep social import: 'Of what use is a college training? A certain amount of meditation has brought me to this as the pithiest reply which I myself can give: The best claim that a college education can possibly make on your respect, the best thing it can aspire to accomplish for you, is this: that it should help you to know a good man when you see him.' The principle here is that only a developed mind can gauge the capacities that are equal to its own, or greater or less. It is an intuitive act, not a numerical demonstration on the basis of tests. The educated will know how to judge 'sound work, slack work, sham work; precision, thoroughness and honesty.' James advocated laboratory and shop work in the lower schools to impart the concrete meaning of these terms at an early age. In adult life this authenticity is the basis of culture and it makes itself felt in a certain tone. ' "Tone," to be sure is a terribly vague word to use, but there is no other, and this whole meditation is over the questions of tone. By their tone are all things human either lost or saved.' In these words, which brother Henry might have written—did write in various forms*—we hear again the leading note, the characteristic tone, of the fastidious and exacting Jamesian mind.

The folly of the "Ph.D. Octopus" lay in this lack of authentic tone. With deep irony, James recounts the sad story of the brilliant Harvard graduate appointed to teach in a neighboring college who turns out not to have a doctorate. His sponsors guarantee his merit, but that is not enough. He must write a thesis, 'padded out in a certain way, and pass our formidable ordeals in subjects perhaps unrelated to his teaching.' Only then could he 'wipe out the stain and bring his college into proper

---

* See for example the end of The Sacred Fount and the remark to Christina Light in Roderick Hudson, "I should know a great character when I saw it." (Ed. Percy Lubbock, New York, 1921, p. 263.)

relations with the world again.' James sums up the episode: 'Human nature is once for all so childish that every reality becomes a sham somewhere.'

Ever since James's day, the octopus has held American higher learning in its grip.* The sham of a required "original contribution to learning" has used up vast amounts of mental energy in all concerned, brought unimaginable anguish to the young scholar and his family, wasted social resources in publishing, storing, and cataloguing the products, and vitiated the very idea of scholarship by demanding it under pressure and of specified bulk.

The resulting inflation is patent: a discovery worth a footnote becomes an article; articles are blown up into books; insignificant subjects are researched and non-subjects (e.g., abstract notions vaguely derived from reading poetry or fiction) are treated at length; the same lives, events, and masterpieces are rehashed again and again under the arbitrary stencil of faddish criticism, history, or psychology. Meanwhile, the standards applied to the research and the writing necessarily vary and, by Gresham's law, tend to decline, but all Ph.D's are equal. The holders are certified—which is indispensable when the practice of telling a good man when you see one has been abandoned.

The consequences may seem remote for society at large, but they are real. The intellectual life of the country is damaged by the diffusion of bad or pointless books; by the common distinction between written work that is genuine and that which is "academic"; by the alienation of whole publics—say, the readers of history or philosophy—through professional prose and ostentatious scorn for the layman.** As we now know, James rightly saw that the Ph.D. was the forerunner of the credentials society. 'America is a nation rapidly drifting towards a state of things in which no man of science or letters will be accounted respectable unless some kind of badge or diploma is stamped upon him, and in which bare personality will be a mark of outcast state. It seems to me high time to cast a critical eye upon this decidedly grotesque tendency. Other nations suffer terribly from the Mandarin disease. Are we doomed to suffer like the rest?'

The answer can be read in the tons of "résumés" and "vitas" that are

* President Lowell of Harvard, a good Jamesian, established the Junior Fellows at Harvard in hopes of breaking the monopoly of the Ph.D. He counted on the prestige of such membership to show that high scholarly ability could exist without the magic letters. But fellows soon found that they needed the degree to get a post, even at Harvard. Several other attempts to kill the octopus or cut off a few tentacles have similarly failed. See Robert Nisbet, "The Octopus Revisited," *Social Research*, Autumn 1979, vol. 46, no. 3, pp. 487–516.

** Note the extended use of this last designation, formerly applied only to those who were not part of the clergy. We have not one culture or two cultures but two hundred, mutually incommunicado.

the paper currency of social worth today. It is a fast-depreciating currency. Every applicant for any job requiring education is covered with prestigious labels like a globe-trotter's suitcase. The competition has got to the point where handbooks exist to teach what certificates and what previous posts are likely to impress and how to organize them into a work of convincing art. For the interviewer can hardly assess the diplomas acquired in good faith so as to "qualify." He is reduced to judging the skill (or rather, the savvy) with which the document has been compiled. He might just as well have begun by developing the ability to judge the applicant himself.

To the end of his life, James questioned the ways of higher education. He thought that college gave 'glibness and flexibility,' but that it did not make citizens wiser voters. He saw, too, that for most men and women the intellectual life as such has no appeal. He therefore, like Robert Hutchins forty years later, favored a three-year undergraduate course leading to the B. A. 'There is a deeply rooted distinction between two sorts of students. The one is born for the theoretic life and is capable of pressing forward indefinitely into its subtleties and specialties. The other class of men may be intelligent, but they are not *theoretical*, and their interest in most subjects reaches its saturation point when the broader results have been reached.' These broader results could be imparted in secondary school if the time spent there were not being wasted as it is now. College would then offer a combined general and special preparation leading to the several professions.

Such a change in the educational system would get rid of many difficulties in the lives of the young as well as in the working of colleges and universities. For one, the tedious debate about "the need for liberal education" and the equally tiresome plans for "giving" it, would come to an end; for there would be no question of specialist scholarship in the high school, so that its graduates would at least have the chance to stretch and fill their minds before entering what is to them the real world.* In these days, when one meets college graduates five or six years after their degree, the striking thing is how few traces of the vaunted "breadth" and "depth" remain. Some women do seem to have kept up habits of cultivation; the men's minds are monopolized by shop and current news. It is not that one expects the details of what they "took" in college to be fresh and active in their talk, but rather some sign of active influence from that expensive past upon the arid present. In this respect, a skilled workman is often, in my experience at least, better educated because self-educated.

---

* Since these lines were written *The Paideia Proposal* has set out the arguments for such a reform and its contents. (New York, Macmillan, 1982.)

An academic man situated as James was for most of his life may be said to carry on three professions at the same time: resident teacher, ambulant lecturer, and writer. It is only habit that makes us think they go well together. A fourth activity—science, scholarship—feeds the other three. But between these, whatever his genius bids a man set forth to the world in books is perpetually cramped. For there is nothing more inimical to writing than talking. The two are indeed rooted in the same impulse—to express, to explain—but one mode of communication disables the mind for the other. To put it concretely, after a day of classroom haranguing, repeating, amplifying for students, the desire to face a blank sheet of paper—never a rosy encounter—is nonexistent. It takes a heroic effort of will to reinstate oneself into the world of one's earlier meditations, lure them out, and recompose them in silent words. And no sooner has a first draft of eight or ten pages been produced than it must be put away and the next day's preparation for class begun. Besides, a university imposes the endurance test of committee work, which in itself enfeebles the mind and entails more writing.*

These conditions absolutely preclude the continuous concentration, the obsession with a subject, that is necessary for writing "a work" in the honorific sense of the term. ('Give me twelve hours of work on one occupation for happiness.') In the last century and this, the fact that professional writing in this country, other than a certain kind of fiction, fails to ensure a livelihood has doubtless deprived the world of many fine and useful books.** Authors without private means have written less than they might and done all their work piecemeal: Emerson never wrote a book. In our day, the academic world has invented the one-year shelter in some far place, where a small herd of the supposedly gravid can give birth, but the device is too artificial to suit every temper, and from William James to Lionel Trilling the norm has been for literary genius to squeeze out its products through the meshes of continual in-

* As the secretary of one such committee, James reported to President Eliot that on the main issue the members had finally reached unanimity, though "on grounds which are incommunicable."

** James was fortunate in having his friend the banker Henry L. Higginson handle the modest inheritance that came from Henry Sr. in 1882. (See the fantasia on money that William addressed to him, *Letters*, I, p. 233 and *passim*.) William's own will shows that he left his wife and children a house appraised at $21,000 and stocks worth $140,000. His copyrights were estimated at $24,000, though the royalties in March 1911 came only to $11.80. By a curious legal reasoning, two of the four children, having been born after the will was made, were declared by the probate court to have been intentionally excluded. Mrs. James corrected the judicial error; the estate repaid to Henry James an outstanding loan of $415; and William's tombstone cost $51.40.

terruption in some university setting.*

That is the main reason why *The Principles of Psychology* took twelve years to write and *Matthew Arnold* nine. The anxiety, too, of work planned but unpursued day after day is galling; it accounts for much of James's nervous irritability and physical symptoms; they were the same, in cause and effect, as when in youth he was starving for the sense of accomplishment. Things being so, it is obvious how cruel and stupid the modern academic policy of "publish or perish" actually is. It fosters nothing but the neglect of teaching and the dilution of scholarship.

That James taught for half of his sixty-eight years and yet managed to leave a body of work so massive and so perfected is something of a miracle. For he has left a legacy to literature, as well as to science and philosophy. As a prose writer, William James ranks with the other American masters—Emerson, Melville, Mark Twain, and Henry James —and he has few or no equals in the language when compared with his peers in philosophy or science.

There is of course no obligation to be both a thinker and a great writer; but when one compares James with other philosophers one is tempted to wonder whether in the world's opinion lucidity and true art may not be a handicap. Clarity exposes every joint of the structure and leaves no difficulties for textual critics to build a career upon. Note how Kant and Hegel have given employment by their ambiguities, how Marx has generated flourishing schools by being obscure and confused, how Stendhal's secretive journals and letters maintain an industry, how even Wagner's lucubrations have lured good minds to tax their strength in the effort to make him a thinker. Nobody could make a name in this fashion by setting up as a professional clarifier of the lucid, of Descartes, Berkeley, or Schopenhauer, Berlioz, Diderot, or James. More than ever today, when interpretation (rebaptized hermeneutics, as if to make my point) is rampant, there is wisdom in being alluring yet inaccessible.

For his own good or ill, James's purpose was just the opposite. He felt the moral obligation to be intelligible: 'to say a thing in one sentence as straight as it can be made, and then to drop it forever.' He hated "oozy writing" or what Darwin envied Spencer for, "the art of wriggling." One must remember that James believed in the worth of philosophy not as a pastime for keen wits but as the answer to a permanent need of mankind; 'the philosophy which is so important in each of us is not a technical matter'; so philosophical utterance must be as ecumenical as religion. On this point he could have invoked the example of Plato and Aristotle, both of whom wrote popular philosophy

---

* This statement applies only to the United States. The English and Continental systems, at least until very recently, were much more favorable for consecutive thought and steady writing.

in dialogue form, though only the former's survives.

One element in such survival is style and the mark of style is individuality in expressiveness. A paragraph by William James can hardly be mistaken for one by anybody else. In an early book review he unwittingly defined his aim: 'As the opinions of average men are swayed more by examples and types than by mere reasons, so a personality as accomplished as Mr. Morley's cannot fail by its mere attractiveness to influence all who come within its reach and inspire them with a certain friendliness toward the faith that animates it. But to be thus widely effective a man must not be a specialist. Mr. John Mill, weighty and many-sided as he is, is yet deficient in the aesthetic direction, and the same is true of M. Littré in France. Their lances lack that final tipping with light that made Voltaire's so irresistible. What Henry IV's soldiers followed was his white plume; and that imponderable superfluity, grace, in some shape, seems one factor without which no awakening of men's sympathies on a large scale can take place.'

Those words give a fair sample of James's style at thirty—a little stiff and self-conscious as yet, but already "tipped with light." Perry, the professional philosopher who was James's respectful biographer, records with some amazement: "In spite of his intermittent resolves to be technical, he could never be *satisfied* with any product of his pen which was not readable." One should add: not simply readable but *exhaustive*, in the sense of conveying a whole meaning in its intended order and atmosphere. In James—as sampling him has shown—the structure is often complex, but the sinuous movement and apt coloring make all clear. The substance is rich in illustrations—cases, historical facts, personal experiences, images and analogies, sometimes dialogue to dramatize an opponent's view—and the tone blends the formal with the colloquial. These features make up a rhetoric of persuasion; it offers perceptions and positions without verbal juggling and propels the argument by affirmation without dogmatism. The effect is of high-powered conversation in which we hear, agreeably, a voice.

Thus a passage written forty years after the book review: 'Place yourself at the centre of a man's philosophic vision and you understand at once all the different things it makes him write or say. But keep outside, use your post-mortem method, try to build the philosophy out of single phrases, taking first one and then another in seeking to make them fit and of course you fail. You crawl over the thing like a myopic ant over a building, tumbling into every microscopic crack or fissure, finding nothing but inconsistencies, and never suspecting that a centre exists.'

This observation should be enough to settle the issue of technical writing in subjects that involve the shape of the mind as much as its contents. A lady reader was shocked by James's style because of its "want of academic dignity," and his dear friend Peirce deplored his "racy writing" as "wrong" for philosophy. But F. C. S. Schiller, James's defender at Oxford, had the wiser view of James's way: "It is absolutely the right way—for you ... and its appeal is world-wide. Unfortunately, there are others who must be dealt with differently. And fortunately we too are capable of other methods. Dewey's primary appeal is to those who like their philosophy difficult and technical and will respect nothing that is not obscure. Mine is to the dialecticians and the logic-choppers and the controversialists. ... My duty is to show them that we can beat them at their own despicable game."*

James achieved ecumenical expression, as others have done, by tireless revision and rewriting. A wording that really exhausts the author's intention comes only from an effort that exhausts the author, too. Taking this truth for granted and acting on it, James was surprised to find that whereas in English he could in one day produce at most twenty-five 8x10 pages in large longhand, he could write forty in French. The reason, of course, was that in a foreign tongue the range of locutions at one's command is limited, which in turn limits self-criticism: one perforce uses the word that presents itself, and that part of meaning which resides in style remains untapped.**

In reading James extensively one comes to distinguish several shadings in his one style. There is the lively-descriptive, which suits the factual cargo of his work in psychology, his scientific papers, and his book reviews; the eloquent-evocative heard in his public addresses; the warmly argumentative of the philosophical essays; and that of the whole man thinking in all possible keys—the style of his letters. Though the intellectual energy never flags, the degree of warmth varies. In reviewing an opponent of his own theory of the emotions, James sounds as uninvolved as a third party. In dealing with the misrepresentations of pragmatism, his good-natured vehemence is that of a friend with nothing to hide. Among the memorial tributes, Emerson is treated with the detachment of one already speaking for posterity, Davidson with the attachment of a brother-philosopher and friend. But James can also be severe when the manner of an opponent or a public attitude exceeds the bounds of indulgent attention.

---

* This division of labor must not be misinterpreted. Behind his chosen form of expression James was "a master of technicalities." And another specialist writes: "Some of the most enlightening and irrefutable pieces of exact thought, extended and constructive, known to me in philosophy, I have found in his pages." (*William James, The Man and the Thinker*, Madison, Wis., 1942, pp. 44–45, 121.)

** It would be a profitable study that would show how much meaning is lost when ideas or facts are set forth in discourse which is exact enough but lacks style—statements strung together without art. James was bothered by Dewey's 'unchained formlessness of expression.' In writers still more obscure, arcanery often differs little from chicanery.

A critic once asked, "May one say that Henry Jr.'s style was an elaboration of his father's and William's a simplification?" I think not. In all three there is a mastery of words and a love of exaggeration, but except for rare unintended echoes, the likeness stops there.* So characteristic and so purposive were their modes of expression that one must say rather, "three men, three styles." Besides, simplification is a relative term. A fault-finding critic could show that William's prose was far from simple. In it are as many French and German words as people object to in Henry Jr.'s—it was a habit of the time to use whatever seemed *le mot juste*. In William, the Latin terms of scholastic logic and philosophy also abound—words and phrases now opaque to a generation neither scholastic nor Latinate. Add that his syntax is much more complex than ours of the 1980s and you might argue that his lucidity is—or rather, has become—discontinuous. That it survives unimpaired in reading is due to the rhythmical force that thoughts perfectly embodied will achieve regardless of diction. Shakespeare is understood even when he cannot be parsed. It comes as no surprise that Graham Wallas thought James could have been a great poet.

For it is by imagery as well that James makes the abstruse easily grasped. Not that he argues by analogy or metaphor; he only illustrates, and at the most telling moment. Among his many original phrases, some curiously anticipate images that have independently become our own. He speaks of the senses as 'tuned receivers'; he uses '*quanta*' for the incoming drops of experience; in describing a theory of creation he sums it up as 'a mere resistless bang' (we say "the big bang theory");** elsewhere he sees: 'the whole universe in its different spans and wavelengths.' In another realm, he warns against desiring a 'pleasure economy,' meaning what we mean by a consumer economy. To add a characteristic phrasing less open to adoption for common use, one might choose at random 'that subtle edge of things where speech and thought expire.' Such are his ways for making sure that his concepts become concretes.

One influence that encouraged James to use imagery and the conversational tone was the lecturing to which he was compelled. As a man of honor he did not simply write an essay and read it aloud more or less audibly: he prepared a lecture. More speakers should remember that

---

* Speaking of echoes, is this William or Henry? "In every hindrance of desire the sense of ideal presence of what is absent in fact, of an absent, in a word, which the only function of the present is to *mean*, is even more notoriously there." It is William in 1895; it could be Henry—and it might be Proust: period style, perhaps, for the moment.

** He also supplies the equivalent of Eliot's "whimper": 'better bring down the curtain before the last act, so that a business that began so importantly may be saved from so singularly flat a winding-up.' (*The Will to Believe,* 168.)

the word means a piece intelligible by ear. Writing a lecture demands a special rhetoric, which could be learned from James's practice: 'This sense of deeper significance is not confined to rational propositions. Single words and conjunctions of words, effects of light on land and sea, odors and musical sounds, all bring it when the mind is tuned aright. Most of us can remember the strangely moving power of passages in certain poems read when we were young, irrational doorways as they were, through which the mystery of fact, the wildness and the pang of life, stole into our hearts and thrilled them. The words have now perhaps become mere polished surfaces for us; but lyric poetry and music are alive and significant only in proportion as they fetch these vague vistas of a life continuous with our own, beckoning and inviting, yet ever eluding our pursuit.'

In these lines, every word and phrase is speakable without stumble or ambiguity, and the rhythms follow the contour of the thought. Note the "special rhetoric": each subject is announced first, the modifiers come after. In speaker's prose one does not begin with some unattached idea whose linking and direction will appear later. In written prose no such caution is needed. James could have inverted clauses: "When the mind is tuned aright, single words, etc."/ "By now, perhaps, the words have become . . ."/ "Only in proportion as they fetch these vague vistas . . ." This "periodic" order of words creates pleasant suspense for the reader but distracts the listener. Again, the speaker is not afraid to repeat: "Words and conjunctions of words," not "words and their conjunctions." Finally, the lecturer falls naturally into a You-and-I relation, which he maintains by a series of: "You might suppose/ I do not mean/ . . . / Most of us can remember/ . . . " and the like—platform courtesies, breathing spells for the listening mind.

Whether in spoken or printed prose, the forward movement that makes it attractive comes from the author's offering his thought not as made but as being made. In possessing that quality, James's style is the perfect mirror of his philosophy, where 'what really *exists* is not things made but things in the making.' And as 'philosophy is only man thinking,' so the great art of writing is to represent matured conceptions as if they were being thought, minted fresh as the eye runs along the lines. Obviously, any genius shows this power at its freest in his correspondence. James was no exception. He is one of America's very few letter writers of the first rank, and he can even take his place beside Byron, Keats, and Flaubert. The test for them all is whether every sample gives a self-portrait of greatness, drawn without reserve or premeditation, while also limning the recipient. When recording his thoughts in these spontaneous works of art, James is a magnifier and dramatist like those two other masters of the private message, Shaw and Berlioz. In all three, the verbal exuberance serves to make emotion an object in the round, or again to create humor, or to signal irony, and at every turn to revigorate perception.

With such lavish resources fully exploited, it may seem paradoxical that James was so profoundly misunderstood, not so much by the public as by professional minds. It was the esthetician Leo Stein who pointed out why James's "vivid, beautiful prose" may be easy to read and hard to understand: "One feels its richness and ignores its precision." The precision resides in each statement as a whole and the whole depicts an unhabitual grouping of ideas or facts. As Stein puts it, this "maintained contact with life" is a cause of his being "difficult"—doubly so, one might add, because the easy quality of the prose does not brace one for a struggle.*

It is not the sense of the words that is refused entrance to the mind, but the implied summons to reorganize all one's familiar ideas. The range of observation, of associations, of learning, of original reflection, of imaginative excursion, that James packs into a paragraph is no doubt enchanting at the time of its reception, but for some the retrospect is bewilderment. Thus C. S. Peirce, Shadworth Hodgson, and others often could not take in some of James's arguments. We saw how such a simple, straightforward, carefully qualified statement as "The Will to Believe" was misunderstood (like *Pragmatism* later) by some of the best minds in the business of thinking. This recurrent "mishearing" puzzled James and made him look for an explanation. He did not ask for agreement, but for a meeting of minds: 'I cry to Heaven to tell me of what insane root my "leading contemporaries" have eaten that they are so smitten with blindness as to the meaning of printed texts. Or are we others absolutely incapable of making our meaning clear? I imagine there is neither insane root nor unclear writing, but that in these matters each man writes from out of a field of consciousness of which the bogey in the background is the chief object. Your bogey is superstition; my bogey is desiccation; and each, for his contrast-effect, clutches at any text that can be used to represent the enemy.' For the same reason, no doubt, artists, looking at each other's work, cannot conceive how it is possible to paint, or compose, "that way."

Some interpreters expectably concluded that their failure to follow

* Some readers of Henry James's short stories have by a comparable confusion imagined an "involved style" where only unusual ideas and attitudes constituted the difficulty.

was due to defects in James's logic, especially since he said that philosophical systems were at bottom visions, chosen not for logical but for
esthetic reasons.* But he also said that 'logic has an imperishable use in
human life [though] it is not to make us acquainted with the essential
nature of reality.' He himself exhibited that 'imperishable use' on every
page. Let any doubter turn back to the endless analyses of rival theories
in the *Psychology;* to the continuous dazzling explication of others' errors in *The Meaning of Truth;* to the thirty-five pages "On Some Hegel-
isms," published in *Mind* in April 1882 and in which classical logic is
like a razor to cut the Hegelian to ribbons; and finally to the letters
again, where James fences like a D'Artagnan with his famous and formidable critics. There are also meditations in which James argues ruth-
lessly—with himself. And as he thought and wrote, so he fashioned his
books. These were not mere collections of essays and lectures with a
sanguine preface hoping that unity would emerge. They were designed.
He rewrote, modified opinion and expression, and cemented the parts,
craftsmanlike, into a logical whole.

All the while, James knew better than his critics that logic is not an
instrument for advancing thought, but only for exposition and partial
verification. One might say it is disemboweled psychology.** When
James discussed the ladder of faith usable in situations where knowledge is wanting, he said plain and loud: 'Not one step in this process is
logical.' Thus the charge of loose thinking is itself loose talking and
inspires the Shakespearean comment

> What we oft do best,
> By sick interpreters ... is not ours,
> Or not allowed.

This does not mean that James's writings form a seamless web. Gaps
and contradictions can be found, some caused by inattention, some by
conflicts unresolved. In that regard they resemble the writings of every

---

* The chief of these critics was his old friend Justice Holmes, whose legal thought in
fact went well beyond James in demoting logic: "The life of the law is not logic but
experience" (James would have said it was both); "The meaning of a sentence [in a stat-
ute] is to be felt rather than to be proved" (James would have dissented). Holmes's other
views—man is born to act; high action makes us believe as right what our doubting minds
could not prove; philosophic systems are only individual insights—are all good Jamesian
utterances based on reflection, not logic. See Francis Biddle, *Mr. Justice Holmes,* New
York, 1942, *passim.*

** As the unjustly neglected thinker Alfred Sidgwick spent a lifetime demonstrating,
sound reasoning is a much wider realm than logic, if only because the latter assumes an
unreal fixity in the sense of words. See his *Process of Argument* (1893) and *Use of Words
in Reasoning* (1901).

Whitehead remarks: "Logic, conceived as an adequate analysis of the advance of
thought, is a fake.... Philosophic thought cannot be based upon exact statements which
form the basis of special sciences." (*Science and Philosophy,* New York, 1948, p. 104.)

thinker without exception. Plato is a nest of contradictions, and if the geometrical Spinoza can be criticized for inconsistency about the meaning of truth after 350 years, or the mathematical logician Whitehead is challenged as philosopher on one point after another through seven hundred pages of celebratory essays, then others too must be allowed slips of the mind and pen.*

The real handicap one notes in James as writer of philosophy is his irrepressible humor. He shares with Swift, Lamb, Samuel Butler, Shaw, Chesterton, and Mark Twain the disadvantage of having used yet one more rhetorical means which, though legitimate in itself and generally pleasing, somehow distracts all but the fittest readers. Most people seize on it as an opportunity to escape from the serious thought just preceding and thus miss the seriousness in the next, the humorous one. The great humorists always run the risk of not being taken thoughtfully, while the normal men of ideas, faithful to solemnity, invariably are.

With all his limitations of temperament and circumstance, James knew what he was about. He gauged accurately the difference between his qualified affirmations and the imposing certitudes he was attacking. 'I am no lover of disorder, but fear to lose truth by the pretension to possess it wholly.' He distrusted bigness in most of the philosophic models available, because—as an English writer put it—"in philosophy and the arts a spacious display creates an illusion of substance." James could have cited as proof the many systems he had studied in the course of acquiring his vast erudition. Superior intellectual honesty (the twin of modesty) explains his long refusal to build a system of his own. When in the last year of his life he undertook a review of his maturest thought, but knew he might not live to finish it, he left instructions that it be called not "The philosophy of—" anything, but "A beginning of an introduction to philosophy." And it, too, is literature.

After seeing what a genius was like and what he did, it is natural to ask: what did those works and utterances accomplish? James would be the first to require a description of the "thing done" in sequel to what he thought and said. Remembering that James was one of those fortunate beings whose life is the carrying out of youthful hopes and fresh per-

* The systematic use of words is sometimes thought to insure logic and the inconsistent use its opposite. Neither is a sure sign. James is inconsistent in using 'copy' in *Pragmatism* where the copy theory is being attacked, but the purpose there is to make a distinction clear to those who espouse that theory. Again, in the last chapter of the *Psychology* and in *Radical Empiricism* 'experience' might seem ambiguous if the context were disregarded. The same is true of 'rational' at times in "The Will to Believe." But no great effort is needed to catch the proper sense.

ceptions, and having followed their unfolding, one need not now assess results in detail or trace out each line of influence. The task has been begun by specializing scholars. They only need to be referred to, with some reflections added that any good reader of James could make for himself.

There are two ways in which a powerful mind affects the world. One is by gathering disciples into a school. After the publication of *Pragmatism* in 1907 it did look as if a school was forming: Dewey, Schiller, Papini, and others put on the mantle of Pragmatism, and Europe and the United States were a-buzz with the new word. Looking back, students found a "pragmatic revolt" in politics, in the law, and in the writing of history, to which on his own account C. Wright Mills added sociology. But well before then, in the decade preceding *Pragmatism*, James was known more ecumenically here and in Europe. A popular French encyclopedia dated 1900 calls James "a physiologist and psychologist who in the last ten years has won for himself a universal reputation." Then the first literal disciples took their own paths, followed by a number of younger Americans—Mead, Lewis, Morris, Woodbridge, Sidney Hook—who variously called themselves neo-realists or pragmatists with a small p. They looked to Dewey as their leader, inevitably. Whitehead accounted for the fact when he said: "Consider John Dewey. In carrying on the philosophy of William James . . . he enormously narrowed it. With James the consciousness of the everpresent complexity and possibility in human experience is always implicit in his writing. Dewey is without it. James's awareness of the wide scope and the interrelations of all questions made him one of the great philosophic minds of history."

One reason Whitehead is such a good judge of James's scope—aside from being himself a mind of the first order—is that he drew so much from the "adorable genius." Not that Whitehead's philosophy is a derivative of James's, but that it takes its rise from the Jamesian revolution and builds on the territory conquered.* Others have acknowledged James's role in their own lives, from Bergson and H. G. Wells to Graham Wallas and Abraham Maslow; a full list would read like a long extract from *Who's Who.* But the conscious debt felt by professional thinkers and artists matters much less than the unacknowledged, un-

* "Whitehead's notion of the actual . . . and the doctrine of prehensions are strikingly close to James's Radical Empiricism." (Andrew J. Reck, in Novak, ed., *American Philosophy and Its Future*, New York, 1968, pp. 156-57.) See also: *The Philosophy of A. N. Whitehead*, ed. Paul A. Schilpp, New York, 1951, especially pp. 64, 275, 282, 307, 489, 494-95, 505, 510, 530, 551, 568, and 598; and Craig Eisendrath, *The Unifying Moment, the Psychological Philosophy of William James and Whitehead*, Cambridge, Mass., 1971.)

conscious absorption, for this last means still wider and deeper effects. So it has proved with James's radiating force.

When the generation of Americans that returned to this country after 1918, the generation which numbered Malcolm Cowley as a leader, then as chronicler, took stock for the first time of "Civilization in the United States" in a book of that title, James's true stature was gauged for the first time. Robert Lowie, the anthropologist, writing the article on Science, opens it by saying that "In even the briefest and most random enumeration of towering native sons, it is impossible to ignore the name of William James. Here for once the suffrage of town and gown, of domestic and alien judges is unanimous. Naturally, James can never mean quite the same to the European world that he means to us, because in the United States he is far more than a great psychologist, philosopher, or literary man. Owing to our peculiar spiritual history, he occupies in our milieu an altogether unique position. He is the solitary example of an American pre-eminent in a branch of science who at the same time succeeded in deeply affecting the cultural life of a whole generation. Further, he is probably the only one of our genuinely original men to be saturated with the essence of old-world civilization. Foreign judgment of James's achievement was consequently not colored by external considerations."*

This estimate remains correct, though no longer vivid in the public mind. In that sieve-like container, he exists as a lovable image, as a man who did good work in his day and has left useful phrases to quote, together with a body of writings that one runs into in anthologies, college courses, and the Britannica "Great Books." But every once in a while the picture Lowie drew glows again in its original colors. Just now—this spring of 1982—the reissue of The Principles of Psychology has again brought amaze and enthusiasm. "Still vital after all these years," exclaims Psychology Today—"a masterpiece." "The sources of his literary genius are mysterious," but "it is not difficult to account for his erudition . . . in science and medicine." Earlier, in 1961, Gordon Allport, writing about the Psychology, Briefer Course had said: "We begin to perceive that the psychological insights of James have the steadiness of a polar star."

There is good reason for these periodic rediscoveries of the genius and good reason also for James's dwelling in the shadows in between: the American mind and much of the European still linger in the Idealist

* Civilization in the United States: An Inquiry by Thirty Americans, ed. Harold E. Stearns, New York, 1922, pp. 152–53. Mention of James also occurs in the articles on philosophy and on literature.

tradition that James combated all his life. In the United States, as Perry Miller and Quentin Anderson have shown, the love of large abstractions and overarching absolutes has not lost its power; and the desiring, willing, subjective mind that James exposed to view continues to hide these activities from itself. In Europe phenomenology looks as if it cared for James's raw and total experience, but it really is still hunting for essences with which to build a system and attain unity. Everywhere, ideologies similarly feed formulas that lend existence an illusory simplicity, while the popular theology of science (not science itself) prolongs the old division between matter and mind, subject and object, knower and known.

All this disregards the several Jamesian revolutions—rejoining knower and known into one universe, re-defining truth and its test, showing the workings of the stream of consciousness and disposing of the heart-and-mind dichotomy, restoring within due limits the right and the will to believe, exploring the unconscious in its relation to religion, genius, and psychopathology, and supplying a vision of what experience is like with nothing left out.

And yet . . . and yet, despite the flat opposition between James and the various tendencies that move the world today, his invisible presence is felt, his influence continues, subterranean. Indeed, if this link with the earlier effect of his work did not exist, it would have been impossible for me to suggest how his thought can still be used. Testimony from others on this point leaves no doubt. Open Piaget's *Biology and Knowledge* (1971) and you find James credited with resisting the resurgence of atomistic doctrines in psychology. That is of course but part of the story. When the American Psychological Association celebrated its seventy-fifth anniversary in 1977, the opening speaker discussed "William James, who is our father who begat us"; and reviewing the work done on questions James opened up, he remarked: "Even if I were to total up all advances in gains and achievements and multiply them by a factor of hope, the total would still not suffice as an adequate tribute to lay at James's feet."

This is direct recognition. More often one has to infer it. Thus when one reads that "Freud's immortal merit" is to have "placed stress on individual psychology," one remembers a main theme of *The Principles*, a decade earlier. And when Freud, again, discovered for himself in *Beyond the Pleasure Principle* (1920) that man cannot fully be explained as an organism driven by instincts, he had been anticipated by James by some thirty years. Perhaps priority does not matter; but then those who profess to chronicle facts ought not to put the later first. The

Jamesian analysis of truth, for example, one finds attributed here and there to others. The Cambridge logician Frank Ramsey, who died young but left a volume of brilliant essays on *The Foundation of Mathematics*, reports that he learned his pragmatism from Bertrand Russell, at the very time when Russell—on again, off again—was busy arguing in print against Pragmatism. The same factual inversion occurs in the statement that "Wittgenstein, even as early as the 1930s admonished: 'Don't ask for the meaning, ask for the use.'"

Fortunately, some scholars are better historians. In a symposium on American philosophy and its future, fifteen years ago, the contributors saw James's hand in many developments. His account of novelty in experience, says one, leads to "expanded inwardness" and "nothing seems to escape him in viewing the interior process." Another, discussing "William James and Claude Monet," finds in James the roots of contemporary "relational esthetics." A third points out how James anticipated the language analysts by asking how we use such common words as "good" and "true," and he goes on to conclude that Jamesian empiricist pluralism ultimately led to the principle that Gödel's theorem established about the impossibility of devising completely consistent systems. Yet another scholar notes that before phenomenology was heard of, James spoke of "we phenomenists" and that the views of James and Husserl "converge."* Even in France, the crude notion of pragmatism as a piece of American trickery does not keep a thinker from devoting his life to "seeking a living philosophy, a science of the practical ... which should be at once thought and action, intellectual order fused with emotion."

Students who assess the work of the Existentialists, Heidegger included, also find James along the path. One who sees no reason but moodiness for their "ontological despair" states his verdict in an echo of the popular lyric: "Everything they have, he has said better; he can write anything better than they." Independently, a second witness shows that James's Will to Believe is an affirmation of the existentialists' "discovery of freedom and authenticity." Meanwhile Hart Crane had found in *The Varieties of Religious Experience* a validation of the realm of visions that he felt the need of as a poet. Still other historians speak of James as "liberating" by virtue of his controlled relativism and his making fundamental "the category of the esthetic." And in the latest edition of the *Dictionary of American History*, James's pragmatism is defined

---

* It was only in 1934 that Sartre discovered in Husserl a point of view that "restored to sensations their original freshness and youth." ("La transcendance de l'ego," quoted by Edouard Morot-Sir in *The Stanford French Review*, Spring 1977, p. 62.)

as "the most sophisticated attempt to reconcile science and religion in the wake of Darwinism." Von Hügel in a long letter to James proffers the same estimate.

Nor is this the end of the tale. Among the historians of science, a specialist on the philosophic background of quantum mechanics and other aspects of non-classical physics assigns James an important place, reminding his readers that Niels Bohr was "strongly influenced by William James" and repeatedly spoke of his characteristic ideas as formative.* In another domain, that of political science, the work of the Chicago philosopher Arthur Bentley explicitly draws on James's empiricism and conception of the self.** And among the very few contemporary thinkers who have attempted to fashion an entire philosophy as James did, Justus Buchler may be regarded as taking up empiricism where James left it and restoring to pragmatism the breadth and flexibility that its first followers restricted.

No wonder that Gail Kennedy called James's influence "penetrating" or that Whitehead in *Science and the Modern World* attributes to James "the inauguration of a new stage in philosophy.... He clears the scene of the old paraphernalia, or rather he entirely alters its lighting."

As for James's shocking reclassification of philosophies as visions, it has also made headway; this status is a logical consequence of individual psychology: the existential taker, moved by his esthetic concerns while also coerced by the pragmatic pressure of fact, arrives at a unique view of things. To which one may add one more note on reverse chronology, this time from the usually irreproachable Ortega, who tells us that the German phenomenologist Dilthey "divined as early as 1895" that a philosophy is at bottom a vision. And Ortega himself takes thought to be "an action for a purpose."

In short, if we take together the work of the phenomenologists, logical positivists, language analysts, existentialists, Gestaltists, behaviorists, Piagetists and, most recent, the disciples of the Perception psychology originating in Denmark (who cite James as a forerunner) we come to see these schools as extensions and refinements upon single aspects of the common thought of the past half century, as an attenuation and a repackaging of 1890 discoveries, among which James's appear fundamental.

* Bohr may have been thinking of James's statement that 'units of approach—drops, buds, steps, or whatever we please to call them—of change come wholly when they do come or do not come at all.' (*Some Problems of Philosophy*, pp. 172 ff., 185.)

** Bentley (1870–1957) is still inadequately known, though the value of his extensive work has been recognized by leading authorities in political science, economics, sociology, law, biology, physics, and mathematics. (See Michael A. Weinstein, "Life and Politics as Plural: James and Bentley, *Journal of Value Inquiry*, Winter 1970–71, pp. 282–91.)

Some thinkers are uncommonly truth-prone, not in the sense of telling the truth but of finding it. The gift is what makes the great scientists. They know the hang of things before the evidence comes in, and above all they know how to frame their intuitions so that these force the world to rethink. James made his revolutionary discoveries because he had, "ahead of time," an inkling of where the truth must lie. It is easy now to see in his letters, articles, and jottings of the 1870s the rootlets from which his intellectual plantation grew. That is why for the jacket of this book I chose a photograph of that decade.

At the other end of his life this divinatory gift was undimmed. In his unfinished chapters on philosophy he was not content to rephrase his considered views; he took up the implications of the latest mathematics and science as they bore on the question of change, all important for his empiricism. His grasp of the function and limitations of concepts enabled him to understand the 'many ways in which the conceptual transformation of perceptual experience makes it less comprehensible than ever,' unless a philosophy of his own kind steps in with new answers to old and new questions.

That some of James's formulations have been distorted and others taken too fragmentarily to be useful was to be expected. But much may be hoped from further studious accounts of the continuities between his mind and ours. Each return to his text in a fresh setting or through the prism of another mind discloses one more face of the mountain and better displays its mass and proportions.

We know from his own words that every philosopher's vision has a center out of which every one of his perceptions radiates. We have followed his glance as well as we could along these radiating lines, sampling as we did so a little of his rich store of incidental wisdom. If at the end we ask ourselves how to characterize that central irreducible truth, I believe the clearest word we could choose would be THICKNESS. It was a favorite with both William and Henry. It stands for the intense awareness of multiplicity—in nature, in persons, in art, religion, and social reality. It is the opposite of the flight into concepts, which more than ever today threatens judgment, action, and the good life. For novelty arises, observations vary with perspective, the world—in short—to keep its thickness and reality must forever be reconceptualized and re-envisioned.

James's last recorded thought, in the sense of an idea with its fringes

filling his consciousness, has already been quoted. It is that his death
seemed to him but a trifling incident. The phrase recalls his earlier
willingness to let others represent him in the hereafter; but was this
abdication not strange for the man who showed that "personality" is an
elemental force among others in the cosmos? Should one surmise that
he grew weary of his own supercharged self—perhaps bored with it—
and looked to death for shelter from those insistent individual traits that
are the very meaning of self? Surely, some such feeling explains why
the loss of even those we love best brings a touch of relief; and this
feeling can without morbidity turn inward. However it was, the power
in James to accept himself could work to accept his own quietus. "And
also Death," as my Jamesian visitor of half a century ago kept saying.
James's mission was done, though not his written work—a fitting end
for the thinker who adopted, and wrote, as his final words: 'What has
concluded that we should conclude in regard to it?'

# Epilogue-Anthology

When James and Bergson began corresponding steadily and paying each other compliments and visits, in the early 1900s, James predicted that as soon as the tide of opinion turned in his friend's favor, the bearing of his work would begin to be found in earlier philosophers, 'but no matter: all the better if you are in some ancient lines of tendency.' In thinking of what James has told us or caused us to think about, the reader has doubtless found his memory stirred into recalling maxims, allusions, perhaps complete statements of parallel thoughts by writers before James. He himself called Pragmatism a new name for some old ways of thinking, and though that caption can hardly be applied to the other parts of his vision, the remark he made to Bergson holds good for himself, as for any thinker: temperaments recur, predicaments also, and the resultant sayings show matching parts.

Having long since taken James as my particular discourser on the world, I was bound to find recollections of his thought quickened when making acquaintance with other writers. Many books on my shelves accordingly carry on the flyleaf notations of contrasts and parallels. The contrasts are instructive but only to be expected; it is the parallels that surprise and entertain by popping up in unlikely contexts and authors. I could compile a fat anthology of "pragmatists *sans le savoir*"—but James prepared us for them. I could also make a book of observations that glance off many of the facets of Jamesian thought, echoes heard ahead of the sounded note. But of course most such utterances are only sidelights—not central to the writer's purpose; or if they do express his main intent, they form part of a different constellation of ideas, which changes the ultimate bearing of the "same" insight. Even Bergson and

James, close in time and in many opinions, were bound for different destinations, as Horace Kallen showed in his lucid study of the pair.

So the worth of parallels lies chiefly in their showing that to similarly 'tuned receivers' experience comes in similar "drops" and inspires similar reflections. That in itself is pleasant to contemplate. I have accordingly made a small selection of "takings" similar to James's and grouped them loosely, to serve as so many small epilogues to topics dealt with along the way. The choice is arbitrary; apart from the pleasure I have just mentioned, it may also suggest something that needs no proof: that I have seldom forgotten James while reading his predecessors in the Great Conversation.

### Pragma: Action and Results

But everything is defined according to its effects and inherent powers, so that when these no longer remain such as they were, it cannot be said to be the same, but only something of the same name.
　　Aristotle, *Politics*, Book I, Ch. II (c. 335 B.C.?)

Beware of false prophets, which come to you in sheep's clothing....
Ye shall know them by their fruits.
　　St. Matthew 7:15–16 (c. A.D. 100)

Whether the speculative and practical intellects are distinct powers? I answer that the speculative and practical intellects are not distinct powers. The reason for this is, as we have said above, that what is accidental to the nature of the object of a power does not differentiate that power.
　　Thomas Aquinas, *Summa Theologica*, Question 79, article II (1256–72)

Tis written: "In the Beginning was the *Word*."
... The *Word*? Impossible so high to rate it
　　If by the Spirit I am truly taught.
Then thus: "In the Beginning was the *Thought*."
　　Is it the *Thought* which works, creates, indeed?
"In the Beginning was the *Power*," I read.
Yet as I write, a warning is suggested
That I the sense may not have fairly tested.
The Spirit aids me—now I see the light!
"In the Beginning was the *Act*."
　　　　　　Goethe, *Faust*. Part I, scene III (1790)

To talk of reliance is a poor external way of speaking. Speak rather of that which relies because it works and is.
　　Ralph Waldo Emerson, "Self-Reliance" (1840)

*Maecenas* to *Augustus*: And since when has action done any harm to thought?
> Alfred de Musset, *Le Songe d'Auguste* (posthumous)


### The Mind, The Stream, "Taking"

The mind has laws, powers, and principles of its own and is not the mere puppet of matter.
> William Hazlitt, *Prospectus of a History of English Philosophy* (1808–12)

Who is there, indeed, that could bear to be judged by even the best of those unnumbered thoughts that course each other, like waves of the sea, through our minds, passing away unuttered and, for the most part, even unowned by ourselves?
> Thomas Moore, *Life of Byron* (1830)

> [The Devil and Peter Bell]
> Each had an upper stream of thought.
> > Shelley, "Peter Bell the Third" (1819)

I have often amused myself with thinking how different a place London is to different people.... A politician thinks of it merely as the seat of government . . . ; a grazier as a vast market for cattle; a mercantile man, as a place where a prodigious deal of business is done upon 'Change; a dramatick enthusiast as the grand scene of theatrical entertainments; a man of pleasure, as an assemblage of taverns and the great emporiums for ladies of easy virtue. But the intellectual man is struck with it as comprehending the whole of human life in all its variety, the contemplation of which is inexhaustible.
> Dr. Johnson to Boswell, July 5, 1763

> There was a child went forth every day.
> And the first object he look'd upon, that object he became.
> > Walt Whitman, "There Was a Child Went Forth" (1873)


### Experience, the Sentiment of Rationality, Truth

This false system of philosophy has been gradually growing up to its present height ... from a wrong interpretation of the word *experience*, confining it to a knowledge of things without us; whereas it in fact includes all knowledge, relating to objects either within or out of the mind, of which we have any direct and positive experience.
> William Hazlitt, *Prospectus of a History of English Philosophy* (1808–12)

One should say not "I think," but "It thinks."
Do not use the word "hypothesis," even less "the-
ory," but "mode of imagining."
Georg Lichtenberg, *Aphorisms* (1799)

This, then, is what we mean by proof: the term simply expresses the
fact that thought takes the direction of least opposing thought; that is,
of least *resistance*. . . . The word proof expresses our feeling that our
thought does go, will go, without possibility of forbidding on our part,
in one direction and not in any other.
James Hinton, *The Art of Thought*, Ch. II (1879)

What is fruitful alone is truth. . . . If I know my relation to myself and
to the external world I call that truth. And thus every man can have
his own truth and yet truth is still one.
Goethe, *Maxims and Reflexions*, No. 98

Those are to be forgiven who possess neither the will nor the power
to judge and have set themselves to finding pure knowledge without
reference to consequences, knowledge—to speak plain—that comes
to nothing.
Nietzsche, "The Use and Abuse of History" (1874)

### Concepts: Origin and Dangers

Since it is not possible for perception to be simple, it is not possible
for a thought to be so, either. A thought becomes simple only by abstraction, but the abstracting is so rapid and so habitual that we do
not notice it.
Diderot, *Phenomena of the Brain: Perception* (1753)

The fool separates his object from all surrounding ones; all abstraction is temporary folly.
Lavater, *Aphorisms on Man*, No. 624 (1775–78)

William James read Bagehot and called *Physics and Politics* 'that
golden little book':

Unproved abstract principles without number have been eagerly
caught up by sanguine men and then carefully spun out into books
and theories which were to explain the whole world. But the world
goes clear against these abstractions, and it must do so, as they require it to go in antagonistic directions. The mass of a system attracts
the young and the unwary; but cultivated people are very dubious
about it.
Walter Bagehot, *Physics and Politics*, Ch. V (1872)

### Thought and Feeling, Utility, Bodily Habit and Mind

It has been thought necessary to make two essentially different things between feeling and thinking, usually called the head and the heart, referring to impressions perceptive and affective. That comes from superficial investigation. There is between those two classes of perception no more difference than a degree more or less of energy and vivacity. It is all one type of *feeling*. All our impressions, affections, perceptions . . . are all very real and indeed the only real things. What we call entities and beings, beginning with ourselves, are secondary.
     Destutt de Tracy, *Elements of Ideology* (1804–18)

The thoughts are to the senses as scouts and spies, to range abroad and find the way to the things desired.
     Thomas Hobbes, *Leviathan,* I, viii (1651)

It is foolish in men to despise the senses . . . I allow not of the distinction there is made 'twixt profit and pleasure.
     Bishop Berkeley, *Commonplace Book,* 546 (1705–1708)

> Assume a virtue, if you have it not.
> That monster, custom, who all sense doth eat
> Of habits devil, is angel yet in this,
> That to the use of actions fair and good
> He likewise gives a frock or livery,
> . . . .
>
> For use almost can change the stamp of nature.
>      Shakespeare, *Hamlet,* Act III, sc. iv (1603)

### Science and Its Limits

That there are some actions so special to Man upon the account of his intelligence and will that they cannot be satisfactorily explicated after the manner of the actings of mere corporeal agents, I am very much inclined to believe.
     Robert Boyle, *The Skeptical Chemist: Some Considerations Touching the Usefulness of Experimental Natural Philosophy* (1664)

### The Will, Freedom, Choice, Faith, Risk

No one believes anything unless he has first thought that it is to be believed. For however suddenly, however rapidly some thoughts fly before the will to believe (and this presently follows in such a way as to attend them in closest conjunction), it is yet necessary that every thing which is believed should be believed after thought has preced-

ed, even though belief itself is nothing else than to think with assent.
>    St. Augustine, "On the Predestination of the Saints," Ch. V
>    (428–29)

The will is caused by the motive which, at the moment of action, lies strongest in the view of the mind. . . . The view is caused by the prevailing inclination. A man does what he does, not becoming every moment a new beginning, but "necessarily" by an inevitable sequence in which the will is a link.
>    Jonathan Edwards (1754), summarized by Perry Miller in
>    *Jonathan Edwards* (1949)

Long before Samuel Butler defined faith as the proposition "I bet that my Redeemer liveth," Pascal had written at length on the necessity of the wager in belief:

Reason has no means of deciding. . . . A game is being played which will come out heads or tails: which will you bet? By reason alone you can choose neither the one nor the other . . . so don't go blaming those who have made a choice—you know nothing to the purpose.—No, I shan't blame them for making this or that choice but *a* choice, for the right thing to do is not to bet at all. —Ah, but you must bet; it's not optional: you are embarked, so which will you take? Come, since you must choose, let's see what will affect you least . . . : You may lose two things, truth and rightness: and you have two things to stake, your knowledge and your happiness. . . . Now do the computation: if you bet that God exists, you win everything. If you lose, you lose nothing. So don't shilly-shally and bet.
>    Pascal, *Pensées*, Article III, No. 233 (1657–59?)

But it *is* possible—as I am most thankful to know—to carry out the resolution "I *will* think of so-and-so." Once fasten the attention upon a subject so chosen, and you will find that the worrying subject, which you desire to banish, is practically annulled.
>    Lewis Carroll, "Rhymes at Midnight" (1883)

Genuine religion contains, not ideas for the understanding but precepts for action. . . . As for dogmas which influence neither actions nor morality, . . . I never trouble myself about them.
>    Rousseau, "Confession of Faith," *Emile*, Book IV (1762)

In all important transactions of life we have to take a leap in the dark. . . . If we decide to leave the riddles unanswered, that is a choice; if we waver in our answer, that too is a choice: but whatever choice we make, we make it at our peril.
>    James Fitzjames Stephen, *Liberty, Equality, Fraternity*, Ch.
>    VII (1873)

## Pluralisms

Swift, who in Gulliver's Voyage to Laputa had ridiculed the concept-work of its inhabitants by describing how they made their ill-fitting clothes by trigonometry, had earlier denounced absolute ideas:

> For what man, in the natural state or course of thinking, did ever conceive it in his power to reduce the notions of all mankind exactly to the same length, and breadth, and heighth of his own? Yet this is the first humble and civil design of all innovators in the empire of reason.
>
> Swift, *A Tale of a Tub*, Section IX, "A Digression concerning Madness" (1704)

> According to their dreadful customs, being all cannibals, they would kill and eat them. . . . But I began, with cooler and calmer thoughts, to consider what I was going to engage in; what authority or call had I to pretend to be judge and executioner upon these men as criminals, whom Heaven had thought fit, for so many ages, to suffer unpunished? . . . How do I know what God himself judges in this particular case? It is certain these people do not commit this as a crime; it is not against their own consciences reproving or their light reproaching them.
>
> Defoe, *Robinson Crusoe*, Part I (1719)

> Unless absolute beauty is that which at all times, in all places, and by all men must be acknowledged as beautiful, I cannot imagine what it means or where it might reside. And that kind of beauty I am sure does not exist.
>
> Berlioz, *Evenings with the Orchestra*, "Fourteenth Evening" (1852)

> Mr. Jenkinson. He sees his own truth. Truth is that which a man *troweth*. Where there is no man there is no truth. Thus the truth of one is not the truth of another.
>
> Mr. Foster. . . . I contend that there is an universal and immutable truth, deducible from the nature of things.
>
> Mr. Jenkinson. By whom deducible? Philosophers have investigated the nature of things for centuries, yet no two of them will agree in *trowing* the same conclusion.
>
> Thomas Love Peacock, *Headlong Hall*, Ch. VIII (1816)

Burckhardt was the historian James would have found most congenial to his own temper, had he known the *Judgments* and the *Reflections* on History, for in Burckhardt's own empiricism, history is neither objective nor subjective, but "participatory"—experience taken two ways—as in Radical Empiricism and its matching pluralism:

This is European: the self-expression of *all* forces, in monuments, pictures, and words, institutions and parties, down to the individual; the full life of the intellect in *all* aspects and directions; and striving of the intellect to leave behind knowledge about *everything* it experiences, not to surrender mutely to world monarchies and theocracies as did the East.

> Burckhardt, *Judgments on History and Historians*, Ch. III (1865–85)

## The Unconscious

One statement from the myriad that might be quoted is enough to show that the awareness of the unconscious is not of today or yesterday:

The key to the understanding of the character of the conscious mind lies in the region of the unconscious.

> Carl Gustav Carus, *Psyche*, opening sentence (1846)

## Self-Acceptance

I maintain that one must be cautious about valuing oneself, and likewise conscientious about giving a true account, high or low.... To claim for oneself less than there is warrant for is silliness, not modesty.... And to claim more is not always presumptuous, it may also be silliness.

> Montaigne, *Essays*, Book II, Ch. VI (1580)

## The Moral Equivalent of War

The deep-rooted feeling expressed by St. Joan of Arc, "When we come to blows we'll see who has the better right," reinforces the thought that to preach "peace at any price" may not be morally or philosophically defensible. The only alternative is an attempt to abate all angers:

Who is bravest? There are always the elements to fight with, stronger than men and nearly as merciless. The only absolutely and unapproachably heroic element in the soldier's work seems to be: that he is paid little for it.

> Ruskin, *The Crown of Wild Olive*, "Traffic" (1866)

## Art vs. Esthetics; Culture vs. Professionalism

I very much regret that his system—is a system. For myself I no longer believe in these various theories within which people keep wanting to imprison the art of sound. Music is free; it does what it wants, and without permission.

Berlioz, "Report to the French Institute" (1866)

To Generalize is to be an Idiot. To Particularize is the Alone Distinction of Merit.

William Blake, "Marginalia on Sir Joshua Reynolds' Discourses, No. 2" (c. 1808)

The great men of culture are those who have had a passion for diffusing, for making prevail . . . the best knowledge . . . ; who have laboured to divest knowledge of all that was harsh, uncouth, difficult, abstract, professional, exclusive; to humanize it, to make it efficient outside the clique of the cultivated and learned, yet still remaining the best knowledge and thought of the time.

Matthew Arnold, Culture and Anarchy (1869)

## Education: Results and Theory

The gentleman is never mean or little in his disputes, never takes unfair advantage, never mistakes personalities or sharp sayings for arguments, or insinuates evil which he dare not say out . . . his disciplined intellect preserves him for the blundering discourtesy of better perhaps but less educated minds; who, like blunt weapons, tear and hack instead of cutting clean, who mistake the point in argument, waste their strength on trifles, misconceive their adversary, and leave the question more involved than they found it. He may be right or wrong; but he is too clear-sighted to be unjust. He is as simple as he is forcible, and as brief as he is decisive.

Cardinal Newman, The Idea of a University (1853, 1873)

The bore of all bores was the third. His subject had no beginning, middle, nor end. It was education. Never was such a journey through the desert of mind: the great Sahara of intellect. The very recollection makes me thirsty.

Thomas Love Peacock, Gryll Grange, Ch. XIX (1861)

## Literary Expression

I know not how it comes to pass that professors in most arts and sciences are generally the worst qualified to explain their meanings to those who are not of their tribe.

Swift, "Letter to a Young Clergyman" (1719-20)

We cannot write well or truly but what we write with gusto. The body, the senses must conspire with the mind. Expression is the act of the whole man, that our speech may be vascular. The intellect is powerless to express thought without the aid of the heart and liver and every member.

           Henry David Thoreau, *Journal*, Sept. 2, 1851

### Philosophy: Visions

The kind of philosophy a man chooses depends upon the kind of man he is. For a philosophic system ... is animated with the spirit of the man who possesses it.

           Fichte, *Science of Knowledge*, Introduction (1794)

My "system" is for serving myself to live by.

           Thomas Carlyle, *On Heroes and Hero-Worship* (1841)

I see the philosophers who are universal skeptics unable to express their main principles in any way at all; they would need a new language, because ours is made up of affirmative statements ... and when they say "I doubt," people leap at their throats to make them admit that they have affirmed at least one thing they don't doubt. They reply that their doubt sweeps everything away like a purge. Sounder than this fantasy would be a question, like the one I use as a motto under the picture of a scale: "What do I know?"

           Montaigne, *Essays*, Book II, Ch. XII (1580)

That famous question was indeed sounder in itself but might not have suited those he criticized, for Montaigne was not a universal skeptic; and still sounder for *him* would have been James's question, which is worth putting again—What has been concluded that we should conclude about it?

# Chronology

1842 William James born, January 11, New York City

1843 Henry James, Jr., born, April 15, New York City

1843–45 First trip to Europe of James family

1848 Alice James born, August 7, New York City

1852–55 Life and schooling in New York City

1855–58 In London and Paris; at *collège* in Boulogne

1858–59 In school at Newport, R.I.

1859–60 At Geneva Academy (= university); summer in Germany

1860–61 In Hunt's studio with La Farge

1861 Enters Lawrence Scientific School at Harvard

1864 Enters Medical School at Harvard
James family moves to Boston

1865–66 In Brazil with Agassiz expedition

1866 James family moves to Cambridge, Mass.

1867 Study in Germany

1869 Receives M.D. at Harvard

1870 Death of Minny Temple (March 8); William's "crisis"
(within the week before or after)

1873–74 Instructor in Anatomy and Physiology at Harvard
Trip to Europe, mostly in Italy

1875–76 Offers first course in psychology; establishes first laboratory
of experimental psychology

1876 Made assistant professor of physiology

1878 Lectures at Johns Hopkins (February)

1878–79 Last year that James teaches physiology
Offers first course in Philosophy ("Phil. 3")

1880 Birth of first son, Henry (Harry)
Made assistant professor of philosophy

1882–83   Travel in Europe
          Death of mother (January) and of father (December), 1882
   1885   Made professor of philosophy
          Death of third son, Herman
   1886   Buys summer place at Chocorua, N.H.
   1889   Builds house at 95 Irving Street, Cambridge, Mass.
   1890   Publishes *Principles of Psychology*
   1892   Death of Alice James (sister) in London (March)
          Publishes *Psychology, Briefer Course*
1892–93   In Europe with his wife and children
          Turns over psychology laboratory to Hugo Münsterberg
1894–99   Intense activity in social and political causes
1896–97   Lowell Lectures on Exceptional Mental States
   1897   Publishes *The Will to Believe and Other Essays* (from years
             1879 through 1896)
   1898   Lecture at Berkeley outlining Pragmatism
   1899   Publishes *Talks to Teachers*
1899–1901 In Europe for rest cures
1901–1902 Gifford Lectures in Edinburgh
   1902   Publishes *The Varieties of Religious Experience*
1904–1905 Henry James revisits the U.S. after 20 years: with William,
             from August 1904 on; July 1905 on
   1905   Trip to Mediterranean countries
   1906   Lectures at Stanford University; undergoes San Francisco
             earthquake
1906–1907 Lowell Lectures on Pragmatism, repeated at Columbia
             University
   1907   Publishes *Pragmatism*
          Resigns from Harvard
1908–1909 Hibbert Lectures at Oxford
   1909   Publishes *A Pluralistic Universe*
          Publishes *The Meaning of Truth*
   1910   In Europe (March-August)
          Dies at Chocorua, August 26
1911–20   Posthumous publications:
          1911   *Some Problems of Philosophy*
                 *Memories and Studies*
          1912   *Essays in Radical Empiricism*
          1920   *Collected Essays and Reviews*
                 *The Letters of William James*
                 *The Letters of Henry James*

# Reference Notes

In the text all passages from the writings of William James are enclosed within single quotation marks. When they come from his works or letters in book form, the following abbreviations designate in these Notes the title and edition used:

Lit. Rem.   *The Literary Remains of the Late Henry James:* Boston, Houghton Mifflin, 1884.

Pr. Psych.   *The Principles of Psychology,* 2 vols.: New York, Henry Holt, 1904.

Ps. Brief   *Psychology: Briefer Course:* New York, World Publishing Co., 1948.

Will Bel.   *The Will to Believe and Other Essays:* New York, Longmans, 1897.

Talks   *Talks to Teachers . . . and Students:* New York, Henry Holt, 1899.

Var. Rel.   *The Varieties of Religious Experience:* New York, Longmans, 1902.

Prag.   *Pragmatism: A New Name for Some Old Ways of Thinking:* New York, Longmans, 1907.

Plur. Univ.   *A Pluralistic Universe:* New York, Longmans, 1909.

Mg. Truth   *The Meaning of Truth: A Sequel to Pragmatism:* New York, Longmans, 1909.

Mem. Stud.   *Memories and Studies:* New York, Longmans, 1911.

Prob. Phil.   *Some Problems of Philosophy:* New York, Longmans, 1911.

Rad. Emp.   *Essays in Radical Empiricism:* New York, Longmans, 1912.

Coll. Ess.   *Collected Essays and Reviews:* New York, Longmans, 1920.

Lett.   *The Letters of William James,* 2 vols.: New York, Longmans, 1920.

| Perry | Ralph Barton Perry, *The Thought and Character of William James*, 2 vols.: Boston, Little Brown, 1935. (The one-volume edition, Cambridge, Mass., 1945, contains three additional letters, pp. 51, 55). |
| Jas. Fam. | F. O. Matthiessen, ed., *The James Family, including Selections from Their Writings*: New York, Knopf, 1947. |
| Murphy | Gardner Murphy and Robert O. Ballou, eds., *William James on Psychical Research*, New York, Viking, 1960. |

As stated in the note on p. 13, many of the extracts from James have been shortened by omissions that are not indicated by dots. James himself similarly abridged or transposed in quoting from his sources in *The Varieties of Religious Experience*. His punctuation I have also occasionally modified, my precedent being the practice of the editor of his *Letters*, his son Henry James. Anyone who wants the full Jamesian text will find it with the aid of the reference below. The page number of this book and the last few words of the quotation will serve as key to the passage.

## Prologue

page

1   who writes novels. Anon., *Pages from a Private Diary*, London, 1899, 144.
and my pride. *Letters of Henry James*, ed. Percy Lubbock, New York, 1920, II, 167.

2   a classic ... important event ... humility. *The Psychiatric Quarterly*, v. 25, 1951, 169; *The Psychoanalytic Quarterly*, v. 21, 1952, 43al; *Journal of Consulting Psychology*, v. 14, 1950, 416–17.

5   by the humanities. Mem. Stud., 312–13.

## The Man

page

6   somewhere else. This anecdote was told me more than once by the late Mrs. Winthrop Ames who, as Lucy Fuller, had been the woman student of the pair to whom James made the remark. But I have taken liberties with the date: Lucy Fuller graduated from Radcliffe in 1900.

10   say infallibly. Henry James, *A Small Boy and Others*, New York, 1913, 118.
The boys come home. Lett., I, 18.
durance again ... long time. William Dean Howells to his father on April 23, 1871. (*Life in Letters*, New York, 1928, I, 164.)

11   God in nature. Henry James, Sr., *Moralism and Christianity*, New York, 1850, 34.

*page*

13 who curse and swear. Henry James, *A Small Boy and Others*, New York, 1913, 147.

soon fatigued. Santayana, *Persons and Places*, II, New York, 1945, 166–67.

skin thereof . . . corrupt and immodest. Lett., I, 94.

say I'm a Student. Henry James, *Notes of a Son and Brother*, New York, 1914, 69–70.

14 mediocre artist. (original in French) Lett., I, 23.

for your father. Lucy Paton, *Elizabeth Cary Agassiz*, Boston, 1919, 88.

of details extends. Lett., I, 65. Besides writing long letters home, James kept a diary during the expedition. Extensive extracts from both have been reprinted in *Four Papers Presented in the Institute for Brazilian Studies*, Vanderbilt University, Nashville, Tenn., 1951, 97–138.

way of thinking. Lucy Paton, op. cit., I, 65.

their lookout. To his mother, December 9, 1865, printed in "William James in Brazil," *Four Papers Presented in the Institute for Brazilian Studies*, op. cit., 135. See also his letter in shaky Portuguese, p. 136.

15 revenge now? Lett., I, 66.

and the bowl. Ibid., I, 96. See also 129.

bodily deadness . . . hibernation . . . psychology. Lett., I, 100.

16 tedious egotism. Lett., I, 99.

wiggle of our will. Lett., I, 152.

16f. purposes of God . . . brotherhood of men . . . evil of restlessness. Lett., I, 130.

17 living brothers. Lett., I, 131.

words and actions . . . my reality. Lett., I, 131–32.

topsy-turvy mind. Lett., I, 62.

through men. Lett., I, 131.

18 into the dark alone. Var. Rel., 160–61. See also Lett., I, 145–47.

19 all one meaning. Perry, II, 356.

fields of action . . . posit life . . . to the world. Lett., I, 147–48.

as a whippoorwill. Lett., I, 157.

other people . . . largest head. G. W. Allen, *William James*, New York, 1967, 170.

20 all my days. Lett., I, 53. The complete letter is given in Perry, I, 218–19.

novel experimenting. Lett., I, 32.

21 a secure belief. Coll. Ess., 5–6.

good for nothing? Lett., I, 82.

23 perception of fact. Coll. Ess., 44–46.

What is the reality? Ibid., 58.

24 not the whole of being. Ibid., 58–60.

to our moral life. Coll. Ess., 11.

constitution of things . . . a common stem. Lett., I, 97.

25 or hatred. Lett., I, 131.

spiritual understanding. Henry James, Sr., "Faith and Science," *North American Review*, 1865, 336–37.

*page*

26  extremely tepid. Harold Larrabee, "Henry James Sr. at Union," *Union Alumni Monthly,* May 1926, 245.

form of man. This was the title of one of Henry Sr.'s books (Boston, 1879). See also Lit. Rem., 49 and n.

doing determines being. Henry James, Sr., *The Nature of Evil,* New York, 1855, 81.

will be the true one. Coll. Ess., 60.

27  or less worth. Ibid., 61.

the important event of 1890. Henri F. Ellenberger, *The Discovery of the Unconscious,* New York, 1970, 762.

28  not impossible she. Richard Crashaw, "Wishes to his Supposed Mistress." James's quoting is in Lett., I, 46.

29  blessed old creatures have. Lett., I, 211.

inaccessible to our sympathy. Ibid., 287.

30  nothing morbid about it. To Kitty James Prince, July 12, 1885, in J. Bixler, *Religion in the Philosophy of William James,* Boston, 1926, 160.

in their company, Lett., I, 188.

and a flock of sheep. Ibid., 196–97.

33  than hitherto. Ibid., 212–13.

the Scratch Eight. Perry, I, 596ff., 606ff.

play tennis in winter. Review of Massachusetts Board of Health Report in *Atlantic Monthly,* v. 34, 1874, 234.

composition generally begins. Wordsworth, Preface to *Lyrical Ballads.*

## The Masterpiece

*page*

34  buzzing confusion. Pr. Psych., I, 488.

35  would be produced. Ibid., I, 24.

suggesters of these. Ibid., I, 20.

36  connected with it. Ibid., I, 347.

which they "know." Ibid., I, vi.

37  is metaphysics. Ibid.

in this book. Ibid., I, vii.

our farther knowledge. Ibid., 192.

38  is conscious of it. Ibid., 197; II, 171 n.

two things, not one. Ibid., I, 278–79.

39  it knows nothing. Ibid., I, 220.

mysterious sort . . . yet in sight. Ibid., I, 687.

systems, involve it. Ibid.

hypnotic trance. Ibid., II, 596.

41  individual minds. Ibid., I, 183.

in the brains of monkeys. See José M. R. Delgado, *Evolution of the Physical Control of the Brain,* American Museum of Natural History, New York, 1965.

holds good of men. Huxley in Pr. Psych., I, 131.

absolute formulas . . . half of existence . . . faithfully attends. Pr. Psych., I, 134–36.

42 brains are up to . . . cellular neurobiology. *Science,* June 8, 1979, 1066; June 15, 1979, 1193.

yaw abruptly . . . stimuli . . . virtually no brain. *Science,* June 16, 1972, 1255; December 12, 1980, 1232.

terra incognita. See also Sir Francis Walshe, "An Attempted Correlation of . . . Hypotheses . . . (about) the Cerebral Cortex," *Journal of the Neurobiological Sciences,* 1964, I, 111–28.

43 blood-soaked sponge. Pr. Psych., I, 98.

strive to discover. William J. McGill, "Neural Counting Mechanisms and Energy Detection in Audition," *Journal of Mathematical Psychology,* 1967, 361, 351.

44 it flows. Pr. Psych., I, 239.

of our consciousness. Ibid.

flights and perchings . . . of our ideas. Ibid., I, 243; II, 528.

45 shimmering of consciousness . . . iridescences . . . regarding the mind. Ibid., I, 241, 235.

silence sounds delicious. Ibid., 240, 234.

46 that come and go. Ibid., I, 196.

my own body does. Ibid., I, 285.

47 to attend to. Ibid., I, 402.

and catch it . . . figure . . . regardless. Ibid., I, 472, 479, 244.

48 a feeling of cold. Ibid., I, 245–46.

48 grasp the nettle. James often used the local equivalent "squeeze the thistle"; e.g., Will. Bel., 153, 274, and the lectures on Exceptional Mental States, passim.

49 have always believed. Pr. Psych., I, 181.

consciousness itself. Ibid., I, 182.

the thought is the thinker. Ibid., I, 342, 401.

50 others continually. Ibid., I, 225.

or disappointments. Rad. Emp., 45.

*ondoyant et divers.* Montaigne, *Essais,* bk. I, ch. I.

*figured* consciousness. Pr. Psych., II, 82.

51 acquired perception. Ibid., II, 78.

squareness, etc. Ibid.

speculation in it. Ibid., II, 81. The remark alludes to *Macbeth,* act III, sc. 4, line 95.

52 ". . . reality! (Loud cheers)." Eddington, *The Nature of the Physical World,* New York, 1929, 283.

subjective interest . . . it is made by it. Pr. Psych., I, 403.

53 system of knowledge. Ibid.

essentially partial . . . of his mind. Will Bel., 220–21.

pain and the brain. Pr. Psych., I, 419.

*page*

56 of our thinking. Ibid., I, 459.

without confusion. Ibid., I, 461.

57 don't mean *that*. Ibid., I, 462.

old conceptions. Ibid., I, 467.

58 perverse sentimentalism. Ibid., I, 479–80.

taken on reality. Plur. Univ., 253; Prob. Phil., 57.

two new conceptions. Pr. Psych., I, 473.

59 low forms of life conceptualize. Ibid., I, 463.

generalities and particulars. Mg. Truth, 144 and passim.

63 never able to forget. Lett., I, 56.

taint of falsity. Descartes, *Rules for the Direction of the Mind*, Rule II.

*esprit de finesse*. Pascal's discussion occurs in Article I of the *Pensées*, Brunschvig edition, Paris, n.d., nos. 1–4.

65 reactive spontaneity. Pr. Psych., I, 103.

66 modes of feeling. Ibid., I, 479n.

geometry become sentiments. *Pensées*, Brunschvig ed., no. 95.

67 so full of weight? Pr. Psych., I, 233.

68 slave of the passions. Hume, *A Treatise of Human Nature*, II, iii.

his seat outside. Pr. Psych., I, 125.

69 a New Hampshire farm. Ibid., II, 448.

entities . . . into each other . . . vengefulness. Ibid., II, 449, 442, 448.

and conditioning. Ibid., II, 449.

afraid or angry. Ibid., II, 450.

make reverberate. Ibid.

72 two pictures. *Science*, N.S. v. IV, no. 88, 318.

preciousness. Lett., II, 87.

72n The articles referred to appeared, respectively, in: *Nation*, July 19, 1894, 49–51; September 20, 1877, 185–86; *Philosophical Review*, 2, no. 5, 590–94; *Nation*, November 9, 1876, 289; *Nation*, 65, 1897, 75.

72 process being aroused. *Nation*, July 19, 1894, 50.

73 n-different-from-m. Pr. Psych., I, 498.

simply as such. *Nation*, September 20, 1877, 186.

in one world. Pr. Psych., I, 508.

74 of our thoughts. Pr. Psych., II, 83–84.

75 tread therein. Ibid., I, 121.

76 never to be undone. Ibid., I, 127.

77 effectively with others. Ibid., I, 404.

shrieking away outside. Alice James, *Journal*, ed. Anna Robeson Burr, New York, 1934, 180.

78 direction . . . psychological rights. Pr. Psych., I, 254, 478n.–79n.

79 it was torn. Ibid., I, 465.

feeling of harmony. Ibid., 466.

artistic inventions. Hermann Helmholtz, *On the Sensations of Tone*, 2nd English ed., New York, 1954, 365.

does not change. Pr. Psych., I, 421.

could not be bored. Pr. Psych., I, 192.

page
80     make new wholes. Ibid., II, 44.

       fainter still. Ibid., II, 71–72.

81     the solemnities. Alice James, *Journal*, ed. Anna Robeson Burr, New York, 1934, 239.

       student's mind. Lett., I, 314.

82     than profound. Ps. Brief., Preface, xii.

## The Test of Truth

page
85     Peirce's article appeared in *The Popular Science Monthly* for January 1878.

       Hodgson's test by practice was reserved for moral issues. See *The Theory of Practice, an Ethical Inquiry*, 2 vols., London, 1870.

86     of our thinking. Prag., 50, 222.

       course of experience. Ibid., 218.

       only principle. Ibid., 61.

       grasp new fact . . . of our experience. Prag., 61–62.

       reports of nature. Prag., 212–13, 57.

87     concrete expediencies. Prag., 232–33.

88     pragmatism's naughty. Matthew Head (John Canaday), *The Congo Venus*, New York, 1950, 203.

89     unkind thing to say. R. C. Woodthorpe, *The Public School Murder*, London, 1932, 242.

       are pests." William Safire, *The New York Times*, August 15, 1975.

       beaded bubbles . . . pragmatic drinker. The allusion is to Keats's "Ode to a Nightingale."

90     . . . if one doesn't. Alan Paton, *Toward the Mountain*, New York, 1980, 59.

       of ideology. Erik v. Kuehnelt-Leddihn, *National Review*, November 14, 1980, 1400.

91     relief and pleasure, Will Bel., 63.

       expectancy. Will Bel., 77.

       "Was Lincoln a Pragmatist?" *New Leader*, September 23, 1957; February 10, 1958.

92     could be free. Letter to Horace Greeley, August 22, 1862, in Roy P. Basler, ed., *Collected Works of Abraham Lincoln*, New Brunswick, 1953, V, 388–89.

       to be based. *New Leader*, loc. cit., 20.

93     no holds barred. Percy Bridgman, *Reflections of a Physicist*, New York, 1950, 351.

       in turn the chemists. Prag., 253.

94     truth upon reality. Prag., 257. Perry, II, 479.

95     sociological movement. See *Essays in Jurisprudence from the Columbia Law Review*, New York, 1963, 66–67, 318.

96     very much reality. T. S. Eliot, "Burnt Norton" in *Four Quartets*.

97     experiences in detail, Prag., 240–41.

*page*

98    what it commemorates? G. K. Chesterton, *Autobiography*, London, 1936, 240.

at the post office. This description of the typical war memorial of the 1920s occurs in Colin Watson's *Bump in the Night*, London, 1963 (1960), 8.

99    quite useless. Wilde, *The Picture of Dorian Gray*, Preface.

by nervous thrills. Santayana, *The Life of Reason*, rev. ed. in one vol., New York, 1954, part IV, ch. 4, p. 317.

102    of my summer. *Letters of Henry James*, ed. Percy Lubbock, New York, 1920, II, 83.

characteristically expounds. Richard A. Hocks, *Henry James and Pragmatistic Thought*, Chapel Hill, 1974, 4–5.

103    what truth is. M. A. De Wolfe Howe, *John Jay Chapman in His Letters*, Boston, 1937, 242–43.

104    statements or beliefs? Perry, II, 477, 485.

105    the very idea of truth. Prag., 192. See also: Mg. Truth, 185–86, and other statements by James in Perry, II, 477–78, 480, 485.

concrete expediencies. Prag., 232–33.

a process. Prag., 226; Mg. Truth, vi.

106    marriage function. Prag., 64.

guide us elsewhere. Prag., 213.

107    bitch-goddess Success. Lett., II, 260.

a given matter. Lett., I, 133.

never laughs. Coll. Ess., 25.

of its answer. *The New York Times*, November 3, 1907; Perry, II, 478–80.

in philosophy. Perry, II, 632.

108    the word "practical." Plur. Univ., 249.

sit in armchairs. *John Jay Chapman in His Letters*, ed. M. A. DeWolfe Howe, Boston, 1937, 432.

## The Varieties of Experience

*page*

109    possible way . . . think clearly. Prob. Phil., 25; Pr. Psych., I, 145.

110    universally discarded . . . a function. Rad. Emp., 3.

are known. Ibid., 4.

both at once. Ibid., 9–10.

111    or what not. . . . things are made. Ibid., 26–27.

plural facts. Ibid., 42.

directly experienced . . . as anything else. Ibid.

111f.   without disfavor . . . thing experienced. Ibid., 44.

112    grade of unity. Ibid., 45.

order generally. Ibid., 45, 44.

minds together. Ibid., 46.

113    all-inclusive fact . . . imagining them. Plur. Univ., 36.

*page*

114 stages of it . . . fathom it. Ibid., 250.

talk as we will. Ibid., 39–40.

115 pictorial nobility. Ibid., 45.

fixed and abstracted. Rad. Emp., 93–94.

as a thing. Ibid., 10.

and concrete . . . bit of experience. Ibid.

116 room is part. Ibid., 11–13.

toward the good? . . . itself complete. Ibid., 34–35.

117 my emotions. Ibid., 153.

or as mental. Ibid.

several heirs. Ibid., 133.

118 sorts of path. Ibid., 62, 63.

begin to understand. Ibid., 133.

leans on nothing. Ibid., 193.

born in the house. Pr. Psych., II, 627.

ignore the rest. Ibid.

120 ever be made. Rad. Emp., 65–66.

name for excess . . . older mass. Plur. Univ., 286.

block universe . . . federal republic. Plur. Univ., 76; 321–22.

somewhere be real. Rad. Emp., 160.

122 marrow of life. Pr. Psych., II, 674n.

123 fundamental phenomenon. Mem. Stud., 102–3.

moral holiday. Prag., 74.

124 darling studies. Letter to J. J. Thelwall, November 19, 1795.

their operations. Ibid., 233.

125 deducing things. Plur. Univ., 107.

what happens. Ibid., 87.

everything that's present. Prag., 215.

out straighter. Preface to Harald Höffding, *The Problems of Philosophy*, New York, 1905, vi.

126 a passion insatiate. Pr. Psych., I, 162.

127 thus arise. Prob. Phil., 51–52.

truth and right. Plur. Univ., 55–56.

vicious intellectualism. Ibid., 60.

their definitions. Ibid., 218.

128 on his own feet. Ibid., 60.

with philosophy. *The Lichtenberg Reader*, ed. Mautner and Hatfield, Boston, 1959, 82.

and overflows. Plur. Univ., 212.

130 future perceptions. Ibid., 52.

possession of reality. Ibid., 272–73.

in its own way. Prag., 259.

131 immutability. Prag., 261–62.

English tradition. Plur. Univ., 16–17.

perspective of events . . . the parts. Ibid., 8.

*page*

132    words to utter. Ibid., 8–9.
       chips of stone. Ibid., 9–10.
       essential interests. Ibid., 11.

133    ways of thinking. Ibid., 87–88; 107.

134    from above. Ibid., 277.
       nor reply. Perry, II, 467.
       known-as. James borrowed this diagnostic term from Shadworth Hodg-
       son and used it throughout his own writings.
       their intellects. Preface to Friedrich Paulsen, *Introduction to Philosophy*,
       trans. Frank Thilly, New York, 1904, vi.
       converse together. Rad. Emp., 275.
       "man thinking" (Pr. Phil., 15) is possibly an echo of the identical phrase
       that Emerson used in 1837 to define "The American Scholar," again in
       reproof of specialism.
       social mates. Prob. Phil., 8.

135    makes hypotheses . . . dogmatism whatever . . . facts of life. Ibid., 15, 26, 27.
       you may pretend. Ibid., 39; 44–45.
       seems pointless. Steven Weinberg, *The First Three Minutes*, New York,
       1977, 154.
       undoubtedly exists . . . familiar . . . caked prejudices. Prob. Phil., 23–24, 7.
       mental background. Ibid., 7–8.

136    perfectly well. Perry, II, 418–19.
       synechism. Ibid., 419.
       my philosophy. Ibid.

138    oozy writing. Lett., II, 237.
       Don't think, look! Quoted in Novak, ed. *American Philosophy and the
       Future*, New York, 1968, 102.
       opening outwards. Quoted in Alice James's *Journal*, ed. Anna Robeson
       Burr, New York, 1934, 121.

140    work out. Rad. Emp., 186.
       elements of things. Ibid., 187; Prob. Phil., 214.

## Freedom and Risk

*page*

144    our welfare. Will Bel., 114.

145    nature's beauty . . . and success. Talks, 232–34.
       remodelled at all. Ibid., 107–8.

146    ideal altitude. Will Bel., 186–87.
       said his say. Ibid., 184.

149    respectively belong. Ibid., 209–10
       aurora borealis. Ibid., 193.

150    ultimately based. Ibid., 194.
       the other way. Ibid., 195.

153    last word. Ibid., 183.
       is impossible . . . and errors. Ibid., 161, 163.
       and so forth. Plur. Univ., 77.

*page*

entering the world. Rad. Emp., 185n.

154 Montaigne: "On Cannibals" in *Essays,* bk. I, ch. 30.

Pascal: *Pensées,* Brunschvig, ed., article V, no. 294.

to adultery. *The New York Times,* October 10, 1981.

156 they belong. Will Bel., 209–10.

157 extinction of slavery . . . honest men only. Lincoln to Charles D. Drake and others, October 5, 1863 (Basler, ed., *Collected Works,* VI, 500).

to kill somebody. Dorothy L. Sayers, *Gaudy Night,* London, 1935, 350, and again, 382, 440, and 472.

such adaptation. October 16, 1854 (Basler, op. cit., II, 270).

161 universal law. Var. Rel., 119.

their significance. Ibid., 10; 13–14.

able to perform. Ibid., 10.

emotions are. Ibid., 14.

energy was only. Humphrey Carpenter, *The Inklings,* New York, 1979, 234.

162 desecrate the universe. Huxley, *Life and Letters,* ed. Leonard Huxley, I, 237.

insufficient evidence. Will Bel., 8.

163 in the voice. Ibid.

each other. Ibid., 9.

making up our minds. Ibid., 11.

to act at all. Ibid., 3.

164 losing the truth. Ibid., 11.

is to lose. *The Journal of Sir Walter Scott,* ed. David Douglas, Edinburgh, 1890: January 26, 1826, 96.

165 regulate our lives! . . . the abyss. Will Bel., 25, 59.

contributed your act. Ibid., 59.

our willing nature. Ibid., 8–9.

166 It was his belief. Hemingway, *A Dangerous Summer,* Kennedy Library, Boston (typescript), 336.

Hope unwilling to be fed. Wordsworth, "Resolution and Independence."

167 face the consequences. Romain Gary, *The New York Times,* December 3, 1980.

of one's own conscience. Perry, II, 301.

168 abuse can go on. Lett., II, 67.

in my life. Ibid., 66.

an enthroned abuse . . . picturesqueness. Mem. Stud., 57–58.

169 Colonel Picquart. Perry, II, 303–4.

169 puts them on top . . . spleen. Lett., II, 90.

170 mob hysteria . . . campaign of education. Ibid., 29.

Lodge's skull. Ibid., 30.

mob psychology. Ibid., 36.

Don't yelp with the pack! Samuel Eliot Morison, *Three Centuries of Harvard,* Cambridge (Mass.), 1936, 413.

must stop. *Boston Evening Transcript,* March 1, 1899.

*page*

171  squinting on the page. Ibid.
     practical men. Perry, II, 294.
     human nature. Mem. Stud., 300-1.

172  determining condition. Ibid., 301, 303.
     and excitements. Ibid.
     to responsibility. *The Atlantic Monthly*, December 1904; reprinted in Mem. Stud., 305.
     to dally with . . . heroic energy. Mem. Stud., 305, 306.
     camping party . . . of the situation. Ibid., 267, 283.
     its own monstrosity. Ibid., 286.

173  against Nature. Ibid., 290.
     choice of the cause. Lett., 28.
     might be—baseball. Morris Cohen, quoted in *City College Alumnus*, December 1980, 11.
     of his higher life. Mem. Stud., 290-91.

174  speed and passion. Perry, II, 299.
     our descendants . . . woman's pains. Talks, 289.
     smashing projectile . . . practical aims. *North American Review*, October 1869, 556.
     children to society, Ibid.

175  a poisoning. Var. Rel., 387.
     of civilization. Lett., II, 273.
     influence a jury. Ibid., II, 67.

176  than himself. Howe, ed., *J. J. Chapman in His Letters* (op. cit.), 202.

177  of the teeth . . . the law. Will Bel., 61-62; 27.
     empirically bad . . . for the tragic. Perry, I, 722; Coll. Ess., 18.
     in our Bible come. Will Bel., 47.

178  sins and suffering. Talks, 268-70.

180  page after page . . . better than another. Lett., II, 122, 123.
     do about it? Will Bel., 50.

## The Reign of William and Henry

*page*

184  and artificial. Rad. Emp., 39-40.

188  art and the world. Henry James, *The Art of the Novel*, ed. R. P. Blackmur, New York, 1950, 79.
     primary motives. Ibid.
     except holiness. J. K. Huysmans, *Les Foules de Lourdes*, Paris, 1906, 107.

189  God was dead. Nietzsche, *The Gay Science* (1882), sec. 125, repeated in the more widely read *Thus Spake Zarathustra* (1883-1891).

191  almost a fury. Henry James, *Art of the Novel*, op. cit., 83.
     permanent presence . . . sense and judgment. Mem. Stud., 319, 320.

194  through a temperament. Zola, *Le roman expérimental*, Paris, 1880, 111.
     already there. *The Early Life of Thomas Hardy*, ed. F. E. Hardy, New York, 1928, January 1887 and January 9, 1889, 242-43 and 283.

page

195  and Schopenhauer. H. R. Rookmaaker, *Synthetist Art Theories*, Amster-
     dam, 1959, 164–65.

     taken twice over. Rad. Emp., 23.

199  in the shadows. Mem. Stud., 147–49.

     wilderness of truth. Mg. Truth, 77.

200  comes back to him. *The Lesson of Balzac*, Boston, 1905, 116.

     a million . . . instrument . . . sees white. Henry James, *The Art of the Nov-
     el* (op cit.), 46.

201  illumination. *The Notebooks of Henry James*, ed. Matthiessen and Mur-
     dock, New York, 1947, 111.

     his own other art. Henry James, *Art of the Novel* (op. cit.), 332.

202  surge of life. *The Notebooks of Henry James*, op. cit., 135

     roaring crowds . . . banal. Ibid., 207, 211.

     encouragements . . . howling desert . . . I do. Ibid., 68.

     and passion. Ibid., 81.

203  its own pocket. Prag., 63.

204  be useful. Ibid., 57.

     conceptual shorthand. Ibid., 212–13, 57.

205  data and laws. Pr. Psych., II, 634.

206  a demonstration. Ibid., 637.

     of the shop . . . constituted neighbors. Will Bel., 131n, 132.

207  are describable. Rad. Emp., 148.

     for them. Prag., 269.

     information theory. C. H. Waddington, *Biology, Purpose, and Ethics*,
     Worcester (Mass.), 1971, 17.

208  all phenomena . . . experiment. E. P. Wigner, "The Unreasonable Effec-
     tiveness of Mathematics in the Physical Sciences," *Communications in
     Pure and Applied Mathematics*, February 1960, 1–14.

     tentative forever. Karl R. Popper, *The Logic of Scientific Discovery*, New
     York, 1961, 278–79, 281.

210  disheartening. Review of H. T. Finck, *Romantic Love and Personal Beau-
     ty*, *Nation*, September 22, 1887, 238.

     simple-minded evolutionist. See, e.g., Pr. Psych., II, 420, 483, 494, 629;
     Will Bel., 253.

     essential data . . . found in X. Review of Darwin's *Variations of Animals
     and Plants under Domestication*, *Atlantic Monthly*, July 1868, 123.

211  and survival . . . for at all . . . of research. Pr. Psych., II, 618n.

     antiseptic substance. *The New York Times*, March 29, 1981.

212  to stand on. *Letters of Henry Adams*, Boston, 1938, II, 407–8.

     delegated to the cerebellum. Pr. Psych., I, 77–78.

213  acquired characteristics . . . terms synonymous. *The New York Times*,
     November 4, 1980, March 2, 1981, April 19, 1982; *Science News*, January
     10, 1981; *Science*, November 21, 1980, July 11, 1980.

214  examination and reform. Strindberg, somewhere in the five volumes of
     *The Blue Notebook* collected in *Werke: Deutsche Gesamtausgabe*, Abt.
     VI, 5–8 Bde.

*page*

215 examined afresh. Plur. Univ., 3.

217 theories of thought. Frazer, *The Golden Bough* (abridged ed.), New York, 1951, 825–26.

218 our national disease. Lett., II, 260.

219 more substantial. Ibid., 277–78.
accepted canons. Ibid., 278.
*once* again! Ibid.

220 pleasing open! . . . crabbed organism. Ibid., 240, 278.

221 divine youth. Perry, II, 274.
truly magnificent (*Germinal*) . . . ran thin. Lett., I, 287; II, 291.
swamps of evil. Eliot G. Fay, "Henry James as a Critic of French Litera-ture," *French-American Review*, II, 1949, 190.
intolerable fluency. Lett., II, 330–31, 335–36.

222 fearing to jar. Perry, II, 274.

223 in your journal. Lett., I, 15.
(Membre de l'Institut). Ibid., II, 330.

225 ungenial act . . . vainer brother. Manuscript letter, Archives of the Ameri-can Academy of Arts and Letters, New York City.

226 play of mind. *Notebooks of Henry James*, op. cit., 323.

## Beyond the Conscious Mind

*page*

228 That it plays. Lowell Lectures on Exceptional Mental States (1896), Houghton Library, Harvard University, I, 4.
its familiarity . . . wonder . . . of reality . . . possible? Ibid., I, 2.

229 F.B.I. and Scotland Yard. *The New York Times*, November 9, 1980; April 21, 1981, and passim.
psychic entities . . . controls. Lowell Lectures (op cit.), I, 5.

230 unconscious idea. Pr. Psych., I, 162ff.
from below. Review of Breuer and Freud, *Psychological Review*, 1894, 1, 199.

231 and parasitic . . . so to speak. Ibid.
from use . . . the other parts. Mem. Stud., 262.
reputation . . . breach is restored. Review of Breuer and Freud (op. cit.), 199.

232 by publishers. Var. Rel., 94.
dangerous method. Lett., II, 327–28.
the real psychology. Perry, II, 123.
pleasant impression. Lett., II, 327.
as an equal . . . a lasting impression. Freud, *Autobiography*, trans. by James Strachey, New York, 1935, 104.
approaching death. Freud, *An Autobiographical Study*, trans. by James Strachey, New York, 1952, 99.

233 views we accept. Freud, *New Introductory Lectures on Psychoanalysis*, trans. by W. J. H. Sprott, New York, 1933, 240.

*page*

realm of reality . . . harmless. Ibid., 219.

relatively trivial. Lowell Lectures (op cit.), IV, 22.

your consideration. Perry, II, 122.

234 an impossibility. In Paul Roazen, *Freud and His Followers*, New York, 1975, 374.

235 theory of types. C. G. Jung, *Two Essays on Analytical Psychology*, New York, 1956 (1912), 64, 184.

too much respect. Var. Rel., 148.

236 because children do. N. C. Starr, Introduction to *Till We Have Faces*, New York, 1968, 11–12.

237 anesthetic revelation. See James's review of B. P. Blood's book on the subject, *Atlantic Monthly*, 1874, 627–29; also Var. Rel., 487, 500.

census of hallucinations. Will Bel., 312.

on trust! Lett., II, 37.

Civil War. Lowell Lectures (op. cit.), IV, 22.

apparently normal. Lowell Lectures (op. cit.), VIII, 67.

a nullity. Ibid., VIII, 70.

238 potency of sex. Review of Mill's *Subjection of Women*, *North American Review*, October 1869, 564.

his hold. Pr. Psych., I, 22.

239 all the data . . . hundred years. Coll. Ess., 490.

arrant humbug. Mem. Stud., 183.

240 rathole life. Ibid., 197; Murphy, 61.

of believing. Will Bel., x.

subconscious constitution . . . in chemistry. Mem. Stud., 191.

intellectual methods. Ibid., 192.

241 resort of despair . . . both of us. Ibid., 198–99.

at the beginning. Ibid., 175.

242 miraculous revelation . . . truth. Edmund A. Opitz, "Lord Gifford's Legacy," *The Freeman*, March 1966, 37–38.

243 point of view . . . deepest dye. Var. Rel., 5–7.

MYSELF alone. Ibid., 9.

sexual life . . . system of thought. Ibid., 10–11.

spiritual significance? Ibid., 13–14.

244 fruits for life. Ibid., 14, 15.

245 with the world. Var. Rel., 88, 136.

all its blood. Ibid., 136, 138.

supply a passage. Var. Rel., 304.

246 poor employment. Ibid., 346–47.

now secure it. Ibid., 430–37.

same quality. Ibid., 508.

so many beads. Ibid., 499–500.

247 Two passages: Lit. Rem., 72, 116.

theological works. Ibid., 116.

conventionalism. Ibid., 72.

moral existence. Ibid., 41, 39.

*page*

theism . . . consciousness . . . energies . . . transcendent. Var. Rel., 521–25.

248 return to it. Ibid., 483–84.

indispensable. Ibid., 515.

249 Disease Center in Atlanta. *The New York Times,* May 10, 1981.

250 no single quality. Var. Rel., 487.

return upon us. Ibid., 525–26.

powers of action. Ibid., 175.

mad and divine. Nietzsche, *Beyond Good and Evil,* Section 188.

common people. Var. Rel., 526.

251 not properly religion. Ibid., 488n.

proper work. Ibid., 245.

genuine form. Lit. Rem., 118–19.

252 interest aroused. Var. Rel., 283.

than it is now. Ibid., 356.

253 great initiation. Ibid., 363.

254 with it in principle. Ibid., 520–23.

judgment of higher law. Var. Rel., 522.

the total fact. Ibid., 523.

255 irresponsible hours. Ibid., 491.

256 vernacular sort. Plur. Univ., 148, 154.

alive and conscious. Ibid., 149.

as an anomaly. Ibid., 150–51.

supreme felicity. Talks, 263.

256 buying a hill and a brook . . . hastened his end. Lett., I, 272–73; II, 90–91; Will Bel., 74–75.

257 of details. Plur. Univ., 181.

thickness . . . ran thin . . . above man. Ibid., 176, 153.

a world elsewhere. *Coriolanus,* act III, sc. 3, line 135.

problematic. Plur. Univ., 308–9.

and morally. Ibid., 311.

258 live on a chance. Var. Rel., 526.

*make* history . . . millennium. Lett., II, 345–46.

259 secondary point . . . how to decide. Var. Rel., 524.

university official . . . keenest order. Murphy, 282.

to the beyond. Perry, I, 173, Lett., I, 130.

fences . . . facts to testify. Mem. Stud., 204.

260 if you believed. Santayana, quoted in Harold E. Stearns, *Civilization in the United States,* New York, 1922, 171.

Francis Child. Murphy, 201.

261 a blessed farewell. Your William. Lett., I, 218–220.

## The Genius

*page*

262 adorable genius. Whitehead, *Science in the Modern World,* New York, 1925, p. 3.

smallness in any respect. My conversations with Whitehead took place not in Cambridge but in Concord, Mass., where he and his wife used to visit Mrs. Frederick E. Lowell during the years 1935-1939.

263   their own line of work. See, for example, Plur. Univ., 398, where James draws attention to Peirce as "a goldmine of ideas for the thinkers of the next generation."

264   to a treadmill. Alice James, *Journal*, ed. A. R. Burr, New York, 1934, 107.
sunlight. J. J. Chapman, *Memories and Milestones*, New York, 1915, 19.
theory of psychology. Peirce, Collected Papers, v. VI; quoted in Perry, I, 541.
unhabitual way. Pr. Psych., II, 110.
will bear fruits. Coll. Ess., 402.

265   quickly bored. *The Monist*, XIX, 1909, 156.
common goods. Pr. Psych., I, 234.
distant joys. Perry, II, 677.
the eagle's race and free. Ibid., 678.

266   write such things. Ibid.
I don't want to go! Lett., II, 9.
with a paving stone . . . satisfaction. George D. Burrage, in Perry, II, 281-82.

267   my university. Perry, II, 9-10.

268   The Chesterton episode is related in H. G. Wells's *Experiment in Autobiography* and quoted in Maisie Ward, *The Life of G. K. Chesterton*, New York, 1943, 377.
imbecile rot. S. N. Smith, *The Legend of the Master*, New York, 1948, 71.
An American Hero. Elizabeth Hardwick, *Mademoiselle*, June 1960, 60ff; reprinted as the preface to her selection of James letters, and again in *A View of My Own*, New York, 1962, 1981.

269   of his will . . . middle of an arch. Perry, II, 673; Lett., II, 259.
rest of life. Pr. Psych., 578-79.
shakes a rat . . . show its power. Mem. Stud., 211-12.

270   engineering problem. Perry, II, 280.
brings to us. Alice James, *Journal*, op. cit., 145. The idea must have been family property. See William's statement of 1869 on p. 19 above.
trifling incident. To Mary W. Calkins, quoted in Julius Bixler, *Religion in the Philosophy of William James*, Boston, 1926, 165.
brief critical hour. Mem. Stud., 19.

273   a cruel death. Shaw, *Sixteen Self-Sketches*, New York, 1949, 73.
ideas of an opponent. Andrew Lang, *Modern Mythology*, London, 1897, 92.
mental perspective. Prob. Phil., 6-7.

274   choose to come. Pr. Psych., II, 370-71.
of its transitions. Ibid., II, 370.
cow weight. Lett., II, 41.
all in one. Pr. Psych., II, 441.

275   to official Harvard. Santayana, *Persons and Places*, v. II, New York, 1945, ch. 7-8, passim.
Professor? What? Perry, II, 504.

*page*

Mrs. Agassiz in Lucy Paton, *Elizabeth Cary Agassiz*, Boston, 1919, 72; Alice Boughton in *Photographing the Famous*, New York, 1928, 98.

276 three parts poetry. J. J. Chapman, *Memories and Milestones*, New York, 1915, 25.

spontaneous and natural. Lucy A. Paton, *Elizabeth Cary Agassiz*, Boston, 1919, 383.

277 a perfect lecturer . . . his apprenticeship. *The Flowers of Friendship: Letters to Gertrude Stein*, ed. Donald Gallup, New York, 1953, 9, 18; Lett., II, 220–21.

276n The third footnote refers to the work of Stephen Kern, *Anatomy and Destiny*, Indianapolis, 1975, 38–39. James's words are quoted from Pr. Psych., 437–38 and n.

278 for hours, for days. F. J. E. Woodbridge, *An Essay on Nature*, New York, 1940, 98–99.

unrequited love. Arthur Train, *Yankee Lawyer*, New York, 1943, 4. Train's recollection is not exact in referring to "the best of all possible worlds." It was the Idealists' perfect universe that James thought flawed by the occurrence of any slightest evil.

like that myself. Elizabeth Sprigge, *Gertrude Stein and Her Work*, New York, 1957, 34. The original source of Miss Stein's relations with James is *The Autobiography of Alice B. Toklas*, New York, 1933, ch. 4.

perfection of rottenness. Lett., II, 122.

279 too good to be true. Ibid., 280.

incarnate boredom. Perry, II, 265.

teacher's use. Talks, 7.

280 in the long run. Talks, 135.

and partly free. Ibid., 196.

loose the effort. Talks, 109, 101, 110.

softer pedagogies . . . learning. Talks, 54–55, 152.

*can* be interesting. Ibid., 55.

moral faculties. Ibid.

281 psychological deduction. Ibid., 37.

in the abstract . . . never-so-little scar. Ibid., 71, 77–78.

often a better one. Ibid., 63.

282 habitual situations . . . before. Ibid., 29.

physical world. Ibid.

what is proposed. Ibid., 114.

283 too docile. Ibid., 6–7.

every generation. Woodrow Wilson, Address to the Association of American Universities, Madison, Wis., 1910.

284 soul of culture . . . virgin-minded youth. James's Preface to E. L. Thorndike, *Elements of Psychology*, New York, 1905, vi; Coll. Ess., 343.

dislikes and disdains. Mem. Stud., 321–23.

when you see him. Mem. Stud., 309.

and honesty . . . lost or saved. Ibid., 311, 323.

laboratory and shop work. Talks, 35–36.

to his teaching . . . shown somewhere. Mem. Stud., 331, 332.

285   suffer like the rest? Ibid., 334.

286   and flexibility . . . wise voters. Lett., II, 41; Perry, II, 298.

have been reached. *Harvard Monthly*, 1890–91, 132–35.

287   for happiness. Perry, II, 679.

288   drop it forever. Lett., II, 277.

technical matter. Prag., 4.

289   can take place. Lett., I, 144n.

not readable. Perry, II, 441.

a centre exists. Plur. Univ., 263.

290   academic dignity . . . racy writing. Perry, II, 465; Peirce is quoted in Michael Novak, ed., *American Philosophy and the Future*, New York, 1968, 88.

despicable game. Perry, II, 508.

forty in French. Lett., II, 219–20.

291   a simplification? Hartley Grattan, *The Three Jameses*, New York, 1932, 78n.

could have been a great poet. Graham Wallas, *The Art of Thought*, London, 1931 (1926), 122.

tuned receivers . . . quanta. Rad. Emp., 126; Prob. Phil., 173–74.

resistless bang. Lit. Rem., 21.

spans and wave lengths. Plur. Univ., 149.

pleasure economy. Mem. Stud., 305–6.

speech and thought expire. Will Bel., 122.

292   our pursuit. Var. Rel., 382–83.

in the making. Plur. Univ., 263; Prob. Phil., 15.

man thinking. Prob. Phil., 15.

293   beautiful prose . . . precision . . . contact with life. Leo Stein, "William James," *American Scholar*, Spring 1948, 163.

the enemy. Lett., II, 208.

294   nature of reality. Plur. Univ., 212.

step . . . is logical. Ibid., 329.

Or not allowed. These lines, with a distracting phrase omitted, are from *Henry VIII*, act I, sc. 2, lines 82–85.

295   Spinoza criticized. T. C. Mark, *Spinoza's Theory of Truth*, New York, 1972.

celebratory essays. *The Philosophy of Alfred North Whitehead*, ed. P. A. Schilpp, Evanston, 1941.

possess it wholly. Var. Rel., 334.

illusion of substance. Gerald Abrahams, *According to the Evidence*, London, 1958, 69n.

introduction to philosophy. Prob. Phil., viii.

296   pragmatic revolts. See W. Y. Elliott, *The Pragmatic Revolt in Politics*, New York, 1928; Cushing Strout, *The Pragmatic Revolt in American History*, New Haven, 1958; C. Wright Mills, *Sociology and Pragmatism*, New York, 1966.

*page*

universal reputation. *Encyclopédie Populaire Illustrée du XXè Siècle,* "Philosophie," ed. F. Buisson, Paris, 1900, 68–69.

minds of history. Lucien Price, *Dialogues of Whitehead,* Boston, 1954, 338.

297   all these years ... a masterpiece ... medicine. *Psychology Today,* April 1982, 52, 53.

a polar star. New York, 1961, Preface, xiii.

298   atomism in biology. Jean Piaget, *Biology and Knowledge,* Chicago, 1971, 98.

father who begat us. David Krech in *Unfinished Business,* ed. Robert MacLeod, Washington, D.C., 1969, 1.

at James's feet. Ibid., 10.

individual psychology. Van Teslaar, ed., *An Outline of Psychoanalysis,* New York, 1925, 261.

299   from Bertrand Russell. Frank Plumpton Ramsay, *The Foundations of Mathematics,* London, 1931, 155.

ask for the use. *Encyclopedia of Philosophy,* New York, 1967, I, 103.

inwardness ... interior process. Michael Novak, ed., *American Philosophy and the Future,* New York, 1968, 74, 83.

relational esthetics. Ibid., 92, 95.

"good" and "true." Paul M. Van Buren in Novak, op. cit., 92, 102.

we phenomenists. See Lett., I, 164, and passim; Rad. Emp., 185n; as well as Bruce Wilshire, *William James and Phenomenology,* Bloomington, Ind., 1968.

converge. Novak, op. cit., 251, 268n.

fused with emotion. Edouard Morot-Sir, "Gaston Berger," *Les Etudes Philosophiques,* October–December 1961, 311–12.

better than they. Julius Bixler, "The Existentialists and William James," *American Scholar,* Winter 1958–59, 80.

freedom and authenticity. R. W. Sleeper, in Novak, op. cit., 294.

need of as a poet. *Letters of Hart Crane and His Family,* ed. T. S. W. Lewis, New York, 1974, 149–50.

category of the esthetic. Michael Novak, op. cit., Introduction, 19.

300   wake of Darwinism. *Dictionary of American History,* New York, 1976, V, 386.

Von Hügel ... same estimate. *Studii Internazionali di Filosofia,* 2. Fall 1970, 117–130.

ideas as formative. Max Jammer, *The Conceptual Development of Quantum Mechanics,* New York, 1966, 176.

penetrating. Gail Kennedy, "Le Pragmatisme," in *Les Grands Courants de la Pensée Mondiale Contemporaine,* Milan, 1961, II, 57–122.

inauguration ... its lighting. *Science and the Modern World,* New York, 1925, 205.

as early as 1895. Ortega y Gasset, *Concord and Liberty,* trans. Helen Weyl, New York, 1963, 177n.

action for a purpose. Ibid., 99, 127.

*page*

  Perception psychology. Franz From, *Perception of Other People*, New York, 1971, 78, 52.
301 comprehensible than ever. Prob. Phil., 172ff., 185.
302 conclude in regard to it? Mem. Stud., 411.

## Epilogue—Anthology

*Page*
303 lines of tendency. Lett., II, 293.
304 tuned receivers. Rad. Emp., 126.
306 golden little work. Will Bel., 232.
308 my Redeemer liveth. Samuel Butler, "Unpublished Extracts from the Note Books," *Life and Letters*, VII, No. 41, October 1931, 301.

# Index

NOTE: The pages given under the several isms refer to all applications of each term and indicate passages about its root idea, regardless of connotation. Thus *Historicism* includes *History*; *Conceptualism* takes in *Concept*; *Theism* supplies references to *God, Voluntarism* to *Will*, and so on. The groupings that result are not only convenient for the purposes of this book, they also throw light on connections often obscured by literary usage.